The Language of Word Meaning

This volume is a collection of original contributions from outstanding scholars in linguistics, philosophy, and computational linguistics exploring the relation between word meaning and human linguistic creativity. The chapters present different aspects surrounding the question of what is word meaning, a problem that has been the center of heated debate in all those disciplines that are concerned directly or indirectly with the study of language and of human cognition.

The discussions are centered around the newly emerging view of the mental lexicon, as outlined in the Generative Lexicon theory, which proposes a unified model for defining word meaning. The individual contributors present their evidence for a generative approach as well as critical perspectives, which provides for a volume where word meaning is viewed not only from a particular angle or from a particular concern, but from a wide variety of topics, each introduced and explained by the editors.

Pierrette Bouillon received a licence in classical philology and a DEA in information science from the University of Brussels, and a doctorate in linguistics from the University of Paris VII. She has been a researcher at ISSCO/TIM, University of Geneva for the past ten years, with particular interest in lexical semantics and machine translation. She has numerous refereed publications in international conferences, journals, and books, and she has served on the programme committees of several international conferences.

Federica Busa is director of knowledge engineering at Lexeme, a company developing natural language technology, in Cambridge, Massachusetts. She has a Ph.D. in computer science from Brandeis University and a Degree in Translation from the University of Geneva School of Translation and Interpretation (ETI), where she initially developed a strong interest in machine translation and lexicography. She is the author of a number of articles on computational semantics for natural language and has served on the committee of both the American and the European chapters of the Association for Computational Linguistics.

Studies in Natural Language Processing

Series Editor: Branimir Boguraev, IBM

Also in the series

The Language of Word Meaning

Edited by

Pierrette Bouillon
University of Geneva

Federica Busa
Lexeme, Inc.

CAMBRIDGE
UNIVERSITY PRESS

PUBLISHED BY THE PRESS SYNDICATE OF THE UNIVERSITY OF CAMBRIDGE
The Pitt Building, Trumpington Street, Cambridge, United Kingdom

CAMBRIDGE UNIVERSITY PRESS
The Edinburgh Building, Cambridge CB2 2RU, UK
40 West 20th Street, New York, NY 10011-4211, USA
10 Stamford Road, Oakleigh, VIC 3166, Australia
Ruiz de Alarcón 13, 28014 Madrid, Spain
Dock House, The Waterfront, Cape Town 8001, South Africa

http://www.cambridge.org

First published 2001

Printed in the United States of America

Typeface Times Roman 10/12 pt.   *System* LATEX 2$_\varepsilon$ [TB]

A catalog record for this book is available from the British Library.

Library of Congress Cataloging in Publication Data
The Language of word meaning / edited by Pierrette Bouillon, Federica Busa.
    p.   cm. – (Studies in natural language processing)
      ISBN 0-521-78048-9
      1. Semantics.   2. Creativity (Linguistics).   3. Generative grammar.
    4. Computational linguistics.   I. Bouillon, Pierrette.   II. Busa, Federica.   III. Series.
    P325 .L295   2001
    401′.43 – dc21
                                                              00-041406

ISBN 0 521 78048 9 hardback

Contents

List of Contributors

Nicholas Asher
DEPARTMENT OF PHILOSOPHY, UNIVERSITY OF TEXAS, AUSTIN, TX
78712, USA
nasher@bertie.la.utexas.edu

Pierrette Bouillon
ISSCO/ETI, UNIVERSITÉ DE GENÈVE, 54 ROUTE DES ACACIAS, 1227
GENÈVE, SWITZERLAND
Pierrette.Bouillon@issco.unige.ch

Federica Busa
LEXEME, INC. (LINGA MOTORS, INC.) 585 MASSACHUSETTS AVE.,
CAMBRIDGE, MA 02139, USA
fede@lexeme.com

Nicoletta Calzolari
ISTITUTO DI LINGUISTICA COMPUTAZIONALE, VIA DELLA FAGGIOLA,
32, 56126 PISA, ITALY
glottolo@ilc.pi.cnr.it

Salvador Climent
LABORATORI DE RECERCA EN LINGÜISTICA COMPUTACIONAL,
UNIVERSITAT DE BARCELONA, SPAIN, GRAN VIA DE LES CORTS
CATALANES 585, BARCELONA 08007, SPAIN
climent@fil.ub.es

Laurence Danlos
TALANA & LORIA, BP 239, 54506 VANDŒUVRE LÈS NANCY,
FRANCE
laurence.danlos@linguist.jussieu.fr

Jerry A. Fodor
CENTER FOR COGNITIVE SCIENCE, RUTGERS UNIVERSITY, PSYCHOLOGY
(ANNEX), BUSCH CAMPUS, NEW BRUNSWICK, NJ 08903, USA
fodor@ruccs.rutgers.edu

Elisabetta Gola
LEXEME, INC. (LINGA MOTORS, INC.), 585 MASSACHUSETTS AVE., CAMBRIDGE, MA 02139, USA
gola@Lexeme.com

Jerry Hobbs
ARTIFICIAL INTELLIGENCE CENTER, SRI INTERNATIONAL, MENLO PARK, CA 94025, USA
HOBBS@ai.sri.com

Jacques Jayez
EHESS-CELITH, 54, BLD RASPAIL, 75006 PARIS, FRANCE
jjayez@dial.oleane.com

Adam Kilgarriff
ITRI, UNIVERSITY OF BRIGHTON, LEWES ROAD, BRIGHTON BN2 4GJ, UK
Adam.Kilgarriff@itri.bton.ac.uk

Alex Lascarides
CENTRE FOR COGNITIVE SCIENCE, UNIVERSITY OF EDINBURGH, 2, BUCCLEUCH PLACE, EDINBURGH EH8 9LW, SCOTLAND, UK
alex@cogsci.ed.ac.uk

Alessandro Lenci
ISTITUTO DI LINGUISTICA COMPUTAZIONALE, VIA DELLA FAGGIOLA, 32, 56126 PISA, ITALY
lenci@ilc.pi.cnr.it

Ernie Lepore
CENTER FOR COGNITIVE SCIENCE, RUTGERS UNIVERSITY, PSYCHOLOGY (ANNEX), BUSCH CAMPUS, NEW BRUNSWICK, NJ 08903, USA
lepore@ruccs.rutgers.edu

James McGilvray
DEPARTMENT OF PHILOSOPHY, MCGILL UNIVERSITY, LEACOCK BUILDING, 855 SHERBROOKE ST. W., MONTRÉAL, QUÉBEC H3A 2T7, CANADA
jim@philo.mcgill.ca

Monica Monachini
ISTITUTO DI LINGUISTICA COMPUTAZIONALE, VIA DELLA FAGGIOLA, 32, 56126 PISA, ITALY
monica@ilc.pi.cnr.it

Julius M. Moravcsik
DEPARTMENT OF PHILOSOPHY, STANFORD UNIVERSITY, STANFORD,
  CA 94305, USA
julius@csli.Stanford.EDU

James Pustejovsky
COMPUTER SCIENCE DEPARTMENT, 258 VOLEN CENTER FOR COMPLEX
  SYSTEMS, BRANDEIS UNIVERSITY, WALTHAM, MA 02254, USA
jamesp@cs.brandeis.edu

Nilda Ruimy
ISTITUTO DI LINGUISTICA COMPUTAZIONALE, VIA DELLA FAGGIOLA,
  32, 56126 PISA, ITALY
nilda@ilc.pi.cnr.it

Patrick Saint-Dizier
IRIT-CNRS, 118, ROUTE DE NARBONNE, 31062 TOULOUSE CEDEX,
  FRANCE
stdizier@irit.fr

Piek Vossen
COMPUTER LINGUISTIEK, UNIVERSITEIT VAN AMSTERDAM, SPUISTRAAT
  134, 1012 AMSTERDAM, THE NETHERLANDS
piek.vossen@hum.uva.nl

Yorick Wilks
AI AND NN RESEARCH GROUP, DEPARTMENT OF COMPUTER SCIENCE,
  UNIVERSITY OF SHEFFIELD, REGENT COURT, 211 PORTOBELLO ST.,
  SHEFFIELD S1 4DP, UK
y.wilks@dcs.shef.ac.uk

Preface

What is the meaning of a word? How can the few hundreds of thousands of words we know be used to construct the many millions of utterances we make and understand in a lifetime? It would appear we need more words than we have available to us, if classical wisdom on this subject is to be believed. The subject, of course, is lexical semantics, and classical wisdom can often be wrong. This field has undergone a radical shift in recent years, in large part because of two developments. First, formal frameworks for word meaning have been developed that greatly simplify the description of lexical classes and their properties. Second, we have at our disposal new compositional techniques that allow us to view word meaning as an integral part of the overall process of semantic interpretation. These and other factors have made the issues relating to "the meaning of a word" some of the most central questions being addressed in the field of linguistics today. In fact, some classic issues have resurfaced with new data and arguments, such as the debate over analyticity and semantic knowledge, as well as the evidence of a distinction (or nondistinction) between lexical and world knowledge.

Waismann (1951) argued for what he called the "open texturedness" of terms. Although he was mainly interested in how the notion applies to the nonexhaustive nature of material object statements and the absence of conclusive verification conditions, there is another sense in which this is an interesting property of language and language use; the infinite variability of reference in language is the direct product of the *essential incompleteness* of terms and their composition. I would like to adopt this image as a characterization of what generative approaches to lexical and compositional semantics are attempting to model. From this perspective, word meanings are malleable and almost actively take on new shapes and forms in novel contexts of use.

By building a notion of "open texture" directly into word meaning, the formal mechanisms that give rise to sentence meanings will themselves ensure that both analytic and contextual aspects of interpretation are available in the model. In other words, it is the very functional nature of how words are modeled that allows them to exhibit their contextual variance, and with this enables the creative use of language.

This view of word meaning leads to an interesting comparison of two very different philosophical traditions in the study of language, namely, ordinary-language philosophy and analytic semantics. These two schools chose very different linguistic units to analyze and from which to start their theorizing concerning language. The ordinary-language philosophers studied words and the functions of words in usage situations. Analytic semantics, on the other hand, derives from the study of sentences, sentence structures, and their propositional content, what has been called the logical syntax of the language (Carnap, 1932). The apparent incompatibility of these two approaches continues to dog certain philosophers, such as Fodor (1998), and has led to a rather pessimistic lack of concern over matters lexical.

The novelty of the generative lexical approach to language is the way in which these traditions and ideas are synthesized. What generative lexicon shares with ordinary language philosophy is a focus on words and word use. What it shares with analytic semantics is of course a concentration on the formalization of rules and types into a coherent and explicable system. The debt to the generative tradition in linguistics is almost too obvious to state: that meanings are compositional and recursive in nature (Chomsky, 1995). Furthermore, the generative devices available to the semantics are both more flexible than conventional approaches to compositional semantics such as Montague Grammar and more constrained than the view resulting from an arbitrary application of lexical rules.

The chapters in this volume constitute one of the first major collections addressing the synthesis of the issues mentioned above within this new paradigm. From the perspectives of philosophy, linguistics, computational linguistics, and lexicography, the fundamental problems of the creative use of language and the open texture of word sense are confronted. Although the contributors do not all agree with the basic principles of the generativity of lexical senses and composition, they have positioned their arguments in relation to this thesis, which is both useful and informative.

If the study of language is to bring us any closer to understanding concepts and the nature of our thoughts, it will be accomplished only by appreciating the importance of word meaning and the realization that compositional semantics is sensitive to word internal knowledge. It is, therefore, the very open texture of our language that reflects the compositionality of our thought.

James Pustejovsky

References

Carnap, R. 1932. *The Logical Structure of Syntax*, Littlefield, Adams and Company.
Chomsky, N. 1995. Language and nature. *Mind*, 104, 1–61.
Fodor, J. 1998. *Concepts*, Oxford, Oxford University Press.
Waismann, F. 1951. Verifiability. In Flew, A. (ed.), *Essays on Logic and Language*, Oxford, Basil Blackwell.

Introduction: Word Meaning and Creativity

Utterers create meanings by using words in context.
Hearers create interpretations.
Patrick Hanks, *SPARKLE Workshop*, Pisa, January 1999.

This quote from Patrick Hanks reflects very closely the spirit of this volume that tackles the relation between word meaning and human linguistic creativity. We are interested in pursuing the view that words are rich repositories of semantic information that people use to talk about the world in a potentially infinite number of ways. Our goal is to tackle the essence of words insofar as they provide a window onto human cognition and the compositional nature of thought. It is thus imperative that a theory of language addresses how lexical items contribute to the peculiar human ability that goes under the label of "linguistic creativity."

It is undeniable that words have "meanings" that go above and beyond the scope of linguistic research: They often carry the weight of a person's own experience. We are not aiming at exploring the unexplorable, but in proving that, given an appropriate set of methodological tools, a formal modeling of word meaning and linguistic creativity can be achieved. *Linguistic creativity* is a "generative" ability to extend the expressive possibilities of language in a potentially infinite number of ways. From the perspective of the lexicon (i.e., word meaning), it is the ability to give new meanings to words beyond their literal use.

As such, the overall task follows the strategy of contemporary generative syntax, which has achieved a basic understanding of how speakers produce and understand novel utterances and has brought simplicity to the great complexity underlying the syntactic structure of sentences. This became possible once the basic data set was isolated and regularities were identified in the massive variability of grammatical expressions.

From the viewpoint of the lexicon, however, creativity looks even more like a miracle. Researchers tend to disagree on what constitutes "linguistic" evidence (as opposed to context-dependent use of words) as well as what is the basic vocabulary for describing regularities in the behavior of lexical items. As a result, lexical semantics has been confined to a narrow domain of investigation, essentially dependent on a specific grammatical framework.

Broader issues surrounding the study of the meaning of words, how it is represented, and how it contributes to syntactic and semantic processing have been the object of controversy among philosophers and the source of serious problems for researchers in computational linguistics and artificial intelligence.

This volume aims to bring together diverse contributions in philosophy, linguistics, computer science, and lexicography to highlight the breadth of the field and, at the same time, to point out how different issues converge around a common need: a framework establishing a set of principled properties of the lexicon and a unified vocabulary for representing word meaning. This cannot be achieved unless researchers isolate the data set to be studied and agree on the way in which these data should be understood.

1   Generativity in the Lexicon

One of the threads that links the contributions to this volume is the attempt to strengthen the foundations for defining the boundary between literal and extended (viz. creative) meanings. This requires two steps:

1. Narrowing and delimiting the definition of a word sense.
2. Defining the compositional processes/rules to extend the sense of a given word.

The second aspect takes advantage of a "strictly limited fragment of world knowledge" (see Asher and Lascarides in this volume) and defines the domains where components of meaning can be shifted. Thus, generativity in the lexicon is about "shifting" meaning in ways and across domains that are not random. To use the metaphors cited by Moravcsik (in this volume): If there is counterfeit money, then there must be real money. If there are meaning shifts, then there must be an underlying literal semantic representation from which the extended sense is projected.

Adopting and expanding Plato's metaphor, if there is a shadow then there must be an object that projects it and a source of light striking that object from a particular angle. In this volume, we take literal meaning to correspond to the object, the extended projection to the shadow, and the source of light to the specific compositional processes at work.

2   Generative Lexicon(s)

In this volume we have explored the lexicon from a particular perspective: a generative approach to word meaning as highlighted by the work in the Generative Lexicon (see Chapter 4 in this volume).

It is important to stress that this volume is not meant to be a defense of the Generative Lexicon (henceforth GL), but rather a way to focus the discussion around a concrete framework that has an important merit: It has taken an explicit stand toward establishing a methodology in lexical semantics and providing its own answer to the basic question of what is word meaning. Although its answers are far from being uncontroversial or complete, such an explicit attempt allows for serious scientific discourse. Our goal is to present different views around a set of basic assumptions made in GL:

a.   The polymorphic nature of words can be studied in a principled way;
b.   There is a semantic vocabulary for structuring word meaning, which provides the input to the rules of semantic composition;
c.   There are generative rules of semantic compositions;
d.   The structuring of word meaning is an empirical question.

The polymorphic behavior of words is reflected in the ability of a lexical item to change meaning in different contexts. Nobody would deny this property of words: most of them appear in different contexts, with different meanings. This is what gives rise to the variability of interpretations and reflects speakers' creativity in using words in a variety of ways.

The more controversial question is how to represent and structure them. One solution is to take an *enumerative* (or monomorphic) approach, where the different senses are listed in the lexicon. This view, however, faces the problem of predicting a priori all the possible senses a word can take in context. As senses are only restricted by the number of possible contexts, it becomes questionable whether a semantics for natural language is even possible.

GL argues that compositional meaning takes place under predictable circumstances, provided there is an adequate set of principles for describing lexical structure. Senses need not be enumerated but can be derived *generatively* from richer representations of words and compositional mechanisms for combining them. The nature of individual lexical representations characterizes literal meaning, which involves two closely tied elements: analytic and conventionalized knowledge. The analytic component is the structuring itself, namely, *qualia structure*; the conventionalized component is represented by the value that fills each qualia role.

Irrespective of any particular framework, anyone studying word meaning has to address these points. We will present solutions within the generative lexicon, as well as alternative views of its critics.

3   Organization of the Volume

The volume is organized into four parts. The first part, *Linguistic Creativity and the Lexicon*, provides the philosophical foundations for the work presented in the book. James McGilvray presents a lucid discussion on the implication of Chomsky's creativity for a theory of the Lexicon. The three subsequent chapters approach the philosophical questions surrounding word meaning in the form of a debate. We have reprinted the debate between Jerry Fodor and Ernie Lepore on one hand, and James Pustejovsky on the other, which appeared in the 1998 spring issue of *Linguistic Inquiry*. In this volume, Yorick Wilks has joined in, contributing the view from three decades of research in artificial intelligence (AI).

Part two of the book, *The Syntax of Word Meaning*, opens with the contribution of James Pustejovsky, who presents new developments in GL, and then moves on to the analysis of fairly standard topics in lexical semantics: verb semantics (Pierrette Bouillon and Federica Busa; Jacques Jayez, and Patrick Saint-Dizier), partitive constructions (Salvador Climent), adjectives (Patrick Saint-Dizier), and causal relations (Laurence Danlos).

The third part of the volume, *Interfacing the Lexicon*, presents contributions on metonymy (Jerry Hobbs) and metaphor (Julius Moravcsik; Nicolas Asher and Alex Lascarides). Here the focus is on the need as well as the feasibility of appealing to structured lexical representations to study those phenomena that are on the edge between the lexicon and pragmatics. These views are challenged in the contribution by Adam Kilgarriff, who presents data against the usefulness of a generative-like approach to sense extension phenomena.

The last part of the book, *Building Resources*, contains contributions on the development of actual resources for natural language processing (NLP) using current developments in lexical semantics. The first two chapters present two aspects of the SIMPLE project: an effort sponsored by the European Commission to develop twelve computational semantic lexicons for the major European languages (Federica Busa, Nicoletta Calzolari, and Alessandro Lenci; Nilda Ruimy, Elisabetta Gola, and Monica Monachini). The last chapter, by Piek Vossen, discusses the EuroWordNet project, whose goal is to build Wordnets for a number of European languages.

Each part of the volume is introduced by a more extensive discussion of the chapters, in order to provide a roadmap for the reader, highlight the common issues raised by each set of papers, and stress their relevance toward our goals.

Pierrette Bouillon
Federica Busa

PART I

Linguistic Creativity and the Lexicon

1   Introduction

FEDERICA BUSA AND PIERRETTE BOUILLON

Lexical semantics has not yet given a satisfactory answer to a crucial question that implicitly or explicitly has been asked by philosophers of language, computer scientists, linguists, and lexicographers, namely, "What is word meaning?" The goal of this part of the volume is to set the stage for subsequent discussion, presenting the issues that confront those investigating language and the mind through the study of the mental lexicon.

The reader should not expect a definite answer. We may gain an insight that word meaning can best be studied as a transparent structure, rather than a black box whose contents escape us. Alternatively, we may choose to take a stand in the debate presented in Chapters 4, 5, and 6, where opposed views are expressed.

There are two broad positions emerging in this part of the volume: One argues for an internal syntax of word meaning (James McGilvray; James Pustejovsky; Yorick Wilks), and the other views concepts as particulars (Jerry Fodor and Ernie Lepore).

McGilvray discusses how word meaning contributes to the creative aspect of language and reaches the conclusion that lexical semantics, as done within a research program such as the Generative Lexicon, is a "branch of syntax, broadly speaking."

Jerry Fodor and Ernie Lepore criticize lexical semantics frameworks that aim at isolating the internal constitution of word meaning. They forcefully argue against the assumption that the content of concepts is constituted by inferential relations, a view that necessarily leads to holism. Alternatively, they take concepts to be atoms with no internal constitution whatsoever, such that all that can be said about word meaning is: "Nothing can be said about word meaning."

In replying to Fodor and Lepore, Pustejovsky presents an internalist view of the lexicon, where qualia structure is the syntax for lexical description, which in turn provides the input to the rules of semantic composition. The role of a syntax of word meaning is precisely that of avoiding holism, while permitting questions concerning the well-formedness of concepts, the combinatorial possibilities of the elements constituting their internal structure (i.e., qualia), and the relations they bear to each other.

Yorick Wilks, approaching the debate from the Artificial Intelligence (AI) perspective, argues against the position of Fodor and Lepore. In this area of

3

research, the semantic import of words ought to be explicitly spelled out if any degree of understanding is to be achieved. In particular, Wilks addresses explicitly the role of inferential relations as key elements that drive "intelligent" natural language understanding and the computational modeling of language. Such a view could be challenged by arguing that the requirements from AI may not mean anything from the perspective of human psychology. The human mind may not be computational in this sense and hence the effort is moot.

Before taking this position – which in our opinion is an unfair criticism – there are still too many avenues of research to be explored. These are addressed in later parts of the volume and include seeking a sound methodology in lexical semantics; addressing the *poverty of the stimulus*, and the ease with which people *prefer* (as opposed to select) certain interpretations and not others in different contexts. These issues are so much at the core of lexical research that their answer determines whether there is a field of investigation at all or whether there should only be lexicographic practice. This is certainly a potential alternative. However, as shown in the last part of the volume, there may not be options after all. Lexicographic practice, in fact, may have some surprises in store for us.

2   Chomsky on the Creative Aspect of Language Use and Its Implications for Lexical Semantic Studies

JAMES McGILVRAY

Abstract

Observations on the creative aspect of language use constrain theories of language in much the way as those on the poverty of stimulus do. The observations as Chomsky discusses them will be explained and their consequences for a semantic theory of the lexicon explored.

1   Introduction

Chomsky began to mention the creative aspect of language use in the early 1960s; his 1964 *Current Issues* discusses it. In 1966, *Cartesian Linguistics* takes it up in detail. At the end of the 1950s he had read extensively in the works of Descartes, Cudworth, Humboldt, and others in the seventeenth to mid-nineteenth centuries "Cartesian linguistics" tradition, and they provided a framework for articulating these ideas. Arguably, though, they were implicit in his review of Skinner and even in *The Logical Structure of Linguistic Theory* (ca. 1955). The creative aspect observations, along with the poverty of stimulus observations, offer a set of facts with which his and – he holds – any science of language must contend. However, he thinks that the lessons of the creative aspect observations in particular are often ignored, especially in dealing with semantic issues such as truth and reference, meaning and content. He may be right. I review the creativity observations and discuss some of their implications and suggestions for a semantic theory of the lexicon. In their light, I discuss briefly James Pustejovsky's different approach.

Chomsky treats the creative aspect and poverty of stimulus observations as facts that a theory of language needs to explain. Here, "explain" amounts to something like "make sense of." A theory of UG explains the poverty of stimulus observations if it portrays the language faculty and its operations in the human mind in such a way that one can see how creatures with the mental capacities the theory deals with would behave in the way the observations indicate. For the poverty observations, a theory that specifies what is innate and that makes defensible claims about just how these innate elements play a role in the computational system of the language faculty (for example, a theory that proposes specific principles and parameters, says how they are represented in the lexicon, etc.) can make sense of how children across the human population so readily and uniformly use language, given in each case a rather thin and skewed data set. As for the creativity facts, the same UG

5

theory of language and the portrait it paints of the language faculty and its place in the mind must show how a paradigm case of intelligent behavior, "language use," can arise, without attempting, of course, to predict what someone would say in any given set of circumstances. Explaining language use means appealing to what the theory says about language and its place in the mind to show how a person's use of language can be stimulus free, unbounded, and innovative, as well as coherent and appropriate to circumstances.

2   The Creative Aspect Observations

The creativity observations are generalizations that anyone with common sense can make by reflecting on what they have experienced; no one needs knowledge of a theory – of language or anything else – to make them. They are also supported by organized and controlled observations. Nothing has shown them to be wrong, or even suspect. Chomsky attributes their first recorded mention to Descartes in the fifth part of his 1637 *Discourse on the method of rightly conducting one's reason and seeking the truth in the sciences*. There they are used as a test of having a mind "as we do," a mind that neither machines nor animals have. Specifically,

> ... [machines and animals] could never use words, or put together other signs, as we do in order to declare our thoughts to others. For we can certainly conceive of a machine so constructed [or animal so trained] that it utters words, and even utters words which correspond to bodily actions causing a change in its organs ... [b]ut it is not conceivable that such a machine [or animal] should produce different arrangements of words so as to give an appropriately meaningful answer to whatever is said in its presence, as the dullest of men can do (p. 140 of Cottingham et al. translation).

Having the observations serve as a test of mind puts them in the right context, for it raises the question of what special capacity humans have that allows them to produce and do what they do.

Notice Descartes' remark, "as the dullest of men can do." The emphasis for Descartes and Chomsky (1966, p. 3f) is on what any speaker displays when she speaks in arbitrary circumstances, not on what some people with special training, insight, or brilliance can sometimes do in specific circumstances when they set their minds to it. The observations are based on ordinary linguistic creativity, not on (say) the extraordinary creativity of the poet. The creativity observations apply universally; that is one reason the sciences of language and mind must take them into account.

To disentangle the different threads in this brief passage from Descartes (and some of his others) and to capture central themes developed later by other rationalists, Chomsky glosses "produce different arrangements of words so as to give an appropriately meaningful answer to whatever is said in its presence" as three distinct but interrelated observations. He uses various labels for them. Taking Mark

Baker's (1995) selection from among these labels[1] the creative aspect amounts to *stimulus freedom, unboundedness,* and *appropriateness.* Stimulus freedom is easy to recognize and illustrate. The idea is that what a person says (out loud or in foro interno) is not causally dependent upon the environment in which the person speaks or thinks. Speaking to her logic instructor after his third effort to explain why C.I. Lewis felt it was important to define strict implication, Gertrude declares her interest in spelunking, or she takes up the topic of the latest U.N. report on the state of the Sudanese economy. It is obvious that there is no prima facie reason to think that there is a "real" causal connection between her circumstances, her uttering words at all, and the specific expression(s) she produces. Perhaps a psychiatrist, soothsayer, or the instructor himself, taking Gertrude's remarks to result from the instructor's earnest efforts, would offer a "causal" explanation of her linguistic output. However, it is not serious causality. It is interpretation of an event as part of a pattern that includes what the instructor said; his position, character, state of fatigue, . . .; Gertrude's character, quirks, aptitude and interest in logic, what else she is doing now, what she wants to do besides what she is doing, . . .; and an unlimitable number of other things. This is not the well-defined causality of serious theory, and – given the apparent impossibility of limiting the factors that might play a role in it – it never will be.

Unboundedness is apparent in the example. Gertrude is not constrained to produce a specific set of sentences. Descartes' remark that there are "different arrangements of words" suggests description of the range available to her in terms of generative rules or principles, but the remark itself seems to be innocent of theoretical commitments. The Port-Royal grammarians may have had generative rules in mind when they made the same observation, but likely Descartes was only observing that the sentences of a natural language come in various configurations and have no apparent limit on length.[2] That this observation is independent of *specific* principles, at least, is obvious from the fact that while virtually everyone agrees that languages provide for various configurations and unlimited length for sentences, there is disagreement on how to account for it – what kind of grammar to construct, what to include in it, and so on. The various *theoretical descriptions* of the phenomenon of linguistic productivity that these attempts yield are disputable.[3] The basic observation is not.

---

[1] In an unpublished manuscript entitled *On The Creative Aspect of Language Use,* Department of Linguistics, McGill University, 1995.

[2] Perhaps Descartes had *some* notion of generativity in mind. It was not unusual to marvel at the way in which the words of a language could be put together from 26 letters. And, as Chomsky notes in (1966, n. 9), Huarte's 1575 *Examen de Ingenios* thought of mind as essentially involving engendering and generating. Chomsky quotes from p. 3 of Huarte: "Wit [ingenio] is a generative power . . . the Understanding is a Generative Faculty." Huarte goes on to describe three degrees of activity or creativity, representing also three degrees or kind of mind that he associates with beast, humans, and divinity (and in rare cases, humans too).

[3] I use "description" as Chomsky does: a generative grammar, if adequate, provides a description, not explanation, of the (infinite) set of sentences/expressions of a natural language.

Stimulus freedom and unboundedness are not enough by themselves to serve as a modern test of minds "like ours." Consider machines. We now understand machines in a way that allows them to produce stimulus free and unbounded sets of language-like entities. Computers provided with a randomizing device and various recursive principles can produce language-like strings that are both. In contrast, Descartes' machines (and all nonhuman organisms also, for all were thought to operate in accord with "instinct" alone) were more limited devices whose operations – supposed to be completely describable in terms of a contact mechanics – were thought to require impulse, received initially from without. So unboundedness and stimulus freedom ruled out Descartes' machines, but not ours.

The unboundedness observation does, however, remain an effective test for mind with animals: no known nonhuman animal has a mind with syntactically productive linguistic capacities "like ours." Animals apparently cannot, in Descartes' language, "use words, or put together other signs, as we do." As Chomsky explains it, this is because animals lack innate knowledge of basic syntactic principles [formal syntactic and phonological ones, certainly, and probably semantic ones (in Chomsky's broadly syntactic sense of "semantic") too]. These principles seem to be beyond the capacity of animals to learn, but that is another matter.

In any case, the third aspect of the creativity observations – appropriateness to circumstance or coherence – seems to constitute a test for linguistic capacities that all machines and animals fail and only (but all) humans can and do pass. The observation is that what people say is usually, perhaps almost always, "appropriate to circumstances" (when judged by another human being). This raises several issues. First is the issue of what counts as a circumstance, which is tightly connected to the issue of which circumstances to take into account. Circumstances must amount to more than just a speaker's immediate environment at time of speech. If a person is telling a fictional tale, what s/he produces is appropriate to what s/he is doing (the task s/he has set), so it is appropriate to the speaker's immediate circumstances in this oblique way. However, it is more important that its content – in one usage of this abused word – be appropriate to the fictional circumstances that s/he relates. If an expression in a fictional tale is also appropriate to current real-world circumstances in some way – where, for example, the tale is an attempt to satirize current government policy – it is less directly appropriate to these real circumstances than it is to the fictional circumstances of the tale. Further, the problems of delimiting what count as the circumstances to which an expression is appropriate by no means stop here. Everyday speech is full of allusions, double-entendres, metaphorical applications to multiple domains (and comparisons between them), and so on. It seems safe to say that it is very unlikely that anyone can come up with a canonical list of items that *must* be included among "circumstances" to which a remark can be said to be appropriate. No doubt this is related to Chomsky's view that language use or language application seems to be beyond the competence of serious science; I return to that topic.

Although the expressions a person produces are almost always appropriate to circumstances, these expressions are stimulus free – that is, they are causally unrelated to things in the speaker's immediate environment. So "being appropriate" is not "being caused by environmental conditions." Nor is it being regularly correlated with environment, although most philosophers and linguists who do semantics seem to think so, for they look to something like correlation to underwrite their view that, semantically speaking, language is related to the world. This is not to say that regular correlation, with or without causation, yields no conception of appropriateness at all. In fact, where immediate environmental conditions correlate regularly with speech and speech in turn regularly correlates with acts and activities that serve the interests of human beings, we have a clear case of speech being appropriate to the circumstances in which it is to be found. In these cases, speech is *functionally* appropriate; it clearly serves a need or goal. However, this functional sense is of no use for the kind of appropriateness we are interested in. Except for the intervention of speech, it is the same form that we attribute to a bee's perceptual and motor states where we can impute to the bee a biologically based need to gather pollen, and it routinely targets flowers that have the pollen it seeks. Nor is it different from the kinds of "speech" Descartes thought animals and machines are capable of. It gives language and speech an intermediary functional role, perhaps likening linguistic production to the states of a calculating device that intervenes between perceptual inputs and any acts and activities that subserve specific needs or desires. This is not the observed ordinary creative use of language. It is conceiving of language as applied to the performance of tasks, jobs, and strategies, or as a device for holding and manipulating "information" and applying it in activity, or as getting its "semantic values" by establishing determinate relations to the things of the world. Use-theoretic, information-theoretic, and most truth conditional accounts of language's semantic aspects appeal to this conception of appropriateness. However, it misses the point and misconceives the task of the theory of meaning too.

There are other ways to put Descartes' and Chomsky's point about appropriateness, but the remarks above suffice. Expressions are almost always recognizably appropriate to circumstances; they are often readily seen to be so. However, there seems to be no articulate scheme(s) or formula(e) that can take a circumstance and a speaker and say of them that such-and-such a set of sentences is appropriate if, and only if, it is used in or with respect to that speaker and set of circumstances. Vague generalizations and question-begging after-the-fact claims do not count, of course. Nothing less than a no-holds-barred theory that specifies exactly what counts as appropriate (given circumstance and speaker) is required of a serious science of language use or of semantics as it is usually understood. It seems that this aspect of Descartes' test for mind not only sets a condition that no machine or animal has managed to meet (or is at all likely to),[4] but it challenges

---

[4] If reflection is not enough to convince, the (larger) Loebner prize competition shows this for machines. And if the many efforts to train apes to produce something like a natural language do not even allow them to meet the unboundedness test, there is no point in speculating about whether they can meet the appropriateness test.

orthodox views of how to construct a naturalistic "semantic theory" for natural languages.[5]

3   How to Explain the Facts: Externalist and Internalist Answers

Whatever their accounts of stimulus freedom (perhaps "complexity of organization") and of unboundedness (perhaps "analogy"), the externalist – Chomsky includes among externalists the empiricist tradition that he discusses in *Cartesian Linguistics* and later – deals with appropriateness by trying to make language use out to be routines that satisfy needs and goals. Human beings might be treated as creatures who are trained to produce linguistic responses to circumstances that the community takes to be appropriate. This move is made by the contemporary tradition that like Wittgenstein treats language as a "game" that fulfills goals (cp Chomsky 1966, p. 10). Humans might be conceived as information-gatherers and agents. Or they might be treated as truth-tellers; some who call themselves Fregeans and who are preoccupied with reference and truth take this tack. For all externalists, language in its semantic aspects is basically a functional device, the essence of which is serving goals, including truth-telling. For them, a theory of language must be externalist, for it must include the things and states of affairs of the world and relations between these and words. It is significant that there is little being said now about semantics so construed that has not been said before, sometimes with more insight. Little, if any, progress has been made in the efforts to construct theories of this domain – a sign that there is no theory to be had and that those who seek one have misconceived the issues. No doubt post-Fregean formal logic and the development of formal systems have helped make it appear that science has been brought to bear on the domain of language use but, formal or not, there are no serious answers of the input-linguistic intermediary-output or contents via relations to the world varieties that can pretend to capture appropriateness by appeal to regularities or routines. Perhaps for naturalistic science to be brought to bear at all on appropriateness of ordinary creative language use, a completely different approach is necessary, one that constructs a naturalistic science of the capacity in the mind that makes it possible for humans to produce expressions that are appropriate to circumstance (and stimulus free and unbounded).

Chomsky, like those in the rationalist tradition before him, abandons the effort to provide a science of language use, except for those aspects of language use that can be dealt with by internalist theories (such as the sciences of language articulation and perception, and perhaps an internalist science of what is found immediately on the other side of the semantic interface, LF/SEM). Instead, he suggests how

---

[5] I assume that naturalistic theories are what is at issue. One can, of course, stipulate a set of semantic values for an expression or set of expressions, and even include these stipulations within a formal theory. But, unless this is taken to be an exercise in how to express contents (and a rather arcane one, in my opinion) and only that, it is difficult to see why one would want to do it. Much the same can be said of attempts to introduce abstract entities as referents of expressions and their parts. For discussion, see McGilvray (1998).

a naturalistic theory can help explain (in the "make sense of" vein) how creative language use is *possible* (cp 1972, p. 13). The rationalist tradition before him made some progress in this regard. It treated language not as a functional device that mediates between perception and action, but as an instrument of free thought and self-expression whose meanings or contents come prespecified, or are innate, so there is no need to try to find content through regularity in "relations to the world." Descartes' own efforts in this regard were not very successful. Like other rationalists, he treated language use as an expression of, or artefact of, coherent "thought," or "reason." In effect, he attributed the special properties of stimulus free and unbounded but appropriate language use to special properties of thought or reason. This allowed him to mobilize important properties of thought – that thought is independent of context and stimulus, can range far and wide, and can be coherent – to make sense of how language use could appear to have these properties. This might appear to beg the question, but not if he can show why *thought* has these properties. He does not, however, offer much by way of doing so. He did, famously, try to say why our internal thoughts can be appropriate to (external) circumstance by appeal to God and His unwillingness to deceive us by populating the world with a mild-mannered Harry (or no Harry at all) when we think or declare that Harry is obstreperous. He did, equally famously, build thought's freedom from circumstance into his view of mind as a separate substance. However, neither of these moves count as contributions to a naturalistic science of thought, at least not now. Furthermore, although Descartes acknowledged that thought is "unbounded," he did not attempt to say what it is about thoughts that allows it to be so.

Unlike Descartes, the Port-Royal grammarians made progress in accounting for thought's unbounded character, for they offered an approximation of Chomsky's early transformational generative grammar, although dealing with judgments (1966), not "strings." That is, they did not clearly distinguish, as Chomsky does, between purely syntactically characterized sentences ("strings") and sentential judgments or thoughts, which are acts of persons and are assumed to have a semantic interpretation. Ignoring Panini, who had no influence on any of these individuals, the Port-Royalists were perhaps the most successful at this task before Chomsky.[6] None of the other Cartesian linguists really got around to attempting to produce generative theories, although they did seem to realize that something needed to be done. Humboldt, for example, for all his fascinating suggestions and insights into the productivity of language, never developed a theory. Well before him,

---

[6] It is worth mentioning a surprising partial exception. In a virtually unknown work called *Menomimi Morphophonemics* that appeared in a rather obscure (to Bloomfieldians) Czech journal in 1939, Bloomfield very uncharacteristically developed the rudiments of a generative theory of morphophonemics (Bloomfield, 1939). No doubt for political or ideological reasons, given the behaviorist orthodoxy of the day and his position as one of its high priests, neither he nor any of his friends mentioned this work again. Chomsky remarks that neither of his teachers at Penn – Harris and Hoenigswald, both of whom were familiar with this work of Bloomfield's and with Chomsky's own very early generative efforts – mentioned to him that Bloomfield had already developed a similar generative theory. He was not aware of Bloomfield's efforts when he did his work.

Cudworth – although speaking of thought, and not explicitly language – remarked on an "innate cognoscitive power" which human minds have that enables them to generate and thus create such a variety of thoughts that they can virtually anticipate (his "prolepsis") any circumstance in which they might be involved.

Chomsky has made two crucial contributions to the rationalist strategy of constructing a theory of an internal capacity that makes sense of the poverty of stimulus observations. One is to offer a serious, well-defended, and justified naturalistic theory of the biological capacity of language. It is a computational theory, but that does not matter; the best current theories of our biological visual capacity are computational too, without being externalist. As a theory of the language faculty, his theory deals with a far less mysterious-looking subject matter than the traditional rationalist's focus on reason or thought. Second, Chomsky's rationalist theory of the language faculty, particularly in its most recent minimalist incarnation, provides plausible and defensible theoretical accounts of properties of the language faculty that make sense of how human beings can use language creatively and recognize its creative use in others.

Stimulus freedom and unboundedness are easy, and in some form or another the machinery for dealing with them has been present in Chomsky's linguistic theories from the beginning. The possibility of stimulus freedom in language use can be seen to result from a modular language faculty. Not just any kind of modularity will do: we need a faculty that utilizes its own resources and with internal prompting produces (in apparent isolation) through its own algorithms items in the form of linguistic expressions that are unique to it and yet that "interface" with relevant other internal biological systems.[7] Chomsky's current "human language computational system" (CHL) does that admirably. As for the unboundedness of creative language use, it is surely the result of a generative system, which, in its present incarnation, consists of a computational system that merges a finite stock of lexical features to produce more complex lexical items, moving features around where required to meet bare output conditions – the effects of which are primarily, perhaps wholly, localized in functional features.

However, although it may be obvious how a form of modularity and the generative system of the language faculty could make stimulus freedom and the unboundedness of linguistic behavior possible, it is less clear how the language faculty can allow for appropriateness of language use. Let us assume that Descartes' "God would not deceive" does not suffice. If not, though, what properties of the language faculty, revealed by the theory of language, could speak to this issue? At times, Chomsky writes as if the language faculty cannot speak to this issue at all and that a theory of it could offer nothing sensible to allow us to understand how language use can be appropriate, while still stimulus free and unbounded. For example, in about the middle of the 1970s, he began to speak of the fact that there had been no progress for millenia in accounting for appropriateness of

---

[7] Chomsky speaks of perceptual and articulatory systems on the one hand, and conceptual-intentional systems on the other.

language use as an example of a mystery for the theory of language, as opposed to a problem (where we at least have an idea of how to proceed). Later, the task of dealing with appropriateness became the insoluble part of "Descartes Problem," the apparently impossible part – unlike speech perception and production – of the task of explaining how language produced by the mind is put to use. However, when Chomsky writes like this, he is just pointing out that the theory of language is and must be internalist; it cannot take what is outside the head as part of its subject matter. However, the way is open to find properties of the language faculty or its products (expressions) that serve the task of explaining how the appropriateness aspect of creative language use is possible.

4   Accounting for Appropriateness

To get a different perspective on the matter, let us look at a bit of recent philosophical history and Chomsky's accommodation of it. Earlier this century, Wittgenstein and others bruited about the distinction between reasons and causes. The distinction, like all those that are technical or verge on it, calls for a decision about what to apply "reason" and "cause" to. However, the point is clear enough without disputing the details: the sciences aim toward well-defined causes while common sense understanding allows its "causes" to include many explanations that would not be accepted in the sciences. Call these explanations "reasons." This distinction is connected to Chomsky's increasingly emphasized (e.g., 1995a) distinction between common sense understanding and scientific understanding. The idea, basically, is that common sense understanding proceeds within a flexible, richly conceptually endowed, open-ended and anthropocentric framework while scientific understanding is specialized for particular frameworks (to theories of specific domains), depends on hard-won concepts for resources, strives to be objective, and is comparatively inflexible. Common sense concepts (**water**) do not serve for the sciences, and scientific concepts (**H_2O**) will never do for common sense with its practical anthropocentric orientation. Nor is scientific description and explanation common sense description and explanation. The former constitutes a domain of causes, the latter a domain primarily of reasons. No doubt reflecting the anthropocentric orientation of common sense, reasons are often reasons for *actions* and are clearly not causes as conceived in the sciences. Take, for example, the idea that something in a person's environment can prompt or serve as an occasion for a remark. Earlier rationalists spoke of something "inciting and inclining" one to do or say something. Chomsky agrees and adds a remark that connects reasons, common sense understanding, and appropriateness: "discourse is not a series of random utterances but fits the situation that evokes it but does not cause it, a crucial if obscure difference" (1988, p. 5).

   To illustrate these connections, recall Gertrude and her discomfited logic instructor. Her profession of interest in spelunking can easily be understood to have been prompted, occasioned, incited, or evoked by her instructor's earnest but tedious efforts. And her reason for saying what she did might well be that she was bored and wanted to change the topic, or perhaps she wanted to inform her instructor – without much subtlety but at least more adroitly than direct statement would – that his efforts were indeed tedious or perhaps she wanted to suggest that following his explanation was equivalent to attempting to explore vast caverns with little light. Anyone hearing the tale recognizes that these are plausible scenarios. And they are not the only ones. There is no one-one nor one-and-specifiable-few correlation between circumstance and action. Circumstances and action can change while the *same explanation* continues to suit: Gertrude's specific remark, the instructor's specific sentences, the room and much of the rest of the environment, the time, etc. Yet reasons can also be modified and modulated, sometimes with great subtlety, to suit the *same situation*: Was it *just* boredom, or did Gertrude have other motivations; was the instructor unsure of himself, inviting doubts about the importance of the topic; was there something else that led Gertrude to be that abrupt; and so forth? All this indicates that the reasons for action that one might appeal to in order to say why a particular remark is appropriate to the circumstances in which it appears are far from the causal explanations that the scientist hopes to establish – where, even though there might be ceteris paribus conditions, one must be able to state (if the science is successful) what needs to be kept the same and what can differ. There is no expectation of nor any hope for anything like this in the domain of common sense understanding and reasons. This is not surprising. The reasons for human action, including linguistic actions, such as statement, expostulation, hinting, cajoling, are as varied and flexible as a particular linguistic action's appropriateness, no doubt because recognizing appropriateness and reasons involves placing human action in one or more of various kinds of patterns of human motivation, desire, interest, character, and belief, as well as changing circumstance. So although linguistic actions are typically appropriate to "suit" and "fit" circumstances, no one should expect a science of why they are. The clear-cut applications and well-demarcated domains of science are foreign here.

Reasons for linguistic action and their associated characteristic, appropriateness of use, cannot be excised from accounts of language use, or pragmatics. They cannot even be quarantined. Both play a central role in practices, such as linguistic communication, that – taken together – constitute the domain of language use. In that regard, Chomsky (1988, p. 5) remarks, "The normal use of language is thus free and undetermined but yet appropriate to situations; and it is recognized as appropriate by other participants in the discourse situation who might have reacted in similar ways and whose thoughts, evoked by this discourse, correspond to those of the speaker." The picture of successful communication Chomsky paints is one of approximation that seems to depend on conceiving of or imagining oneself reacting to circumstances in similar ways to another in order to come to some decision about what the other intends. Ignoring the complex details, the emphasis for current purposes must be on how people manage to conceive of how they might have reacted, given some circumstances. The answer cannot be given in terms of large overlap in beliefs, interests, and the like, with or without Davidson's "charity." Arguing for this overlap in beliefs, interests, and the like presupposes that their contents are accessible to others and to the extent that conformity in belief, and so on, is required for communication to take place, makes understanding someone with different beliefs and interests difficult, perhaps impossible.

The key to a different, internalist approach to understanding others lies in Chomsky's view of content as found in natural language expressions themselves, where these are taken to provide in their semantic and formal features endless numbers of *perspectives* that can be used to cut up the world in ways that suit human needs and interests. These anthropocentric perspectives are what make it possible for creative language use to be appropriate to circumstance, and the innate features that make them up allow for enough commonality in how people can describe circumstance to allow for communication.

To emphasize what is at stake, keep in mind that if the remarkable practices involved in understanding one another are possible, and if appeal to commonality of belief begs the question, the alternative is that something about the mind and its products must underwrite such normally effortless operations. Not only do we seem to be able to describe the free linguistic actions of people, understand them, and gain insight into them and the reasons they are produced, we also seem to be able, with remarkable ease, to comprehend a whole range of nonlinguistic actions with which humans are concerned, quickly recognizing who is the giver, what is given, to whom or what it is given, how the status of the given thing, the donor, and receiver have changed, and so on. Our routinely performed feats do not stop with comprehending events in which humans are the agents. We recognize that the tree bends to the wind, the sun rises in the sky, and so on, and can presume that others can recognize these also. In other words, from a very early age we have and apply the folk psychology and folk physics that make up common sense understanding. We have their elements down pat, even though we rarely, if ever, articulate them (we do not need to). Further, we apply them without appealing to something such as Descartes' God to provide assurance that our practices will net us successes. Properties of the language faculty itself and the theory of the language faculty that details these properties provide a naturalistic answer to how linguistic activities can be appropriate to circumstance – not by correlating circumstance and words directly but by providing humans with the machinery that makes this possible.

In recent work, Chomsky has increasingly been emphasizing the anthropocentricity of the concepts that the lexical items of natural languages provide to human use – to our efforts to state or question, comment, or cajole, or do any of the many things that we do with language. In his informal discussions of LF/SEM, for example, he emphasized that these interfaces, produced by the operations of the computational system of the language faculty from a limited stock of lexical items with their phonological, formal, and semantic features, provide – especially through their semantic features – "*intricate and highly specialized* perspectives from which to view [selected aspects of the world], *crucially involving human interests and concerns even in the simplest cases*" (1995a, p. 20; emphasis added). The emphasis on intricate and highly specialized perspectives and on the fact that they seem to be essentially devoted to human interests and concerns suggests how a feature of the language faculty could make sense of appropriateness. If the concepts embodied in semantic features that lexical items provide the computational system that produces SEMs/LFs are both rich and essentially devoted to human interests, it is no surprise that the complex configurations in which these concepts appear at SEM/LF provide the extraordinarily diverse (but sufficiently structured that they are accessible) set of "contents" needed to deal with how humans use language to relate to the world – or to fictional worlds, for that matter. They allow – virtually invite – one to raise and speak to the issues that are of interest to creatures like us.

Simple illustrations help clarify this. The first appeals to a feature of at least some nominal concepts. Assume on reasonable grounds that many nominals of natural language lexicons provide for *both* an abstract and a concrete application or "reading" – an important form of polysemy. Chomsky discusses **book** and mentions that it gets both readings in "the book I'm writing will weigh 5 pounds" (1995b, p. 236). It is not clear how to theoretically represent this fact about **book** and other nominal concepts. Pustejovsky, who favors a categorial grammar in (1995), represents it by using dot product terminology; Chomsky, who favors a computational-derivational approach coupled to a version of lexical decomposition (judging by 1995b, but see also Chomsky's approving comments on Humboldt's version in 1966), tends to advert in his informal exposition to the admittedly inadequate but tried and useful +/−ABSTRACT (or +/−CONCRETE). There are serious issues of lexical composition and computation to settle here, but however they are settled, it is plausible to assume along with Chomsky that *both* "readings" are available at SEM/LF: they have to be, or else "Harry's book is on the way" and endless numbers of other expressions would have to (implausibly) be represented with two SEM/LFs to allow for the abstract reading as opposed to the concrete, and the choice of which of these two SEMs to assign in a particular case would have to depend on context, individuals involved, purpose, and so on – all those factors, largely indeterminate unless one has common sense and is au courant with the relevant discourse context – that make one reading appropriate as opposed to another. Assuming that the concept admits both readings, the point is clear. **Book** and many other nominal concepts, perhaps all, allow for considerable flexibility in the ways in which they are applied *by virtue of features that are intrinsic to them and that they provide for use or application.* They are *intricate* perspectives indeed, particularly when one takes into account the almost endless variety allowed by combination with other lexical items ("heavy book": to read or carry?) and by various structures (under "the book" / "The book strikes me / . . .").

Nominals also make Chomsky's point about being essentially tied to human interests and concerns. Take **house**. Chomsky makes the usual points about this being a container word sharing certain properties with other container words, but also remarks that having the concept **house** is possessing something that essentially involves human interests and concerns. The argument in favor of this claim was nicely made near the end of the seventeenth century by the Cambridge Platonist Ralph Cudworth (whose views and works Chomsky cites, especially in connection with the issue of how language relates to and constitutes the world; 1966; 1997). Cudworth wanted to show that the concept **house** has to be innate and did so, in part, by demonstrating that the concept is (in spite of superficial appearances) both so highly complex and tied to human interests and concerns and yet readily available at a young age to everyone across the human population that it is impossible to conceive of a way in which it could have been learned through the senses, and equally impossible to conceive of an animal acquiring, or having available beforehand, just *that* concept. He pointed out that to have the concept **house** is to know that houses must be built by humans from certain appropriate materials, to know they serve human interests, and to know that one might be asked to speak to questions about how commodious, inviting, efficiently arranged, and beautiful a house is. These are all relevant to the concept, and the fact that *everyone* has such knowledge and everyone knows what kinds of questions to ask and answer when someone speaks about houses is inexplicable unless this "information" about relevant forms of inquiry and concern is part of the concept itself – unless these various lines of concern and inquiry are invited by the nature of the (lexical) concept. They must be, otherwise it would not be clear to everyone that these are relevant issues. It is difficult, of course, to know how to represent all this information or, perhaps better, to represent the vectors that a perspective that includes the concept **house** includes. Pustejovsky does so by developing a formalism that locates these various areas of concern in "qualia structure," with different specific and characteristic qualia assigned for specific lexical items. There is much in common between his view here and Chomsky's, for good reason. Pustejovsky's structure is derived from the work of Moravcsik, who got it from Aristotle, and on several occasions Chomsky has mentioned Moravcsik's 1975 and more recent 1990 work. Although how to theoretically represent all this is not settled, the basic, intuitive point is clear: what might be called the intrinsic semantic structure of nominals reflects Aristotle's classification of four "causes" (reasons or explanations, in the terminology I adopted). It is becoming increasingly apparent that this structure, given the degree to which it figures in nominals in the lexicons of all natural languages, is innately fixed. There is little doubt that the structure helps explain why the complex perspectives provided by SEM/LFs are "relevant" to human concerns; they are (in part) because the nominal lexical concepts that contribute to them are configured in ways that suit human concerns about where something came from (its origin), what it is made of, what it does,[8] and so forth. Because these internal

---

[8] I am not by any means claiming that all expressions that result from computationally possible combinations of lexical items are usable or "interpretable." Some are too long and/or involve embeddings that cannot be readily parsed, and hence are unusable. Others are perfectly parsable, but there is little use for them; the (in)famous "Colorless green ideas sleep furiously" is an example. Moreover, some sentences are usable that are not computationally workable: "the child seems sleeping," for example. The point is that the concepts contained in lexical items are (generally) "designed for use" by creatures like us. Whether they are, or in certain combinations can be, put to use is another matter.

intrinsic contents, when used, structure a term's application in the cognitive perspective they contribute to, they guide our thought and imagination. And, given circumstances, they help make certain applications plausible and appropriate, and others not.

Perhaps verbs make the point even more effectively. Many of the causative verbs are obviously agentive, calling for an agentive thematic structure. Even when apparent nonagents appear in agent roles ('The plane sank the ship'), the expression seems to be understood as agentive. This suggests strongly that human agency is at the core of the basic idea of bringing about some changes – in "causality" as it is often understood in the common sense framework. This highlights the anthropocentric characters of the concepts provided by large numbers of natural language verbs.

In any case, we now have answers to how linguistic expressions produced by the human language faculty make the creative aspect of language use possible. The faculty is modular, hence we get stimulus freedom. It is generative, hence affords unbounded numbers of expressions. Further, the concepts that go into expressions seem virtually "designed" to deal with circumstances in ways that reflect our concerns. Therefore, it is no accident that we, who have these concepts, can produce expressions that are appropriate to circumstances. Nor, sharing the biology that we do, is it as difficult to see how we manage to understand others when they produce expressions that they then transmit by auditory or visual signals which, when we receive them, give us the occasion to create expressions for which we imagine applications that are similar to those given by the person who spoke.

These points are connected to Chomsky's minimalist program requirement that expressions be legible to other biological systems at the interface levels PF/PHON and LF/SEM. There the other systems impose bare output conditions that constrain what can appear at the interface. For LF/SEM (PF/PHON is irrelevant for present purposes), one has to have indications of tense, binding, theta role, and so on – all clearly relevant to interpretation. However, the point about the anthropocentricity of the concepts provided by LF/SEMs is largely independent of this. The minimalist program emphasizes that this is a fact about the features and structure of lexical items themselves, not about the computational system. Perhaps there are evolutionary reasons for these features and structure, but that is a topic for another occasion. For the moment, it is enough that the minimalist program picture of the language faculty, like the picture that all of Chomsky's various theories of language provide (only more so), explains how creative language use is possible by placing meanings inside a modular faculty inside the head, by providing enough of them that one will not run out, and by making sure that they suit human interests, that they are apt for interpretation by humans (where this involves, presumably, reference and truth).

5   A Science of Meaning is an Internalist Syntactic Science

Creativity observations obviously have consequences for semantic theories of the lexicon. Taking a "serious" science of language to be one for which it is possible to state under what conditions a principle, process, rule, or procedure applies, the creativity observations rather strongly suggest that any serious science of language had better be an "internalist" one. (An externalist theory would be one that in any way relies essentially on some thing, condition, or state outside the head.) If there were to be a theory of successful reference as that is usually understood (where a word, inside the head, is used to refer to something outside the head), success in reference could only be defined within the theory if it included things in the world within its subject matter. If it did, familiar objections would arise, such as that this makes the theory a theory of everything and that referential success is a normative notion, hardly the subject matter of science. The creativity observations add another major objection to the list: reference is a form of human action – something that people do with words, not something that words do all by themselves – and human actions are not subject to serious science. The reasons are obvious from the above: There is no theoretically definable and determinate relationship between words and things. To have one is to be able to state the conditions under which it does not apply, and that is not possible. Things look bad, then, for a referential semantic *theory*, at least as reference is usually understood. Trying to construct a semantic theory of the lexicon that relies on reference, or its bedfellow truth, is wasted effort.

One can, of course, introduce the term "reference" as a theoretical term and define it over a domain that is itself specified by a theory. That would satisfy the conditions mentioned above. However, it is difficult to see why one would want to do this. Chomsky himself suggests such a move, though with tongue firmly in cheek. Beginning in 1981 (p. 324), continuing in 1986, and culminating in his 1993 *Explaining Language Use*, Chomsky mentioned the possibility of introducing a "relation R" to stand between expressions (LF/SEMs, technically) and a theoretically introduced domain of elements – perhaps semantic values, perhaps "things," perhaps abstract entities. He notes, however, that if this is seen as a contribution to a serious theory of an aspect of the language faculty – as, say, a contribution to a "theory of content" or "theory of meaning" for SEM/LFs – it must be read (so far as he is concerned) "as a part of syntax," as a contribution to an internalist theory of UG/I-languages. If so, it is not "real reference," if by that is meant some sort of a relationship, established when a person uses a word, to something "outside the head." It is instead a contribution to an internalist science of language and is either explanatorily and descriptively adequate to its domain (and hopefully illuminating), or not; it is proposed as a branch of syntax, broadly speaking. Because its domain is virtually invented with the introduction of the theory, no doubt it can be made descriptively adequate, although perhaps only in a Pickwickian sense.

However, it is hard to see the point of the exercise. A straightforward theoretical description of SEM/LFs in terms of features and the generative computational system that produces them avoids the misleading appearance of being a "theory of reference" in the other, externalist sense.[9]

If the creativity considerations show that a theory of meaning or content (and so, in a sense, "semantic theory") must be internalist, they are not quite enough to show that meanings or contents inside the head also have to be located in the language faculty and, at least initially, in lexical items. It is at least conceptually possible that SEM/LFs (syntactic objects that they definitely are) must, in order to serve a "semantic function," stand in some kind of relationship (perhaps "Relation R," perhaps indexing, perhaps linking) to something *elsewhere* in the head – to something in, say, a semantic space, a set of concepts, a set of semantic values, a belief-space, or what have you. Chomsky, however, made a compelling argument against this kind of a move (1997). His argument relies on establishing a theoretical and methodological symmetry between the study of phonological and semantic features. If PHONs are plausibly theoretically defined "sounds," he suggests, then SEMs should be theoretically defined "meanings." He wants to show that meanings have the same status as sounds, for both are defined in terms of interfaces that are the products of, and thus located "in," a broadly syntactic computational engine that begins with and combines set of lexical features and introduces nothing but lexical features – his "inclusiveness condition" (1995b, p. 228).

The argument proceeds by eliminating alternatives to holding that sounds and meanings are located in the language faculty. Assuming that the alternatives must locate sounds and meanings somewhere else inside the mind/brain, let us see what they might be:

> Consider a "Mentalese" alternative ... Instead of taking LI [a lexical item] to include I-sound and I-meaning [sounds and meanings as theory-defined over an I-language], let us assume that one or the other is missing, or perhaps both. Accordingly, either SEM, PHON, or both are missing at the interface levels (1995b, p. 10).

The aim then is to show that linguistic theory and theorizing go awry with "Mentalese" alternatives. Including running up against poverty of stimulus considerations among the things that go wrong if one tries to construct a "Mentalese" theory and focusing on PHON, he continues:

> To learn a language is to acquire rules that map LI into some other system of mind, Mentalese, which is interpreted to yield (aspects of) I-sound and I-meaning. If I-sound is missing, then LI is mapped into P-mentalese [phonetic mentalese]. If I-meaning is missing, then LI is mapped into S-mentalese [semantic or meaning-mentalese]. Or both. Language itself has

---

[9] I discuss this move of Chomsky's in more detail (McGilvray, 1998) in connection with an article of Larson and Ludlow's.

no phonology/phonetics, or no semantics, or neither. These are properties
of Mentalese . . .

For concreteness, consider . . . the words of (2), or the words "persuade,"
"force," "remind" for X in (3):

(2) chase, lace, follow

(3) John X-ed Mary to take her medicine.

Suppose the corresponding LIs lack I-sound and that Peter has learned to
map them into regions of P-mentalese that have phonetic interpretations.
Peter knows a lot about the regions and their interpretations. Thus "chase"
rhymes with "lace"; "persuade" and "force" begin with lip constriction,
though in different ways, and "remind" does not; etc. Standard approaches
assign these properties to FL [the language faculty], taking them to be
represented in PHON. The P-Mentalese alternative adds an extra layer of
complexity, and raises new problems, for example: What component of
LI indicates the region of P-Mentalese to which it is mapped, if not the
I-sound (as conventionally assumed)? At what point in the computation
of an expression does the mapping of P-Mentalese take place? How are
universal and particular properties of sound expressed in the interpretation
of P-Mentalese? For good reasons, such questions have not been raised,
and we may drop the matter (1995b, pp. 10–11).

Anyone proposing this for sounds would have to demonstrate that it is plausible
to think that all the knowledge that a speaker has about sound (which Chomsky,
of course, along with everyone else, sensibly places in the language faculty) is
mentally represented elsewhere, would have to show how it is acquired or learned,
and show how it is systematically linked to the language faculty through (for
example) a demonstration of how it bears on the generation of a sentence from
lexical items. It is far simpler to assume (and sensible theoreticians do assume)
that sound-relevant features (i.e., phonological features) are in an I-language's
set of lexical items, and therefore the language faculty as parameterized for an
I-language, from the start, and that the computation that leads to a sentence deals
with these features along with others. No one seriously proposes moving sounds
into Mentalese. They do, however, propose it for meanings:

Consider the semantic analogue. We now assume that LIs have only I-
sound and uninterpreted formal properties, and that Peter has learned how
to map them into regions of S-Mentalese, which have semantic interpretation. Peter knows a lot about these regions/interpretations too. Thus if
Tom chased Bill then Tom followed Bill with a certain intention, not conversely; if X = "persuade" in (3), then John's efforts were a partial success
(Mary came to intend to take her medicine, but may not have done so);
if X = "force," John succeeded, but differently (Mary took her medicine,
whatever her intentions); if X = "remind," John may have failed (Mary
may not have been paying attention), but if he succeeded, then Mary came

to remember to take her medicine. The [I-language or FL] picture assigns the relevant properties to FL, taking them to appear in SEM by virtue of operations on LIs and the constructions in which they appear. The S-Mentalese alternative adds an extra layer of complexity and raises new problems analogous to those of the phonetic component (1995b, p. 11).

Therefore, if someone seriously proposes moving meaning out of the language faculty to some other place in the mind, s/he must answer questions about how the rich and anthropocentric "information" or knowledge about links between concepts (**intend, persuade**) and the like is acquired and represented, and how it bears on the production of a sentence (how a lexical item's semantic information participates in the generative theory that produces expressions). If meanings are located in the language faculty and, specifically, in lexical items (from which expressions are produced), these questions are answered – as Chomsky's minimalist program account answers them.

The same argument applies to other attempts to place meanings or knowledge of meaning elsewhere, whether in a different mental capacity, outside the head, or in abstract entities. Consider representing semantic knowledge as a matter of assigning semantic values to an expression/word. The same issues arise: how do "semantic values" represent the knowledge of meaning we have, how is knowledge of semantic values acquired, how do semantic values bear on computation, and how do people gain and maintain access to the domain? The proposal comes to appear silly, as Chomsky intends. As sensible people place sounds in lexical items and the language faculty, so sensible people place meanings "in" the language faculty and its generated products, expressions.

It is arguable, of course, that these theoretically defined linguistic meanings or intrinsic contents cannot be what contribute to our dealings with the world, that they are not concepts that play a direct role in describing and remonstrating. The response to this is that they are not, of course, all that is involved in our dealings. Vision, (nonlinguistic) audition, touch, facial recognition, and other faculties of the mind also contribute. However, it is surely fair to say that they constitute our linguistic concepts, even though in a particular case their contribution is a cooperative venture involving various faculties. Moreover, as we have seen, these linguistic concepts/meanings certainly seem to be virtually designed for our use; they are anthropocentric, serving our interests and our need for concepts that configure the things of the world in ways that we can deal with. A semantic science reflects these facts in lexical semantic features.

6   The Semantics of the Lexicon and Variability in Meaning and Interpretation

Chomsky's minimalist program seems to be tied to a specific conception of the lexicon and its role. Lexical items must have phonological, formal, and semantic features. These have to be sufficiently richly specified that a theory of them, of

UG, and of the computational system *alone* yields all language-faculty internal "decisions" about their co-occurrence and, furthermore, provides everything at PHON and SEM that is needed there. (A theory's lexical specification of features need not, however, *fully* specify features: To the extent that some feature is fixed in UG, or determined by another feature, given UG, only the "exceptional" feature need be mentioned. Thus, from the fact that "horse" is an N, it follows from UG that it will be assigned a case. That it is third person singular, that it has the semantic feature ANIMATE, and that it is associated with the sound it is do not follow from and are not a part of UG; these must be lexically specified [1995b, pp. 235–7].) The linkage between, on the one hand, phonological and, on the other, formal plus semantic features displays what Chomsky calls "Saussurean arbitrariness." Although within a specific natural language community's I-language set, phonological parameters may correlate with that natural language's formal parameters (so that Englishy sounds correlate with English head parameter settings, and so on), nothing but the need to communicate with others prevents the sound "arthritis" within a specific Englishy I-language from being associated with the concept **disease of the limbs** or, for that matter, with **broad-leafed tree** (1997, pp. 24–5). Chomsky insists, for good reason, that there is no natural connection between specific sounds and specific meanings and therefore, for the purposes of linguistic science, the connection is arbitrary. Its arbitrary nature is reflected in the computational system's splitting off of phonological/phonetic processing "after" Spell Out; after that, there is no further "communication" between the two interfaces. It is also reflected in the nature of the processing: to all intents and purposes, the processing from Select/Numerate to SEM is uniform, operating in accordance with Merge and Move/Attract alone, while that from Spell Out to PHON almost certainly involves specialized processing needed to meet the bare output conditions imposed by other systems at PHON (1995b, 228; n.10, p. 381). Formal and semantic features are more closely tied to each other, given that both appear (except for functional features) at SEM. In fact, one can think of semantic features as rather like fine-grained formal features. Perhaps, however, it is better to conceive of their relationship the other way around: formal are coarse-grained semantic features. A brief experimentation with interpretation at deep structure aside, Chomsky's settled view seems to be that so-called syntactic processing has always had a semantic aim – to produce a semantically "interpretable" tool. From the beginning in *The Logical Structure of Linguistic Theory* and *Syntactic Structures*, where he proposed a "use theory" to deal with how these tools are used by people, Chomsky's syntactic work has been oriented toward the production of meanings that can be used by people to effect their ends, where their production is determined within the language faculty, but open to interpretation or application afterward.

Much of this is rather old hat. The list of features to be included in a lexicon has been characteristic of Chomsky's grammars since *Aspects*; the devolution onto lexical features and their role in processing of more and more of the responsibility for the direction a derivation takes and for "decisions" about whether a computation crashes or not has been a characteristic of the principles and parameters framework since the early 1980s; it only culminates in its purest form yet in a few lectures and in chapter 4 of *The Minimalist Program* (1995b) where X-bar gets absorbed, and perhaps even QR. This point is emphasized, moreover, by what Chomsky has to say about Select/Numerate. Apparently, they leave no feature undecided.

Chomsky seems to think that the lexical features that play a role in computation should be *fully* specified so that a lexical item's role in derivation is fully determined. Consider a strategy that "underspecifies" features, letting later computation add features or further specify some. For instance, one might suggest starting a derivation with a rather thin specification for the V "wash" – perhaps only that it is a V and requires an agent and an object – and let the issue of whether to make it past or present depend on later computational "decisions," including which other words it is Merged with. This, however, raises the question of on what grounds or principles these decisions are to be made and it gives the computational process more to do – undesirable on minimalist assumptions and regrettable if these processes are to proceed blindly, without intervention. A better strategy is to list all the possible options for the lexical item and choose among them before computation even begins (1995b, pp. 237–9). This requires that the lexicon list the options available for a lexical item unless these options are already predictable from UG, as is the fact that "wash" will get some tense features. However, Chomsky thinks that the best strategy is to have fully specified lexical items placed in the Numeration of lexical items: "The optional features of a particular occurrence of 'book' (say, [accusative], [plural]) are added by either [numeration or select] presumably by [numeration], a decision that reduces reference sets and hence computability problems" (1995b, p. 236). On either this or the prior strategy, N/S provides a fully specified set of lexical items over which the computation proceeds. On these assumptions, computation is straightforward, and it is fully determined whether a computation with a particular set of features crashes or reaches the interfaces.

Of course, nothing is said about how Numeration is determined; that is not a job for a theory of the language faculty and the features that play a role in it. Nor, certainly, does a computation that leads to a fully formed SEM close off all options to a speaker. Although a computation might be fully determined, there are still choices for the interpreting speaker and/or the other systems to which SEMs "speaks." Uses are not predetermined, which is exactly what the creative aspect needs. What a nominal is used to refer to, where in discourse a sentential expression appears, whether the content of the expression is held true or not, whether it is treated ironically, and so on, is all up for grabs. As mentioned before, some lexical features allow for changes in emphasis and focus. The features of **book**, for example, allow that this single lexical item, in its various possible configurations (accusative, nominative, singular, plural), can be "read" as referring to *either* a physical object *or* an abstract container of information, or *both*. Notice that no choice is made as computation begins; [+/−abstract] or [physobj.info] migrates to SEM along with the other features of the lexical item, oblivious to various merges and moves (although words with which it co-occurs might serve to skew interpretations in one direction rather than another). When there, it provides a very useful special form of ambiguity that seems to be characteristic of natural languages.

The internalist implications of the creativity observations seem to be far-reaching.

7 Pustejovsky and a Generative Lexicon

Creativity of language use really is a matter of use and not something that a serious theory should try to deal with within the theory itself. Assuming that in language we are concerned with generative theories, the point is simple: A serious theory will try to introduce a well-defined set of primitives (features, in the case of Chomsky's minimalist program) and detail how the generative procedures they are subject to produce some "outputs" (PHON and SEM). The theory itself is, then, "deterministic" and deals with a cognitively impenetrable domain. It might conceivably allow for options, late lexical insertion, and so forth, but on the whole, it leaves no room for a person with his or her creative urges to intervene. Basically, creativity is a property of actions of human beings who use linguistic "tools" for all sorts of reasons and, although linguistic expressions are tools used in carrying out the actions we think of as describing and explaining (and cajoling, conjecturing, . . .), the theory of these "tools" and how they are produced from largely innate feature sets is not a theory of human actions and the roles of words in them. This sets the context in which to view how a naturalistic theory of language makes sense of the creativity observations. A deterministic theory, operating with innate features, shows how the language faculty can produce endless numbers of interest-relevant perspectives. Given that these are properties of the language faculty and its outputs, we can make sense of the creativity observations. The point is like one Chomsky made early in *Language and Mind* (1972, p. 13) where he pointed out that it could not be an aim of a linguistic theory to explain linguistic behavior, a paradigm case of intelligent behavior. However, it could be an aim of linguistic theory to explain how intelligent behavior of this sort is possible.

With this in mind, consider Pustejovsky's (1995) suggestion that among the most pressing problems for lexical semantics is "Capturing the *creative use of words* in novel contexts" (p. 5). The issue is what he has in mind by "creative use" and what by "capturing." By creative use he seems to have in mind *generative* in one of the ways he wants to make lexical theory generative (p. 42f): regulated polysemy, or the generation of "new senses," by a process he calls "co-composition," largely for the nonlexicalized kinds of cases. This is not, I take it, something that people do, therefore perhaps it is best to avoid speaking of *use*. It is not entirely clear that as he conceives of the matter, it is something that happens in the language faculty either, and to insist that it must be one or the other may be a false dilemma. Nevertheless, it would be useful to have some clarification on the matter. My impression, however (and it is only that), is that Pustejovsky does not have human intervention in mind. If so, co-composition could be proposed to form a part of the theory of the operations carried out in the language faculty and so could help say how creative language use is *possible* in Chomsky's sense. If that were the case, Pustejovsky would have in mind by "capturing the creative use of words" explaining how the creative use of words is possible. On the other hand, this does not suit his statement and practice, and the formal theory he offers does not divorce truth and reference from computation, which makes his version of computation look very different from that of a Chomsky-inspired language faculty with lexical items merging and moving by virtue of their features to yield a semantically potent expression that can be used by a person for all sorts of linguistic tasks. Therefore, it is difficult to see whether, or how, Pustejovsky could follow Chomsky's route. The creativity facts make the alternative he seems to choose look unappealing; it seems to be committed to an externalist semantics, with the consequence that there is no serious theory to be had. Contrast in this respect the operation Pustejovsky calls "type coercion." This can be seen as an internal syntactic operation; in fact, Pustejovsky cashes out some forms of coercion in terms of the *Knowledge of Language* notion of a canonical syntactic form (1995, p. 132f). The explication of coercion in terms of "reconstructing" (1995, p. 116) is, though, another matter, which looks a bit like human intervention.

There is an alternative that I have not emphasized. Chomsky often speaks (e.g., 1995a; see also 1982) of the language faculty as consisting of the computational system or "cognitive system" that produces SEM/LFs from lexical feature sets *plus* various "other systems" in the head. If so, there would be another position for regulated polysemy principles – or some of them – that would take them out of the sphere of what people do and would place them back within the sphere of what happens in the language faculty, which we can assume is beyond intervention. They could be placed among the various "cognitive systems" to which SEM/LF gives "instructions." Chomsky is very tentative about what these systems might be, insisting only that they are on the other side of SEM/LF and help constitute bare output conditions at SEM/LF. However, they are fully "inside the head" – not accounts of reference or behavior, for example. In the case of PHON/PF, it is reasonably clear that they will include speech production and perception systems. However, there is nothing equally clear in the semantic sphere. Chomsky sometimes gestures toward something that he calls "i-belief systems" and refers to the work of Bromberger and others, but this is gesturing. He also sometimes refers to the work of some of his students (notably, Danny Fox) as moving in the direction of saying what is on the other side of the interface. It would be very interesting to have a firm proposal about what these systems are, and a clear account of how they related to SEM/LF. Perhaps Pustejovsky's co-composition would fit in here, although it is tempting to hope that aspects of it can be dealt with in the computational system that produces SEM/LFs.

There is still another alternative. Trying to deal with what people do with their words and sentences in explaining and describing the world should not be a part of a serious semantic theory. What, then, does one say to Pustejovsky's second sentence in the introduction to *The Generative Lexicon*, where he says, "Lexical semantics is the study of how and what the words of a language denote"? If "denote" amounts to something like "refer by use of the term on the part of a person," it would seem that he is committing his theory to providing an account of what people do with words, very often creatively. However, it does not seem to be intended as that. Interestingly, moreover, the concept of denotation involving the activities and intentions of persons – "real reference", or "real denotation" – plays no important role in his theory and its statement. If so, it is quite possible that his concept of denotation could be taken to be Chomsky's Relation R. Relation R appropriates model theory for syntax while denaturing it of what the externalists want it to be. If his "denote" were taken to be Relation R, much of Pustejovsky's valuable contribution to lexical semantics could be seen as a contribution to an internalist semantics – a branch of syntax, broadly speaking.

References

Baker, M. 1995 *The Creative Aspect of Language Use*. Unpublished manuscript, Department of Linguistics, McGill University.

Bloomfield, L. 1939. Thenomimi Morphophonetics. *Travaux du cercle linguistique de Prague*, Prague.

Chomsky, N. 1959. Review of Skinner. *Verbal Behavior Language* 35: 26–58.

Chomsky, N. 1964. *Current Issues in Linguistic Theory*. Mouton, The Hague.

Chomsky, N. 1966. *Cartesian Linguistics*. Harper and Row, New York.

Chomsky, N. 1972. *Language and Mind*. Harcourt, Brace, Jovanovich, New York.

Chomsky, N. 1975 [ca 1955]. *The Logical Structure of Linguistic Theory*. Plenum Press, New York.

Chomsky, N. 1981. *Lectures on Government and Binding*, Dordrecht: Foris.

Chomsky, N. 1982. *Lectures on Government and Binding*. Foris, Dordrecht.

Chomsky, N. 1986. *Knowledge of Language*. Praeger, New York.

Chomsky, N. 1988. *Language and Problems of Knowledge: The Managua Lectures*, Cambridge, MA: MIT Press.

Chomsky, N. 1993. *Explaining Language Use*. Manuscript published in Tomberlin (ed.), *Philosophical Topics* 20: 205–231.

Chomsky, N. 1995a. Language and Nature. *Mind* 104: 1–61.

Chomsky, N. 1995b. *The Minimalist Program*. MIT, Cambridge, MA.

Chomsky, N. 1997. *Internalist Explorations*. To appear in a volume of papers in honor of Tyler Burge, ed. Bjorn Ramberg.

Cudworth, R. 1976 [1731]. *A Treatise Concerning Eternal and Immutable Morality*, Garland, New York. Reprint of (1731), posthumously edited by Chandler, Bishop of Durham.

Descartes, R. 1988 [1637]. *Discourse on Method*. Trans. Cottingham et al., *Selections*, Cambridge University Press, Cambridge.

Huarte, J. (1575). *Examen de Ingenios*. Trans. Bellamy (1688).

McGilvray, J. 1998. Meanings are Syntactically Individuatated and Found in the Head. *Mind and Language* 13: 225–280.

Moravcsik, J. 1975. Aitia as Generative Factor in Aristotle's Philosophy. *Dialogue* 14: 622–636.

Moravcsik, J. 1990. *Thought and Language*. Routledge, London.

Pustejovsky, J. 1995. *The Generative Lexicon*, MIT Press, Cambridge, MA.

3   The Emptiness of the Lexicon: Critical Reflections on J. Pustejovsky's "The Generative Lexicon"

JERRY A. FODOR AND ERNIE LEPORE

Abstract

We consider Pustejovsky's account of the semantic lexicon (Pustejovsky, 1995). We discuss and reject his argument that the complexity of lexical entries is required to account for lexical generativity. Finally, we defend a sort of lexical atomism: though, stricly speaking, we concede that lexical entries are typically complex, still we claim that their complexity does not jeopardize either the thesis that lexical meanning is atomistic or the identification of lexical meaning with denotation.

1   Introduction[1]

A certain metaphysical thesis about meaning that we will call Informational Role Semantics (IRS) is accepted practically universally in linguistics, philosophy, and the cognitive sciences:[2] the meaning (or content, or "sense") of a linguistic expression[3] is constituted, at least in part, by at least some of its inferential relations. This idea is hard to state precisely, both because notions like metaphysical constitution are moot and, more importantly, because different versions of IRS take different views on whether there are constituents of meaning other than inferential role, and on which of the inferences an expression occurs in are meaning constitutive. Some of these issues will presently concern us, but for now it will do just to mention such familiar claims as that: it's part and parcel of "dog" meaning 'dog'[4] that the inference from "x is a dog" to "x is an animal" is valid; it's part and parcel of "boil" meaning 'boil' that the inference from "x boiled y" to "y boiled" is

---

[1]   This paper was published in *Linguistic Inquiry*, 29:2, 1998.

[2]   By a "metaphysical thesis about X" we simply mean a thesis about which properties of Xs are essential. By stipulation: If theory T holds that it is metaphysically necessary that Xs are Ys, then T says that being Y is metaphysically necessary for being X, and that being Y is "constitutive" of Xness.

[3]   The corresponding doctrine is generally supposed to be true of the meaning (content/"sense") of mental entities like concepts and beliefs. Our discussion is intended to apply, mutatis mutandis, to either version of IRS.

[4]   Cited forms are in double quotation marks. Emphasized expressions are in italics. Expressions enclosed in single quotation marks stand for semantic values (e.g., meanings or denotations). Semantic representations are in full caps. However, citation conventions in quoted passages are as per the quoted text.

valid; it's part and parcel of "kill" meaning 'kill' that the inference from "x killed y" to "y died" is valid; and so on (see Cruse, 1986, Chap. 1 and passim).

IRS brings in its train a constellation of ancillary doctrines. (We are neutral about whether these ancillary doctrines are literary entailed; that would depend on how IRS is formulated.) Presumably, for example, if an inference is constitutive of the meaning of a word, then learning the word involves learning that the inference holds. If "dog" means 'dog' because "dog" $\longrightarrow$ "animal" is valid, then knowing that "dog" $\longrightarrow$ "animal" is valid is part and parcel of knowing what the word "dog" means; similarly, learning that "x boiled y" $\longrightarrow$ "y boiled" is valid is part and parcel of learning what "boil" means; and so forth.

IRS also constrains grammatical theories because, on standard versions of the IRS view, the *semantic lexicon*[5] of a language is supposed to be the component of a grammar that makes explicit whatever one has to (learn/) know to understand the lexical expressions of the language. IRS implies that meaning-constitutive inferences are part of the *semantic lexical entries* for items that have them. Lexical entries are therefore typically complex objects ("bundles of inferences") according to standard interpretations of IRS. It is this latter thesis that will primarily concern us in the present discussion. For reasons that we have set out elsewhere, we doubt that IRS can be sustained (Fodor and Lepore, 1992); a fortiori, we doubt the cogency of arguments that take IRS as a premise. The primary question in what follows will be *whether there are any persuasive arguments for the complexity of lexical entries that do not presuppose IRS.* Our main interest in Pustejovsky (hereafter JP) is that he purports to provide such an argument.

Here is how we will proceed: The natural alternative to the claim that lexical entries are typically complex is the claim that lexical entries are typically atomic (i.e., they lack internal structure). We propose to adopt a version of this claim as a sort of null hypothesis: namely, that the only thing a lexical entry specifies is the denotation of the item it describes. Here again, we scant the details for the moment. Roughly, however, the lexical entry for "dog" says that it refers to 'dogs'; the lexical entry for "boil" says that it refers to 'boiling'; and so forth.[6] We will try to show that all the standard arguments for rejecting this null hypothesis, Pustejovsky's included, either depend on assuming IRS or are independently unsound.

In sections 2 and 3, we consider Pustejovsky's (1995) account of the semantic lexicon; in particular, we discuss and reject his argument that the complexity of lexical entries is required to account for lexical generativity. In section 4, we consider whether our default theory, lexical atomism, might not actually be true. We argue that, strictly speaking, it probably is not; strictly speaking lexical *entries* are

---

[5] In what follows, *lexicon* always means 'semantic lexicon' unless we are explicit to the contrary.

[6] If it's assumed that it's necessary that dogs are animals, then, of course, whatever denotes a dog denotes an animal. However, according to the present view, the lexical entry for "dog" does *not* provide this information; it says only that "dog" denotes 'dogs'. Correspondingly, according to the present view, knowing that dogs are animals is *not* necessary for knowing what "dog" means.

typically complex. However, we claim that they are complex in a way that does not jeopardize either the thesis that lexical *meaning* is atomistic, or the identification of lexical meaning with denotation.

2   Pustejovsky's Theory

We take the theory of the lexicon that Pustejovsky (hereafter JP; Pustejovsky, 1995) holds to be firmly within the IRS tradition. In particular, like other proponents of IRS, JP thinks that word meanings are constituted by inferences, hence that knowing what a word means involves knowing (some of) the inferences in which it participates. In fact, he apparently thinks (what IRS does not strictly require) that understanding a token (e.g., an utterance or inscription) of an expression involves actually drawing some of the inferences that the words that are tokened license: "the structuring of taxonomic information . . . is not simply an exercise in domain modeling; it is necessary for driving *the inferences that a language reasoning system must perform in order to understand a sentence*" (Pustejovsky, 1995, p. 19, our emphasis). As usual with IRS-motivated theories of meaning, it is taken for granted that the semantic lexicon should somehow formally specify the inferences by which meaning (/knowledge of meaning/sentence understanding) is constituted.

We stress this because JP occasionally writes as though it were not the specification of *inferential roles* but rather the specification of *denotations* with which lexical semantics is primarily concerned: "Lexical semantics is the study of how and what the words of a language denote" (1995, p. 1). However, this is a little misleading. Roughly, according to JP, lexical entries specify denotations via their *meanings*, so that, for example, coextensive expressions may well be assigned distinct lexical entries.[7] Thus, "John bought the book from Mary" and "Mary sold the book to John" are made true by the same event; but they differ, according to JP, in a property of "headedness" or "focus" that they inherit from the lexical entries of their respective verbs. Patently, however, "headedness" is not a property of denotations ("things in the world") but rather of denotations *as represented*. JP says that "[h]eadedness is a property of all event sorts . . . " (p. 72); but he can't really mean that. What he must really mean is that it's a property of all (semantically well-formed) representations of event sorts (in English).

Similarly, one of JP's characterizations of an "event structure" specifies an event e_3 such that "there is no other event that is part of e_3" (p. 69). However, clearly, all events have parts (down to whatever physics determines is the microstructure of the universe). What JP means is really that no other event is *represented as* (or implied as) part of e_3 by the form of words that expresses the event. Here again,

---

[7] Whether JP thinks that the semantic representations that the lexicon specifies actually *determine* denotations is unclear from the text, though there are passages that suggest he does. For example, discussing the "qualia structures" that constitute the lexical entries for nouns, he says that they "contribute to (or, in fact, determine) our ability to name an object with a certain predication" (1995, p. 85).

what the semantics is telling us about is not (or not just) what a word represents, but how it represents it – in effect, not just the word's denotation but also its sense.

We do not mean to insist on what are, probably, not confusions but a matter of being casual about the use/mention distinction. However, it is important to us to contrast JP's sort of project with a bona fide denotational semantics, according to which satisfaction conditions, and properties defined in terms of them, are the only semantic features of linguistic expressions that lexical entries specify. In fact, JP enumerates a variety of constraints on semantic theories that a purely denotational lexicon clearly could not meet, hence that are supposed to motivate a richer notion of lexical semantic representation than a denotational lexicon could provide. With one exception, these are familiar from discussions in lexical semantics dating as far back as Katz and Fodor (1963). Consonant with our overall project, we propose to discuss them relatively briefly, putting aside the ones that are motivated either by IRS or by other assumptions what we regard as tendentious. This will leave for section 3 to consider what we take to be JP's main line of argument and the main contribution of his book: the claim that only if lexical entries are typically complex can the generativity of the lexicon be captured – a fortiori, that an atomistic lexicon would fail to explain "how words can take on an infinite number of meanings in novel contexts" (p. 42).

As far as we can make out, other than the considerations about generativity, JP offers three kinds of arguments for complex lexical representations; we take these up in sections 2.1–2.3

2.1   *Interlexical Semantic Relations*

Lexical semantics is required to specify "how words are related to one another" (Pustejovsky, 1995, p. 23), including, in particular, relations of "synonymy, antonymy, hyponymy and lexical inheritance, meronymy, entailment and pre-supposition." [8]

Clearly, a lexical entry that says only that "dog" refers to 'dogs' will not thereby specify, for example, that dogs are animals (hyponymy); a lexicon that says only that "bachelor" refers to 'bachelors' will not thereby specify that "bachelor" means the same as "unmarried man" (synonymy), and so on. In fact, barring appeal to meaning postulates (of which JP disapproves; see pp. 54, 110), the only way of capturing such relations in the lexicon would seem to require complex lexical entries (e.g., ones that include ANIMAL in the entry for "dog" and UNMAR-RIED and MAN in the entry for "bachelor"). In short, if the lexicon is constrained to capture "interlexical relations," then it is neither atomistic nor purely denotational.

---

[8] JP says nothing about how to decide which lexical relations are on the list of interlexical relations to which grammars must be responsive, or whether the enumeration he provides is supposed to be complete.

The question, however, is how to motivate imposing this constraint on lexical entries and here the problems are formidable. The basic issue is this: all the relations JP enumerates are species of *analyticity* (lexical entailment); so, in effect, he is requiring that the lexicon reconstructs the notion of *analytic inference*. However, this notion is notoriously problematic, and not just for familiar Quinean reasons. Arguably, there simply is no such notion. If so, then the program of lexical semantics that JP advocates cannot be carried out. This is, to be sure, a large issue, and it has implications for many projects other than JP's. Suffice it, for present purpose, to stress just two points.

First, Quine's own doubts about analyticity are part of his larger skepticism about necessity. However, the two need to be distinguished because analyticity does not follow even if necessity is granted. Suppose, for example, that "dog" —→ "animal" is necessary; that is suppose nothing could be a dog that wasn't an animal. Remember that semantic lexicons are supposed to be repositories of (and only of) meaning-constitutive inferences, that is, of those inferences that one has to be prepared to draw on pain of not understanding the word in question. It seems clear, given this condition, that the *necessity* of an inference is not, per se, sufficient for its meaning constitutivity. "Two" —→ "prime" is necessary if anything is, but it is implausible that you can't know what "two" means unless you know that two is prime. Similarly, it's presumably necessary that what is square isn't circular, but it's implausible that you can't know what "square" means unless you also know what "circle" means. Such examples are legion.[9] The moral is that even if we had a theory of necessity, it wouldn't, all by itself, give us a theory of synonymy, antonymy, hyponymy, and the like; it wouldn't even certify the possibility of such a theory. Even if it were perfectly certain that the distinction necessary/contingent is principled, that would not be a reason for believing in analyticity (or, a fortiori, in synonymy, antonymy, hyponymy, and the like).

Second, and worse, even if analycity is real, it is perfectly possible to doubt that it is connected, in anything like the way that lexical semanticists generally suppose, with facts about "what the speaker/hearer knows qua speaker/hearer." To see this, assume for the moment that semantics is purely denotational, so that the lexicon consists solely of a compendium of "disquotational" truths like " "red" denotes (the property) 'red'," " "dog" denotes (the property) 'dog'," " "two" denotes (the number) 'two'," and so on. It is perfectly possible for someone who believes in this sort of lexicon to hold that each of these disquotational truths is analytic – that is, that the truth of each is guaranteed just by the semantics of English together with logic. However, it would not follow from there being analyticities in *that* sense that grasping the truths of disquotation is a necessary condition for speaker/hearers to know the lexicon of their language. It is, for example, not

---

[9] Transitivity severely compounds the problem. Because it's necessary that what's circular isn't triangular, it follows that you can't know what either "square" or "circle" means unless you know what "triangle" means. And so on ad infinitum.

plausible that understanding the word "red" requires knowing what quotation is, or having a concept of denotation, or the concept of property, and so on.

Nor would it follow that, by underwriting this notion of analycity, the lexicon would thereby underwrite synonymy, antonymy, and the rest. Suppose X and Y are absolute synonyms; and suppose that their lexical entries are, respectively, the disquotational principles "X denotes Xs" and "Y denotes Ys"; and suppose both of these disquotational principles are analytic. Still, nothing that is in (or that follows from) the lexicon says that X and Y are synonyms. That is because nothing that is in (or that follows from) the lexicon says that 'being X' and 'being Y' are the same thing. On the present assumptions, then, the lexicon supports a notion of analyticity but not of synonymy.[10]

The moral, so far, is as follows: There is a tendency among lexical semanticists to think that synonymy, antonymy, hyponymy, and the like must be bona fide linguistic phenomena because, after all, linguists have spent such a lot time studying them; "Thus I refute Quine," Samuel Johnson might have said. However, in fact, their bona fides depend on very strong, and very dubious, semantical assumptions, for which, to our knowledge, no serious defense is on offer. Methodology cannot constrain the lexicon to reconstruct analytic inference if, in fact, there is no such thing.

These remarks apply to lexical semanticists at large; but in fact JP's theory faces even greater problems, because many of the inferences that he thinks lexical entries determine (e.g., from "want a cigarette" to "want to smoke a cigarette"; see below) are "defeasible" (p. 46), hence not even strictly necessary. One might reasonably feel that if the necessity of an inference does not imply the semantic relatedness of its lexical constituents, no weaker modality is likely to do so. JP's comments on these sorts of issues tend not to be illuminating. For example, "[O]ne fairly standard definition states that two expressions are synonymous if substituting one for the other in all contexts does not change the truth value of the sentence where the substitution is made. . . . A somewhat weaker definition makes reference to substitution relative to a specific context. For example, in the context of carpentry, "plank" and "board" might be considered synonyms, but not necessarily in other domains . . . " (p. 23). However, neither notion of synonymy can be right because, on the one hand, no two words substitute, salve veritate, in every context (see Mates, 1950); and, on the other hand, any two words substitute, salve veritate, in some context (e.g., "elephants" and "asteroids" substitute in the context "are often bigger than a breadbox"). One could perhaps counter this objection if one had an account on how to individuate semantic "domains"; but JP provides none.

JP does not address the problem that is implicit in making notions like "defeasible inference" respectable as a basis for semantic theory, namely, the problem of

---

[10] An "informational" semantics – one that construes meaning in terms of nomic or causal world-mind connections – might have very much this character. By contrast, lexical semantics simply takes for granted that semantic facts are basically epistemological – that they are grounded in facts about what speaker/hearers know about thir language. We think that lexical semantics is ill advised to assume this. For discussion, see Fodor and Lepore, 1992; Fodor, 1994; Fodor, 1998.

distinguishing what the language tells one from what one knows about the world. "[My wife uses the subway every day] . . . is a near paraphrase of 'My wife travels on the subway every day,' an interpretation that is made possible by our knowledge of what the function of a subway is" (p. 87). However, if the interpretation is indeed made possible by what we know about subways, then the conclusion should be that the two sentences are not "near paraphrases" in any sense that semantic theory is concerned with. If lexical entries really do express meanings, then what's in the semantic lexicon is information about words, and not information about the world. That's why it's perfectly possible both to understand "Sarah likes to use the subway" and to wonder what she likes to use it for.

If IRS is true, then there must be some answer to the questions "what distinguishes linguistic knowledge from world knowledge?" and "what distinguishes lexical entailment from mere necessity?" IRS guarantees that some interlexical relations are meaning constitutive, and should thus be specified by lexical entries, even if it's not quite clear which ones these are. In the present discussion, however, we are explicitly *not* taking IRS for granted. We are, therefore, impressed by the difficulty of saying with any clarity which interlexical relations are the semantically relevant ones, or how they should be individuated. Accordingly, in what follows we will assume that the failure of an atomistic, denotational lexicon to capture such relations as synonymy, hyponymy, and the rest is not a decisive argument against it.

2.2   Semantic Well-formedness

JP writes, "I will introduce a notion of *semanticality* analogous to the view of grammaticality [*sic*] . . . , but ranging over semantic expressions rather than syntactic structures. Semanticality refers to the semantic well-formedness of expressions in a grammar" (p. 40).

No doubt, if there is such a property as semanticality, the lexicon should contribute to determining it. The trouble is that it's not clear what property it might be. JP provides no general characterization, and the few examples he offers are not transparent.

Consider pleonasms like: "?Mary kicked me with her foot" and "?Mary buttered the toast with butter" (p. 40). On any account, what's wrong with these sentences is that the prepositional phrase adds nothing to what the rest of the sentence says, so a Gricean imperative ("Be informative") is violated. We suppose JP must think that the locus of the redundancy is the meaning of the verbs; anyone who knows what "buttering" means knows that it's done with butter. This consideration does not, however, argue unequivocally that the lexical entry for "butter"$_{tr}$ is COVER WITH BUTTER or the like. Suppose that the dictionary says only that "butter"$_{tr}$ refers to 'buttering.' Still, anyone who knows this, and knows what 'buttering' is, can tell that the sentences in question are redundant. It seems that this kind of "unsemanticality" does not, after all, argue for "a level of representation in the semantics, which operates according to its own set of constraints" (p. 42).

Here are some of JP's other examples of semantic ill-formedness (p. 41):

(1)   a.   ?John began the dictionary.
       b.   ??Mary began the rock.

According to JP, these are "semantically odd because of what we normally associate with the semantic possibilities of a noun such as "dictionary" and "rock" " (p. 41). We're inclined to think, on the contrary, that there's nothing wrong with (1a) at all; and that, if there's anything wrong with (1b), it's that one can't imagine what it was that Mary began to do with (/to) the rock. Given a clue (e.g., she began, in either sense, to paint it), the perplexity vanishes and so does the intuition that something is awry with the sentence.

The trouble, in a nutshell, is this: If capturing semantic well-formedness is to be a constraint on representations of lexical meanings, hence on lexical entries, it has to turn out that what's wrong with a semantically ill-formed sentence is that *what it means* is defective, not just that it would be "normally" or "generally" hard to "readily" interpret without contextual support. It's not clear that any of JP's examples have this property. Indeed, it is not clear that there *is* such a property as defectiveness of meaning as distinct from ungrammatically, necessary falsity, and any of a variety of kinds of pragmatic malfeasance. Barring more persuasive examples, or an independent argument for "a level of representation in the semantics" whose rules would determine the semantic well-formedness conditions for expressions, we are inclined to doubt that failure to mark (1a,b) and the like as defective militates very strongly against purely denotational lexical entries.

2.3   Distribution

It is a widely held view that the semantic properties of a lexical item "give rise to" (p. 19) its syntactic properties: Syntactic distribution is somehow determined or explained by, or is anyhow predictable from, meaning; so a lexicon that represents only denotation would miss linguistically salient generalizations. In this spirit, Higginbotham (1994) remarks that "... the meanings of lexical items systematically infect grammar. For example, ... it is a condition of object preposing in derived nominal constructions in English that the object be in some sense 'affected' in the events over which the nominal ranges: that is why one has ... *algebra's discovery* (*by the Arabs*) [but] not **algebra's knowledge* (by the Arabs)" (p. 102). Similarly, according to JP, "the diversity of complement types that a verb or other category may take is in large part also determined by the semantics of the complements themselves" (p. 10).

It is, however, notoriously difficult to assess the claimed correlations between lexical semantics and syntactic distribution, because one is never told what the semantic representations themselves mean. What, exactly, is it for an object to be "in some sense 'affected' by an event"? [11] This imprecision tends to undermine the supporting examples. So, for example, JP says that the difference between "John is running" ("Therefore, John has run") and "John is building a house" ("*Therefore, John has built a house") "is whether an action is homogenous in nature or has a culmination of some sort" (p. 16). Well, one might have thought that the process of "starting to run" has a culmination of *some* sort – namely, running. But "John is starting to run" $\longrightarrow$ "John has started to run" looks fine (cf., "John is starting to build a house" $\longrightarrow$ "John has started to build a house," etc.). Our point isn't that this is a counterexample to JP's generalization; rather, it's that the generalization is formulated so imprecisely that one can't tell whether it's a counterexample. JP's emendation to "having a culmination" ("culminates in a changed state, i.e., . . . is an accomplishment" [p. 16]) doesn't help a lot. Does it rule "starting to run" in or out? By what criterion? After all, *culminates in* is a *technical* term when it's used this way (as are, for example *agent, patient, theme* as they are used in the theory of θ-roles, and to which the present points apply mutatis mutandis). Assuming *culminates in* without explication in the language used to specify the semantics of lexical entries thus begs the key issue: whether predicates that are syntactically similar to "build" do, in fact, share anything *semantic*. [12]

In fact, we know of no cases in the lexical semantics literature where the semantic end of putative semantics/syntax correlations has been made out with sufficient clarity to permit the claims to be evaluated.

Another of JP's examples (p. 10) is given in (2). Compare:

(2)   a. The woman ate her meal quickly.
        b. The woman ate quickly.
        c. The dog devoured the cookie.
        d. *The dog devoured.

Why can speakers drop the direct object of "ate" but not of "devoured"? The explanation, according to JP, is "while "eat" denotes an activity of unbounded duration (at least lexically), "devour," one might argue, denotes a transition. . . . [D]evour . . . carries a completive implicature that is absent from *eat*" (p. 11).

There is some uncertainty about how much JP is claiming here; if (as seems likely; see pp. 9–12 passim) JP thinks that the fact that "eat" is lexically represented as denoting an unbounded activity explains why its object can be dropped (i.e., that it provides a sufficient condition), then he must believe that there could not be a word that means what "eat" does but does not allow its direct object to delete.

[11] If you think your intuitions tell you, ask them whether algebra was more, or less, "affected" by being discovered by the Arabs than the electric light was being discovered by Edison. Our intuitions say such questions are plain nonsense.

[12] Another way to put this point is that, on the kind of theory JP advocates, lexical entries express *senses*, not just denotation. However, the sense of *culminates in* is at least as obscure as the sense of "build," so it is hard to see how appealing to the one could much illuminate the other.

This claim is remarkably strong and there is no reason to suppose that it is true. Notice that all of the following are bad, though unbounded activities are apparently involved in each: "*John stroked"; "*John ground (/his teeth)"; "*John pounded"; "*John smelled (/the salt air)"; and so on.

However, maybe, unboundedness is a *necessary* condition for the direct object to delete? Apparently not, because "win," "lose," and "tie" are surely bounded and "John won/lost/tied" ⟵ "John won/lost/tied the race" seems fine. In any avent, the usual problem crops up; we can't really evaluate the proposal because we don't really know what it is for an expression to "denote an activity of unbounded duration (at least lexically)." For example, nobody eats forever; why doesn't that make "eat" bounded? Also, why doesn't the "change of state" from eating to not eating that occurs when one stops eating constitute "a transition," just as much as the cessation of devouring that occurs when one stops devouring? If "devour" carries a completive implication, why is "She never finished devouring her meal" all right? Even supposing that "devour" does carry a completive implication, so too, surely, does "finish eating." However, "The woman finished eating her meal" is perfectly fine, although "*The woman finished devouring" isn't.

The fact is, nobody knows what, if anything, it is for a word to denote a transition; so nobody knows whether "devour" does. Similarly, we believe, for the other claims about the semantic determinants of syntactic distributions with which the lexical semantics literature abounds. What's worse, it's possible to wonder, in such cases, whether there really are two different things to correlate. Perhaps the intuition that "devour," but not "eat," is *semantically* completive is just a hypostatic misconstrual of one's *syntactic* knowledge that the first but not the second verb takes a direct object mandatorily. You can't correlate a thing with itself; that is why Pooh never caught a Woozle. (See Milne, 1957. For further discussion, with further examples, see Fodor, 1998.)

Finally, suppose that, despite the unconvincingness of the examples and the imprecision of the metalanguage that is used to describe them, it really is true, in God's eyes as it were, that (some or all) syntax is semantically driven. Would that show that there's something more to lexical representations than denotations? Not obviously. For, even if it's the fact that "devouring" is a transition that explains why "devour" has to have an object, why should knowledge of this fact count as part of what the speaker/hearers know about "devouring" rather than as part of what he knows about 'devouring'? A priori, it seems as reasonable that syntax should be driven by what people know about what a word denotes as that it should be driven by what they know about what the word means. Barring some principle for choosing between these two interpretations, we do not see how the putative influences of semantics on syntax could count in favor of a semantics of lexical meanings *rather than* denotations.

So much for the polemical background. Although one finds all these sorts of arguments in JP's book, they have a considerably older provenance, and JP's treatment of them is not more convincing than what earlier discussions offer.

What makes JP's book interesting is his argument from the semantic generativity of the lexicon to the semantic complexity of lexical entries. We turn to that now.

3   Generativity

A word about method: JP develops considerable apparatus in setting out his proposals about lexical generativity, and neither his notation nor his exposition is strikingly perspicuous. Therefore, we will in most cases not reconstruct the technical details. Instead, we will consider several of his examples of how his theory applies to the analysis of linguistic data. We will try to show that these analyses do not work, but our main purpose is not to impugn them; rather, it is to illustrate the character of the theory and of its defects. We claim that JP's failures to get the data right are principled and show that there is something wrong with the *kind* of account of the lexicon he endorses. We aren't, in short, just quibbling about cases.

JP's discussion of generativity starts by invoking the distinction between "polysemy" and mere accidental homonymy.[13] Intuitively, the paradigm of polysemy is the kind of quasi ambiguity exhibited by the "believe" in "John believes Mary," on the one hand, and "John believes that 2 is less than 3," on the other. However, according to JP, polysemy can also be exhibited by expressions that, unlike "believe" in this example, are syntactically homogeneous; for example, the "window" that JP says means 'aperture' in "He crawled through the window" and the "window" that means 'physical object' in "The window is rotting." Similarly, JP thinks "good," though it has only one lexical entry, means something different in "good knife" and "good secretary."

Many linguists have shared JP's sympathy with Weinreich's (1959) complaint that standard treatments of the semantic lexicon fail to reconstruct the difference between polysemy and mere homonymy. In effect, by postulating distinct lexical entries for each meaning of a polysemous term, "sense enumeration lexicons" (SELs) miss "[t]he fact that [the] two senses [of a polysemous expression] are logically related . . . " (p. 37). However, on JP's view, the fact that "believe" or "window" (or "use"; see below) seem to take on different, but related, senses in their various contexts, is itself just a special case of the perfectly general fact that "words can assume a potentially infinite number of senses in context . . . " (p. 105). Correspondingly, the theorist's goal is to capture the context sensitivity of lexical meaning "while limiting the number of senses actually stored in the lexicon" (p. 105), that is, without proliferating lexical entries beyond necessity.

To see how this is to be accomplished, let's start with JP's treatment of the polysemy of "bake." Prima facie, "bake" is polysemous between a "creative activity" as in "bake a cake" and a "change-of-state predicate" as in "bake a potato."

---

[13] Terminological stipulation: We take ambiguity to be the generic property of which polysemy and homonymy are species.

"Intuitively we would like to capture the fact that the former objects are prototyp-
ically brought about by the activity they are in composition with..." (p. 123) –
that is, that "certain objects come into being by virtue of an activity which can
otherwise simply change the internal state of an object" (p. 98).

The kind of "sense enumeration" analysis that JP wishes to reject might distinguish two lexical entries for "bake": CREATED versus HEATED UP, or something
of the sort. JP's account, by contrast, has a single lexical entry for "bake" and distinguishes the semantics of "bake a cake" from the semantics of "bake a potato" on
the basis of a difference in the lexical representations of the object nouns "cake"
and "potato": "...we can derive both word senses of verbs like *bake* by putting
some of the semantic weight on the NP. This view suggests that, in such cases, the
verb itself is not polysemous. Rather, the creation sense of *bake* is contributed in
part by the meaning of *a cake*, by virtue of it being an artifact" (p. 124).

This treatment is characteristic of JP's general approach; indeed, much of the
book consists of applying it to a wide variety of examples. Notice, in particular, the
idea that the sense of "governing" expressions is inherited partly from their lexical
entries, but partly also from the semantics of the expressions that they govern
in a context. According to JP, this is true not just of the relation between verbs
and their complements but also, for example, of the relation between adjectives
and the nouns they modify (e.g., "good" inherits FOR CUTTING from "knife" in
"good knife"; p. 129). Notice also that pursuing this strategy *places constraints
on the lexical contents of the governed expressions.* "Use" can inherit TO RIDE
ON from "subway" in "use the subway" only if the "telos" (function) of a subway
is part of the entry for "subway." Likewise, the creative sense of "bake a cake"
can emerge from the occurrence of ARTIFACT in the entry for "cake" only if that
entry specifies the information that cakes are artifacts; and so on. In effect, the
more context sensitive the meanings of governing expressions are supposed to be,
the richer must be the lexical entries for the expressions that they govern. So, JP's
standard tactic for arguing that there is a certain piece of semantic information
in the lexical entry for a noun is to show that there is a context in which the
information is inherited by a verb to which the noun functions as a complement
or by an adjective that modifies the noun, and so on.

Because, in all these respects, JP's analysis of "bake" is paradigmatic, the failure
of the analysis is characteristic of the general inadequacy of the theory. We turn to
considering this analysis at some length.

To begin with, suppose that JP is right and the reason that "bake" in "bake a cake"
means 'create' and "bake" in "bake a potato" means 'warm up' is that cakes are
artifacts and potatoes are "natural kinds." However, would that explain why the two
"bake"s aren't merely homonyms? According to JP, "[Artifacts] such as cookies,
cakes and bread are typically baked. The process of baking, modulo such objects,
is a creative activity, while relative to objects such as potatoes, carrots and other
natural kinds, it is simply a change of state predicate.... [T]o classify the verb *bake*
as having both senses lexically specified is to miss the semantic generalization..."

(p. 98; See also p. 47). Apparently, on this account, what makes the two "bake"s not merely homonyms is that both express the same "process of baking" that, in one case, constitutes a creative activity and, in the other case, merely effects a change of state.

However: By what criterion do both kinds of baking count as the same process? What decides that the "bake" in "bake a cake" (hence creating one), denotes the same activity as the "bake" in "bake a potato" (hence heating one)? (Whereas, presumably, "bank" is homonymous because the "bank" in "bank a check" counts as a *different* process from the "bank" in "bank a plane.") This is just the polysemy problem all over again; all that's happened is that it has been kicked upstairs from the semantics to the ontology: Whereas we used to worry about how to count senses, we are now invited to worry about how to count processes. Six of one, half a dozen of the other.

However, for the sake of the argument, let's put ontological qualms aside and go back to the linguistics.

If the creative sense of "bake" is determined by something that it inherits from its direct object – and if "bake" and "cake" are themselves univocal – then "bake a cake" must have *only* the "creative" reading. However, in fact, "bake a cake" is ambiguous. To be sure, one can make a cake by baking it; but also one can do to a (preexistent) cake just what one does to a (preexistent) potato: put it in the oven and (noncreatively) bake it. Because "bake a cake" is ambiguous and "cake" is univocal, it must be that "bake" is lexically ambiguous (specifically, polysemous) after all, contrary to JP's analysis.

The ambiguity of "bake a cake" shows that JP is wrong about the polysemy of "bake." However, it does not show that he is wrong about "cake" being lexically marked as an artifact. Indeed, at first blush, it looks as if *only* distinguishing artifacts from "natural kinds" could account for the differences between "bake a cake" and "bake a potato," because the latter appears to have only the noncreative reading. Maybe some of JP's program can be saved after all.

However, in fact, even assuming that the lexicon distinguishes artifacts from natural kinds is not enough. Notice that although knives and trolley cars are artifacts, "bake a knife" and "bake a trolley car" resist a creative reading quite as much as "bake a potato" does. However, if "bake a cake" is heard as creative because "cake" is marked as denoting an artifact, then *bake a trolley car* should be heard as creative too. Clearly, something has gone wrong.

In fact, there's a striking difference between JP's informal account of "bake" and what he actually puts in the examples of lexical entries that he offers. According to the informal account "the creation sense of *bake* is contributed, in part, by the meaning of *a cake*, by virtue of it being an artifact" (p. 124). However, the lexical entry for "cake" specifies not that *cakes are artifacts*, but, in effect, that *cakes are made by baking* (p. 123). (Compare JP's discussion of "co-compositionality.") Presumably, this is required in order to distinguish *cake* from "potato," on the one hand, and from *knife*, on the other: the entry for "potato" says potatoes are a "natural kind," and "knife" is presumably lexically specified for some means of production other than (and exclusive of) baking.[14] In short, in order to explain why "knife" doesn't select the creative sense of "bake," JP is required to claim that you don't know what any term for an artifact means unless you know how that kind of artifact is made. If, like the present authors, you don't know how pencils are made, you don't know what "pencil" means.

The right story is surely this: as far as the language is concerned, "bake" is polysemous and "bake a potato" and "bake a knife" are both ambiguous. What makes "bake a potato" and "bake a knife" sound funny is a thing about the world, not a thing about the words: everybody knows that you can't make either a potato or a knife by baking them. If you didn't know this, you would hear the ambiguity, as indeed you do in "John is baking something" or "what is John baking?"[15] Contrary to JP's analysis, "bake" is lexically ambiguous and the semantics of "bake NP" offers no argument that the lexicon contains ontological information.

However, is the "bake" case representative? We will briefly look at some of JP's other examples. We claim that JP offers no convincing cases where the meaning of a governing expression is modulated by the lexical content of the expressions that it governs. In fact, it is our view that this never happens.

Consider JP's treatment of "begin." The idea is that "begin" (/"finish") picks up the "telic role" of its direct object (pp. 115–117). This is to account for such inferences as (3a–c).

(3)   a. ... begin a book $\longrightarrow$ ... begin to read a book
       b. ... finish a cigarette $\longrightarrow$ ... finish smoking a cigarette
       c. ... begin a beer $\longrightarrow$ ... begin drinking a beer etc.

It's this sort of example that provides JP's primary evidence that information about function is part of the lexical entry for "book," "beer," and the like.

On second thought, however, the analysis of "begin" doesn't work; It is not, in general, the case that if what NP denotes has a function, then "begin NP" means "begin to use NP to perform its function." "Begin a car" doesn't mean "begin to drive a car"; "begin a thermometer" doesn't mean "begin to measure the temperature"; and so on. "Enjoy," another of JP's salient examples of a verb that incorporates the telic role of its direct object (p. 88), fails for the same sort of reason. JP notes cases like "enjoyed the meal" $\longrightarrow$ "enjoyed eating the meal." However, his account incorrectly predicts the well-formedness of "*enjoyed the doorknob," "*enjoyed the federal government," "*enjoyed the carpet tack," all of

---

[14] How one gets such exclusion (/inclusion) relations to hold among semantic representations without, in effect, resorting to meaning postulates is a traditional, and unsolved, problem in the literature on lexical semantics.

[15] Assuming that gapping is semantic, JP's theory requires that "John baked the potatoes and Mary the cookies" means that Mary heated up the cookies, not that she made them. We don't think that prediction is true either. We suspect that gapping *is* semantic, and that it distinguishes polysemy from true homonymy; hence "*he banked the plane and the check."

which are bad. The first and last of these examples are especially problematic for JP's account because "enjoyed using the doorknob (/carpet tack)" is fine.

Indeed, "use" may seem more suitable for JP's purpose than "begin" or "enjoy," because if X uses Y, where Y is something that has a (conventional/typical) use, then the invited inference is that X uses Y for what Y is used for. (Even so, there's something odd about ". . . used a glass of beer," ". . . used a meal," and the like.) In fact, however, "use" raises a thorny problem for JP's account because it's perfectly possible to use things that don't have uses: a rock to break a window, snow to make a snowball. ("Enjoy" works this way too because one can perfectly well enjoy things that have no function, such as the clement weather or dancing the eightsome reel. These examples raise a serious question about which JP has little to say: What happens if a verb makes a demand on an argument that the lexical entry of the argument doesn't satisfy?

JP's view may be that, if the governing expression demands X in the lexical entry for the governed expression and that entry is not marked for X, the resulting phrase is interpreted as existentially generalized in respect of X. We infer this from JP's treatment of "Mary believes John" (pp. 120–122). According to JP, "believes" wants a proposition in the lexical entry for its direct object, which, however, the lexical entry for "John" presumably doesn't contain. Although the mechanism by which it is achieved is unclear to us, JP's solution is that the interpretation of *Mary believes John* contains an existential quantifier over the required propositional argument: something like "Mary believes what John communicated."[16] Assuming that "believe John" constitutes a precedent for "use a rock," then "John used a rock" should come out meaning something like "John used a rock to perform some function."

If, however, that is the treatment that JP has in mind, it's certainly untenable. The problem is that, given interpretive mechanisms that strong, it becomes unclear how a combination of a verb with an NP argument could ever *fail* to be interpretable. For example, JP's own analysis of "begin a rock" is undermined; it should be (but isn't) heard as meaning 'begin to use a rock for something'. Likewise, why doesn't "John asserted a rock" mean 'For some rock-involving proposition P, John asserted P'? Conversely, why doesn't "Bill used that John is tall" mean 'For some function F, Bill used the proposition that John is tall to perform F' (compare "Bill used

---

[16] In particular, according to JP, the semantic representation of "Mary believes John" is the existential generalization of the p_2 in BELIEVE($^\smallfrown p_2$JOHN))(MARY) (p. 122). The problem is: Where does the propositional constant p_2 in this formula come from? Surely not from the lexical entry for "John," because "John" doesn't mean anything propositional? As JP himself says, "Unlike the case of . . . "the book" . . . the [proposition] type required by selection [is not part of] the [lexical] interpretation of the complement" (p. 121). As far as we can tell, JP never suggests an answer to this question. ("About" raises a structurally analogous problem, because it seems to govern an event in "a book about Vietnam" [i.e., "about the Vietnam War"] but not in "a book about Nixon." Where does this event come from? JP says only that "about" "covers" objects of two different ontological types in the two cases – which, we suppose, is just to say that it's polysemous.)

John's being tall to illustrate the effect of diet on growth")? In order to argue for telic roles in the lexical entry for NP arguments, what's really needed is a verb that picks the telic role when there is one and that yields unsemanticality when there isn't one. But, as far as we know, there is no such verb.[17]

Let us summarize the argument so far. JP's general strategy is to explain the apparent polysemy of governing expressions by appealing to the semantic heterogeneity of the objects they govern: If X is a governing expression that is prima facie A/B polysemous, assume that the expressions that it governs are lexically cross-classified as being either A or B.

We know of no cases where this strategy works. For one thing, it predicts that an A/B polysemous expression should be univocal in the A direction when it governs a univocal A-expression, whereas, in all the cases we can think of, A/B polysemous expressions are A/B ambiguous in both A and B contexts (cf. "bake a cake"). Furthermore, the claim that governing expressions inherit semantic content from and only from the lexical entries of the expressions they govern fails in both directions: "begin" inherits a "telos" from "a cigarette" but not from "a car," and the propositional construal of "believes John" cannot derive from the lexical entry for "John," and so on.

We conclude the following:

1. Apparent polysemy is generally real; the reason "bake" seems to be lexically ambiguous is that it is. This is compatible with a denotational semantics on the assumption that baking (creative) and baking (warming up) are different processes. JP provides no grounds for doubting this assumption.

2. There is no evidence that the meaning of governing expressions is ever modulated by the semantics of the expressions that they govern. For all the arguments show so far, "bake" behaves the same way in "bake a cake" and in "bake a potato" (it's ambiguous in both); "enjoy" means the same thing in "enjoy a cigarette" as in "enjoy the sunset" (it means 'enjoy'); "good" means the same thing in "good knife" and in "good car" (it means 'good'); and so on. If "bank" means something different in "bank a check" and "bank a plane," then "bank" is not polysemous but homonymous, and the context effects are not modulation but selection.

4   Compositionality and Logical Form

We start this section by distinguishing two kinds of issues that JP's treatment generally runs together: on the one hand, questions about the *complexity* of lexical

---

[17] On pages 137ff, JP provides an (unconvincing) explanation of "John asked me (/*wondered) the temperature." But he doesn't consider why, given that "John wondered what the temperature is" is well formed, the statement "John wondered the temperature" doesn't have a reading on which "the temperature" is "coerced" to an interrogative proposition.

entries; and, on the other hand, questions about the *generativity* of the lexicon. As we have shown, JP typically argues for lexical complexity by claiming that it is needed to account for generativity. ("Cake" must contain ARTIFACT in order to account for the polysemy of "bake"; "telephone" must contain a "telos" in order to account for the polysemy of "use"; and so on.) However, in principle, the issues are dissociable. Someone who agrees with us that JP's arguments for lexical complexity are unconvincing and who shares our suspicion that content is just denotation could wonder, nonetheless, whether a denotational lexicon might not be generative. So let's turn to this.

Suppose, for the sake of the argument, that the lexical entry for "cake" contains MADE BY BAKING. What happens next? Actually, JP tells two different accounts, though he does not acknowledge they are distinct. First, the lexicon is generative; "cake" contributes MADE BY BAKING to the meaning-in-context of "bake," thereby bestowing a "creative" sense on the verb. "Thus, we can derive both senses of verbs like *bake* by putting some of the semantic weight on the NP. This view suggests that, in such cases, the verb itself is not polysemous [i.e., it has only one lexical entry]. Rather, the creation sense of *bake* is contributed in part by the meaning of *a cake* . . . . The verb appears polysemous because certain complements . . . add to the basic meaning by co-composition" (p. 124).

Second, "The semantics *for the VP* [our emphasis] *bake a cake* results from several operations. . . . The operation of co-composition results in a qualia structure for the VP that respects aspects of both constituents" (p. 124). "The result of co-composition is a semantic representation *at the VP level* [our emphasis] that is identical in structure to the lexical form for a creation verb such as *build* " (p. 125). According to this second account, the lexicon isn't generative after all; "cake" never contributes anything, at any level, to the representation of "bake." Rather, "cake" contributes its lexical content (atomistic or otherwise) to the interpretation of the VP "bake a cake" (as does, mutatis mutandis, "bake").

Our polemical reason for insisting on the difference between these two accounts is that it is news if the lexicons of natural languages are generative; everybody always thought they were just lists. However, it is no news that there's an infinity of VPs.[18]

However, we have a second reason for stressing the distinction: though we're very dubious that the meaning of a word is ever a function of its context, we have no doubt at all that (barring idioms) the meaning of a phrase is always a function of the meanings of its lexical constituents. In short, all semanticists, whatever they may think about the generativity of the lexicon, have to face the problem of compositionality – the problem, that is, of saying how lexical semantics

---

[18] We are not, by the way, denying that JP's two accounts are compatible. Perhaps he thinks that "cake" adds to the interpretation of "bake a cake" by modulating the meaning of "bake." Our point is that evidence that "cake" contributes to the meaning of "bake a cake" is neutral as to whether the lexicon is generative.

contributes to determining the semantic interpretation of phrases. Although we take the question to be very largely moot, we are inclined to think that the exigencies of the compositionality problem really do require that lexical entries cannot just specify denotations even assuming denotation is all that there is to content.

Consider the phrase "want a beer"; and assume – what, to be sure, is tendentious – that the right interpretation of this phrase is "want to have a beer"[19] whereas, by contrast, the right interpretation of "drink a beer" is just 'drink a beer'. How does the theory that derives the meanings of phrases from the meanings of their lexical constituents ensure this difference of interpretation?

One way would be to agree with SEL that there are two "want"s, differing somehow in meaning, one of which takes an infinitival complement and one of which takes an NP. Here we agree with JP; this treatment is too unrevealing to be plausible. In particular, it misses the equivalence of "wants a beer" and "wants to have a beer"; and it fails to explain why, if Bill wants to drink a beer and Mary wants a beer, then they both want something and they both want to have something[20]; and it fails to explain why the two *wants* are in complementary distribution. So, what's the right way to handle "want"?[21] Roughly, we think, like this: "Want" denotes the relation that holds between x and y when and only when *x is a creature and y is a state of affairs* (or whatever kind of thing infinitive expressions like "to have a beer" denote), *and x wants y*.[22] The way to avoid the lexical polysemy is to maintain that "want" denotes this relation both in "wants a beer" and in "wants to have a beer"; that is, it denotes this relation whether its complement is an infinitive or an NP.

Of course, this proposal faces an immediate problem: a beer isn't a "state of affairs" (i.e., it isn't the sort of thing that infinitival complements denote). Then how could "want a beer" and "want to have a beer" denote the same relation? This is just the polysemy problem over again; how can the semantics ensure that expressions of the form "want NP" get the same semantic value (viz., the same denotation) as corresponding expressions of the form "want INF" without assuming two lexical

---

[19] In JP's account, of course, this is *not* the right interpretation; it is part of the account that "want" is generative and that "want a beer" means "want to drink a beer." We will return to this presently.

[20] You should be prepared to admit this even if you doubt there is something (viz., to have a beer) that Bill and Mary both want or both want to have.

[21] We are concentrating on whether "want NP" is polysemous and ignoring the questions that are raised by its intentionality (viz., by the opacity of the NP position to existential generalization and substitution of coreferentials). If you like, assume that "wants" expresses an "intentional relation," and plug in your favorite account of them.

[22] Actually, the talk of creatures, states of affairs, and the like is entirely heuristic. That is because, on the present view, the lexicon is not required to specify a *sense* for "want" but only required to say what "want" denotes. Perhaps, if x wants y, then, necessarily, x is a creature and y is a state of affairs. However, a purely denotational lexicon is not required to say that this is so, any more than it is required to say that dogs are animals or that 2 is prime. A denotational theory thus avoids the commitments to unanalyzed semantic entities and properties ("agents," "patients," "events," "transitions," "being in some sense affected," etc.) by which, as we have remarked above, standard views of lexical semantics are plagued.

entries for "want"? Or, to put the same question in slightly different terms, how does a compositional semantics operate to assign the interpretation 'wants to have NP' to expressions of the form "wants NP"?

Here is our proposal: A lexical entries is allowed to be complex. If it is, it specifies (a) a meaning (viz., content, viz., denotation) and (b) a rule of composition that contributes to determining the *logical form* of the phrases of which the item is a constituent.

A (very) schematic derivation of the interpretation of expressions of the form "wants X" (where X is a lexical item) should serve to introduce the general idea. We assume that the semantic interpretation proceeds, node by node, from the bottom to the top of a (surface) syntactic tree. In the present case, the crucial steps are as follows:

Domain:

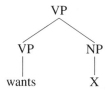

Stage 1:

> *Input*: $\langle wants_V, X_{NP} \rangle$
> *Operation*: Assigns lexically specified semantic interpretations.
> *Output*: Interpretations of (viz., assignments of denotations to) the lexical nodes: Assigns to the V node the set of ordered pairs $\langle y,x \rangle$ such that y wants x, and assigns to the NP node the lexically specified denotation of *X*.

Stage 2:

> *Input*: The domain tree with the lexical nodes interpreted as per stage 1.
> *Operation*: Interprets the node VP
> *Output:* VP is assigned "{y: y wants to have F(X)}" where *F(X)* designates the interpretation that *X* receives in stage 1.[23]
> *Note:* We assume that the operation in stage 2 is driven by a composition rule that is part of the lexical entry for "want": namely, if the constituents of VP$_i$ are $\langle$"wants"$_V$, X$_{NP}\rangle$, then the interpretation of VP$_i$ is 'want to have F(X).'

Several comments (in no particular order):

1. The derivation of "wants to drink a beer" assumes that the surface syntax of that sentence is not relevantly different to its logical form. The

---

[23] If the sentence under interpretation is of the form *NP$_1$ wants X*, a later cycle will identify y with the denotation assigned to NP$_1$.

composition rule assigns to the VP node the set "{y:y wants to drink a beer}." In this case, the composition rule is presumably not lexically governed; this is the unmarked treatment for phrases consisting of a verb with an infinitive complement.

2. Notice that, according to this proposal, "want" *never* means (denotes) anything except a relation between a creature and a state of affairs, not even in "wants a beer" (i.e., not even in an expression where its surface complement *fails* to denote a state of affairs). Therefore, "want" isn't polysemous; it's *content* is absolutely context invariant. We're as far from a generative lexicon as it is possible to get.

   The cost of this univocality is complex lexical entries, which determine not only the content of an item but the logical syntax of the phrases to which they contribute their content.

3. The proposed mechanism does the same sort of job that JP's notion of "type coercion" is designed to do. There are, however, differences other than the fundamental one that distinguishes a semantics of complex lexical senses from an atomistic lexical semantics of denotations. For example, it's part of what we take to be the context insensitivity of "want" that it always introduces the same "light verb" into the VP it governs. This repeats the remark we made in footnote 18: we assume that "wants a pretzel" means 'wants to have a pretzel' not 'wants to eat a pretzel.' The meaning of "want" doesn't decide what one can want a pretzel for.

   Indeed, we think, exactly contrary to JP, that it is this consideration that distinguishes expressions like "want," which introduce light elements, from expressions like "use," "enjoy," and "begin," which don't. In our view, the semantic interpretation of "use NP" is the set '{y: y uses NP}'. Part of the evidence for this is that there is no relation (other, of course, than using) that y has to have to the NPs that y uses. Contrast the necessary truth that every y that wants NP ipso facto wants to have NP.

4. There is a variety of lexically governed effects on logical form other than light verb introduction. For example, we think it is plausible that "good" introduces a quantifier into the interpretation of "good NP"; roughly, a good NP is one that is good for *whatever it is* that NPs are supposed to be good for (cf., Ziff 1960). Notice that this treatment makes "good" context *in*sensitive; "good" quantifies over the function of the NP it modifies, and the way it does so is independent of which NP it is. Because the meaning of "good" is context independent, the lexical entry for the NP need not specify a "telos"; so the semantics of "good knife" provide no argument that "knife" has a definition that includes its function. (This is just as well because, as JP himself remarks (p. 43), "good children" and "good weather" are perfectly fine, though neither children nor the weather have functions. See above for the corresponding point about "enjoy" and "use.")

5. Our discussion has not assumed that there is a *level* of logical form at which, for example, "want a beer" is represented as WANT TO HAVE A BEER. On our account, all that happens is that wanting to have a beer (material mode) is assigned as the denotation of the expression "wants a beer." Our treatment is, however, compatible with positing an explicit level of logical syntax should there prove to be any reason to do so; we have no views on the matter for present purposes.

We close with two pending questions: The first strikes us as not very urgent but the second is vital.

First, what about polysemy? We do not have a theory of polysemy beyond the suggestion, implicit in the preceding, that where it is sensitive to the syntactic structure of the context, polysemy belongs not to the theory of content but to the theory of logical form. That leaves lots of residual cases like "lamb" ('meat' vs. 'animal'), "window" ('the opening' vs. 'what fills the opening'), "newspaper" ('the thing you read' vs. 'the organization that publishes it').

We suspect that there is nothing interesting to say about such cases; the meanings of words can partially overlap in all sorts of ways, so there are all sorts of ways in which polysemous terms can differ from mere homonyms. Nothing in the literature convinces us that there are powerful generalizations to state.[24]

Surprisingly, JP apparently shares this view so far as the polysemy of *nouns* is concerned (see pp. 90–95). In cases like "lamb" and "window," JP does exactly what SELs do: He has branching lexical entries that allow one to say, for example, that "lamb" always means 'physical object', but doesn't always mean 'animal' or always mean 'food.' This is really unavoidable, given JP's architecture: governing expressions get their ambiguity from what they govern, so the governed expressions have to get theirs from the lexicon. Of course, as JP himself points out when discussing SELs, appealing to branching entries to distinguish polysemy from homonymy is a merely notational solution. It "accounts for the data, but in a *post hoc* fashion, without making any predictions as to whether a particular datum should be possible or not" (p. 42). "Bank" 'river' versus "bank" 'building' is presumably homonymy rather than polysemy, but both "bank"s, like both "lamb"s, mean (hence are "branches" of the representation that corresponds to) 'physical object.'[25] Nor is it clear why, if nouns can be really (viz., lexically) polysemous, verbs can't be too.

---

[24] There is a semiproductive generalization according to which terms for tastes double as terms for personalities: "sweet," "bitter," "sour," "tart," "acid," "bland," "salty," and so on. Could anyone really suppose that lexical semantics should be required to capture this regularity? And, if not, why should it be required to capture the polysemy of "window," "door," "newspaper," and the like?

[25] The function of JP's dot operator (see pp. 92ff) is not clear to us, but we suspect that it has the effect of allowing components of lexical entries to combine freely, in the way that features do. If that's the right reading, then JP's lexical entries are even less constrained than those of classical SELs such as Katz and Fodor (1963).

Second, Prima facie, our notion of coercion is more constrained than JP's. For example, it cannot turn out that the content of one expression ever depends on the content of another; it is not allowed that "want NP" sometimes means 'want to eat NP' and sometimes means 'want to drink NP.'

Nevertheless, we do allow that the logical role of an expression can be determined by the lexical entries of the forms that govern it; "beer" is the logical object of "drink" in "want to drink a beer," but it is the logical object of "have" in "want a beer." This departs from the most rigorous notion of compositionality, according to which each constituent contributes its content and only its content to its hosts, and the effect of a constituent on its hosts is absolutely context independent.

The entirely rigorous notion of compositionality seems to us almost certainly not attainable. For example, "want" and the like to one side, it is a truism that *logical* vocabulary is typically defined "in use" (i.e., in a grammatical context), so that the lexical entry for (as it might be) "the" determines the logical role of the NP in "the NP" and does so in a way that is specific to "the"; presumably the logical role of the NP in "an NP" is quite different. Indeed, it is arguable that the lexical content of "the" is exhausted by what it says about the logical form of *the NP*.[26]

However, if pure compositionality can't be had, it also can't be that just anything goes. What we've said is tantamount to saying there can be context effects on what a lexical item contributes to logical form but not on what it contributes to content. However, because we don't know how to be rigorous about the form/content distinction, we're not persuaded that the notion of coercion that we've sketched actually succeeds in constraining the ways that a constituent can affect its hosts. Which is to say that, although we're sure that language is compositional, we don't know what the claim that it is amounts to. That, and not polysemy and the like, seems to us to be the main problem of lexical semantics.

References

Cruse, D. A. 1986. *Lexical Semantics*. Cambridge University Press, Cambridge.

Fodor, J. A., and Lepore, E. 1992. *Holism, A Shopper's Guide*. Blackwell, Oxford.

Fodor, J. A. 1994. *The Elm and the Expert*. MIT Press, Cambridge, MA.

Fodor, J. A. 1998. *Concepts*. Oxford University Press, Oxford.

Higginbotham, J. 1994. Priorities of Thought. *Aristotelian Proceedings Supplement* 68: 85–106.

Jackendoff, R. 1992. *Languages of The Mind*, MIT Press, Cambridge, MA.

[26] By contrast, the lexical entry for "and" is, of course, not exhausted by the compositional rule it gives; it also must supply a denotation, so as to distinguish between sentences of the logical form $P \& Q$ and sentences of, for example, the logical form $P \lor Q$, $P \to Q$, and so forth. (Likewise with the entries for "all" and "some." If this is right, then there are perhaps four kinds of lexical entries: ones that specify only a composition rule ("the," "a"), ones that specify only of a denotation ("Tom," "eat"), ones that specify both ("want," "believe," "good"), and ones that specify neither (expletives and the "do" of "do"-support).

Katz, J., and Fodor, J. A. 1963. The Structure of a Semantic Theory. *Language* 39: 170–210.

Mates, B. 1950. Synonymity. *University of California Publications in Philosophy* 25. Reprinted in L. Linsky, *Semantics and Philosophy of Language*, Urbana: University of Illinois Press, 1952, 111–138.

Milne, A. A. 1957. *The World of Pooh*. E. P. Dutton, New York.

Pustejovsky, J. 1995. *The Generative Lexicon*. MIT Press, Cambridge, MA.

Weinreich, U. 1959. Travels through Semantic Space. *Word* 14: 346–366.

Ziff, P. 1960. *Semantic Analysis*. Cornell University Press, Ithaca.

4 Generativity and Explanation in Semantics: A Reply to Fodor and Lepore

JAMES PUSTEJOVSKY

Abstract

In this article, I address the remarks made in Fodor and Lepore's article, "The Emptiness of the Lexicon: Critical Reflections on James Pustejovsky's *The Generative Lexicon*," regarding the research program outlined in Pustejovsky (1995). My response focuses on two themes: Fodor and Lepore's misreadings and misinterpretations of the substance as well as the details of the theory, and the generally negative and unconstructive view of the study of semantics and natural language meaning inherent in their approach.

1 Methodological Preliminaries[1]

I would like to address the remarks made in Fodor and Lepore's (henceforth, FL), "The Emptiness of the Lexicon: Critical Reflections on James Pustejovsky's *The Generative Lexicon*" (in this volume), regarding the research program outlined in Pustejovsky (1995). My response focuses on two themes: FL's misreadings and misinterpretations of the substance as well as the details of the book, and the generally misguided and unconstructive view of the study of semantics and natural language meaning inherent in their approach.

In contrast to this approach, I have proposed a framework, Generative Lexicon Theory, that faces the empirically hard problems of how words can have different meanings in different contexts, how new senses can emerge compositionally, and how semantic types predictably map to syntactic forms in language. The theory accomplishes this by means of a semantic typing system encoding generative factors, called "qualia structures," into each lexical item. Operating over these structures are compositional rules incorporating specific devices for capturing the contextual determination of an expression's meaning.

Perhaps the biggest disappointment in FL's critique of Generative Lexicon Theory is to not even recognize the relevance of polysemy as a key aspect to linguistic creativity, and a window into the generative nature of thought. As a result, their discussions of what they call "compositionality" and "productivity" are beside the point, even if they were correct. The truth of the matter is that language meaning is dirty. Wittgenstein, Searle, and others have shown us that. However, discovering

---

[1] This paper was published in *Linguistic Inquiry*, 29:2, 1998.

what in a speech act is responsible for our ability to convey the richness and diversity of meaning with such finite lexical resources is a task both more deserving than the null-hypothesis offered up by FL, and more amenable to empirical investigation than they suggest.

In the following discussion, let us not lose sight of our goal, namely a theoretically sound, empirical investigation of language meaning. To this end, mental representations are justifiable when, postulating them provides us with a theory that connects to the observables (i.e., the data under investigation) in a superior fashion, and satisfies some notion of simplicity to this end, when compared with other theories. Hence, the unobservables must do more than earn their keep; they have to be cheaper than the competition. In the rest of this article, I will outline what I think can be said about natural language semantics, and how this position is both defensible and preferable to FL's silence over the many semantic phenomena demanding explanation.

2   Generative Lexicon Theory and Knowledge of Language

Before discussing of the criticism presented in FL's article, the goals of the Generative Lexicon Theory and related theories of language semantics will be discussed. In the study of meaning, our aim is to provide an adequate description of how our language expressions have content, and how this content appears to undergo continuous modification and modulation in new contexts. Furthermore, when possible, we attempt to establish an explanation for why this might be the case. Hence, along the way, we should adopt only those theoretical entities that are justified and justifiable in light of the data we examine. Generative Lexicon Theory is in large part motivated by the desire to see what contribution lexical information makes toward the overall semantic interpretation of sentences. The important questions along the way are not so different from those asked by many language researchers. These can be stated as follows:

1. Given our finite means, what is the nature of our knowledge that allows us to adapt to an unbounded number of contexts, and successfully use our language to talk about the world in these contexts?

2. Is this knowledge associated with the linguistic representations themselves, which act as mediators between "meaning" and "referring practices"?

3. By what standards can we evaluate theories of linguistics and semantics? Should these standards be different from those of other empirical sciences?

The position adopted in Generative Lexicon Theory is that the human linguistic capacity is a reflection of our ability to categorize and represent the world in particular ways. What is uniquely human is not an extensional language per se so much as the generative ability to construct the world as it is revealed through language and the categories it employs. Language is a natural manifestation of this faculty for generative categorization and compositional thought. In particular, the ability to categorize "co-compositionally" is argued to be characteristic of human behavior uniquely. This is the ability to take a category and refine or redefine its use in a novel way or a new context. The continuous refinement and redefinition of what roles an object plays in our environment, and how we conceptualize that object as having different properties in different contexts is the process of co-composition (e.g., as with the different meanings of the adjective "fast" in "fast car," "fast typist," "fast waltz," or the verb "open" in "open a door," "open a box," or "open a file"; cf. Pustejovsky, 1995, and references therein for discussion).

Perhaps a useful comparison of the two approaches under discussion can be seen in the attitude to the following quotation from Davidson (1968):

> Language is the instrument it is because the same expression, with semantic features (meanings) unchanged, can serve countless purposes.

In spite of their major disagreements with Davidson's holism, this is essentially the position adopted by FL is their article. In my view, this has matters completely upside down. Rather, the situation is more fully stated as follows:

> Language is the instrument it is since the same expression can serve countless purposes because the semantic features (meanings) change in context.

Yet the ability of linguistic expressions to "adapt" their meanings to fit a specific context is nothing mysterious or inexplicable. The semantic potential of language is not to be explained in terms of ad hoc devices. Rather, it is the result of an appropriately expressive and adequately constrained generative system, devised essentially to this end. That is, the recursive devices underlying semantics remain unchanged, giving rise to new meanings. In fact, what makes language so uniquely expressive is the way it seems to embrace meaning shifts such as polysemy. FL simply ignore this fact and try to deny that it is an issue or even a real phenomenon. Some examination of the data will help demonstrate my point.

What is polysemy, why is it so central to language, and why can it not be ignored? To answer these questions, let me review briefly three major themes in the study of polysemy and what has concerned and motivated each tradition. The first systematic formal treatment of inherent polysemy comes arguably from the philosophy of language, in works such as Geach (1971), and Lambek (1958), where it was acknowledged that sentential operators such as "not" in English can be logically treated as predicate operators, through a type-changing operation. Montague (1970) employs a different type-changing rule to allow for a uniform treatment of noun phrases, and Gazdar (1980), Partee and Rooth (1983) and others, extend the notion of type-shifting to allow for polymorphic conjunction.

The second tradition concerns the formal treatment of polyvalency phenomena in verbs. Klein and Sag (1985), for example, extend the range of type-shifting operations to relate the multiple subcategorization possibilities for verbs such as "believe" and "prefer." Seeing the formal applicability as well as the descriptive utility of such type-shifting operations, work in semantics started providing for more flexible interpretations of types for a variety of phenomena (cf. Partee, 1992 for a review).

Interestingly, one set of polysemy phenomena has been largely ignored by the mainstream semantic community, yet it has had a long tradition of analysis within lexicographic and lexical semantic circles. These phenomena, known as regular, systematic, or logical polysemy (cf. Apresjan, 1973; Nunberg, 1979; Ostler and Atkins, 1992; Pustejovsky, 1991; Weinreich, 1964, 1972) appear to be qualitatively different from the cases mentioned above, and involve sense modulations and perspectival shifts over the meanings of words. For example, nouns such as "newspaper," "book," "lunch," and "exam" are logically polysemous between different aspects or facets of the noun's meaning.

(1)   a. Mary doesn't believe <u>the book</u>.
       b. John sold <u>his books</u> to Mary.

(2)   a. Eno the cat is sitting on yesterday's <u>newspaper</u>.
       b. Yesterday's <u>newspaper</u> really got me upset.

(3)   a. Mary is in Harvard Square looking for the Bach <u>sonatas</u>.
       b. We won't get to the concert until after the Bach <u>sonata</u>.

(4)   a. I have my <u>lunch</u> in the backpack.
       b. Your <u>lunch</u> was longer today than it was yesterday.

(5)   a. The phone rang during my <u>appointment</u>.
       b. My next <u>appointment</u> is John.

In each of these cases, the same noun denotes in two ways; "book" refers to both propositional content and a physical object, "lunch" to both food and an event, "appointment" to both an event and an individual, and so forth.

One of the goals of Generative Lexicon Theory has been to unify these diverse conceptions of syntactic variation, type shifting, and regular polysemy within a systematic formulation of the general nature of semantic compositionality, and in particular, the processes giving rise to creative changes in meaning.

It is interesting to speculate on why these concerns haven't been part of the logical tradition in natural language semantics. It is fair to say that Russell and Frege (and the early analytic tradition) were not interested in language as a purely linguistic phenomenon, but simply as the medium through which judgments can be formed and expressed. Hence, there is little regard for the relations between senses of words, when not affecting the nature of judgment, for example, within intensional contexts. Nineteenth century semanticists and semasiologists, on the other hand, viewed polysemy as the life force of human language. Bréal, for example, considered it to be a necessary creative component of language, and argued that this phenomenon better than most in semantics illustrates the cognitive and conceptualizing force of the human species (see Bréal, 1897).

For Erdmann also, polysemy is a necessary part of the functioning of language itself. The "Vieldeutigkeit" of a word can refer either to a constructional ambiguity, such as inheres in the modal distinction in the meaning of "play" in "Mary played the violin" (between the activity of playing a violin and the ability to perform that action), or to the polysemy of an expression that alters its meaning in context, as with adjectives such as "good" and "fast" (see Erdmann, 1900; Stern, 1931). The early theories of semasiology attempted to account for meaning shifts in language and in particular, for how an expression (i.e., word or phrase), changes its meaning in context in definite and definable ways. Erdmann's discussion of metonymy, for example, is similar to the view expounded here on how the meaning, and with it, the referential potential of an expression changes in a context in specific ways.

Although sense enumeration approaches to meaning construct a Linnaeus-like museum of word senses, with genus and species neatly classified and separated into distinct cases, in Generative Lexicon Theory the methodology has been to construct differential structures that have functional behaviors. More specifically, (i) the semantics of lexical items are underspecified expressions, (ii) every element in a phrase may function "actively" in the composition of the phrase, and (iii) the notion of word sense only emerges at the level of the sentence, namely, its "sense in context."

Generative Lexicon Theory is concerned with the following problems:

(a) Explaining the polymorphic nature of language;
(b) Characterizing the semanticality of natural language utterances;
(c) Capturing the creative use of words in novel contexts;
(d) Developing a richer, co-compositional semantic representation.

One of the most crucial aspects of the theory is that the representation and treatment of polysemy is central to the way one structures linguistic theory generally and one's theory of meaning in particular. Thus, the first step in examining the meaning of a word is to see the range of polysemies it exhibits. The point is that most current theories of lexical semantics, and by virtue of their incorporating these theories, theories of compositional semantics, have been unable to account for the expressive and creative power of word sense. Words generally have fixed meanings in frameworks adopting this thesis. The ability to change the sense of a word in these systems arises only by virtue of creating a new sense or lexical item, or by some sort of unconstrained meaning postulate.

As argued in Pustejovsky (1995), something fundamental is being missed in this approach; namely, the logical relationship *between* the senses, which is tantamount to explaining what sense-combinations are possible in a language. This is directly analogous to the (descriptive or theoretical) usefulness of establishing transformations such as movement to account for syntactic variation. The necessary first step is to observe the variation, but the interesting step is establishing what the relationship is between the forms, e.g., as with indicative and *wh*-transformed constructions. The theory of movement, for example, however formulated, postulates the existence of empty categories or their formal equivalent, and with such entities comes the need to provide closure on their distribution. This methodology has been at the core of generative linguistics since the 1960s, and is one of the general strategies adopted here for modeling language meaning as well.

Another crucial assumption in Generative Lexicon Theory is that, rather than assuming a fixed set of *primitives* to describe word meaning, we assume a fixed number of *generative devices* that are used to construct semantic expressions. Just as a formal language is described more in terms of the productions in the grammar than in terms of its accompanying vocabulary, so a semantic language is defined by the rules generating the structures for expressions rather than the vocabulary of primitives itself. It is for this reason that the semantics is called a generative lexical theory.

For the purpose of the following discussion, a *generative lexicon* can be characterized as a system involving at least four basic levels of linguistic representation (see Grimshaw, 1990; Parsons, 1985; Williams, 1981; and references in Pustejovsky, 1995):

1. ARGUMENT STRUCTURE: Specification of number and type of logical arguments.
2. EVENT STRUCTURE: Definition of the event type of an expression and its subeventual structure.
3. QUALIA STRUCTURE: A structural differentiation of the predicative force for a lexical item.
4. LEXICAL INHERITANCE STRUCTURE: Identification of how a lexical structure is related to other structures in the type lattice.

A set of generative devices connects these four levels, providing for the compositional interpretation of words in context (see Pustejovsky, 1995). The exact nature of these devices determines the polymorphic expressiveness of the semantics in fairly restrictive ways. These devices include *type coercion, subselection,* and *co-composition.*

Examining the theory in a bit more detail, I will assume that word meaning is structured on the basis of four generative factors, or *qualia roles,* that capture how humans understand objects and relations in the world and provide the minimal explanation for the linguistic behavior of lexical items (these are inspired in large part by Moravcsik's (1975, 1990) interpretation of Aristotelian *aitia*).

> FORMAL: the basic category that distinguishes the object within a larger domain;
> CONSTITUTIVE: the relation between an object and its constituent parts;
> TELIC: the object's purpose and function;
> AGENTIVE: factors involved in the object's origin or "coming into being."

The qualia structure is at the core of the generative properties of the lexicon, because it provides a general strategy for creating increasingly specific concepts with conjunctive properties. As an illustration of this view, consider the properties of nominals such as "rock" and "chair." These nouns can first of all be distinguished on the basis of semantic criteria that classify them in terms of general categories such as `natural_kind`, `artifact_object`. Although very useful, this is not sufficient to discriminate semantic types in a way that also accounts for their grammatical behavior. A crucial distinction between "rock" and "chair" concerns the properties that differentiate `natural_kinds` from `artifacts`: Functionality plays a crucial role in the process of individuation of artifacts, but not of natural kinds. This is reflected in grammatical behavior, whereby "a good chair," or "enjoy the chair" are well-formed expressions reflecting the specific purpose for which an artifact is designed, but "good rock" and "enjoy a rock" are semantically ill-formed because for "rock" the functionality (i.e., TELIC) is undefined. Exceptions arise when new concepts are referred to, such as when the object is construed relative to a specific activity, as in "The climber enjoyed that rock"; "rock" itself takes on a new meaning, by virtue of having telicity associated with it, and this is accomplished by co-composition with the semantics of the subject NP.

Although "chair" and "rock" are both `physical_object`, they differ in their mode of coming into being (i.e., AGENTIVE): artifacts are made by humans, "rocks" develop in nature. Similarly, a concept such as "food" or "cookie" has a physical manifestation or denotation, but also a functional grounding, pertaining to the relation of "eating." These apparently contradictory aspects of a category are orthogonally represented by the qualia structure for that concept, which provides a coherent structuring for different dimensions of meaning.

These facets make up the qualia structure for a lexical item. A simple schematic description of a lexical item, α, using this representation is shown in (6):

$$(6) \quad \begin{bmatrix} \alpha \\ \text{ARGSTR} = \begin{bmatrix} \text{ARG1} = x \\ \ldots \end{bmatrix} \\ \text{QUALIA} = \begin{bmatrix} \text{CONST} = \textbf{what } x \textbf{ is made of} \\ \text{FORMAL} = \textbf{what } x \textbf{ is} \\ \text{TELIC} = \textbf{function of } x \\ \text{AGENTIVE} = \textbf{how } x \textbf{ came into being} \end{bmatrix} \end{bmatrix}$$

Adopting these assumptions, we are well-positioned to address the question of what constitutes a well-formed concept from the perspective of conceptual acquisition, lexical semantics, and issues of computability. In turn, an answer to those questions relates directly to the following issues:

1. Why do we learn the categories we do when we do?
2. Are there natural constraints on what we can in principle conceptualize?

Furthermore, specific formal proposals for how semantics might be structured enables us to address a range of questions in acquisition: How can early patterns of language production and comprehension be used as evidence for the structuring of concepts outlined above? Psychological studies can be devised, focusing on how factors such as lexical frequency, priming, and simple associative strength fare, when pitted against those inheritance principles that follow from formal and computational theories such as Generative Lexicon (see Keil, 1989; Pustejovsky, Keil, and Pollack, 1997).

3   Underspecification in Semantics

The most effective way of countering FL's rejection of the position in Pustejovsky (1995) is to illustrate the scope and diversity of the phenomena they have failed to consider, and to review how these are addressed within Generative Lexicon Theory.

Over the past several years, there has been a resurgence of interest in questions relating to the messiness of word meaning. Inspired by a few early researchers who admitted the complexity of sense determination and the fixing of reference (see Fauconnier, 1985; Kayser, 1988; and Nunberg, 1979), much of the work in semantics and computational linguistics is now expressly concerned with the representation and processing of polysemous lexical items and phrases.

I believe the reasons for this resurgence are two-fold. First, there is now an appreciation of the fact that systematic or logical polysemy is formally related to the problem of semantic selection and polyvalency, making the treatment of polysemy much more relevant to theoretical work on issues of syntactic form and polymorphic behavior. Second, formal mechanisms are now available for the analysis of these constructions, which allow them to be viewed as an integral component of the lexicon and the semantics, as opposed to off-line, noncompositional processes of sense extension or metaphorical interpretation. It is these mechanisms that form the backbone of compositional operations in Generative Lexicon Theory.

3.1   *Nominal Polysemy*

In this section, I argue that, given the appropriate machinery, we can in fact model the syntactic and semantic behavior of polysemous nominal types in natural language. In particular, I study one class of nominals that has been particularly difficult to model formally, namely, nouns such as "lecture," "prize," "book," and "lunch." Members of this class, I have argued, must be represented as complex structures rather than simple types, as they do not allow for simple conjunctive typing or interpretation.

I will first illustrate why these nouns are formally problematic for conventional semantic treatments, such as that assumed by FL. To begin, consider the semantic distinction underlying our conceptions of "food" and "lunch." How are these nouns distinguished semantically? We obviously understand the concept of food as something paraphrasable by dictionary definitions such as 'edible substance or material.' All that seems to be required to minimally capture the meaning of the noun "food" is some characterization of the relation between the property of 'substance' and that of 'edible,' relative to a class of certain individuals, e.g., humans. Our conception of "lunch," however, seems more complex, because it makes reference to a specific period or event in the day as well. Unlike "food," it may refer to either the substance or event. For "food," one might simply conjoin or unify these properties to give a specific intersective property of 'edible substance'. This assumes that modally subordinating properties such as 'edible' have no internal structure, a tenable position only if one is willing to make liberal use of meaning postulates as off-line inferences in the compositional process of interpreting sentence meanings.

Contrary to the rather ad hoc approach to representation briefly suggested above, I will assume a mechanism employing significantly more machinery for representing the analytic knowledge associated with words. On this view, the modal subordination of the predicate indicating the use of the substance is given an explicit representation, distinct from the material aspect of "food." This is accomplished in the following manner. Assume that for a concept such as "food," we can separate the characteristic property from the functional aspect. Let us associate these with the FORMAL and TELIC roles, respectively. Minimally, then, the notion "food" is a concept making reference to distinct and orthogonal facets of knowledge, each expressing a different explanation of this concept.

Continuing with the example above, we can imagine that "food" as a concept is formed by conjoining or unifying "orthogonal" values from FORMAL and TELIC qualia roles, as illustrated schematically in (7).[2]

$$
(7) \quad
\begin{bmatrix}
\textbf{food} \\
\text{ARGSTR} = [\text{ARG1} = \texttt{x : substance}] \\
\text{QUALIA} =
\begin{bmatrix}
\text{FORMAL} = \texttt{x} \\
\text{TELIC} = \texttt{eat(e,y,x)}
\end{bmatrix}
\end{bmatrix}
$$

---

[2] I will assume the qualia are partial functions over types, as presented in Pustejovsky (1998) and Asher and Pustejovsky (forthcoming) – namely, from types to a specific mode of description, be it formal, material, an event description, or an individual event (the FORMAL, CONST(ITUTIVE), TELIC, and AGENTIVE roles, respectively). Here, I define the qualia for a type α as follows:

a. $Formal(\lambda x[\alpha(x)]) = \lambda x[Q(x)] \leftrightarrow \alpha \subseteq Q$

b. $Const(\lambda x[\alpha(x)]) = \lambda y[Q(y)] \leftrightarrow \forall x[\alpha(x) \rightarrow \exists y[Q(y) \land made - of(x, y)]$

c. $Agentive(\lambda x[\alpha(x)]) = \lambda e[\psi(e)] \leftrightarrow \forall x, e'[\alpha(x, e') \rightarrow \exists e' \exists y[\psi(e') \land e' \prec e \land make(e', y, x)]]$

d. $Telic(\lambda x[\alpha(x)]) = \lambda y \lambda e \exists x[\phi(e, y, x)] \leftrightarrow \lambda y \forall x \forall e \forall y[\psi_\alpha(e, y, x) >, \exists e'[(\phi(e', y, x) \land e < e']]$

In the representation of the TELIC, ψ_α denotes the appropriate circumstances of doing something to an x of type α, and $>$ is the default conditional of Asher and Morreau (1991). Intuitively, the qualia relate modes of description of an object. Whereas the FORMAL is treated as reference to the supertype and CONST returns the material mode of the object, notice that both AGENTIVE and TELIC make reference to events, but in very different ways. Whereas the AGENTIVE identifies a set of individual events associated with the object, the TELIC refers to an event description, namely that which under all appropriate circumstances (ψ) is by default interpreted as the object's purpose. See Busa (1996) and Pustejovsky (1998) for discussion.

Let us refer to such structures as *unified types*, as represented in (8a), and analyze the orthogonal values of the qualia roles as logical conjunction, as in (8b), where P_F and Q_T, are the values associated with the FORMAL and TELIC qualia, respectively.[3]

(8)   a.
$$\begin{bmatrix} \sigma\_\tau \\ \text{ARGSTR} = [\, \text{ARG1} = x \,] \\ \text{QUALIA} = \begin{bmatrix} \text{FORMAL} = P(x) \\ \text{TELIC} = Q(x) \end{bmatrix} \end{bmatrix} \Rightarrow$$

b. $\lambda x[P_F(x) \wedge Q_T(x)]$

For the interpretation of the noun "food," this would give the expression in (9).

(9) $\lambda x[substance_F(x) \wedge \lambda y \lambda e[eat_T(e, y, x)]]$

The qualia can, in fact, be structured by the conjunction of properties for many semantic classes of nominals. For example, we might view an artifact as something having an AGENTIVE quale value; that is, "having been made":

(10) $\lambda x \exists y \exists e[P_F(x) \wedge make_A(e, y, x)]$

Putting the above concept together with a specific FORMAL value, such as a physical object, gives rise to the concept of a *physical artifact*, which can also be modeled as the conjunction of predicates (or unification of types). A propositional artifact, such as a *speech act*, would be constructed in a like fashion (see Pustejovsky, 1997 for discussion).

This method, in fact, permits us a general strategy for creating increasingly specific concepts with conjunctive properties. *Unified types* can be seen as structured by orthogonal dimensions or perspectives, rather than as inheriting properties from multiple parents in a homogeneous property structure. One would not want to allow the free structuring or combinatorics of conjunctive properties, however, because this would generate more nonsense than well-formed concepts. The question of what constitutes a well-formed concept is at the core of lexical semantic research, and it is necessary for any theory to address this issue directly in how representations are structures and generated. FL are silent on this issue and the phenomena generally.

This is not surprising, however. Basic categorization as well as how word meanings combine to form complex structures in a lattice of types is something that neither Carnap nor Quine ever imagined as part of the "linguistic" machinery available to a semantic theory. Both observed – positively and negatively, respectively – that meaning postulates will, with equal force, relate one expression to another (Carnap, 1956; Quine, 1961). The discussion of the type system underlying

---

[3] The event description of "eating," which is the value of the TELIC role, is treated formally as an *analytic generic*, describing a functional aspect of the major mode of predication, namely the FORMAL. See Pustejovsky (1998) for more details.

linguistic expressions is relevant because FL assume that there is no such structure because there is no evidence for it. The data suggest otherwise, however, because the modes of inheritance for concepts associated with linguistic expressions are not arbitrary. The model of inheritance we construct is itself the means of overcoming the arbitrariness of meaning postulates or mentalese inferences.

Generative Lexicon Theory assumes, in fact, that there is no multiple inheritance per se in natural language semantics. What appear to be instances of concepts which inherit from multiple superordinates are in fact either *typed orthogonal inheritance* structures or *complex types.*

The qualia provide us with typed orthogonal information of the appropriate sort for the former class above. Let us assume that a concept is well formed only if it inherits from a single parent within a given quale. Under this assumption, then, the only way to form more complex lexical or phrasal expressions would be by unifying predicates from distinct and orthogonal qualia. This is, in fact, what I proposed earlier for the noun "food."

Yet even the above logic is inadequate to allow words such as "book" and "lunch" to "denote" contradictory types, as the data in (1)–(5) seem to suggest. What is interesting about these pairs is that the senses of the nominals are related to each other in a specific and nonarbitrary way.

The apparently contradictory nature of the two senses for each pair actually reveals a deeper structure relating these senses, called a *complex type* (or *dot object*, see Pustejovsky, 1994). For each sense pair, there is a relation that "connects" the senses in a well-defined way. I will characterize this structure as a Cartesian type product of n types, with some additional constraints, to be described below. The product $\tau_1 \times \tau_2$, of types τ_1 and τ_2, each denoting sets, is the ordered pair $<t_1, t_2>$, where $t_1 \in \tau_1, t_2 \in \tau_2$. There exists a relation R between the elements of τ_1 and τ_2, namely, $R(t_1, t_2)$. This relation must be seen as part of the definition of the semantics for the dot object. Intuitively, the dot object can be thought of as an abstraction of the relation between the types, where the types are abstracted together. Hence, the dot operator, unlike the Cartesian product, is not a commutative product. The set of relations, $\{R_i\}$, can be seen as specialized type product operators, where the specific relation is built into the constructor itself:

(11) $\{R_i\} = \cdot_{R_1}, \cdot_{R_2}, \ldots, \cdot_{R_n}$

For nouns such as "book," "disk," and "record," the relation R is a species of "containment," and shares grammatical behavior with other container-like concepts. For example, we speak of information *in* a book, articles *in* the newspaper, as well as songs *on* a disc. This containment relation is encoded directly into the semantics of a concept such as "book" – i.e., $hold(x, y)$ – as the FORMAL quale value. For other dot object nominals such as "exam," "sonata," and "lunch," different relations structure the types in the Cartesian product (see Pustejovsky, 1995 for discussion). Let us say that, for any dot object, α, defined as a Cartesian product,

$\tau_1 \cdot \tau_2$, the following must hold:

(12) $\lambda x.y \exists R[\alpha(x : \tau_1.y : \tau_2) \wedge R(x, y) \ldots]$

The lexical structure for "book" as a dot object can then be represented as in (13).

(13)

$$
\begin{bmatrix}
\textbf{book} \\
\text{ARGSTR} = \begin{bmatrix} \text{ARG1} = \text{y:information} \\ \text{ARG2} = \text{x:phys\_obj} \end{bmatrix} \\
\text{QUALIA} = \begin{bmatrix} \text{information.phys\_obj} \\ \text{FORM} = \text{hold(x,y)} \\ \text{TELIC} = \text{read(e,w,x.y)} \\ \text{AGENT} = \text{write(e',v,x.y)} \end{bmatrix}
\end{bmatrix}
$$

This translates roughly to the following logical expression:

(14) $\lambda x.y \exists e' \exists v [book(x: \text{physobj}.y: \text{info}) \wedge hold(x, y)$
        $\wedge \lambda w \lambda e[read(e, w, x.y)] \wedge [write(e', v, x.y)]]$

Nouns such as "sonata," "lunch," and "appointment," on the other hand, are structured by entirely different relations, as explored below. What is important to note, however, is that the dot object construction (i.e., the type product) allows otherwise contradictory types to be combined into a single type.

The notion of a complex type proves useful for explaining the polysemy associated with process-result nominalizations, such as "construction" and "examination" (see Grimshaw, 1990). Consider the senses of the noun "construction" in (15a)–(15c).

(15)   a. The house's <u>construction</u> was finished in two months.
        b. The <u>construction</u> was arduous and tedious.
        c. The <u>construction</u> is standing on the next street.

In Pustejovsky (1995), it is suggested that a dot object actually allows us to capture all three senses. Informally, we can imagine this class of nominalizations as a type product (i.e., a dot object) of the two subevents constituting the transition event denoted by the verb. In some sense, the only thing different about this dot object is the typing on the dot elements and the specific relation that structures them. Thus, whereas a "book" is a dot object composed of information and physobj and is structured by the relation of containment, "construction" is a dot object composed of process and state, related by the temporal relation in the event structure of exhaustive precedence, namely, $<_\alpha$. It is interesting to speculate briefly on the semantic contribution of the *-ion* nominalizing morpheme more generally. For any verb with a complex event structure, application of the *-ion* nominalizer produces a dot object nominal, with a polysemy reflecting the types of the subevents from the verb's event structure. Hence, from the left-headed transition verb "examine," the nominalization "examination" denotes a dot object with process and state dot elements, as illustrated below (see Pustejovsky, 1995 for details):

(16)

$$
\begin{bmatrix}
\textbf{examination} \\[4pt]
\text{EVENSTR} =
\begin{bmatrix}
E_1 = \texttt{process} \\
E_2 = \texttt{state} \\
\text{RESTR} = <_\infty
\end{bmatrix} \\[20pt]
\text{ARGSTR} =
\begin{bmatrix}
\text{ARG1} = \text{[1]}
\begin{bmatrix}
\texttt{animate\_ind} \\
\text{FORMAL} = \texttt{physobj}
\end{bmatrix} \\[14pt]
\text{ARG2} = \text{[2]}
\begin{bmatrix}
\texttt{physobj} \\
\text{FORMAL} = \texttt{entity}
\end{bmatrix}
\end{bmatrix} \\[26pt]
\text{QUALIA} =
\begin{bmatrix}
\texttt{event\cdot event} \\
\text{FORMAL} = \texttt{examine\_result}(e_2, \text{[1]}) \\
\text{AGENTIVE} = \texttt{examine\_act}(e_1, \text{[1]}, \text{[2]})
\end{bmatrix}
\end{bmatrix}
$$

Another example of a dot object is seen in the semantics of the noun "exam." What is interesting about "exam" is that it can refer to either the questions that compose the event of the examination, or the event of the examining itself, as illustrated in (17).

(17)   a. The exam lasted for several hours.
       b. Bill was confused by the exam.

Questions, like any information objects, may also have physical manifestation, but need not (e.g., an oral exam). The ambiguity arises from the combination of the inherent polysemy possible in the type of information object of $\texttt{question}$, and the $\texttt{event}$ of the examination. In this case, the relation that structures the two dot elements in the type product refers directly to the "asking" event.

The range of complex types we encounter in natural language is quite broad and rich, including the following type combinations:

(18)   a. $\texttt{physobj\cdot info}$: e.g., "book," "record";
       b. $\texttt{event\cdot event}$: e.g., "construction," "examination";
       c. $\texttt{event\cdot question}$: e.g., "exam";
       d. $\texttt{event\cdot food}$: e.g., "lunch," "dinner";
       e. $\texttt{event\cdot human}$: e.g., "appointment."

For each of these type products, there is a unique relation, R_i, that structures the types. Cases that I have not examined here include nouns such as "prize," "sonata," and the more complicated concepts of "city" and "organization."

FL can avoid the empirical and technical problems associated with accounting for the nominal polysemy data examined above, because they deny there is any systematic observation to model. Yet the data speak for themselves, and we are left wondering what, in FL's view, constitutes regularity or systematicity in the domain of our investigations.

3.2   *Verbal Polysemy*

Lexical semanticists have traditionally taken enumerated senses in different contexts or with different selected phrases as characterizing the full range of meanings for a word. This is quite standard and is a descriptivist starting point for doing the deeper work of semantic analysis. On this point, FL do not mention the considerable literature on this topic (see Apresjan, 1973; Atkins, Kegl, and Levin, 1988; Levin, 1985, 1993; and Ostler and Atkins, 1992). The fact is that sense distinctions, such as those pointed out by Levin and others, are real phenomena, but that is not the real issue.[4] The interesting question is rather: How do the specific senses emerge and what is the relationship between them? The manner in which a semantic theory accounts for this, I take to be one measure of its success.

There are many ways in which a verb can be seen as exhibiting polysemous behavior. Intuitively, we might separate these into syntactic and semantic polysemies. The former deals with polyvalency, object deletion, and the general properties of argument expression, as illustrated by the following well-studied data (see Fillmore, 1986; Jackendoff, 1992; Levin, 1993; Levin and Rappaport, 1995).[5]

---

[4]   FL miss the point regarding the polysemy of "bake." Of course the phrase "bake the cake" can still refer to the "heating" or change-of state sense. Co-composition is not an obligatory semantic rule, and the expression is formally ambiguous, just as "John drank two wines" can refer to portions or kinds. Regarding the "bake" data, French and Italian differ from English in an interesting way. Neither language allows this polysemy, and "*faire*" and "*fare*" must be used in the "create" context. In Pustejovsky (1989), it was suggested that this sense-alternation is related to a larger set of crosslinguistic differences, and is apparently linked to the phenomena of resultatives as well as manner and motion conflations (see Levin, 1985 and Talmy, 1985), owing to the presence or absence of event composition rules of a particular sort.

[5]   Concerning the distinction between "butter" and "kick": These data don't involve merely an appeal to the oracle of Grice. Rather, the reason to introduce a notion such as semanticality is of course to explain the many ways that a descriptive oracle such as Gricean maxims accords with the data. For example, one might suppose that the Gricean maxim "Be informative" would obviate the need to express the direct object in (i):
(i) The murderer killed.
Furthermore, operating with Gricean maxims alone, we could "explain" why redundancy would rule out the sentence in (ii):
(ii) Mary began Mary to read the book.
because we obviously *know* what "beginning" means, just as we know what "buttering" means.
On this view, we could even study verbs such as "wash" in English (iiia) and "*sich waschen*" in German (iiib) to examine crosslinguistic informativeness quotients in terms of FL's appeal to "Grice's oracle":
(iii) a. Mary washed.
(iii) b. Marie hat sich gewascht.
We could then begin to study the associated inferences with verbs that carry uninformative complements, as in German, as compared with verbs whose complements may be dropped, by convention, as in English.
    As this small exercise shows, anything can be explained by appeal to a general enough mechanism, with the subsequent lack of theoretical interest or scientific merit.

(19) a. Mary began to read the novel.
      b. Mary began reading the novel.
      c. Mary began the novel.

(20) a. Mary ate (her meal) quickly.
      b. Mary devoured *(her meal) quickly.

(21) a. John carved a doll (out of the wood).
      b. John carved the wood (into a doll).

The latter type of polysemy can be seen as dealing with the different but related senses of a verb, as shown in (22) and (23).

(22) a. Mary enjoyed the movie last night.
      b. John enjoys his morning coffee.
      c. Bill enjoyed Kundera's last book.

(23) a. John opened the door.
      b. Mary opened the letter.

In (22), the specific meaning of the verb "enjoy" differs for each sentence, as does the meaning of "open" in (23).

According to Generative Lexicon Theory, this distinction between polysemy types is largely arbitrary and difficult to maintain, when the phenomena are examined in more detail, as illustrated in (24) an (25).[6]

(24) a. John gave a talk to the academy today.
      b. John gave a talk today.
      c. *John gave a book today.

(25) a. Mary showed a movie to her guests.
      b. Mary showed a movie.
      c. *Mary showed a record.

Unlike the previous sentences here, two dimensions of the linguistic behavior of these verbs are being modulated: (a) the arity of the verb complex; and (b) the meaning of the verb itself. Hence, in these examples we see polysemy as both syntactic variation in the complement structure and semantic mutability effects in the verb.

I take it to be one of the goals of natural language semantics to explain the shifts in interpretations above, and, when possible, to explain the compositionality involved in such cases.[7]

---

[6] FL make reference to the "unconvincingness of the examples and the imprecision of the metalanguage that is used." The examples in chapter 2 of Pustejovsky (1995) are in most cases simply the standard repertoire illustrating specific alternations or grammatical phenomena. As far as the "imprecisions of the metalanguage" are concerned, where the example of "devour" is mentioned, chapter 2 doesn't even introduce the Generative Lexicon-like formalism. FL don't distinguish the metadiscussion from the specific formal proposal put forth later in the book.

[7] The grammatical distinction raised between "eat" and "devour" points to several long discussions in the literature, none of which FL reference. The question is not whether the feature

That is, what is it about the meaning of the nouns "talk" in (24b) and "movie" in (25b) that allows a reinterpretation of (i.e., a co-composition with) the verb meaning in each example? Such data are at the core of illustrating the underlying nature of how natural language meanings are constructed and modulated in new contexts, yet FL offer no explanation for such phenomena.

Generative Lexicon Theory provides an explicit model for how such meaning shifts and polyvalency phenomena interact. From the discussion above, we can see how the qualia structure provides the structural template over which semantic transformations may apply to alter the meaning of a lexical item or phrase.[8] These transformations are the generative devices mentioned above, such as type coercion, selective binding, and co-composition, which formally map the expression to a new meaning. For example, when we combine the qualia structure of an NP with that of a governing verb, a richer notion of compositionality emerges (i.e., *co-composition*), one that captures the creative use of words. Consider, for example, how the NPs, both in subject and complement position contribute toward further specifying the interpretation of the verb "use" in the following examples

[+/- completive] adequately distinguishes the behavior of the two verbs, but rather, what knowledge of our language is responsible for the inviolable linguistic distinctions that, however learned, appear to be as natural and automatic as face recognition in visual processing. In other words, how much can be said about the phenomena, or about semantics in general?

According to FL, not very much can be said. We know by demonstrative proof that the feature [+/- completive] fails to distinguish between the above-mentioned verb pair, so there is *no* systematic semantic distinction possible. FL state (seec. 1.3) that "nobody knows what, if anything, it is for a word to denote a transition." This is, of course, incorrect, any way it's interpreted. First, as speakers we clearly and obviously make distinctions that are essentially classifications and subsequent judgments about our constructions of the world. From an intuitive point of view, "transition" in the basic sense seems to be one of the first things we learn (see Carey, 1985; Keil, 1989; Markman, 1989; Michotte, 1954). We appear to know unconsciously how our grammar expresses duration, completion, and the gradations in between the two, whether these distinctions are realized morphologically, syntactically, or semantically.

Regarding the observable distinctions between the verbs "eat" and "devour," here are the facts:

	"eat"	"devour"
object drop	YES	NO
imperative	YES	NO
object of "force"	YES	NO
aspectual particles	YES	NO
object depictives	YES	NO
resultatives	YES	NO

One of the fundamental analytical tools in linguistics and semantics is to group elements by the clustering of properties they exhibit. The distinction above is ripe for the classic clustering of data, suggesting us that we have a lexical distinction on our hands.

[8] Regarding the discussion of the interpretation of aspect: now FL accuse me of fabricating the imperfective paradox. However, it is neither my own invention nor a will-o'-the-wisp, but rather a cold hard fact of language (see Bach, 1986 and references cited therein).

taken from Pustejovsky (1995):

(26)   a. John used the new knife on the turkey.
          b. Mary has used soft contact lenses since college.
          c. This car uses unleaded gasoline.

In sentence (26a), our knowledge of knives as tools that can cut permits an economy of expression, whereby mention of the particular activity of cutting may be ellipsed. Similarly, in (26b), contact lenses are visual aids, and the use of them refers to the act of "wearing" them. The utility of a verb such as "use" is that it is semantically *light*, or simply *underspecified*, with respect to the particular activity being performed. The factors allowing us to determine which sense is appropriate for any of these cases are twofold: (a) the qualia structures for each phrase in the construction; and (b) a richer mode of composition, which is able to take advantage of this qualia information. The mechanism of *type coercion* operates along similar lines, allowing us to account for how the contextualized meanings for the verb "enjoy" emerge as the result of qualia-based information supplied by the different complements in (22a)–(22c). Although there are certainly any number of ways of enjoying something, our understanding of these sentences is facilitated by default interpretations of properties and activities associated with objects. The qualia of an object can be seen as the initial points from which to construct interpretations that would otherwise be ill formed. Hence, the TELIC roles for "movie," "coffee," and "book" somehow project the activities of "watching the movie," "drinking his morning coffee," and "reading Kundera's last book," respectively, to the interpretation of the VP. Although the specific interpretation of what activity is being enjoyed is only suggested by the complement, the typing of the complement as a controlled event description is unavoidable and an inviolable part of our knowledge of the verb "enjoy."

As mentioned above, it is the generative mechanisms that allow us to model word meaning in a dynamic way, forming the backbone of the compositional operations in Generative Lexicon Theory. Although the lexical representations are richer, they are motivated to account for the linguistic generalizations in the observable data. Introducing more abstract and linguistically motivated descriptions has a number of advantages: (a) to allow for a correct treatment of argument selection, to limit the production of unmotivated ambiguous parses; (b) to permit a correct "reconstruction" of the full explicit metonymic constructions; (c) to introduce a clear distinction, whenever possible, between basic meanings and derived meanings that are produced generatively.

It has been noted (as in FL's remarks) that the application of these generative mechanisms must restricted by semantic factors (cf. Godard and Jayez, 1993; Jackendoff, 1996; Pustejovsky, 1995), which are in turn reflected in sensitivity to certain sense alternations as well as to grammatical restrictions that could be conceived along similar lines as subjacency violations (e.g., a sort of metric to determine the relation and distance between constituents in a syntactic tree, see Pustejovsky, 1997 for discussion).

Because Generative Lexicon Theory adopts the view that polysemy is an essential property of natural language and not a problem that must be avoided, in order to construct a semantic theory, it is important to account for the degree of polysemy of different lexical items as the result of their semantic type. Hence, it is an empirical question as to how much of the syntactic behavior of a lexical item is determined by the semantic typing. As an illustration of this point, consider, for instance, the verbs "tell" and "read." A verb such as "read" permits complements of type physical object (e.g., "John read a book"), as well as complements of type information (e.g., "John read a story"). Conversely, "tell," uniquely selects for a complement that is of type information and does not allow *book* as its complement, i.e. "*John told a book." Similarly, certain verbs of transfer such as "get" or "rent" can refer to both directions of transfer, thus allowing multiple expressions such as "John got a book for Mary" (give), and "John got a book from Mary" (take). In contrast, verbs such as "give" and "sell," which are fully specified for the directionality of the transfer, do not allow the same range of prepositional phrases that is licensed in the previous cases. Finally, a variety of verbal alternations, among which is the causative/unaccusative alternation, also fall into this set of phenomena. Verbs such as "sink" and "break" allow different grammatical forms as the result of the polysemy that they carry. According to the analysis given by Pustejovsky and Busa (1995), the causative form is expressed as a transitive sentence (e.g., "the enemy sank the boat"), and the unaccusative form as an unaccusative sentence (e.g., "the boat sank"). This availability of multiple syntactic forms for underlyingly polysemous lexical items contrasts with the unique expression of fully specified semantic forms such as the predicate "arrive," which uniquely licenses unaccusative forms (e.g., "the children arrived"). As discussed in Pustejovsky (1996), in order to properly capture these distinctions and treat them as a property of the lexicon, it is necessary to introduce new distinctions concerning the properties of semantic types. More specifically, verbs that allow a multiplicity of expressions, such as "read," "get," "sink," have a complex relational type (i.e., *polymorphic type*), and verbs such as "tell," "take," and so on, have a *simple semantic type* (see Pustejovsky, 1997).

4   Discussion

The position that FL take in their remarks to my work can be characterized as a strong methodological dualism, in Chomsky's (1995) sense, where the standards for any semantic theory are set unnaturally high and are unattainable by any empirically motivated framework – unlike research in chemistry or physics, for example, where observation and theory find some comfortable balance. The alternative to this view, as offered up by FL, might be able to meet such standards, because their theory, working without explicit mechanisms and operating over no particularly identifiable body of data, satisfies, in their view, at least two criteria: (a) rejecting analyticity, and (b) maintaining compositionality. I will not explore these issues here in any depth, but a few brief remarks are in order (see Pustejovsky, 1997 for discussion).

4.1   *Evaluating Semantic Theories*

First, why is the issue of analyticity relevant to the discussion here? FL disagree with Quine's radical holism and his position on conventionalized meaning, yet they accept his proposal – because there is little argument to call it a conclusion – that there is no viable distinction between analytic and synthetic expressions. In fact, although we can evaluate the descriptive and explanatory powers of a semantic framework quite independently of this issue, it is interesting that all of FL's recent criticisms on the representational hypothesis in natural language semantics crucially rely on the impossibility of such a distinction possible (see Fodor and Lepore, 1992, 1996; Lepore, 1994). What this view entails, among other things, is the following: There is nothing in the form of the semantic representation associated with a word that can be identified inviolably as part of its meaning. However, this is surely suspect. Consider the distinction illustrated in (27) and (28), between the English verbs "enjoy" and "like."

(27)   a. Mary enjoys watching movies.
        b. Mary enjoys movies.

(28)   a. Mary likes to watch movies.
        b. Mary likes watching movies.
        c. Mary likes movies.
        d. Mary likes for John to watch movies with her.
        e. Mary likes that John watches movies with her.
        f. Mary likes it that John watches movies with her.

As argued in Pustejovsky (1995), it is our knowledge associated with the verb "like"that allows the syntactic variation seen in (28), rather than the limited complementation patterns in (27). To understand this verb is to know (in the sense employed in Chomsky, 1986) that "like" expresses an attitude toward any type, which, in Generative Lexicon Theory, enables it to appear with the broadest subcategorization variability possible. The verb "enjoy" in (27), on the other hand, expresses a more specific relation of how the subject participates in an event description denoted by the complement phrase. This distinction is not just a pragmatic one, revealing different conventions of usage for the two verbs, but arises from the underlyingly distinct types selected for by these verbs. When I understand what the 'like'-relation is in contradistinction to the 'enjoy'-relation, I manifest a conceptual and categorical distinction between the two intensions. Hence, for example, the only way for a speaker to understand (29a) is in relation to the inviolable conditions laid out by "enjoy" 's semantics; in other words, there must be some controlled event description relative to the room key such that I could enjoy it.

(29)   a. ?!I enjoyed the key to my room.
         b. I like the key to my room.

Such a condition, however, is not present in (29b) with the verb "like," because it expresses a different attitude towards its argument.

Analyticity need not require the concepts of definition and substitution, as conventionally assumed (cf. Quine, 1961).[9] It does presuppose, however, a specific mode of identification in the computation of the expression. In other words, computing containment relations over the predicate relative to the subject in a sentence assumes a very impoverished notion of how to calculate the meaning of an expression. The fact of the matter is that any descriptively adequate view on the semantics of natural language requires computations far more involved than this. How is analyticity determined when richer models of meaning (such as Generative Lexicon Theory) are employed for description and computation? This is answered in part by saying that, in the process of determining the interpretation of a sentence, we can identify subprocesses that are analytic in nature and those that are not. At best, FL's concerns for avoiding the analyticity trap are obviated by the developments in linguistic theory and semantic formalisms over the past few years.[10] At worst, they stand in the way of clarifying real semantic distinctions in natural languages, which, in my opinion, are associated only with the strongly predictive and testable hypotheses of appropriately rich theories.

When we view the discussion of analyticity and underlying semantic knowledge in this light, FL's notion of compositionality, and how it fails in Generative Lexicon Theory and other representational frameworks becomes irrelevant to the evaluation of semantic theories. Consider the sentence in (30a).

(30)   a. That is a rattling snake.
         b. It is rattling.
         c. It is dangerous.

Lepore (1994) raises the question of how (30c) is any less a part of the meaning of (30a) than (30b) is, because, if a theory has no principled view on how to distinguish the relations between the types of knowledge coming from words, then they are equally strong and relevant inferences in the computation of this sentence. Fodor and Lepore (1996) make the same argument regarding compositionality as that given above. To hold the belief that "brown cows" are dangerous, when neither "brown" nor "cows" contains hints of danger, is, they argue, devastating to the view that meanings are constructed compositionally from word meanings.[11] The

---

[9] However, see Katz, 1990. Katz does adopt this position, and further argues that Quine's thesis has never been substantiated by linguistic data.

[10] One might argue that, independent of recent developments in semantic theory, Quine's proposal and FL's use of it are irrelevant to theory construction for language meanings (cf. Chomsky, 1995).

[11] This issue relates to the problem of inheritance and the attribution of default properties to individuals in a class. The argument as given has no force, without clarifying what is "typically" the case (or perhaps even "analytically" so) for cows.

reasoning here, however, is circular, because it is assuming that all inferences associated with the composition of these expressions have equal force. This position confuses the set of possible, identifiable inferences with those that are automatic and unsurprising in this expression. By analogy to phonology, there are many possible inferences regarding the word "cat." By "composition" in this sense of the word, "cat" is associated with lots of propositional knowledge; for example, it rhymes with "bat," it has the same number of syllables as "ball," and it ends with the same sound as "permit" and "caught," and so forth (see Chomsky, 1995). These are all inferences that we as speakers of English can associate with the word "cat." However, this does not represent the intrinsic properties of "cat," as modeled by the theory of phonology, any more than the above considerations speak to the concerns of compositionality in semantics.

The interpretation of compositionality as merely "licensing an inference" has really very little to do with the standard notion of constrained composition in any serious semantic framework. Most workable views on this topic do not include the range of all implicatures or invited inferences that may accompany an expression, as contained in the part-structure of an expression and determined by composition. This is perhaps one of the most exciting questions in contemporary semantics, but is exciting and approachable *only* by making semantic distinctions that FL believe are arbitrary or nonexistent.

4.2   Conclusion

I have tried to clarify how FL's remarks both distort the views and facts presented in Pustejovsky (1995), and convey an unfortunately pessimistic message for how to conduct research in natural language semantics. This is remarkably reminiscent of early attempts to dismiss generative syntactic analyses for language, by reducing syntactic variation to mere "effects of semantics and pragmatics." Underlying any differences about what constitutes the data, the major distinction in our positions is this: Generative Lexicon Theory is concerned with explaining the semantic properties of natural language.[12] On this matter, what have FL proposed?

1. Regarding semantic differentiation involving argument structure and object drop phenomena, FL deny that any generalizations are possible and are silent on this question.
2. Concerning the conditions for and constraints on coercion, FL deny that any systematicity or generalization is possible, but are silent on what is responsible for the observable regularities of behavior.

---

[12] There are several other major lacunae in FL's account of how language connects to the world, but space does not permit discussion of these questions here. One serious problem concerns the basic principles of individuation and persistence that the language provides to the referring individual. That is, how does atomism distinguish between the denotation of 'dog' and 'all dogs' or 'some dogs'? Providing some sort of mechanism to do just this leads us back to structured representations (see Moravcsik, 1990 and Pustejovsky, 1997 for discussion).

3. For polysemy phenomena in verbs and nouns, FL claim to not understand the relevant examples and doubt that they are real phenomena in any case. Hence, even in the face of observable systematicity, they are silent on this issue.

4. Regarding the qualia structure and how the generative factors contribute to word meaning, FL provide no explanation for how qualia-related inferences and not arbitrarily any others are asscoiated with the meanings of lexical items. Yet they provide no system predicting how interpretations should be performed.

5. Finally, regarding cross-linguistic phenomena, their account is unable to say anything of interest about how languages vary systematically along a number of semantic parameters, including coercion and type selection, because such generalizations would be arbitrary or conventionalized at best.

A theoretical framework should be evaluated and judged on the merit of the theory relative to how effectively it accounts for the observables, in our case, language meanings. It is a theoretical question whether linguistic knowledge plays any privileged role in the determination of the content of an utterance. It is also, however, empirically tangible in nature, as I have demonstrated, where for each phenomenon examined, the knowledge associated with an expression is clearly linguistic and not elsewhere. To paraphrase the words of one philosopher, any serious competing theory of language meaning, "would appear to owe a detailed account of these phenomena that avoided [such] mentalistic postulations. The dignified silence that they have so far maintained on such matters does not really amount to an argument" (Fodor, 1968:86).

Acknowledgments

I would like to thank Noam Chomsky, Julius Moravcsik, Federica Busa, Peter Cariani, Nicholas Asher, Richard Alterman, Ray Jackendoff, Jens Allwood, Victor Poznanski, Michael Morreau, Paul Buitelaar, and Bob Ingria, for commenting on various drafts of this article, and for help in framing the argument and refining specific points. All remaining errors are, of course, my own.

References

Apresjan, J. 1973. Regular Polysemy. *Linguistics* 142: 5–32.

Asher, N., and Morreau, M. 1991. Common Sense Entailment: A Modal Theory of Nonmonotonic Reasoning. *Proc. 12th International Joint Conference on Artificial Intelligence*, Sydney, Australia.

Asher, N., and Pustejovsky, J. (forthcoming). *The Metaphysics of Words*. Manuscript, Brandeis University and University of Texas.

Atkins, B.T., Kegl, J., and Levin, B. 1988. Anatomy of a Verb Entry: From Linguistic Theory to Lexicographic Practice. *International Journal of Lexicography* 1: 84–126.

Bach, E. 1986. The Algebra of Events. *Linguistics and Philosophy* 9: 5–16.

Bréal, M. 1897. *Essai de sémantique (Science des significations)*. Hachette, Paris.

Busa, F. 1996. *Compositionality and the Semantics of Nominals*. Doctoral Dissertation, Brandeis University, Waltham, Mass.

Carey, S. 1985. *Conceptual Change in Childhood*. MIT Press, Cambridge.

Carnap, R. 1956. *Meaning and Necessity*. University of Chicago Press, Chicago.

Chomsky, N. 1975. *Reflections on Language*. Pantheon, New York.

Chomsky, N. 1986. *Knowledge of Language, Its Nature, Origin, and Use*. Praeger, New York.

Chomsky, N. 1995. Language and Nature. *Mind* 104: 1–61.

Davidson, D. 1968. On Saying That. *Inquiries into Truth and Interpretation*. Oxford University Press, Oxford.

Erdmann, K. 1900. *Die Bedeutung des Wortes: Aufsätze aus dem Grenzgebiet der Sprachpsychologie und Logik*. Avenarius, Leipzig.

Fauconnier, G. 1985. *Mental Spaces*. MIT Press, Cambridge.

Fillmore, C. 1986. Pragmatically Controlled Zero Anaphora. *BLS* 12: 95–107.

Fodor, J. 1968. *Psychological Explanation*. Random House, New York.

Fodor, J., and Lepore, E. 1992. *Holism: A Shopper's Guide*. Blackwell, Oxford.

Fodor, J., and Lepore, E. 1996. The Red Herring and the Pet Fish: Why Concepts Still Can't Be Prototypes. *Cognition* 58: 253–270.

Fodor, J., and Lepore, E. 1998. The Emptiness of the Lexicon: Critical Reflections on J. Pustejovsky's *The Generative Lexicon*. *Linguistic Inquiry* 29:2, 269–288. Also published in this volume.

Gazdar, G. 1980. A Cross-categorial semantics for coordination. *Linguistics and Philosophy* 3: 407–409.

Geach, P.T. 1971. A Program for Syntax. *Synthese* 22: 3–17.

Godard, D., and Jayez, J. 1993. Towards a proper treatment of Coercion Phenomena. *Proc. EACL*. Utrecht University, Utrecht, 168–177.

Grimshaw, J. 1990. *Argument Structure*. MIT Press, Cambridge, MA.

Jackendoff, R. 1992. Babe Ruth Homered His Way into the Hearts of America. In T. Stowell and E. Wehrli (eds.), *Syntax and the Lexicon*. Academic Press, San Diego, 155–178.

Jackendoff, R. 1996. *The Architecture of the Language Faculty*. MIT Press, Cambridge.

Katz, J.J. 1990. *The Metaphysics of Meaning*. MIT Press, Cambridge.

Kayser, D. 1988. What Kind of Thing is a Concept? *Computational Intelligence* 4: 158–165.

Keil, Fr. 1989. *Concepts, Kinds, and Cognitive Development*. MIT Press, Cambridge.

Klein, E., and Sag, I. 1985. Type-Driven Translation. *Linguistics and Philosophy* 8: 163–202.

Lambek, J. 1958. The Mathematics of Sentence Structure. *American Mathematical Monthly* 65: 154–170. Also in W. Buskowski, W. Marciszewski, and J. van Benthem (eds.), 1988, *Categorial Grammar*. John Benjamins, Amsterdam, 153–172.

Lepore, E. 1994. Conceptual Role Semantics. In S. Guttenplan (ed.), *A Companion to the Philosophy of Mind*. Blackwell, Oxford.

Levin, B. 1985. Introduction. In B. Levin (ed.), *Lexical Semantics in Review*. Lexicon Project Working Papers 1, Center for Cognitive Science, MIT, 1–62.

Levin, B. 1993. *Towards a Lexical Organization of English Verbs*. University of Chicago Press, Chicago.

Levin, B., and Rappaport Hovav M. 1995. *Unaccusatives: At the Syntax-Lexical Semantics Interface*. MIT Press, Cambridge.

Markman, E. 1989. *Categorization and Naming in Children*. MIT Press, Cambridge.

Michotte, A. 1954. *La Perception de la causalité*. Publications Universitaires de Louvain, Louvain.

Montague, R. 1970. Universal Grammar. In R. Thomason (ed.), *Formal Philosophy: Selected Papers of Richard Montague*. Yale University Press, New Haven.

Moravcsik, J. 1975. Aitia as Generative Factor in Aristotle's Philosophy. *Dialogue* 14: 622–636.

Moravcsik, J. 1990. *Thought and Language*. Routledge, London.

Nunberg, G. 1979. The Non-uniqueness of Semantic Solutions: Polysem. *Linguistics and Philosophy* 3: 143–184.

Ostler, N., and Atkins, B.T. 1992. Predictable Meaning Shift: Some Linguistic Properties of Lexical Implication Rules. In J. Pustejovsky and S. Bergler (eds.), *Lexical Semantics and Knowledge Reperesentation*. Springer Verlag, Berlin, 87–100.

Parsons, T. 1985. Underlying Events in the Logical Analysis of English. In E. LePore and B. P. McLaughlin (eds.), *Actions and Events*. Basil Blackwell, Oxford, 235–267.

Partee, B. 1992. Syntactic Categories and Semantic Type. In M. Rosner and R. Johnson (eds.), *Computational Linguistics and Formal Semantics*. Cambridge University Press, Cambridge.

Partee, B., and Rooth. M. 1983. Generalized Conjunction and Type Ambiguity. In R. Bäuerle, U. Egli, and A. von Stechow (eds), *Meaning, Use, and Interpretation of Language*. Walter de Gruyter, Berlin, 361–383.

Pustejovsky, J. 1989. Issues in Computational Lexical Semantics. *Proc. Fourth European ACL Conference*, April 10–12, Manchester, England.

Pustejovsky, J. 1991. The Generative Lexicon. *Computational Linguistics* 17: 409–441.

Pustejovsky, J. 1994. Semantic Typing and Degrees of Polymorphism. In C. Martin-Vide (ed.), *Current Issues in Mathematical Linguistics*. North-Holland, Amsterdam, 221–238.

Pustejovsky, J. 1995. *The Generative Lexicon*. MIT Press, Cambridge.

Pustejovsky, J. 1996. *Lexical Shadowing and Argument Closure*. Manuscript, Brandeis University.

Pustejovsky, J. 1997. *Multiplicity of Meaning*. Manuscript, Gustaf Stern Memorial Lectures, Gothenburg, Sweden.

Pustejovsky, J. 1998. The Semantics of Lexical Underspecification. *Folia Linguistica* XXXII.

Pustejovsky, J., and Busa, F. 1995. Unaccusativity and Event Composition. In P. M. Bertinetto, V. Binachi, J. Higginbotham, and M. Squartini (eds.), *Temporal Reference: Aspect and Actionality*. Rosenberg and Sellier, Turin, 159–178.

Pustejovsky, J., Keil, F., and Pollack, J. 1997. *Semantic Categories in Natural Language: Representation, Acquisition, and Computation*. Manuscript, Brandeis University and Cornell University.

Quine, W.V. 1961. *From a Logical Point of View*. MIT Press, Cambridge.

Stern, G. 1931. *Meaning and Change of Meaing. With special reference to the English Langage*. Indiana University Press, Bloomington.

Talmy, L. 1985. Lexicalization Patterns: Semantic Structure in Lexical Forms. In T. Shopen (ed.), *Language Typology and Syntactic Description* 3. Grammatical Categories and the Lexicon, Cambridge University Press, Cambridge, 57–149.

Weinreich, U. 1964. *Webster's Third*: A Critique of its Semantics. *International Journal of American Linguistics* 30: 405–409.

Weinreich, U. 1972. *Explorations in Semantic Theory*. Mouton, The Hague.

Williams, E. 1981. Argument Structure and Morphology. *The Linguistic Review* 1: 81–114.

5   The "Fodor"-FODOR Fallacy Bites Back

YORICK WILKS

Abstract

The paper argues that Fodor and Lepore (1998) are misguided in their attack on Pustejovsky's *Generative Lexicon*, largely because their argument rests on a traditional, but implausible and discredited, view of the lexicon on which it is effectively empty of content, a view that stands in the long line of explaining word meaning (a) by ostension and then (b) explaining it by means of a vacuous symbol in a lexicon, often the word itself after typographic transmogrification. Both (a) and (b) share the wrong belief that to a word must correspond a simple entity that is its meaning. I then turn to the semantic rules that Pustejovsky uses and argue first that, although they have novel features, they are in a well-established Artificial Intelligence tradition of explaining meaning by reference to structures that mention other structures assigned to words that may occur in close proximity to the first. It is argued in Fodor and Lepore's view that there cannot be such rules is without foundation, and indeed systems using such rules have proved their practical worth in computational systems. Their justification descends from line of argument, whose high points were probably Wittgenstein and Quine that meaning is not to be understood by simple links to the world, ostensive or otherwise, but by the relationship of whole cultural representational structures to each other and to the world as a whole.[1]

1   Introduction

Fodor and Lepore (FL from here on; 1998) have saddled up recently and ridden again at the Windmills of Artificial Intelligence (AI): this time against Pustejovsky's *Generative Lexicon* (Pustejovsky, 1995: FL call the work TGL), so as to make an example for the rest of us. I want to join in because FL claim they are part of a wider movement they call *Informational Role Semantics* (which I will call IRS as they do), and I count myself a long-term member of that movement. However, their weapons are rusty: They wave about as their sword of truth an old and much satirised fallacy, which Ryle (1957) called the "Fido"-FIDO fallacy: that to every word corresponds a meaning, be it abstract denotation (as for FL), a concept, or

---

[1] "One might say: the ostensive definition explains the use – the meaning – of a word when the overall role of the word in language is clear. Thus, if I know that someone means to explain a color-word to me the ostensive definition "That is called '*sepia*'" will help me to understand the word" (Wittgensein, 1953, p. 30).

a real world object. The special quality of the fallacy is the simple one-to-one mapping, and not the nature of what corresponds to a word.

In the first part of this paper I want to show that the fallacy cannot be pressed back into service: It is old and overexposed. It is important to do this (again) even though, as the paper progresses, FL relent a little about the need for the fallacy, and even seem to accept a part of the IRS position. However, they do this as men convinced that, really and truly and after all concessions are made, the fallacy is still true. It is not, and this needs saying yet again. In the second part of the paper, I will briefly touch on issues specific to Pustejovsky's (JP) claims; only briefly because he is quite capable of defending his own views. In the third and final part, I will make some points to do with the general nature of the IRS position, within AI and computational natural language processing, and argue that the concession FL offer is unneeded. IRS is a perfectly reasonable doctrine in its own right and needs no defense from those who really believe in the original fallacy.

2   "Fido" and FIDO

Fodor and Lepore's dissection of JP's book is, and is intended to be, an attack on a whole AI approach to natural language processing based on symbolic representations, so it is open to any other member of that school to join in the defense. IRS has its faults but also some technological successes to show in the areas of machine translation and information extraction (e.g., Wilks et al., 1993), but is it well-founded and philosophically defensible?

Many within IRS would say that does not matter, in that the only defense lexical or other machine codings need in any information processing system is that the system containing them works to an acceptable degree; but I would agree with those who say it is defensible, or is at least as well-founded as the philosophical foundation on which FL stand. That is, I believe, one of the shakiest and most satirised of this century, and loosely related to what Ryle (1957) called the "Fido"-FIDO fallacy: the claim that to every word corresponds a concept and/or a denotation, a view that has crept into everyday philosophical chat as the joke that the meaning of life is life′ (life prime, the object denoted by "life").[2]

It is a foundation of the utmost triviality, that comes from FL (op.cit., p. 1) in the form:

(1)   The meaning of "dog" is DOG.

They seem to embrace it wholeheartedly, and prefer it to any theory, like TGL, offering complex structured dictionary entries, or even any paper dictionary off a shelf, like Webster's, that offers even more complex structures than TGL in a form of English. FL embrace an empty lexicon, willingly and with open eyes: one

---

[2] Fido′ or Fido-prime are common notations for denotations corresponding to words. FL seem to prefer small caps FIDO, and I will use that form from their paper in the argument that follows.

that lists just DOG as the entry for "dog." The questions we must ask, though the answer is obviously *no* in each case, are:

- is (1) even a correct form of what FL want to say?
- could such a dictionary consisting of statements like (1) serve any purpose whatever, for humans or for machines?
- would one even need to write such a dictionary, supposing one believed in a role for such a compilation, as opposed to say, saving space by storing one as a simple rule for capitalizing any word whose meaning was wanted?

The first of these points brings back an age of linguistic analysis contemporary with Ryle's, in particular the work of writers like Lewy (1964); put briefly, the issue is whether or not (1) expresses anything determinate (and remember it is the mantra of the whole FL paper), or preferable to alternatives such as:

(2)   The meaning of "dog" is a domestic canine animal

or

(3)   The meaning of "dog" is a dog

or even

(4)   The meaning of "dog" is "domestic canine animal"

not to mention

(5)   The meaning of "dog" is "dog."

The two sentences (2) and (3) are perfectly sensible, depending on the circumstances: (2) is roughly what real, non-Fodorian, dictionaries tell you, which seems unnecessary for dogs, but would be more plausible if the sentence was about marmosets or wombats. (3) is unhelpful, as it stands, but perhaps that is accidental, for if we translate it into German we get something like:

(3a)   Die Bedeutung von "dog" ist ein Hund

which could be very helpful to a German with little or no knowledge of English, as would be:

(2a)   Die Bedeutung von "dog" ist ein huendliche Haustier.

To continue with this line of argument one needs all parties to accept the reality of translation and its role in argument: that there are translations, at least between close languages for simple sentences, and no amount of philosophical argument can shift that fact. For anyone who cannot accept this, there is probably no point in arguing about the role of lexicons at all.

Both (2) and (3), then, are sensible and, in the right circumstances, informative: they can be synonymous in some functional sense because both, when translated, could be equally informative to a normal fluent speaker of another language. But (4) and (5) are a little harder: their translations would be uninformative to a German when translated, because translation does not translate quotations and so we get forms like:

(5a)   Die Bedeutung von "dog" ist "dog"

and similarly for a German (4a) version of the English (4). These sentences therefore cannot be synonymous with (3) and (2) respectively. But (4) might be thought no more than an odd form of a lexical entry sentence like (3), spoken by an English speaker.

But what of (1); who could that inform about anything? Suppose we sharpen the issue by again asking who its translation could inform and about what:

(1a)   Die Bedeutung von "dog" ist DOG.

(1a) tells the German speaker nothing, at which point we may be told that DOG stands for a denotation and its name is arbitrary. However, that is just old nonsense on horseback: it implies that the English speaker cannot understand (1) either, because DOG might properly be replaced by G00971 if the final symbol in (1) is truly arbitrary. It is surely (3), not (1), that tells us what the denotation of "dog" is, in the way language is normally used to do such things.

DOG in (1) is simply a confidence trick: it is put to us as having the role of the last term in (3). When and only when it is in the same language as the final symbol of (3) (a fact we are confidently assured is arbitrary) it does appear to point to dogs. However, taken as the last term in the synonymous (1a) it cannot possibly be doing that for it is incomprehensible, and functioning as an (untranslated) English WORD, exactly as in the last term of (5). However, as we saw, (5) and (3) cannot be synonymous, and so DOG in (1) has two incompatible roles at once, which is the trick that gives (1) interpretations that flip uncontrollably between the (nonsynonymous) (3) and (5). It is an optical illusion of a sentence.

In conclusion, then, (1) is a dangerous sentence, one whose upper case-inflation suggests it has a function but which, on careful examination, proves not to be there: it is either (case-deflated) a form of the commonsense (3), in which case it loses its capitals and all the role FL assign to it, because it is vacuous in English, or just a simple bilingual dictionary entry in German or some other language. Or it is a form or (5), uninformative in any language or lexicon but plainly a triviality, shorn of any philosophical import.

Those who still have worries about this issue, and wonder if capitalizing may not still have some merit, should ask themselves the following question: which dog is the real DOG? The word "dog" has 24 entries even in a basic English dictionary like Collins, so how do FL know which one is intended by (1)? If one is tempted to reply, well DOG will have to be subscripted then, as in DOG_1, DOG_2, etc., then I shall reply that we will then be into another theory or meaning, and not one of simple denotations. My own suspicion is that all this can only be understood in terms of Fodor's *Language of Thought* (1975), and that DOG for FL is a simple primitive in that language, rather than a denotation in the world or logical space. However, we have no access whatever to such a language, though Kay among others has given arguments that, if anything like a LOT exists, it will have to be subscripted (Kay, 1989), in which case the role of (1) will have to be rethought from scratch. All the discussion above will still remain relevant to such a development, and the issue of translation into LOT will then be the key one. However, until we can do that, and in the presence of a LOT native speaker, we may leave that situation aside and await developments.

The moral for the rest of the discussion, and the role of IRS and TGL, is simple: Some of the sentences numbered above are like real, useful, lexical entries: (3) is a paradigm of an entry in a bilingual lexicon, where explanations are not crucial, while (2) is very like a monolingual lexical entry, where explanations are the stuff of giving meaning.

3   Issues Concerning TGL

The standard of the examples used by FL to attack TGL is not at all challenging; they claim that JP's:

(6)   He baked a cake

is in fact ambiguous between JP's 'create' and 'warm up' aspects of "bake," where baking a cake yields the first, but baking a potato the second. JP does not want to claim this is a sense ambiguity, but a systematic difference in interpretation given by inferences cued by features of the two objects, which could be labels such as ARTIFACT in the case of the cake but not the potato.

"But in fact, 'bake a cake' is ambiguous. To be sure, you can make a cake by baking it; but also you can do to a (preexistent) cake just what you can do to a (preexistent) potato: viz. put it in the oven and (noncreatively) bake it" (op.cit. p. 7).

From this, FL conclude, "bake" must be ambiguous, because "cake" is not. However, all this is absurd and untrue to the simplest facts. Of course, warming up a (preexistent) cake is not baking it; who ever could think it was? That activity would be referred to as warming a cake up, or through, never as baking. You can no more bake a cake again, with the other interpretation, than you can bake a potato again and turn it into an artifact. FL like syntactically correlated evidence in semantics, and they should have noticed that a "baked potato" is fine but a "baked cake" is not, which correlates with just the difference JP requires (cf. baked fish/meat).

It gets worse: FL go on to argue that if ARTIFACTs are the distinguishing feature for JP then "bake a trolley car" should take the creative reading because it is an artifact, completely ignoring the fact that the whole JP analysis is based on the (natural) assumption that potatoes and cakes both share some attribute like FOOD (as trolley cars do not), which is the only way the discussion can get under way: being a FOOD is a necessary condition for this analysis of "bake" to get under way.

FL's key argument against TGL is that it is not possible to have a rule, of the sort JP advocates, that expands the content or meaning of a word in virtue of (the meaning content of) a neighboring word in a context, namely, a word in some functional relation to the first. So, JP, like many in the IRS tradition argues that in:

(7)   John wants a beer

the meaning of "wants" in that context, which need not be taken to be any new or special or even existing sense of the word, is to be glossed as 'wants to drink a beer.' This is done by a process that varies in detail from IRS researcher to researcher, but comes down to some form of:

(8)   X wants Y $\Rightarrow$ X wants to do with Y whatever is normally done with Y.

An issue over which AI researchers have differed is whether this knowledge of normal or default use is stored in a lexical entry or in some other computational knowledge form such as one that was sometimes called a script (Schank and Abelson, 1997) and thought of as indexed by words but was much more than a lexical entry. It is not clear that one needs to discriminate between structures, however complex, if they are indexed by a word or words. JP stores the inference captured in (8) within the lexical entry under a label TELIC that shows purpose. In earlier AI systems, such information about function might be stored as part of a lexical semantic formulas attached to a primitive GOAL (Charniak and Wilks, 1976[3]), or (depending on its salience) within an associated knowledge structure.[4] Some made the explicit assumption that a system should be sufficiently robust that it would not matter if such functional information was stored in more than one place in a system, perhaps even in different formats.

For FL all this is unthinkable, and they produce a tortuous argument roughly as follows:

- "Fido"-FIDO may not be the only form for a lexicon, but an extension could only be one where an expansion of meaning for a term was independent of the control of all other terms, as it is plainly not in the case of JP's (8).
- Any such extension would be to an underlying logical form, one that should also be syntactically motivated.

---

[3] In preference semantics (Wilks) "door" was coded as a formula (that could be displayed as a binary tree) such as:
(THE((PLANT STUFF)SOUR) ((((THRU PART)OBJE) (NOTUSE *ANI))GOAL) ((MAN USE) (OBJE THING)))
where the subformula:
(((THRU PART)OBJE) (NOTUSE *ANI))GOAL)
was intended to convey that the function of a door is to prevent passage through an aperture by a human.

[4] Such larger knowledge structures were called pseudo-texts (Wilks, 1980) in preference semantics (to emphasize the continuity of language and world knowledge): one for "car" (written [car]) would contain a clause like [car consume gasoline] where each lexical item in the pseudo-text was an index to a semantic formula (in the sense of note 3) that explicated it.

FL then produce a complex algorithm (op.cit. p. 10) that expands "want" consistently with these assumptions, one which is hard to follow and comes down to no more than the universal applicability (i.e., if accepted it MUST be applied to all occurrences of "want" regardless of lexical context) of the rule:

(9)   X wants Y $\Rightarrow$ X wants to have Y.

This, of course, avoids, as it is intended to, any poking about in the lexical content of Y. However, it is also an absurd rule, no matter what dubious chat is appended to it about the nature of "logical form."
Consider:

(10)   a. I want an orange.
          b. I want a beer.
          c. I want a rest.
          d. I want love.

(10a) and (10b) seem intuitively to fit the IRS rule (8) and the FL rule (9). (10c) might conform to some appropriate IRS coding to produce (from (8)): X wants to experience a rest, but the apparently felicitous application of FL's (9), yielding, X wants to have a rest, is purely fortuitous, since "have a rest" is a lexicalised form having nothing at all to do with possession, which is the only natural interpretation of (9). This just serves to show the absurdity of FL's *content-free* rule (9) because its application to (10c) cannot possibly be interpreted in the same way as it was when producing "X wants to have a beer."

Only the IRS rule (8) distinguishes appropriate from inappropriate applications of rules to (10c). One could make the same case with (10d), where the FL rule (9) produces only ambiguous absurdity, and the applicability of the IRS rule (8) depends entirely on how the function of "love" has been coded, if at all. However, the purpose of this section has been not to defend an IRS view or rule (8) in particular but to argue that there is no future at all in FL's grudging, context free, rule (9), in part because it is context free.

JP's specific claim is not that the use of rule (8) produces a new sense, or we would have a new sense corresponding to many or most of the possible objects of wanting, a more promiscuous expansion of the lexicon (were it augmented by every rule application) than would be the case for "bake a potato/cake" where JP resisted augmentation of the lexicon, though other researchers would probably accept it. Nor is this like the application of *normal function* to the transformation of:

(11)   My car drinks gasoline

in Wilks (1980) where it was suggested that "drink" should be replaced by the structure for "consume" (as in Footnote 4 below) in a context containing broken preferences (unlike (7)) and where augmentation of the lexicon would be appropriate like (11) and if the *relaxation*, as some would call it, became statistically significant, as it has in the case of (11).

It is not easy to pin down quite why FL find the rule (8) so objectionable, because their rule (9), like (8), is not, as they seem to believe, distinguished by logical form considerations. The traditional (Quine, 1953) logical opacity of "want" is such that inferences like (8) and (9) can never be supported by strong claims about logical form whose transformations must be deductive, and one can always want X without wanting Y, no matter what the logical relations of X and Y. Hence, neither (8) nor (9) are deductive rules, and FL have no ground in context-dependence to swallow the one but not the other.

Contrary to what FL seem to assume, an NLP algorithm to incorporate or graft part of the lexical entry for one word (e.g., "beer") into another (e.g., "want") is not practically difficult. The only issue for NLP research is whether and when such inferences should be drawn: At first encounter with such a collocation, or when needed in later inference, a distinction corresponding roughly to what is distinguished by the oppositions forward and backward inference, or data-driven and demand-driven inference. This issue is connected with whether a lexical entry should be adapted or a data base of world knowledge and, again contrary to FL's assumptions, no NLP researcher can accept a firm distinction between these, nor is there one, any more than a firm analytic-synthetic distinction has survived decades of skepticism.

One can always force such a distinction at trivial cost into one's system, as Carnap (1947) did with his formal and material modes of sentences containing the same information:

(12)   f. "Edelweiss" has the property "flower"
        m. An Edelweiss is a flower

but the distinction is wholly arbitrary.[5]

JP's treatment of more structural intensional verbs like "believe" is far more ingenious than FL would have us believe, and an interesting advance on previous work: It is based on a richer notion of default than earlier IRS treatments. JP's position, as I understand it, is that the default, or underlying, structure associated with "believe" is "X believes p" where p is expanded by default by the rule:

(13)   X believes p $\Rightarrow$ X believes (Y communicates p).

FL of course object again to another expansion beyond their self-imposed limit of context-freeness for which, as we saw, there is no principled defense, while failing to notice that (13) is in fact context-free in their sense.

For me, the originality of (13) is not only that it can expand forms like:

(14)   John believes Mary

---

[5] Provided one remembers always that forms like:
"Edelweiss" has nine letters
is in material mode even though it could look like the formal mode. The formal mode of what it expresses is:
"Edelweiss" has the property "nine letters."

but can also be a general (context-free) default, overriding forms like:

(15)   John believes pigs eat carrots

as the more complex:

(16)   John believes (Y communicates (pigs eat carrots))

which is an original expansion according to which all beliefs can be seen as the result of some communication, often from oneself (when Y = John in (16)). There certainly were default expansions of "believe" in IRS before JP but not of this boldness.[6]

4   Some General IRS Principles

Once (Wilks, 1971, 1972) I tried to lay out principles for something very like IRS, and which still seem to underlie the position arrived at in this discussion; it would be helpful for FL to see IRS not simply as some form of undisciplined, opportunistic, discipline neighboring their own professional interests. Let me restate two of these principles that bear on this discussion:

- Meaning, in the end, is best thought of as other words, and that is the only position that can underpin a lexicon- and procedure-based approach to meaning, and one should accept this, whatever its drawbacks, because the alternative is untenable and not decisively supported by claims about ostension. Quine (1953) has argued a much more sophisticated version of this for many years, one in which representational structures are only compared against the world as wholes, and local comparisons are wholly symbolic. Meanings depend crucially upon explanations and these, formally or discursively, are what dictionaries offer. This solution to the problem is indeed circular, but not viciously so, because dictionaries rarely offer small dictionary circles (Sparck Jones, 1966) like the classic, and unsatisfying, case where "furze" is defined as "gorse," and vice versa. Meanings, in terms of other words, is thus a function of circle size: furze gorse is pathological, in the sense of unhelpful, yet, because a dictionary definition set is closed, and must be circular, not all such circles can be unhelpful or dictionaries are all and always vacuous.

  On the other hand, FL's original position of the section 2 above, is not really renounced by the end of their paper, and is utterly untenable, not only for the analytic reasons we have given, but because it could not form the basis of any possible dictionary, for humans (seeking meaning explanations) or for NLP.

---

[6] In preference semantics (Wilks, 1972) "believe" had a lexical entry showing a preference for a propositional object, so that "John believes Mary" was accepted as a preference-breaking form but with a stored expansion of the object in the lexical entry for "believe" of a simple propositional form (Mary DO Y) not a communication act like TGL.

Indeed, as we pointed out earlier, no lexicon is needed for the "dog"-DOG theory, because a simple macro to produce upper-case forms will do, give or take a little morphological tweaking for the "boil"-BOILING cases.

- Semantic well-formedness is not a property that can decidably be assigned to utterances, in the way that truth can to formulas in parts of the predicate calculus, and it was hoped for many years that *syntactically-well formed* would be assignable to sentences.

This point was made in some detail in Wilks (1971) on the basis that no underlying intuition is available to support semantic well-formedness,[7] because our intuitions are dependent on the state of our (or our machine's) lexicons when considering an utterance's status, and that we are capable of expanding our lexicons (in something like the ways discussed in this paper) so as to bring utterances iteratively within the boundary of semantic well-formedness, and in a way that has no analogy in truth or syntax. Thus, no boundary drawing, of the sort required for a decidable property, can be done for the predicate semantically well-formed. Belief in the opposite seems one of the very few places where JP and FL agree, so further discussion may prove necessary.

References

Carnap, R. 1947. *Meaning and Necessity*. University of Chicago Press, Chicago.

Charniak, E., and Wilks, Y. (eds.) 1976. *Computational Semantics*. Amsterdam, North Holland.

Fodor, J., and Lepore, E. 1998. The Emptiness of the Lexicon: Critical Reflections on James Pustejovsky's *The Generative Lexicon*. *Linguistic Inquiry* 29:2, 269–288. Also published in this volume.

Fodor, J. 1975. *The Language of Thought*. Crowell, New York.

Kay, M. 1989. The Concrete Lexicon and the Abstract Dictionary. *Proc. Fifth Annual Conference of the University of Waterloo Centre for the New Oxford English Dictionary*, Oxford.

Lewy, C. 1964. Entailment and Propositional Identity. *Proc. Arist. Soc.* LXIV.

Pustejovsky, J. 1995. *The Generative Lexicon*. MIT Press, Cambridge, MA.

Quine, W.V.O. 1953. *From a Logical Point of View*. MIT Press, Cambridge, MA.

Ryle, G. 1957. The Theory of Meaning. In C.A. Mace (ed.), *British Philosophy in Mid-Century*. Allen and Unwin, London.

Schank, R., and Abelson, R.P. 1977. *Scripts, Plans, Goals and Understanding*. Lawrence Erlbaum, Hillsdale NJ.

Sparck Jones, K. 1966. *Dictionary Circles*. Technical Memorandum SP-3304, System Development Corporation, Santa Monica, California.

---

[7] This property must intuitively underlie all decidability claims and procedures: Goedel's proof that there are true but undecidable sentences in a class of calculi only makes sense on the assumption that we have some (intuitive) way of seeing those sentences are true (outside of proof).

Wittgenstein, L. 1953. *Philosophical Investigations*. Blackwell, Oxford.

Wilks, Y. 1980. Frames, Semantics and Novelty. In D. Metzing (ed.), *Frame Conceptions and Text Understanding*. de Gruyter, Berlin.

Wilks, Y. 1971. Decidability and Meaning. *Mind* LXXX.

Wilks, Y. (1972). *Grammar Meaning and the Machine Analysis of Language*. Routledge, London and Boston.

Wilks, Y., Pustejovsky, J., and Cowie, J. (1993). DIDEROT: automatic data extraction from text using semantic analysis. *Proc. ARPA Conference of Human Language Technology*. Morgan Kaufmann, Princeton, NJ and Menlo Park, CA.

PART II

The Syntax of Word Meaning

6   Introduction

FEDERICA BUSA AND PIERRETTE BOUILLON

The contributions in this section are centered around a set of common themes:

1. developing a theoretical vocabulary sufficiently rich to understand how word meanings compose;
2. developing and motivating frameworks for lexical semantics with explanatory force;
3. analyzing cross-linguistic data for achieving linguistically independent models.

Although each contribution approaches the problems from different angles and different data sets, they all highlight the richness of the information carried by words in context. The real challenge, as it emerges from the papers, is whether it is possible to establish a clear boundary between people's *words* and people's *worlds* or experiences. The goal is to understand whether there is a level of representation that is independent of specific contextual variations, while accounting for the novel use of words in different contexts.

The authors reach different conclusions: some reject structured representations of lexical information, others show that it is precisely in the structuring of the lexicon that we can achieve an understanding of how meaning changes in context.

The first paper by James Pustejovsky presents recent developments in GL, focusing on the role of qualia structure as a syntax for creating new concepts. The paper addresses fundamental questions on the well-formedness of concepts, the combinatorial possibilities within a generative mental lexicon, and how these principles are motivated by linguistic evidence.

The contribution by Jacques Jayez focuses on the meaning variations of the French verbs *"suggérer"* (suggest) and *"attendre"* (wait). He argues that the compositional interpretation of these verbs is crucially determined by extra-linguistic/contextual factors, and, as a result, localized/static representations of word meaning are inadequate. This conclusion is meant to point out the shortcomings of the Generative Lexicon, which he takes to be a framework relying on local/static representations unable to cope with context.

Pierrette Bouillon and Federica Busa present an alternative view on the French verb *"attendre"* (wait) and extend their account to Italian. The use of qualia structure for representing verb meaning is quite different from Jayez's understanding of qualia-based representations as static structures. Here, the distinction between static and dynamic components of lexical representation is made clear by separating qualia roles (i.e., the elements of the theoretical vocabulary for structuring word meaning) from their actual values. Although the latter may be viewed as static, localized, or "speaker" dependent components, the former are not and should not be confused or made analogous to the values assigned to each role (this may vary from context to context and from speaker to speaker).

The paper by Patrick Saint-Dizier presents possible extensions to qualia structure for modeling the compositional behavior of verbs and adjectives. The meaning shifts that are analyzed rely on a view of qualia similar to that of Bouillon and Busa, although Saint-Dizier argues that the TELIC quale would appear to be the most productive role in compositional processes.

The paper by Salvador Climent investigates a range of partitive constructions. In his account, qualia also represents a level of "syntactic"-like description of the compositional operations that derive the interpretation of complex nominals.

The paper by Laurence Danlos closes this section with a study that relates word meaning to discourse, providing a useful bridge to the next part of the book. Danlos analyzes causal relations in discourse, showing that it is possible to understand certain extra-linguistic facts (interpreting causation) from a linguistic perspective, involving the internal complexity of events.

The general methodology and assumptions that emerge from this part of the volume appear to support McGilvray's view of the role of a generative approach to the lexicon: Word meaning needs a syntax to account for the compositional properties that are at the basis of linguistic "creativity." Qualia roles are the closest candidates to best represent an adequate abstract vocabulary over which the compositional processes can be defined. In this sense, we believe that we have moved further ahead toward achieving a clear distinction between strict lexical knowledge and more general common sense knowledge. The ways in which this can be demonstrated and even accomplished is the topic of the next part of the volume.

7   Type Construction and the Logic of Concepts

JAMES PUSTEJOVSKY

Abstract

I would like to pose a set of fundamental questions regarding the constraints we can place on the structure of our concepts, particularly as revealed through language. I will outline a methodology for the construction of ontological types based on the dual concerns of capturing linguistic generalizations and satisfying metaphysical considerations. I discuss what "kinds of things" there are, as reflected in the models of semantics we adopt for our linguistic theories. I argue that the flat and relatively homogeneous typing models coming out of classic Montague Grammar are grossly inadequate to the task of modeling and describing language and its meaning. I outline aspects of a semantic theory (Generative Lexicon) employing a ranking of types. I distinguish first between natural (simple) types and functional types, and then motivate the use of complex types (dot objects) to model objects with multiple and interdependent denotations. This approach will be called the *Principle of Type Ordering*. I will explore what the top lattice structures are within this model, and how these constructions relate to more classic issues in syntactic mapping from meaning.

1   Language and Category Formation

Since the early days of artificial intelligence, researchers have struggled to find a satisfactory definition for category or concept, one which both meets formal demands on soundness and completeness, and practical demands on relevance to real-world tasks of classification. One goal is usually sacrificed in the hope of achieving the other, where the results are muddled with good intentions but poor methodology.

Such comments are not restricted to classic AI approaches to knowledge representation alone, however, but are appropriately applied to the bulk of research done in theoretical linguistics on lexical representation as well. By rushing to describe a body of data from the perspective of syntactic structure and the resulting logical form, most assumptions regarding the underlying semantic "primitives" or categories used by the theories are opportunistic and do not impact on the question of whether the representations are conceptually appropriate or fitting. Thus, what is typically missing in these accounts of knowledge representation is the luxury of posing the fundamental questions of *sufficient reason*, perhaps the most basic of questions regarding concept construction. These include the following:

1. How can we choose between competing representation languages?
2. What makes one feature or category more appropriate or more suitable than another for constructing an ontology?
3. What justifies the admission of a feature or category into the ontology?
4. How are these categories put together to make larger ones (principle of compositionality)?
5. Can we quantify the size or complexity of our categories?

In this paper, I approach these issues from the combined perspectives of linguistic semantics and computational linguistics. What I hope to illustrate here is a fairly different approach to modeling categories, but one that I believe is both philosophically intuitive and linguistically motivated. I describe a framework within which we can construct increasingly complex types from a set of basic building blocks. The units of composition will correspond to conceptual categories that are primitive, but in no way fixed or static. Rather, these underlying units are highly functional in nature, and are structured according to a theory of semantic underspecification. The result is a type constructional system of concepts based in part on the classic Aristotelian notion of substance, together with the generative mechanisms recently developed in Generative Lexicon Theory. These include *qualia structure*, the *Principle of Orthogonal Inheritance*, and *Dot Object Construction*.

On this view, the resulting architecture of the upper concept lattice is structured into three domains: entities, qualities, and events. Each domain is itself structured by a type ordering relation, from simpler to more complex types. In this paper, I discuss a tripartite system, the simplest model employing the mechanisms of orthogonal inheritance and dot object construction. The resulting type structure is as shown in the Figure 7.1 below. The simples types in each domain are *Natural*

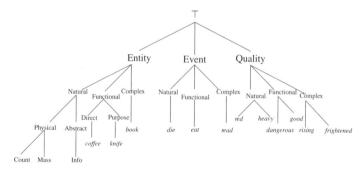

Fig. 7.1. Tripartite concept lattice.

Types, from which all others are grounded types are constructed.[1] *Functional Types*, on the other hand, combine qualia-based information from AGENTIVE and TELIC modes of explanation with a ground type, as we see below. *Complex Types* (or dot objects) are even richer in structure and are formed by the application of a type constructor, creating a type which is the reification of a specific *relation* between two types. I argue that this is a desirable characterization of natural categories and is strongly motivated by the linguistic data. Perhaps the most desirable consequence of this architecture of types is that we can provide distinct algebras of subtyping behavior for each type rank. In other words, the criteria for partitioning a type in the domain of Naturals to create subtypes will be very different from those that create subtypes in the Functional types and Complex types.

Before beginning our investigations into category structure, let me present some of the theoretical assumptions I will be making regarding the structure of the lexicon, and how this impacts our model of semantics. I assume that human cognitive abilities are manifested in the languages we speak and that central to this capability is the mental lexicon. Research in Generative Lexicon Theory points to a view of the mental lexicon that is neither that of a classical dictionary nor that of a warehouse of data within an information processing system. Rather, the lexicon is coming to be viewed as a complex, dynamic, and yet coherent system of knowledge, serving as the interface between structural linguistic operations and the compositional rules that create meaning. Such a design reflects some of the basic assumptions that have motivated generative linguistics over the past forty years. The computational perspective of generative lexicon theory entails studying how the combinatorics of semantic expressions is a reflection of the compositionality of thought itself. There are two questions central to this area:

1. What is the nature of our lexical knowledge that allows us to deploy a finite number of words in an unbounded number of contexts, and to successfully use our language to talk about the world in these contexts?
2. Is this lexical knowledge really separable from our ability to categorize and classify concepts in the world?

In this paper, it will be assumed that the first glimpse of our concepts comes from the lexicalization strategies employed in language. Equally important are the compositional processes giving rise to more complex concepts. This does not entail, however, a Whorfian position of conceptual relativism tied to linguistic behavior. Rather, this view is consistent with the belief that it is the logic of concepts itself which is parameter driven, and to which the generative mechanisms of GL are ultimately linked.

Generative Lexicon theory assumes that semantic descriptions, as constructed from lexical expressions, make use of four kinds (levels) of linguistic

---

[1] Ungrounded types correspond to those concepts which are functional in nature, without reference to specific ground values, such as tool and so on. See below for further discussion.

representations. These are listed below:

1. ARGUMENT STRUCTURE: Specification of number and type of logical arguments.
2. EVENT STRUCTURE: Definition of the event type of an expression and its subeventual structure.
3. QUALIA STRUCTURE: A structural differentiation of the predicative force for a lexical item.
4. LEXICAL INHERITANCE STRUCTURE: Identification of how a lexical structure is related to other structures in the type lattice.

The motivation for such apparently rich representations is actually grounded in a fairly conservative strategy of linguistic description matching semantic explanation. Consider, for example, how a conventional view on semantics models a verb such as "build" as a relation between individuals, e.g., $\lambda y \lambda x[build(x, y)]$. Recognizing the state of affairs of "building" itself as an individual gives rise to a neo-Davidsonian single event-place interpretation (cf. Parsons, 1990) of the relational reading:

(1)   **Events as individuals**: $\lambda y \lambda x \lambda e[build(e, x, y)]$

Furthermore, linguistic and semantic evidence suggests that many causatives are in fact not logically atomic from the perspective of event structure, but have internal events of their own. This gives rise to another enrichment in the logical form associated with the verb, where subevents are associated with subpredicates, corresponding to some logical *portion* of the verb's meaning:

(2)   a. **Subevents as individuals**: $\lambda e_2 \lambda e_1[\ldots]$
       b. **Subpredicates for the subevents**:
           $\lambda y \lambda x \lambda e_2 \lambda e_1[build_1(e_1, x, ..) \wedge build_2(e_2, y, ..)]$

Within GL, it has been argued that a further enrichment of this decompositional approach is motivated by both semantic and syntactic data; namely, the introduction of *qualia* structure as a cross-categorial representational tool. Briefly, qualia are Aristotelian "modes of explanation" for an entity or relation. They are defined in Pustejovsky (1995) with the following characteristics:

> FORMAL: the basic category which distinguishes it within a larger domain;
> CONSTITUTIVE: the relation between an object and its constituent parts;
> TELIC: its purpose and function;
> AGENTIVE: factors involved in its origin or "bringing it about".

For relations, the qualia act in a similar capacity to thematic relations, but where the individual qualia are possibly associated with entire event descriptions, and not just individuals. Something like the expression in (3) would correspond to "build":

(3)   a. **Qualia Identify the Substructures**:

b. $\lambda y \lambda x \lambda e_1 \lambda e_2 [\text{AGENTIVE} = [build_1(e_1, x, \ldots)]$
    $\wedge \quad \text{FORMAL} = [build_2(e_2, y, \ldots)]$
    $\wedge \quad \text{TELIC} = \ldots$
    $\wedge \quad \text{CONST} = \ldots]$

It can be seen that motivation for three of the four levels of representation in GL are tied to fairly familiar methodological strategies.[2] Viewed more conceptually, the qualia structure can be seen as providing functional tags to words, linking the words to a network of concepts.

(4)

$$\begin{bmatrix} \alpha \\ \text{ARGSTR} = \begin{bmatrix} \text{ARG1} = x \\ \ldots \end{bmatrix} \\ \text{EVSTR} = \begin{bmatrix} \text{E1} = e_1 \\ \ldots \end{bmatrix} \\ \text{QUALIA} = \begin{bmatrix} \text{CONST} = \textbf{what } x \textbf{ is made of} \\ \text{FORMAL} = \textbf{what } x \textbf{ is} \\ \text{TELIC} = \textbf{function of } x \\ \text{AGENTIVE} = \textbf{how } x \textbf{ came into being} \end{bmatrix} \end{bmatrix}$$

Returning to the questions posed at the beginning of this section, we can now at least approach the major concern of this paper: namely, what kinds of things are there and can there be, conceptually? In the remainder of this paper, I turn to answering this question with the help of qualia structure. I will suggest that the qualia be deployed as the organizing principle of the logic of concepts.

2   Toward a Generative Type System

Conventional approaches to knowledge base design follow a standard strategy of creating an upper model of concepts, and based on subsumption relations, specializes these concepts accordingly to specific types as needed in a domain. Although it is standard to separate things from actions and qualities, beyond this initial partition, there is little agreed upon. For example, within the domain of entities (or things), much is left to interpretation, and multiple inheritance is conventionally a crucial tool to model the relationships between, for example, the concepts "food" and "apple," or "animal" and "pet." How are we to model concepts that seem to inherit from multiple basic types, and what constraints can be imposed on the construction of such concepts, because this seems an unduly powerful mechanism of concept formation?

---

[2] The fourth, *Lexical Inheritance Structure*, relates to the very structure of categories themselves, the major topic we address later in this paper.

Consider, for example, the questions that arise when categorizing the relatively simple concepts below.

(5)   a.   "stick": individual physical entity;
       b.   "rock": mass or individual physical entity;
       c.   "apple": individual, possibly given purpose;
       d.   "sandwich": individual, with purpose, prepared artifactual;
       e.   "cookie": individual, with purpose, baked artifactual;
       f.   "father": relational concept between individuals;
       g.   "boss": relational concept between individuals;
       h.   "friend": long-term stage-level relational concept;
       i.   "student": short-term stage-level relational concept;
       j.   "audience": short-term stage-level concept;
       k.   "laundry": mass noun bipolar stage-level;
       l.   "groceries": mass noun monopolar stage-level;
       m.   "human": agentive intentional individual.

The first and most obvious distinction in our conceptual partitioning of the world involves the notion of natural kind. Hence, while "sticks" and "rocks" are naturally occurring entities, "sandwiches" and "cookies" are not. "Apples" are certainly natural kinds, but they like other natural objects can be grouped in other types of categories that do not include naturally occurring entities, such as "cookies," for example, which are artifacts. Distinguishing between the concepts "father" and "boss" involves understanding the various social and functional roles that are possible between individuals. Such roles are typically identifiable eventualities, but needn't be; similar remarks hold for "student" and "friend."

Some concepts are bound more directly to a specific activity or event, and because of this, the referring potential of words associated with such concepts is integrally linked to this defining event. For example, understanding the concept of "audience" is possible only by reference to the event which the individuals are engaged in attending. Hence, an audience might remain a "crowd" even after it is actively attending to a particular event, but it is no longer an audience; in other words, audiences are audiences of some event. Concepts such as "laundry" and "groceries" are similarly defined relative to an activity that must be identified in order to properly understand them. However, unlike "audience," these nouns do not behave relationally; rather, the activity is incorporated into the way the objects are identified. In fact, "laundry" is interestingly ambiguous because of this fact; it can refer to the dirty clothes that require cleaning, or to the clean clothes that have just been cleaned. The noun "groceries" appears to prefer the interpretation of 'recently selected (food) stuff' and not 'to be selected (food) stuff,' although this is somewhat unclear.

Conventional approaches to lexicon design and lexicography are relatively liberal with forming taxonomic structures where they seem appropriate, as informed by word senses in the language. A quick glance at the top concepts in WORDNET illustrates that the goal of this lexicographic exercise is to catalogue words as characterized by fairly local clusterings of semantic properties.

{act, activity}   {natural object}
{animal, fauna}   {natural phenomenon}
{artifact}   {person, human being}
{attribute}   {plant, flora}
{body}   {possession}
{cognition, knowledge}   {process}
{communication}   {quantity, amount}
{event, happening}   {relation}
{feeling, emotion}   {shape}
{food}   {state}
{group, grouping}   {substance}
{location}   {time}
{motivation, motive}
{food}

As with many ontologies, it is hard to discern a coherent global structure for the resulting classification beyond a weak descriptive labelling of words into extensionally defined sets. Abstracting away much of the top structure in the figure above, notice that WORDNET handles both contrastive ambiguity and complementary ambiguity (polysemy) in the same way; namely, by allowing multiple inheritance from the word denoting multiple concepts (cf. Pustejovsky, 1995 for discussion). Hence, for a polysemous noun such as "book," the classification strategy associates the different senses with different synsets, the two most important, perhaps, being `artifact` and `mental`, as shown in Figure 7.2.

It is not the goal of this paper to examine the shortcomings of WORDNET. What is important to point out, however, is the extreme difficulty facing semanticists when attempting to add ontological richness to a formal type system for language. WORDNET, of course, does not pretend to model lexical items in formal terms; many approaches to ontology construction, however, do formalize the categories

Fig. 7.2. Classic taxonomy of entities.

as types, with no concern for what categories there can and should be. In the next section, I will argue that there are principled and intuitive methods for designing a lexicon, on metaphysical grounds. I will discuss three points relating to the design of an ontology as a type sytem:

(a)   The qualia are in fact generative coherence relations between types;
(b)   There is a formal *ranking* in the complexity of types;
(c)   The structure of these types is exploited in composition.

In what follows, I will map out how the qualia allow us to differentiate categories of concepts, at first broadly, and then quite specifically.

3   The Natural Types

In this section, I begin with an exploration into the basic distinction between natural kinds and artifacts; this is one of the oldest categorical distinctions made in the literature, and exercises philosophical discourse to the present (see Putnam, 1975; Quine, 1962; others). There are several questions that pertain to this distinction, including the satisfaction conditions on membership in a category, but what will concern us presently is the difference in how natural kinds are *evaluated* relative to artifacts. I will argue that the major discriminant in distinguishing between natural kinds and artifacts is *intentionality*; intentionality is expressed in relation to the AGENTIVE and TELIC qualia in GL. This will form the basis for ranking the types for the kinds of things there are into a hierarchy of types, the *Principle of Type Ordering*.

Consider, for illustration, the use and meaning associated with the two nouns "chair" and "rock" in the contexts below, where "!" will indicate a semantic anomaly.

(6)   a. This is a good <u>chair</u>.
        b. !This is a good <u>rock</u>.

(7)   a. Mary enjoys that <u>chair</u>.
        b. !Mary enjoyed the <u>rock</u>.

On a very basic level, the evaluative predicates present in these examples refer to the <u>function</u> of the object or material; hence the judgments in these sentences are functional ones. For natural kinds such as "rock," "tiger," and so on, this is only possible when we have reconceptualized the concept to also carry some intention along with it. For example, if rocks are judged relative to how good they are for climbing on, then the sentences in (6b) and (7b) are well-formed enough. Similarly, although "apples" are natural kind plant products, we can categorize them as a food stuff, a category that is typically grouped into natural kinds as well. Other sorts of food stuff, such as cookies and cakes are, however, artifactual in nature, but what are the discriminant properties that tell us this is so? On this view, classifying them as foods does not tell us what category they belong to, but reference to an event of creation would do just that. Hence, although there are some diagnostics for determining what is natural or not, they do not appear to relate to intentionality.

In order to better understand how intentionality affects the conceptualization strategies in our thought, imagine a language, $\mathcal{L}_N$, without intentionality. We will say that all words and their compositions are *Natural Types*. Differentiation of the types in this language is accomplished by the FORMAL quale:

(8)   a. stick, lion, pebble
          b. water, sky, rock

$\mathcal{L}_N$ is closed under the operation, CONSTITUTION:

(9)   a. wood stick; $\lambda x \exists y [stick(x) \wedge wood(y) \wedge made\_of(x, y)]$
          b. cloud sky; $\lambda x \exists y [sky(x) \wedge cloud(y) \wedge made\_of(x, y)]$

$\mathcal{L}_N$ is not closed under AGENTIVE (Coming into Being), however, because this quale involves reference to an intentional action toward the entity. Hence, these are invalid forms: i.e., the "passive" predicates below entail agency:

(10)   a. *carved stick*; $\lambda x \exists e [stick(x) \wedge carved(e, x)]$
         b. *chipped stone*; $\lambda x \exists e [stone(x) \wedge chipped(e, x)]$

These would be in the Natural types only if these predicates are interpreted non-intentionally, viz., as undirected action.

Following the notation in Asher and Pustejovsky (1999), I will interpret the conventional feature-based qualia structure of GL in terms of an algebra of types, operating under very restrictive rules of combination. For example, instead of the feature structure in (11), where constitution as a quale is a feature value, we can represent this aspect of the meaning as integrally part of the basic type structure itself.

(11)   a. $\begin{bmatrix} x \\ \text{QUALIA} = \begin{bmatrix} \text{FORMAL} = \sigma \\ \text{CONST} = \tau \end{bmatrix} \end{bmatrix} \implies$

         b. $x : \sigma \text{\textcircled{c}} \tau$

Hence, what is needed is a way to represent both FORMAL and CONST as being legitimate aspects of a type in $\mathcal{L}_N$:

(12)   If σ and τ are types in $\mathcal{L}_N$, then $\sigma \text{\textcircled{c}} \tau$ is also in $\mathcal{L}_N$, where $\text{\textcircled{c}}$ expresses the constitutive relation, as defined in GL.

From the examples above, we would thus have the following types in $\mathcal{L}_N$, ignoring the actual composition rules giving rise to the compound interpretations:

(13)   a. wood stick; *stick*$\text{\textcircled{c}}$*wood*
         b. cloud sky; *sky*$\text{\textcircled{c}}$*cloud*

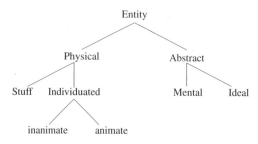

Fig. 7.3. Upper natural type lattice.

Unless specified explicitly, an explicit constitution for an entity is not entailed. However, for physical entities, *some* constitution is entailed for that type. It is important to point out that this analysis states that the constitutive qualia relation is primary and extensional in nature.[3] Viewed in isolation, the set of natural types $\mathcal{N}$ is not very informative or illuminating, but they provide the necessary building blocks on top of which to define our other types.

Given these assumptions, the upper lattice structure of the natural types will refer only to unintentional objects and will have the structure shown in Figure 7.3.

Now consider the predicates that select for just these natural types. In other words, once we have defined the natural type entities, we are in a position to define the natural predicates and relations that correspond to these types. First, let us review some notation. I assume a *typing judgment*, $g \vdash \alpha : \tau$, with respect to a grammar to be an assignment, g, an expression, α, and a type, τ, such that under assignment g, the expression α has type τ. In the case of the natural types, I will also assume the following equivalence:

(14) $g \vdash x : \alpha \in \mathcal{N} =_{df} g \vdash x : e_n$

---

[3] In Pustejovsky (1998b), the formal type structural distinction between individuals and mass concepts is handled by an explicit *linkage* between the CONST(TITUTIVE) and FORMAL in the qualia structure. Thus, (i) was the abstract feature representation for a mass term such as "water," while (ii) modeled count nouns such as "boy" and "stick."

$$(i) \quad \begin{bmatrix} \alpha \\ \text{QUALIA} = \begin{bmatrix} \text{FORMAL} = \boxed{1}_a \\ \text{CONST} = \boxed{1} \end{bmatrix} \end{bmatrix}$$

Individuals where $a \neq b$:

$$(ii) \quad \begin{bmatrix} \alpha \\ \text{QUALIA} = \begin{bmatrix} \text{FORMAL} = a \\ \text{CONST} = b \end{bmatrix} \end{bmatrix}$$

With the present type notation, this can be handled in a parallel fashion with the CONST type constructor ©.

Then, for the construction of predicates from natural types, we have the following: for the predicates below, e_n and $\underline{t}$ are in the set of Natural Types, $\mathcal{N}$, structured as a join semi-lattice, $< N, \sqsubseteq >$;

(15) a. die: $e_n \to \underline{t}$;
      b. touch: $e_n \to (e_n \to \underline{t})$;
      c. be under: $e_n \to (e_n \to \underline{t})$;
      d. give: $e_N \to (e_N \to (e_N \underline{t}))$.

The predicate and relational types that result from natural type entities are just those predicates and relations that are natural types themselves.

Observe that the propositions formed by the composition of a natural predicate with a natural type entity will be *brute propositions*, making use of brute entities, i.e., natural types. Examples of such propositions are given below:

(16) a. The rabbit died.
      b. The rock touches the water.
      c. The ants are under the tree.

It is interesting to compare this to Anscombe's (1958) and Searle's (1995) proposals regarding "brute facts," where facts are classified according to the kinds of participant descriptions they contain. This is very much in line with the research strategy here: in fact, as we shall see, the qualia and the principle of type ordering will allow us to enrich this "fact classification" even further.

So far, I have outlined a simple class of types for entities and relations, $\mathcal{N}$ and $\mathcal{N} \times \mathcal{N}$. Now let us explore how these types are deployed in composition in syntax. First, we turn to the manner in which subtypes in the lattice, $\mathcal{N}$ are accepted in selective contexts. As in Pustejovsky (1995), we express a *subtyping coercion* relation, Θ, for these judgments as follows:

(17) $$\frac{x : \sigma_1, \quad \Theta[\sigma_1 \sqsubseteq \sigma_2] : \sigma_1 \to \sigma_2}{\Theta[\sigma_1 \sqsubseteq \sigma_2](x) : \sigma_2}$$

This says that, given a variable x of type σ_1, which is a subtype of σ_2, there is a coercion possible between σ_1 and σ_2, which changes the type of α in this composition, from σ_1 to σ_2. The typing relation between the subtype rock and the type selected by a governing verb "throw," for example, namely phys_obj, is respected by this coercion relation, Θ. Similarly, because the concept rabbit is subtyped under animal, it falls under the same coercion operation. Both are shown below in (18) and a composition is illustrated in (19), where the type for the verb "die" is *animal* $\to \underline{t}$;

(18) a. $\Theta[rock \sqsubseteq phys\_obj] : rock \to phys\_obj$
      b. $\Theta[rabbit \sqsubseteq animal] : rabbit \to animal$

(19)

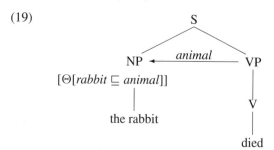

Adjectives will be typed in a similar fashion to predicates, selecting directly for a natural type and thereby becoming *natural qualities*, as shown in (20) below.

(20)   a. red: $e_n \rightarrow \underline{t}$;
        b. heavy: $e_n \rightarrow \underline{t}$.

Ignoring for now how the semantics of attributive modification treats the type differently, we see a straightforward composition in (21).

(21)

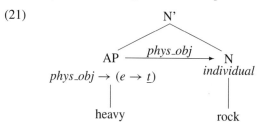

Given the above representation for FORMAL and CONST qualia as a specialized kind of composite type structure, it is no surprise why adjectives such as "old" in the noun phrase "an old ring" appear to be able to predicate of either quale, FORMAL or CONST.

(22)

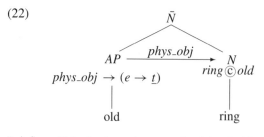

Briefly, within the type structure for "ring," either quale is satisfied by the type restrictions of the adjectival, giving rise to the two interpretations below. Although the CONSTITUTIVE interpretation is not as acceptable as the FORMAL, assume composition allows for type selector functions (cf. Pustejovsky, 1995) such as Σ_1 and Σ_2 below, thus solving the classic mereological puzzle discussed in Bach (1986) and Link (1998).

(23)   a. $\Sigma_1[ring\textcircled{C}old]$: *ring*: "the object is old as an artifact";
        b. $\Sigma_2[ring\textcircled{C}old]$: *old*: "the constitution of the ring is itself old".

This states essentially that, when there are distinct values (types) for the CONST and FORMAL, the selective ability of adjectives such as "old" allows for a nonspecific interpretation.

An even more interesting ambiguity that arises with the selective properties of "old" is when it assumes the interpretations of "former" and "previous," as in "an old car" and "and old girlfriend," vs. "an old friend," which assumes either a FORMAL modification or a TELIC modification, preferably the TELIC; i.e., a friend that one has known for a long time. These were discussed briefly in Pustejovsky (1995) and have recently been discussed more fully in Bouillon (1997) and Bouillon and Busa (forthcoming). In the present discussion, these interpretations can only be available for functional types, the class of concepts to which we turn presently.

4   Functional Types

Up to this point we have discussed only natural types. In some fairly obvious sense, these types refer to real objects that are identified through classic principles of individuation. However, $\mathcal{L}_N$ is not a very expressive language, because any trace of intentionality is absent. This is what the operations of the TELIC or AGENTIVE qualia do; they introduce intentionality, giving rise to the generation of our first *virtual types*, concepts referring to natural types that are colored by intentional descriptive content. For example, the identification of any of the natural types "stick," "stone," or "water," as functioning in the capacity of the activities of "hitting," "throwing," or "drinking," respectively, is a compositional operation that is not supported by $\mathcal{L}_N$.

(24)   a. Introduction of TELIC:
        b. hitting stick; not in $\mathcal{L}_N$;
        c. throwing stone; not in $\mathcal{L}_N$;
        d. drinking water; not in $\mathcal{L}_N$.

The introduction of TELIC above generates a functional description for an entity without of course creating a new entity in the world. Hence, we have a new domain of entities in our type system, the **Functional Types**, $\mathcal{F}$, which are virtual, in that from a realist perspective, each is still identifiable by the properties that satisfy its being a natural type, which forms the *ground* for the functional type.

The other aspect of intentional description is associated with the AGENTIVE quale. Starting again with natural types, we can identify *artifacts* as those naturals with identified AGENTIVE and TELIC roles (see Pustejovsky, 1995). Natural artifacts are those naturals with no expressed purpose or TELIC associated with them; the Adj-N cases in (25) are a good example of this interpretation.

(25)   a. Introduction of AGENTIVE:
        b. carved stick; not in $\mathcal{L}_N$;
        c. flaked stone; not in $\mathcal{L}_N$;
        d. boiled water; not in $\mathcal{L}_N$.

We will call such concepts "semi-intentional," when reference only to AGENTIVE is made. In these examples, the natural type has been transformed or modified from its original state, but not brought into existence by the referenced activity (event). Clearly, real artifactual concepts such as "table," "knife," and "computer," are intentionally defined by reference to both AGENTIVE and TELIC. In fact, for such objects, it is difficult to imagine creation without purpose.

Other concepts that are semi-intentional in nature are types involving individuals where a relational state is defined in terms of the AGENTIVE quale. For example, the classification of two natural types individual humans as entering into the relations of "brother" or "father" also constitutes a semi-intentional type. Reference to the functional relation of two individuals through the TELIC however, is a purely intentional relation, such as illustrated in the examples in (26).

(26)   a. Introduction of TELIC for human:
        b. boss;
        c. friend.

Combining both TELIC and AGENTIVE for humans gives rise to concepts such as "wife" and "president," where social function and social modes of creation are folded into one concept and one lexicalized item. Not surprisingly, the relations associated with such types will also be functionally defined, e.g., "elect," "vote," "marry" (see below).

A large subclass of such nouns, the *agentive nominals*, has been studied recently in Busa (1996), and Busa et al. (1999), where TELIC and AGENTIVE values for nouns such as "violinist" and "pilot" characterize the relation that the individual has to its defining event or event descriptions. For the nouns presented above, institutionally defined roles such as "boss," "president," or "wife" make reference to events through the TELIC or AGENTIVE.

For the present discussion we will interpret the feature-based representations of qualia structure as types, adopting and extending the framework introduced in Asher and Pustejovsky (1999).[4] In earlier treatments of types in GL (Pustejovsky,

---

[4] In Asher and Pustejovsky's (1999) Dot Logic, no explicit distinction is made in the type structure between the qualia roles; in other words, they are all introduced as tensor types to a base type, σ, i.e., $\sigma \otimes \tau$. The basic set of types there is defined as follows:
   (i)   If σ and τ are types, then so is $(\sigma \rightarrow \tau)$
   (ii) If σ and τ are types, then so is $(\sigma \bullet \tau)$.
   (iii) If σ and $\tau_1, \cdots \tau_n$ are types, then so is $(\sigma \otimes (\tau_1 \cdots \tau_n))$.
In the present work, I adopt the basics of the Dot Logic, but also introduce explicit reference to qualia by name, i.e., $\sigma \otimes \tau_T$ and $\sigma \otimes \tau_A$, for reference to TELIC and AGENTIVE, respectively. Furthermore, here CONST is introduced as a type operation, $\sigma \copyright \tau$, directly on the base type.

1995), unified types were represented as the result of a meet of two types from the type lattice, $\sigma \sqcap \tau$, where

(27)   a. $\sigma = [_\sigma \ldots [Q_F = \alpha]]$
        b. $\tau = [_\tau \ldots [Q_T = \beta]]$

In Dot Logic, the tensor type constructor $\otimes$ introduces a quale-relation as part of the type directly, $\sigma \otimes \tau_T$.

(28)   a. $g \vdash x : \alpha =_{df} g \vdash x : e_n$
        b. $g \vdash x : \alpha \otimes \beta_T =_{df} g \vdash x : e_f$,
            where $x : \alpha \otimes (\ldots \beta_i \ldots) \wedge Telic(x, y) \to y : \beta_i$

For example, the feature-based qualia structure for a noun such as "beer," shown in (29),

(29)
$$\begin{bmatrix} \textbf{beer} \\ \text{ARGSTR} = [\,\text{ARG1} = \text{x:liquid}\,] \\ \text{QUALIA} = \begin{bmatrix} \text{FORMAL} = \text{x} \\ \text{TELIC} = \text{drink}(e^P, \text{y}, \text{x}) \end{bmatrix} \end{bmatrix}$$

can be viewed directly as a type as follows:

(30)   beer: *liquid* $\otimes$ *drink$_T$*

Similarly, the unified type for `phys_artifact_tool`, shown in (31)

(31)
$$\begin{bmatrix} \textbf{phys\_artifact\_tool} \\ \text{ARGSTR} = \begin{bmatrix} \text{ARG1} = \text{x:phys\_obj} \\ \text{D\_ARG1} = \text{y:human} \end{bmatrix} \\ \text{QUALIA} = \begin{bmatrix} \text{FORMAL} = \text{x} \\ \text{TELIC} = \text{R}(e^P, \text{y}, \text{x}) \\ \text{AGENTIVE} = \text{make}(e^T, \text{y}, \text{x}) \end{bmatrix} \end{bmatrix}$$

can be represented as a type as follows:[5]

(32)   *phys_obj* $\otimes$ *make$_A$* $\otimes$ ϵ_T

In the previous section, natural predicates were defined in terms of natural entity types. In what follows, we will show how functional predicates are defined in terms

---

[5] Just as the original Dot Logic was extended to include the constitutive type operator, ©, we could complete the extension to map isomorphically to the complete set of qualia by partitioning the tensor type constructors into an AGENTIVE operator, @, and a TELIC operator, $*$. Then, the type in (32) would be represented as *phys_obj* @ *make* $*$ ϵ.

of functional entities. As a result of this, it will be shown how the predicate inherits the intentionality of its arguments directly. Assume e_f is in the set of Functional Types, $\mathcal{F}$, structured as a join semi-lattice, $< F, \sqsubseteq >$. Consider the predicates below;

(33)   a. spoil: $e_f \rightarrow \underline{t}$;
        b. eat: $e_f \rightarrow (e_n \rightarrow \underline{t})$;
        c. feed: $e_f \rightarrow (e_f \rightarrow (e_f \rightarrow \underline{t}))$.

Below are examples of *functional propositions* composed from functional entities and functional predicates, i.e., functional types;

(34)   a. The beer spoiled.
        b. The rabbit ate the carrots.
        c. The rabbit fed the bunny the food.

The judgments expressed by the above propositions entail brute (or natural) propositions, but go beyond them as they also express judgments of intentional content, which natural propositions do not. To illustrate how this separation in judgment is actually calculated compositionally, consider the sentence below in (4).

(35)   The beer fell.

If a functional expression such as "the beer" is predicated by a natural event expression, then the natural proposition is denoted by virtue of the base natural type constituting the expression, i.e., *liquid*, as shown in the derivation below:

(36)

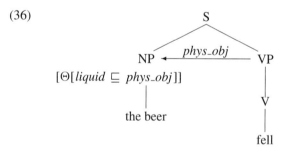

However, in the context of a functional predicate, such as the verb "spoil," the same expression denotes both a natural proposition and a functional proposition, as explained below. Because the predicate "spoil" selects for not just a natural type, $\mathcal{N}$, but a *functional type*, $\mathcal{F}$, as its subject, the general type of the predicate "spoil" is $e_f \rightarrow \underline{t}$, and specifically it is typed as (37):

(37) $phys\_obj \otimes \epsilon_T \rightarrow \underline{t}$

Therefore, functional type selection is selection of not only the base type but of the functional component as well, as illustrated below.

(38)

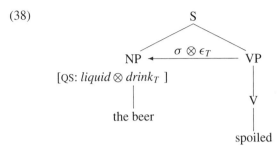

There are two logically distinct components to what is asserted by this sentence: (a) some physically tangible event is implicated relative to a quantity of liquid (this is the brute proposition); (b) the event is intentionally described as a spoiling, and the liquid is beer (this is the functional proposition).

5   A Complex Type Language $\mathcal{L}_C$

$\mathcal{L}_C$ introduces types containing a coherence relation between (at least) two natural or functional types. The resulting objects are also *virtual types*:

(39)   a. `phys_obj·info`: e.g., "book," "record";
         b. `event·event`: e.g., "construction," "examination";
         c. `event·question`: e.g., "exam";
         d. `animal·rational`: e.g., "person".

(40)   a. Introduction of DOT:
         b. book; not in $\mathcal{L}_F$;
         c. money; not in $\mathcal{L}_F$.

For the predicates below, e_C is in the set of Complex Types, C, structured as a join semi-lattice, $< C, \sqsubseteq >$:

(41)   a. play: $e_C \to \underline{t}$, or $e_C \to (e_C \to \underline{t})$;
         b. read: $e_C \to (e_C \to \underline{t})$;
         c. buy: $e_F \to (e_C \to (e_C \to \underline{t}))$.

Examples of *complex propositions* making use of complex entities and complex relations are shown below:

(42)   a. The music played.
         b. The man read the book.
         c. The man bought the food from the vendor.

Notice, further, how selection by the predicate "read" of a noncomplex type such as "story" results in a coercion of the complement to that required by the governing predicate:

(43)

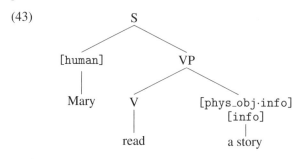

The coercion operations projecting one type from the complex type are a special case of *type pumping* (or projection), defined as Σ_1 and Σ_2 below. These two operations, together with the dot object itself form the definition of the type cluster called a lexical conceptual paradigm (lcp):

(44) $\text{lcp} = \{\sigma_1 \cdot \sigma_2, \Sigma_1[\sigma_1 \cdot \sigma_2] : \sigma_1, \Sigma_2[\sigma_1 \cdot \sigma_2] : \sigma_2\}$

(45)   a. $\Sigma_1[\text{info} \cdot \text{phys\_obj}]:\text{info}$
        b. $\Sigma_2[\text{info} \cdot \text{phys\_obj}]:\text{phys\_obj}$
        c. $\text{info} \cdot \text{physobj\_lcp} = \{\text{info} \cdot \text{phys\_obj}, \text{info}, \text{phys\_obj}\}$

In the case of a predicate that actually selects for only one component in the type complex of the complement, such as that shown below with the verb "believe," type pumping allows the propositional interpretation of the complex type to project and satisfy the selectional constraints of the predicate.

(46)

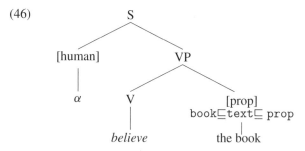

The type derivation below shows both the application of the type pumping operator, Σ, and the subtyping relation, Θ. The complex type interpretation of "book" essentially allows for two subtyping relations, one of which is $\alpha \sqsubseteq S'$:

(47) $$\frac{\Sigma_1(\text{info} \cdot \text{phys\_obj}) : \text{info}, \quad \Theta[\text{info} \sqsubseteq \text{prop}] : \text{info} \to \text{prop}}{\Theta[\text{info} \sqsubseteq \text{prop}](\Sigma_1(\text{info} \cdot \text{phys\_obj})) : \text{prop}}$$

(48)   a. Mary believes the book.
        b. **believe(^Θ(Σ_1(the-book)))(Mary)** $\Rightarrow$
        c. **believe'(^Θ(the-book:info))(Mary)** $\Rightarrow$
        d. **believe'(^the-book:prop)(Mary)**

6   Coercion Revisited

In this section, I will discuss briefly the consequences of the present type system for operations of type coercion. Following the basic formulation of type coercion in Pustejovsky (1995), as a semantic operation that converts an expression, α, to the type expected by a governing function, β, it was suggested that α has a set of type shifting operators, Σ_α, associated with it, which may operate over an expression, changing its type and denotation. These operators are the qualia themselves and the resulting types are the values of the qualia. Following the standard GL analysis of coercion in complement position,[6] I will assume that the verb "enjoy" selects for an eventual function, that is, an unsaturated event description (see Pustejovsky, 1993, 1995 for discussion). Thus, although the NP "her coffee" does not satisfy the typing environment of the governing verb "enjoy," it is coerced to the appropriate type by the operation of *type coercion*. The compositional processes in the grammar results in the coercion of the NP complement "her coffee" into an event description, whose subject is controlled by the predicate "enjoy."

(49)

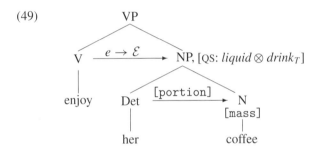

The exact value of the predicate in this event description is mediated by two factors, described in (50) below.

(50)   a.   SPECIFICATION IN COERCION: For a coercing predicate β and its argument α, the specification is controlled by the following two factors:

           b.   the selectional specificity of the coercing predicate;

           c.   the aliases, Σ_α, available to the argument being coerced. There are two types of aliases for an expression:

               (i)   Globally available methods of type-shifting, such as *grinding* and *packaging*;

               (ii)   Locally available values in the qualia structure of an expression, such as TELIC and AGENTIVE events.

---

[6] I assume some version of function application with coercion (FAC), as stated below:

     FUNCTION APPLICATION WITH COERCION (FAC): If α is of type c, and β is of type <a,b>, then,

     (i)   if type c = a, then $\beta(\alpha)$ is of type b.

     (ii)   if there is a $\sigma \in \Sigma_\alpha$ such that $\sigma(\alpha)$ results in an expression of type a, then $\beta(\sigma(\alpha))$ is of type b.

     (iii)   otherwise a type error is produced.

The property exhibited by coercing predicates such as "enjoy" is interesting because the verbs do not seem to ever fail in coercion. That is, although there may be no obvious or "proximate" interpretation for the sentences in (51), there are legitimate default readings available, even in the absence of qualia-derived interpretations. The two sentences in (51) for example, are cases in point.

(51)   a. Mary enjoyed the rock.
         b. John enjoyed the flower.

Namely, Mary might enjoy the way a rock feels, and John the way a flower looks or smells, all of which are perceptual experiences. For such top-typed experiencing predicates, it is hard to imagine a semantically ill-formed "enjoying event." In such cases where the complement is a functional type, the natural component of a functional type can be selected and is itself coerced into the selected type. For this reason, I shall refer to such type changing contexts as *Natural Coercions*. Returning to the example in (49), the same structure viewed as undergoing a natural coercion results in the following interpretation:

(52)   VP, $\lambda x \lambda e \exists y : liquid\ [enjoy(e, x, \text{EXP}(x, y))]$

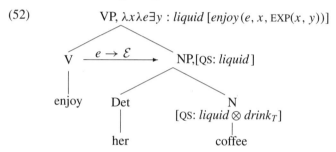

Hence, natural coercions (such as with "enjoy") impose an event description interpretation on its complement, even in cases where the complement itself does not directly carry such information.

Evaluative predicates, on the other hand, such as "good" and "effective," impose functional descriptions on their arguments, and as such shift the order or rank of the argument to a functional type.

(53)

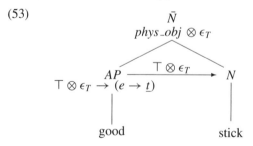

With the introduction of type order (or *rank*), it is possible to classify the kinds of coercion operations a bit more precisely than has been accomplished thus far. There

COERCION TYPES	Rank-preserving	Rank-shifting
Domain-preserving	*Subtyping* (54a)	*Evaluative Predicates* (54c)
Domain-shifting	*Natural Coercion* (54b)	*Imposed Telic* (54d)

Fig. 7.4. Table of coercion relations.

are two parameters that can help us distinguish the types of coercion operations that occur in grammar. One refers to the integrity of the type within its rank, while the other refers to the rank itself. For example, coercions preserving the order of the type will be called *Rank-preserving*; this is where an expression $x : \alpha \in \mathcal{N}$, remains in $\mathcal{N}$ after the application of coercion. A coercion not having this property is said to be *Rank-shifting*. A coercion is *Domain-preserving* when the coerced expression α is not shifted from its domain (i.e., entities, events, or properties) during the coercion. If this is not the case, the coercion is said to be *Domain-shifting*. These properties are summarized in the table below.

The sentences in (54) contain instances illustrating the distinct coercion types referred to in Figure 7.4.

(54)   a.   Mary threw the rock.
           b.   John enjoyed the flower.
           c.   The water spoiled.
           d.   John began the rock.

The actual complement in (54a) is a subtype of that selected for by the verb "throw," as seen above in (18). The coercion in (54b) has already been discussed, while (54c) is a clear example of a natural type instance being coerced to a functional interpretation. The aspectual coercion in (54d) combines this functional interpretation with a domain-shift to a controlled event description. Because both parameters are being positively deployed in this example, this sentence is clearly the hardest for which to find a natural interpretation.

7   Elements of Type Construction

In this section, I turn to two of the questions posed in the first section of the paper, regarding how discriminant features are chosen for constructing the relationship between types within each type lattice. These questions are repeated below:

1.   What makes one feature or category more appropriate or more suitable than another for constructing an ontology?
2.   What justifies the admission of a feature or category into the ontology?

The extensions to GL I have been outlining above are an attempt to answer just these questions; they provide us with two new strategies for type construction:

(a)   The criteria for subtyping are distinct to each type rank; that is, each level of type is structured according to distinct partitioning strategies;

(b)   Underspecification over the different levels of representation in GL allows for parameterizable views on specialization relations in the type system.

To make these points clearer, I will first discuss briefly how the type-subtype relation in the natural type lattice, $\mathcal{N}$, is structured. Then, I show how the same relation in the domain of functional types, $\mathcal{F}$, must be characterized in terms of a subtyping relation making reference to event descriptions. The goal of the following sections is not to actually "construct" the types corresponding to the natural lattice, but to rather understand what local constraints exist within the lattice, and how they are structured relative to the global constraints in the type system. Because of space, I will have little to say about the subtyping relation in the rank of complex types, but see Pustejovsky (forthcoming) for discussion.

The premise of the current work is that it is the lexicalization strategies in a language that give us our first glimpse of the concepts behind our thoughts. Equally important of course are the compositional structures that give rise to new concepts. Constructing a model for how our meanings are built up and modified in context has always been at the very center of Generative Lexicon Theory. The consequences of adopting such a thesis are that ontological considerations are unavoidable when studying categories and have to be seriously addressed when studying the compositional processes involved in language. Although the discussion so far has focused on the structure of the tripartite type system and the effects of this logic on the consequent descriptive and explanatory mechanisms in Generative Lexicon theory, in this section, I would like to touch on some of the assumptions underlying the construction of the types themselves, as seen from underlying conceptual principles. The remarks in this section will be brief, and for a longer treatment of these issues, the reader is referred to Pustejovsky (forthcoming).

As described above, the global algebraic constraints on the type system are uniform but weak in nature. Understanding the partitionings at different levels of the type system involves appreciating what discriminant predicates, D_i, have been employed to generate the subtypes in a particular sublattice. To begin with, following some general assumptions in knowledge representation (see Johansson, 1989; Simons, 1987; and Smith, 1982), I assume that there are metalanguage predicates which act to generate partitions on the upper level of the type system. For the domain of natural types, $\mathcal{N}$, this will involve reference to the set of *logical discriminants* (L-discriminants), which are essentially a priori categorization schemas, as in Carnap (1928).

Earlier we discussed the structure of the natural lattice $\mathcal{N}$, but we did not address the issue of what logical coherence existed in the lattice beyond the minimal constraints imposed by the join semi-lattice structure. In other words, many constructional issues remain as to how the type system is built, and according to what principles. For two entities in the set of natural types, σ, $\tau \in \mathcal{N}$, where $\sigma \sqsubseteq \tau$, then there must exist a *tangible discriminant predicate, D*, such that D partitions τ into a nonempty set of two or more types, one of which includes σ. Hence, in accord with the intuition that the downward structure in the semilattice of types corresponds to the addition of more information to the concepts modelled, as we proceed down the structure we effectly are conjoining properties expressed by the discriminant D_i at that level. However, not all discriminants can be represented as being of the same type, and we must be able to distinguish the way in which properties may predicate of individuals. Clearly the nature of predicate opposition is crucial to better understanding the different modes of predication. For example, the classic distinction between contradictories and contraries suggests at least two sorts of predicate opposition.

(55)   a. Bill is healthy
    a′. Bill is not healthy.
  b. Bill is sick.
    b′. Bill is not sick.

(56)   a. Jan is male.
    a′. Jan is not male.
  b. Jan is female.
    b′. Jan is not female.

Sentences ((55)a,b), involving *polar opposites* such as "healthy/sick," are typically viewed as contraries, while ((55)a,a′) are contradictories. While contradictories ((55)a,a′) and ((56)a,a′) usually follow from an interpretation of *not* as "weak negation" (cf. Horn, 1989; von Wright, 1959), the contradictories present in ((56)a,b) and ((56)a′,b′) cannot be the result of weak negation alone: properties such as "male" and "female" are inherently contradictory when applied to its naturally predicated type, i.e., `animal`.

Rather than suggesting that predicate pairs such as "male/female" make reference to internal negation in their semantics, I will propose that the type structure that models such predicates is simply a Boolean semilattice. Similarly, although "healthy" and "sick" can be partially modeled in terms of negation, there is a stronger constraint that can be imposed on how polar opposites relate to one another through the semantics of a scalar semilattice with poles. It is the interpretation of the semilattice rather than the predicates themselves that makes reference to the operations of negation and ordering. Thus, discriminant properties (both logical and natural) are typed according to the kind of opposition involved. Assuming some basic notion of a property sortal array and the type defining it, let us make the following assumptions:

(57)   a. Property semilattice:

   b. $<\Sigma, \tau, \sqcup, \sqsubseteq >$ *realizes* a predicate P, where Σ is a sortal array of types, τ is a local top type for this sortal array, such that $\sigma_i \in \Sigma$ for $\sigma_i \sqsubseteq \tau$.

Let us now define the simplest opposition as a 2-element property semilattice:

(58)   a. Binary Property:

   b. $< \sigma_1, \sigma_2, \tau, \sqcup, \sqsubseteq >$ *realizes* a binary predicate P, where τ is a local top type for this sortal array, such that $\sigma_1, \sigma_2 \sqsubseteq \tau$.

   c.

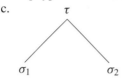

Examples of adjective pairs with this behavior include "male/female" (natural type), "married/unmarried" (functional type), and so forth.

(59)   Gendered

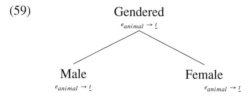

These are examples of natural discriminants, but L-discriminants will be classified by similar means. For example, let us return to the discussion of generating the upper level of the natural type entity lattice. Assume the type phys_obj is partitioned by the L-discriminant, *individuated*, generating the structure in (60).[7]

(60)   phys_obj

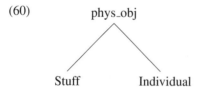

In some cases, however, the partitioning of the natural types does not follow from the application of logical discriminants but from naturally identifiable properties associated with the members of a set; these may be natural or functional discriminants. In the construction of the natural types, they must be naturals, however. For example, the sublattice associated with the type animal is arguably constructed according to natural discriminants, such as "flying" (D_3), "walking" (D_4), and "swimming" (D_2), as informally illustrated below in (61):

---

[7] The type phys_obj itself is the result of L-discriminants, but we will gloss over this for the current discussion.

(61)

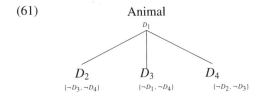

I will assume that there are constraints on the possible combinations of discriminants defining a partitioning, but I will not address these issues here. In the above structure, a legitimate subtype is constructed from those expressions with only one positive discriminant value for the three predicates in question. This generates a shallow structure for animal types as shown below.

(62)

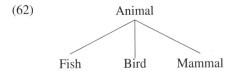

It should be noted that, in general, the discriminants used to create the natural types are both logical and natural predicates.

In addition to the types of discriminant predicates encountered so far, it is possible to justify several other classes of opposition structures. One of the most prevalent in natural language lexicons is the privative/nonprivative opposition pairing. Examples of adjectives with this behavior include fully lexicalized pairs such as "dead/alive," as well as privative anchors with a lexical gap, such as "bald." The type structure accounting for this ordering is given as follows:

(63)   a. Binary Ordered Property:
       b. $< \sigma_1, \sigma_2, \tau, \sqcup, <, \sqsubseteq >$ *realizes* a binary predicate P, where τ is a local top type for this sortal array, such that $\sigma_1, \sigma_2 \sqsubseteq \tau$, and $\sigma_1 < \sigma_2$.
       c.

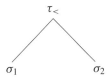

The nature of polar attributes such as "sick/healthy" and "tall/short" is defined in terms of a sortal array with distinguished elements.

(64)   a. Polar Property:
       b. $< \Sigma, \tau, \sqcup, <, \sqsubseteq >$ *realizes* a predicate P, where Σ is a sortal array of types, τ is a local top type for this sortal array, such that $\sigma_1, \ldots, \sigma_n \in \Sigma$

for $\sigma_i \sqsubseteq \tau$, and $\sigma_i < \sigma_{i+1}$, and there are two poles, σ_1, and σ_n, that are distinguished sorts.

c.

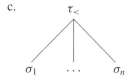

Thus far, I have focused on the construction of types within the naturals. Let us now turn briefly to a discussion on subtyping relations in the domain of functional types, $\mathcal{F}$. Unlike the natural types, where subtypes are defined in terms of natural tangible discriminants, subtyping in $\mathcal{F}$ operates in an entirely different manner, namely, in terms of functional behavior. Thus, the domain of $\mathcal{F}$ will appear to be socially arbitrary and less consistent cross-linguistically, because the lexicalization illustrates socially dependent concepts rather than the more universally grounded discriminants of the naturals.

As a case in point, consider the semilattice associated with the functional concept beverage. The conventional qualia structure for beverage is shown in (65), while the corresponding type structure is *liquid* $\otimes$ *drink$_T$*.

$$(65) \quad \begin{bmatrix} \textbf{beverage} \\ \text{ARGSTR} = \begin{bmatrix} \text{ARG1} = \text{x} : \texttt{liquid} \end{bmatrix} \\ \text{QUALIA} = \begin{bmatrix} \text{FORMAL} = \text{x} \\ \text{TELIC} = \texttt{drink}(\text{e}^P, \text{y}, \text{x}) \end{bmatrix} \end{bmatrix}$$

The subtypes of beverages, as exemplified in our language lexicalizations, are classified according to functional principles (i.e., the TELIC) rather than natural discriminants, such as with animals or trees. Hence, we have drinks that wake us up, drinks that refresh us, drinks that relax us, and so forth. The operative discriminants are all functionally defined, however. As a lattice structure, the ground type (the natural base) for beverage is `liquid`, and the tensor type value for the TELIC is specialized according to the particular subtype activity. This is illustrated in (66) below.

(66)

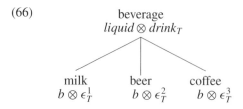

The first thing to note about this structure is that the functional discriminants can be *uniquely* determined for the subtypes of the functional type. For example, a beverage might be defined in terms of its use in a religious cerimony (e.g., "altar wine"). The complement of this discriminant is not particularly informative for the other sorts in the array. The second point to make regarding functional subtyping in $\mathcal{F}$ is that in many cases there is no justifiable natural subtyping relation between two types. Thus, materially, a table is a table, but the functional specification that determines that a work table is different from a kitchen table is not necessarily part of the discriminant family in $\mathcal{N}$.

Another fact illustrated by the structure in (66) is that functionally defined objects have multiple TELIC roles through inheritance, where some values are more proximate than others. In the case of "coffee," for example, it would appear to be the following:

(67) $liquid \otimes drink_T \otimes \epsilon_T^3$

where the "discriminating" quale value (relative to beverage) is that it is used for keeping one alert. However this cluster of properties is to be described – here it is modeled as controlled event descriptions – this is a more proximate description of the drink than that associated with beverages in general.

Although this functional type description for the types under beverage seems motivated, this appears to have some problematic consequences for how coercion exploits the events associated with the objects, as shown in the sentence below.

(68)   John finished the coffee.

If coercion is defined as selecting the outermost type of the object by the governing verb, then we have a puzzle, because the proximate TELIC of "coffee" is actually defined relative to how it is distinguished from the other beverages. However, this gives the wrong results, as the derivation below illustrates.

(69)

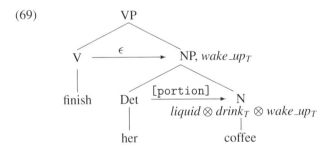

This would predict that the interpretation of the sentence is "finishing (the effects of) the coffee," which is obviously incorrect. What is clearly going on is an embedding or recursive structure with the type structure, where the TELIC of TELIC is referenced. As a qualia structure, this would correspond to something like (70), where the inherited TELIC is embedded as the AGENTIVE of the proximate TELIC, and whose TELIC value is "waking up."

(70)

$$
\begin{bmatrix}
\textbf{coffee} \\
\text{ARGSTR} = \begin{bmatrix} \text{ARG1} = x : \texttt{liquid} \\ \text{D\_ARG} = y : \texttt{human} \end{bmatrix} \\
\text{QUALIA} = \begin{bmatrix} \text{FORMAL} = x \\ \text{TELIC} = \begin{bmatrix} \text{TELIC} = \texttt{wake\_up}(e^T, y) \\ \text{AGENTIVE} = \texttt{drink}(e^P, y, x) \end{bmatrix} \end{bmatrix}
\end{bmatrix}
$$

Abstracted as a type structure, this would be simply *liquid* $\otimes$ (*drink$_T$* $\otimes$ *wake_up$_T$*). Given these assumptions, the coercion will now select the appropriate TELIC value, as illustrated in (71) below.

(71)

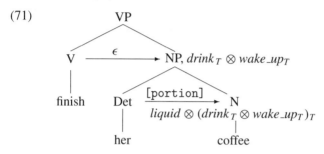

8   The Conceptual Architecture

In this paper, I have presented a new architecture for a type structure corresponding to the concepts of natural language expressions. First, I abstracted away from the conventional type feature structure interpretation of qualia structure to present concepts as ground types and type constructions. The qualia structure of (72) becomes a typing specification as shown in (73).

(72)

$$
\begin{bmatrix}
x \\
\text{QUALIA} = \begin{bmatrix} \text{CONST} = \tau \\ \text{FORMAL} = \alpha \\ \text{TELIC} = \epsilon_T \\ \text{AGENTIVE} = \epsilon_A \end{bmatrix}
\end{bmatrix}
$$

(73) $x :$
$$
\begin{bmatrix}
\alpha \\
\text{QUALIA} = \begin{bmatrix} \text{\textcircled{c}} = \tau \\ \otimes = \epsilon_T \\ \otimes = \epsilon_A \end{bmatrix}
\end{bmatrix}
$$

Furthermore, I have motivated a three-way distinction of increasingly complex

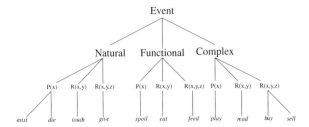

Fig. 7.5. Event/relation lattice.

types (or ranks), as summarized below:

(a) NATURAL TYPES: Predication from the domain of substance, e.g., the qualia FORMAL or CONST.

(b) FUNCTIONAL TYPES: Predication includes reference to either AGENTIVE or TELIC qualia.

(c) COMPLEX TYPES: Cartesian type formed by Dot Object Construction.

Similarly, the domains of relations and properties are also partitioned into three ranks:

(a) NATURAL EVENTS: Arguments in the predicate or relation are only from the domain of substance, e.g., the qualia FORMAL or CONST.

(b) FUNCTIONAL EVENTS: At least one argument in the predicate or relation is a functional type, f, e.g., makes reference to either AGENTIVE or TELIC qualia.

(c) COMPLEX EVENTS: At least one argument in the predicate or relation is a complex type, e.g., a type formed by Dot Object Construction.

The resulting top structure of the types denoting events is shown in Figure 7.5.[8]

Although we have yet to discuss the typing of attributive properties, a few remarks are in order. Just as with the distinctions seen in entities and relations, attributes can be usefully distinguished as ordered according to the same principles, as suggested in the type structure in Figure 7.6.

---

[8] Following Pustejovsky (1998b), I assume that there is an order of predicates, given as 1-place, 2-place, and 3-place relations. Furthermore, I assume that for 1-place predicates, the constraints on sortal domains discussed above apply. For 2-place predicates, the following *Relational Class Constraints* apply:
(i) Constraints on 2-place Relation, R_2:
Reflexivity; Symmetry; Antireflexivity; Antisymmetry.
For 3-place relations, we have the following constraints operative:
(ii) Constraints on 3-place Relation R_3:
Partial Pairwise Reflexivity; Partial Pairwise Symmetry; Partial Pairwise Antireflexivity; Partial Pairwise Antisymmetry.

Fig. 7.6. Property lattice.

The same patterns of entailment hold for judgments involving the different modes of attribution as with the relations. These phenomena are discussed further in Pustejovsky (forthcoming).

Given what we have presented, the overall architecture of the type system is summarized in Figure 7.7.

In this paper I have outlined a methodology for the construction of ontological types based on the dual concerns of capturing linguistic generalizations and satisfying metaphysical considerations. I have tried to show that the flat and homogeneous formal typing models are too weak to model and describe language and its meaning. To fill this gap, I have presented extensions to Generative Lexicon Theory employing a ranking of types, distinguishing between natural types and functional types, and then complex types. I concluded with a discussion of how the different ranks of types have distinct operations defining the type-subtype relation. This is important for lexicon design, because it shows how conventional models of type structures are too homogeneous in structure for capturing the semantic richness behind natural language expressions.

Appendix: Interpreting the Qualia

The remarks below will hopefully clarify some of the formal aspects of the qualia structure as presented in the discussion above. These explanations are adapted from Pustejovsky (1998a).

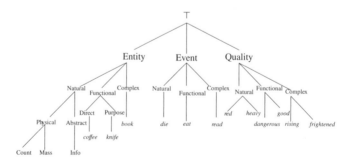

Fig. 7.7. Tripartite concept lattice.

Assuming that the FORMAL as defined above has a natural interpretation, we begin with a suggestive translation of the constitutive mode, CONST:

(74) $Const(\lambda x[\alpha(x)]) = \lambda y[Q(y)] \leftrightarrow$
$\qquad \forall x[\alpha(x) \rightarrow \exists y[Q(y) \wedge made\_of(x, y)]$

(75) a.
$$
\begin{bmatrix}
\textbf{snowball} \\
\text{ARGSTR} = \begin{bmatrix} \text{ARG1} = x \\ \text{D-ARG1} = y \end{bmatrix} \\[2ex]
\text{QUALIA} = \begin{bmatrix} \text{FORMAL} = \texttt{ball(x)} \\ \text{CONST} = \texttt{snow(y)} \end{bmatrix}
\end{bmatrix} \Rightarrow
$$

b. $\lambda x[ball(x) \wedge const(x) = \lambda y[snow(y)]]$

The AGENTIVE quale makes reference to the mode of coming into being:

(76) $\forall x, e[\alpha(e, x) \rightarrow \exists e'\exists y[\psi(e') \wedge e' \prec e \wedge make(e', y, x)]]$

(77) a.
$$
\begin{bmatrix}
\textbf{wine} \\
\text{ARGSTR} = \begin{bmatrix} \text{ARG1} = x \\ \text{D-ARG1} = y \end{bmatrix} \\[1ex]
\text{EVENTSTR} = [\text{D-E1} = e] \\[1ex]
\text{QUALIA} = \begin{bmatrix} \text{FORMAL} = \texttt{liquid(x)} \\ \text{AGENTIVE} = \texttt{make(e, y, x)} \end{bmatrix}
\end{bmatrix} \Rightarrow
$$

b. $\lambda x[wine(x) : formal(x) = \lambda x[liquid](x) \wedge agentive(x)$
$\qquad\qquad\qquad\qquad = \lambda e[\psi(e)]]$

Making reference to TELIC enriches the structure even more:

(78) $Telic(\lambda x[\alpha(x)]) = \lambda y \lambda e \exists x[\phi(e, y, x)] \leftrightarrow$
$\qquad \lambda y \forall x \forall e \forall y[\psi_\alpha(e, y, x) > \exists e'[(\phi(e', y, x) \wedge e < e']]$

In this representation of TELIC, ψ_α denotes the appropriate circumstances of doing something to an x of type α, and $>$ is again the default conditional of Asher and Morreau (1991).

Applying this interpretation to the artifactual liquid "wine" gives the following expanded interpretation:

(79) $\lambda x \exists e[wine(e, x) : formal(x) = \lambda x[liquid(x)]$
$\qquad \wedge\ agentive(x) = \lambda e[\psi(e)]$
$\qquad \wedge\ telic(x)\ =\ \lambda e \lambda y[drink(e, y, x)]]$

Then, with the full definitions of TELIC and AGENTIVE substituted, this expression becomes:

(80)　　$\lambda x \exists e', e, y[wine(e, x) : formal(x) = liquid(x)$
　　　　$\wedge\ agentive(x) = [\psi(e') \wedge e' \prec e \wedge make(e', y, x)]$
　　　　$\wedge\ telic(x) = \lambda y \forall e[\psi_{wine}(e, y, x) > \exists e'[(drink(e', y, x)]]]$

This expression now captures our intuitions about a qualia-based interpretation of word meanings; in this case, that wine is a particular liquid made for the purpose of drinking.

Acknowledgments

This paper is a revision of "Specification of a Top Concept Lattice: Version 1.0," a manuscript from April, 1998, where the basic proposal for a tripartite type structure was proposed. Subsequent work on the SIMPLE model (Busa et al., 1999) implemented and greatly expanded on this proposal and contributed significantly to pointing out several gaps in the original model. The present paper has profited greatly from the work done in the SIMPLE group, as well as from other colleagues. In particular, I would like to thank Nicholas Asher, Federica Busa, Jose Castano, and Bob Ingria for useful comments and suggestions to this paper. All remaining inconsistencies are my own.

References

Anscombe, G. E. M. 1958. On Brute Facts. *Analysis* 18: 3.

Asher, N., and Morreau, M. (1991). Common Sense Entailment: A Modal theory of Nonmonotomic Reasoning. In Proc. to the 12th International Conference on Artificial Intelligence, Sydney, Australia, 387–392.

Asher, N., and Pustejovsky, J. 1999. The Metaphysics of Words. manuscript. Brandeis University and University of Texas.

Bach, E. 1986. The Algebra of Events. *Linguistics and Philosophy* 9: 5–16.

Bouillon, P. 1997. *Polymorphie et sémantique lexicale : le cas des adjectifs.* Presses Universitaires du Spetentrion, Lille.

Bouillon, P., and Busa, F. (forthcoming). Where's the polysemy? A study of adjective-noun constructions. *Proc. Second Workshop on Lexical Semantics Systems,* Pisa, Italy.

Busa, F. 1996. *Compositionality and the Semantics of Nominals,* Ph.D. Dissertation, Brandeis University.

Busa, F., Calzolari, N., Lenci, A., and Pustejovsky, J. 1999. Building a Semantic Lexicon: Structuring and Generating Concepts. *Proc. IWCS-III,* Tilberg, The Netherlands.

Carnap, R. 1928. *The Logical Structure of the World,* University of Chicago Press, Chicago.

Horn, L. R. 1989. *A Natural History of Negation.* Chicago, University of Chicago Press.

Johansson, I. 1989. *Ontological Investigations,* Routledge, London.

Link, G. 1998. *Algebraic Semantics in Language and Philosophy.* CSLI, Cambridge University Press, Cambridge.

Parsons, T. (1990). *Events in the Semantics of English,* MIT Press, Cambridge, MA.

Pustejovsky, J. 1993. Type Coercion and Lexical Selection. In J. Pustejovsky (ed.), *Semantics and the Lexicon.* Kluwer Academic Publishers, Dordrecht, The Netherlands.

Pustejovsky, J. 1995. *The Generative Lexicon.* MIT Press, Cambridge, MA.

Pustejovsky, J. 1998a. Generativity and Explanation in Semantics. *Linguistic Inquiry*, 29:2, 289–311 .

Pustejovsky, J. 1998b. Specification of the Top Lattice. manuscript. Brandeis University.

Pustejovsky, J. 1999. The Semantics of Lexical Underspecification. *Folia Linguistica* XXXII.

Pustejovsky, J. (forthcoming). *Language Meaning and The Logic of Concepts*. MIT Press, Cambridge, MA.

Putnam, H. 1975. The Meaning of 'Meaning.' *Mind, Language, and Reality: Philosophical Papers* 2: 215–271.

Quine, W. V. 1962. *Word and Object*. MIT Press, Cambridge.

Searle, J. 1995. *The Construction of Social Reality*, Free Press, New York.

Simons, P. 1987. *Parts: A Study in Ontology*. Clarendon Press, Oxford.

Smith, B. (ed.) 1982. *Parts and Moments: Studies in Logic and Formal Ontology*. Philosophia, München.

von Wright, G. 1963. *Norm and Action: A Logical Inquiry*. Routledge and Kegan Paul, London.

8   Underspecification, Context Selection, and Generativity

JACQUES JAYEZ

Abstract

The idea that semantic representations are *underspecified*, that is more abstract than the specific interpretations obtained in various contexts, is by now current in lexical semantics. However, the way in which underspecified representations give rise to more precise interpretations in particular contexts is not always clear. On one view, context provides missing information, for instance because it contains salient entities that can be referred to. I consider here the symmetric dependency, in which lexical elements impose certain semantic profiles to the contexts they fit in. I show that, although they are highly underspecified, those profiles cannot be reduced to a general semantic frame, unlike what is proposed in Pustejovsky's *Generative Lexicon*, and that their semantic adaptability reflects the highly abstract and similarity-based character (vagueness) of the predicates that help to define them.

1   Introduction

Recent work about the relation between lexical items, context, and interpretation has highlighted two notions of *underspecification* (see van Deemter and Peters, 1996 for various points of view). In some approaches, underspecification amounts to code ambiguities in an efficient way, to avoid carrying a set of alternatives during the interpretation process (Reyle, 1995). In the domain of the lexicon, underspecification sometimes takes the form of information enrichment. Instead of positing multiple lexical homonymous entries, researchers tend to prefer a complex information structure, in which the existence of various subparts accounts for the flexibility of interpretation (Copestake and Briscoe, 1995; Pustejovsky, 1995). Which subpart(s) is (are) then accessed in the interpretation process depends either on the selection restrictions of other items or on general discourse organization principles. The first case is illustrated by compositional procedures like "coercion" (Pustejovsky, 1995), the other case by various discourse constraints (Asher and Lascarides, 1995; Lascarides and Copestake, 1995, Lascarides et al., 1996). The present paper pursues this general line of reasoning about the specific problem of *context selection*.

It is well-known that certain items are appropriate only in certain types of contexts. For example, hierarchy/politeness markers or constructions depend on social relations and interactional situations (Brown and Levinson, 1987). More generally, many works in cognitive linguistics assume that meaning is underspecified and the context provides the necessary clues to flesh it out (Fauconnier, 1997). However,

124

there is a complementary mechanism of *context selection*, in which some lexical items impose constraints on the types of context in which they can occur.

In this chapter, I illustrate this mechanism by studying three French verbs: *"faire penser à"* (≈ to call to mind), *"suggérer"* (≈ to suggest) and *"attendre"* (≈ to wait or to await), which give a good idea of the complexity and flexibility of context selection. I start with some uses of *"faire penser à,"* whose treatment encompasses the main aspects of context selection. Then I turn to two shorter examples (some uses of *"suggérer"* and *"attendre"*), which expand on the general theme of semantic *vagueness*.

In section 4, I discuss the connection between vagueness and semantic flexibility. It is well-known that lexical items can be used in highly different contexts, which cannot be enumerated in advance. This reusability can be called *generativity*, by analogy with the similar properties of grammatical structures. The analysis of context selection suggests that semantic constraints are too local to explain generativity, in contrast with what is proposed in the framework of *Generative Lexicon* (Pustejovsky, 1995). Lexical items behave essentially as idiomatic units that package small sets of partly related senses, and, in this respect, resemble the *constructions* of Constructional Grammar (Fillmore et al., 1988; Goldberg, 1994; Jurafsky, 1993; Kay, 1998). Generativity reflects rather the inherent vagueness of the primitives that semantic representations use.

2   Introducing Context Selection with a Nontrivial Example

In this section, I consider the French verb *"faire penser à"* with a nonanimate subject in two of its constructions illustrated by (1a) and (1b)–(1d). There is also a VP complement construction, which I ignore here because it is relatively unproblematic.

(1)   a. *La violence du   vent fait   plutôt penser   que c'est un*
          The violence of the wind makes rather think–INF that it is a
          cyclone qui   se prépare
          typhoon which is coming
       b. *Ce   chat fait   penser   à un tigre*
          This cat   makes think–INF of a tiger
       c. *L' atmosphère du   lieu fait   penser   à un tableau*
          The atmosphere of the place makes think–INF of a   painting
          de Corot
          by Corot
       d. *La violence du   vent fait   plutôt penser   à un*
          The violence of the wind makes rather think–INF of a
          cyclone[1]
          typhoon

---

[1]   It should be noted that the adverb *"plutôt"* (rather) is necessary for the example to be fully natural. I return to this problem in section (2.2).

With a sentential complement, "*faire penser*" means roughly 'to evoke,' 'to point to,' etc. So, (1a) can be paraphrased as 'The violence of the wind suggests that a typhoon is coming.' This sense will be noted by the label **resemble–hint**. With a nominal complement, "*faire penser*" has two main senses. The first is illustrated by (1b) or (1c) and can be glossed by 'to resemble.' (1b) means 'This cat resembles a tiger.' (1c) means 'The atmosphere of the place resembles that of a painting by Corot.' Let us note this sense by **resemble**. The second is illustrated by (1d) and can be glossed again by 'to evoke,' 'to point to,' etc. (1d) means 'The violence of the wind suggests that there is or will be a typhoon.' So, this second sense is actually the **resemble–hint** sense of the clausal construction. It is plausible that the **resemble** sense and the **resemble–hint** sense are connected, as they are for the French "*évoquer*" and "*suggérer*" and their English counterparts 'to evoke' and 'to suggest.' The **resemble** sense is used when there is a direct resemblance between properties of objects, individuals, or situations. The **resemble–hint** sense is used when the subject of the verb denotes an abstract object[2] in the sense of Asher (1993), that is an event, a fact or a proposition that (i) resembles some other abstract object typically found in the kind of situation (indirectly) denoted by the NP complement and (ii) might be explained by assuming that this situation obtains or obtained. Clearly, (i) is conducive to (ii) in many contexts. For instance, (1d) means that the actual wind resembles the kind of wind which is to be found in typhoons and might be explained by assuming that a typhoon is coming. In spite of their semantic similarity, constructions where the two senses emerge are subject to different constraints. In the following, I consider only the **resemble–hint** sense, which is by far the more difficult to describe.

2.1   *The Sentential Complement Construction*

In this chapter, I use an HPSG–style representation (Pollard and Sag, 1994) as consistently as possible to clarify the connection between subcategorization and semantic selection (or, more generally, semantic constraints). In HPSG, lexical or phrasal linguistic signs are represented as typed feature structures (Carpenter, 1992). A typed feature structure $\mathcal{F}$ is a finite conjunction of equations $\bigwedge F_i = v_i$, where the F_i's are features (or *attributes*) and the v_i their typed values. A sketchy graphical representation for the sentential complement case is given in Figure 8.1.

Feature structures are delimited by square brackets. Lists of elements are delimited by angle brackets. The features are in small caps, while the types are in boldface. The value of a feature can be a feature structure (of a certain type) or an atomic type (in boldface, because it is a type). Usually, the types can be atomic or

---

[2] Examples where the subject denotes another type of entity are at best marginal. For example, *La* $^{?or??}$*maison fait penser qu'il y a eu une tempête* (The house (lit. makes think) that there was a storm), or *La* $^{??}$*maison fait penser à une tempête* (The house (lit. makes think of) a storm), under the interpretation 'The state of the house suggests that there was a storm.'

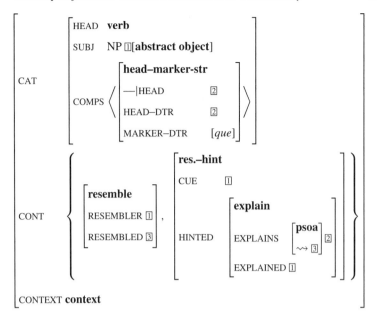

Fig. 8.1.

stand for (partially specified) feature structures. For example, the type **verb** stands for a feature structure that contains information about the morphological status (finite, infinitive, etc.) of the verb, its status as an auxiliary (yes or no), etc. The same is true for major preterminal categories (nouns, adjectives, etc.). For every category, the main syntactic information is stored in the value of a feature CAT. The HEAD feature holds the main syntactic properties (the type **verb** for a verb, **noun** for a noun, etc.). The feature SUBJ contains the subject and the feature COMPS the list of complements. Normally, an ARG-S feature contains the subcategorization list of the lexical item. Because, in the cases considered here, it is always the concatenation of the list values of SUBJ and COMPS, I will omit it. The CONT feature points to the semantic structure associated with the syntactic subcategorization (or, more generally, the syntactic configuration). Note that, in the present case, it is a list of feature structures. The roles of the main participants show as features and receive self-explaining labels (N–or, N–ed, N–ee, etc.). The feature CONTEXT points to contextual information (of type **context**), which is left undetermined at the moment.

The reader should pay special attention to two points. First, the tags $\boxed{1}$, $\boxed{2}$, etc. are pointers to the CONT values of the structure they are appended to. For instance, NP $\boxed{i}$ denotes the CONT value of a NP structure. Having pointers to CONT values allows us to handle the semantic information more easily. Second, I adopt Davis' (1996) proposal that semantic structures (the members of CONT) be explicitly typed. So, in Figure 8.1, the type of the first element of the CONT list value is

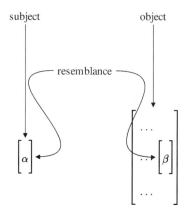

Fig. 8.2.

resemble. The type of the second element is **resemble–hint** (**res.–hint** for short), etc. The types of the structures determine the attributes and the range of values that belong to the structure. The type **psoa** (for 'parameterized state of affairs') is that of propositional contents.

In Figure 8.1, the object complement of "*faire penser*" is a structure headed by a clause (a sentence, in French) with a marker–daughter (such as "*que*" in French or "*that*," "*for*" in English, etc.). The CONTENT value reflects the intuitive analysis proposed above. The first element expresses the resemblance relation that holds between the denotation of the subject and some substructure, tagged as ③, in the denotation of the complement. In general, we cannot know in advance that role is filled by the element that resembles the denotation of the subject. For example, in (1a), the intuitive interpretation is that the wind is as violent as the kind of wind that is to be found in typhoons. This is awfully vague, but it is not possible to discuss here the various models of analogy that exist in the semantic and AI literature (see French, 1995, for a broad perspective). For clarity, I will impose the following simplistic condition: at *some* level of analysis, the feature structure that corresponds to the complement head of the verb must host a substructure that is linked to the denotation of the subject by the resemblance relation. This is illustrated in the next schema. (see Figure 8.2).

Formally, we have to require that β be one of the substructures of the denotation of the object head. This is what the symbol $\leadsto$ says in Figure 8.1. It is understood as a type. So, we say that a structure $\mathcal{F}$ is of type $\leadsto\mathcal{F}'$:

(2) $\leadsto x$ **Type** Let $\mathcal{F}$ be a feature structure. $\mathcal{F}$ is of type $\leadsto\mathcal{F}'$ whenever $\mathcal{F}'$ is the value of one of the features of $\mathcal{F}$ or some value of a feature in $\mathcal{F}$ is of type $\leadsto\mathcal{F}'$.[3]

---

[3] This notion is quite similar to that of *functional uncertainty* in Lexical Functional Grammar (see Kaplan and Maxwell, 1988).

The feature structure that hosts the ⤳ constraint is the denotation of the sentential complement and the value of EXPLAINS in the structure of type **res.–hint**. In this latter structure, the CUE is the denotation of the subject, that is the information that 'points to' what is HINTED, namely that the denotation of the sentential complement explains the denotation of the subject. So, in the sentential complement construction, the **resemble–hint** sense shows underspecification on the entity that the denotation of the subject resembles.

2.2   The Problem of Nominal Complements

At first sight, the case of NP complements is not extremely different and the corresponding feature structure is that of Figure 8.1 with minor syntactic adaptation. However, we noted above that example (1d) needed the adverb "*plutôt*" to be natural. This observation is not isolated, as evidenced by the following contrasts.

(3)   a. *La   réaction des   marchés fait   penser   qu' il y a*
            The reaction of the market   makes think–INF that there is
            une crise monétaire
            a   crisis monetary

         b. *La   réaction des   marchés fait   penser   à *?*une crise*
            The reaction of the market   makes think–INF of   a   crisis
            monétaire
            monetary

         c. *La   réaction des   marchés fait   plutôt penser   à une*
            The reaction of the market   makes rather think–INF of a
            crise monétaire
            crisis monetary

         d. *Les résultats du   groupe font penser   qu' il y a eu*
            The results   of the holding make think–INF that there was
            une mauvaise gestion
            a   mismanagement

         e. *Les résultats du   groupe font penser   à *?*une*
            The results   of the holding make think–INF of   a
            mauvaise gestion
            mismanagement

         f. *Jean pense que le   groupe a   des difficultés de trésorerie,*
            John thinks that the holding has difficulties   of cash–flow,
            mais les résultats font   penser   á une mauvaise gestion
            but   the results   make think–INF of a   mismanagement

         g. *Jean pense que le   groupe a   des difficultés de trésorerie,*
            John thinks that the holding has difficulties   of cash–flow,

> *mais les résultats font   plutôt penser   à une*
> but   the results   make rather think–INF of a
> *mauvaise gestion*
> mismanagement

h. *Les résultats du   groupe font   plutôt penser   à une*
   The results   of the holding make rather think–INF of a
   mauvaise gestation
   mismanagement

The regularity that emerges from these examples (and from many similar ones) is the following. When *"faire penser à"* is used in its **resemble–hint** sense, nominal complement are not very natural unless they are connected with a proposition in the context. In cases like (3f), the proposition is already in the context. It expresses the opinion of John that the holding is experiencing cash-flow difficulties. The nominal complement stands for the proposition that there is some kind of mismanagement and the sentence with *"faire penser à"* indicates that it is rather the mismanagement that explains the poor results of the holding. In cases like (3h), because of the adverb *"plutôt"* (rather), there is a presupposition that some relevant proposition already exists in the context. Many examples that sound strange are significantly improved by adding *"plutôt"* (rather), *"même"* (even), *"aussi"* (too), *"seulement"* (only), etc. It is well-known from the literature on focus that those adverbs are associated with focus-background phenomena.[4] It is generally assumed, at an intuitive level, that such adverbs give access to 'alternative propositions,' which differ from the actual proposition with respect to the identity of the focus. For instance, "John saw only Mary" asserts that John saw Mary and negates alternative propositions of form "John saw x," where x is different from Mary. Similarly, "Mary will rather choose John" asserts that Mary will choose John, but points to alternative propositions of form "Mary will choose x," where x is different from John. The effect of focus adverbials is then to force the assumption that there is some alternative proposition in the context.

2.3   A Simple Constraint-Based Approach

Verbs like *"faire penser,"* *"évoquer"* (to evoke), and *"suggérer"* (to suggest) behave in a similar way. We can say that such verbs inspect the value of CONTEXT to find some alternative proposition, which has been introduced in previous discourse or is forced by a focus adverbial. Clearly, we are not concerned here with the general definition of "alternativeness." Alternativeness is (partly) different from adverb to adverb and depends on the conception of "parallelism" one entertains, that is on the way in which propositions are compared. I will assume that the current litterature on focus adverbials and general models of parallelism, such as Pullman's (1997) approach, allow us to define a reasonable notion of alternativeness. I will use

---

[4] See Rooth 1985 and 1992; Krifka, 1992; Bonomi and Casalegno, 1993; Nølke, 1983 for some descriptive and formal properties of such adverbs.

the black box-like predicate *alternative*(x, y) without trying to substantiate its content.[5]

In contrast, the notion of context inspection is crucial. The NP complement construction is not "passive" with respect to the context. It either requires that some relevant information be already present in it or uses the presupposition that it is, in the case of focus adverbs. This shows that the representation of Figure 8.1 is not sufficient. We need a device that *checks* the availability of some information in the context. We cannot simply use unification here because unification forces existence. If we declare some contextual content, this content will be introduced in the context by the mechanism of unification, whereas we want it to be *retrieved* from the context. There are two mains options to augment unification. One is to use dynamic notions from the object–oriented paradigm (as proposed in Jayez and Godard, 1995). This option is powerful but complex. The other solution is to add external constraints to feature structures. I will follow this track here, because of its simplicity. I will assume that feature structures are equipped with a feature CONSTRAINTS, which contains conditions that are not amenable to unification.

The value of CONSTRAINTS indicates that the context contains an alternative proposition 4 with respect to the denotation of the complement. I assume that CONTEXT has a feature PREVDIS that contains a list of the contents associated with previous sentences. Therefore, if there are n previous contents up to the current point of discourse, PREVDIS will contain a list of form ⟨1, ..., n⟩. The resulting feature structure for *"faire penser à"* + NP is shown below. (See Figure 8.3).

In a sentence like (3f), the value of 4 corresponds to the proposition 'John thinks that the holding is experiencing difficulties of cash-flow.' It is an alternative with respect to the suggested explanation for 1 (the denotation of the subject), that is 2, the denotation of the complement. How does this mechanism interact with adverbs like *"plutôt"* (rather)? Standard tests on adverb scope in French (Molinier, 1984) tend to show that *"plutôt"* is a VP adverb.[6] In HPSG, adjuncts have a special feature MOD, which contains information on the phrase to which they are adjoined. I assume that *"plutôt"* introduces in the CONTEXT|PREVDIS of the VP to which it is adjoined at least one psoa, which is an alternative with respect to the VP. The detailed way in which it can be done is outside the scope of the present description, because it involves the general treatment of focus and background in HPSG (see Engdahl and Vallduví, 1996 for a survey). Such psoa's can then be retrieved at a later stage of the compositional process.

Under this representation, the verb imposes constraints on previous discourse. Although these constraints remain abstract, they are not on a par with general

---

[5] Any candidate definition for this predicate should incorporate the observation that parallelism and alternativeness extend beyond simple argument structure correspondence. For instance, "John thinks that Mary is late" and "Sue is late" are 'parallel' in a suitable sense, as evidenced by the possibility of sentences like "John thinks that Mary is late, but, in fact, SUE is late." (3f) shows the same parallelism.

[6] This is not a crucial point, because the present assumptions could be adapted to sentential adverbs.

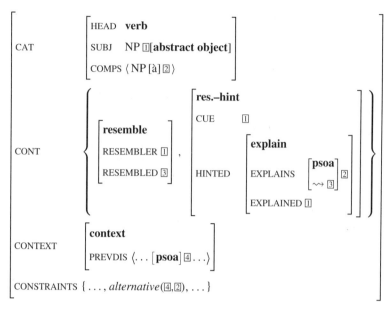

Fig. 8.3.

semantic or pragmatic principles. Any analysis of the *alternative* and RESEMBLE relations[7] can be incorporated in the representation to narrow the set of possible candidates. So the *factors* of vagueness are identified and can be acted upon to increase precision.

3   Shadow Meanings

3.1   The "suggérer" Case

With a nonanimate subject, the verb "*suggérer*" (to suggest) is similar to "*faire penser à*." I consider here the animate subject case, illustrated by the following two examples.

(4)   a. *J' ai suggéré Jean (à Marie)*
            I suggested John (to Mary)
        b. *J' ai suggéré (à Marie) qu' on aille*$_{subj}$ *nager*
            I suggested (to Mary) that we go   swimming

For "*suggérer*" to be felicitous with animate subjects, what is suggested must be a certain *choice*, not an explanation for the truth or occurrence of some abstract

---

[7] Note that RESEMBLE could be taken out of the regular feature set and put into CONSTRAINTS. I chose to favor the similarity with Figure 8.1.

object, in contrast with the semantic structures of Figures 8.1 and 8.3. Let us start with the *"que"*–clause construction, which, as in the *"faire penser"* case, is easier to describe.

The *"suggérer que P"* Construction

The paraphrase of a construction x (animate) *"suggère que"* y *"à"* z (animate) is: x suggests that z choose y as the preferred course of action. The author of the suggestion cannot simply predict or describe what is going to happen. That is why, in languages such as French or English, the indicative mood, which indicates descriptions or predictions, is marked after *"suggérer"* or "suggest," for the sense considered in this section. The subjunctive, the mood of *modus irrealis*, constitutes the unmarked option. Optative verbs like *"souhaiter"* (to wish) or *"désirer"* (to desire) also demand the subjunctive mood. The difference between suggestion and desire is that z (the suggestee) must take some action, if she follows the suggestion, whereas nothing such is required for desire. That is why *"suggérer"* is strange when its clausal complement expresses something that evades the control of the suggestee under normal circumstances.

(5)   *Je* $^{??}$ *suggère que tu   ne sois*$_{subj}$ *pas malade*
        I   suggest that you be   not ill

Moreover, the control must be intentional. Even if a causal factor has the power to bring about some state of affairs, one may not ask the suggestee to use this factor in a covert way.

(6)   *Je* $^{??}$ *suggère que le   courant d'air raffraîchisse*$_{subj}$ *la   pièce*
        I   suggest that the draught   cool   the room
        (Intended interpretation: 'I suggest that you create a draught to cool the room')

(6) is not felicitous because the complement clause does not mention any intentionally controlled action. Neither is it possible that the clausal complement denotes a state.[8]

(7)   *Je* $^{??}$ *suggère que tu   connaisses*$_{subj}$ *le   résultat*
        Je   suggest that you know   the result

Summarizing, in this construction, *"suggérer"* introduces a proposition denoting an action (co–)controlled by the suggestee. The suggestee must be different from the suggestor. That is why, in the construction *"suggérer à z de y"* (to suggest to z to y), where *"suggérer"* is an object equi verb, the *"nous"* (us) pronoun is very strange (*"Je"* $^{??}$ *"nous suggère de"* = I suggest to us to).

---

[8] This is particularly clear for states that correspond to uncontrolled Carlsonian individual-level properties (being intelligent) or Vendlerian states (knowing, loving, being parked in the street, etc.). However, we need a more complete analysis to evaluate seriously the compatibilities and incompatibilities.

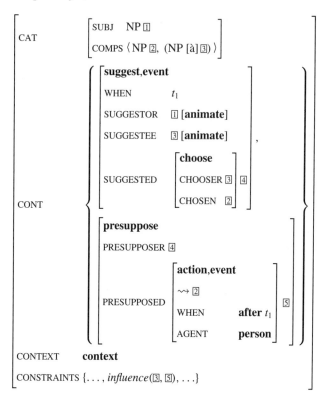

Fig. 8.4.

The *"suggérer"* + *NP* construction

This construction is semantically less clear. The paraphrase for *x* *"suggère"* *y* (*à z*) (*x* suggests *y* (to *z*)) is: *x* suggests that a person *z* choose *y* to play some role in a future action (the choice's theme), which is (indirectly) controlled by the same person *z*. The main difference with the clausal complement case is that the controlled action remains implicit. We have the following representation (Figure 8.4).

This representation says that the suggestor suggests to the suggestee to choose somebody or something that/who plays some role in a future action controlled by some person. The choice presupposes[9] that the chosen entity plays some role in the future action. It is not necessary that the chosen entity be animate, as evidenced by sentences like *Je suggère sa machine pour faire les calculs* (I suggest her machine

---

[9] The plausibility of the implicit future action survives negation and interrogation. For instance, if *Jean a suggéré Marie* (John suggested Mary) means that John suggested Mary to do A (an action), the negation (*Jean n'a pas suggéré Marie*) means that John did not suggest Mary to do A and the question (*Est-ce que Jean a suggéré Marie?*) means 'Did John suggest Mary to do A?'. This shows that the future action is presupposed.

to do the computation), under the interpretation 'I suggest that we choose her machine to do the computation.' As in the clausal complement case, the theme of the choice (the value of PRESUPPOSED) may not be a future state of affairs on which the suggestee has absolutely no control, whence the oddity of (8).

(8)   *Jean ne savait pas qui viendrait   à coup sûr cet après–midi.*
        John did not know who would come for sure   this afternoon.
        J' $^{??}$*ai suggéré Marie*
        I   suggested Mary

(8) is strange because it means that John ignores who will come, not who should be chosen to be sent. It is not necessary that the suggestee be the unique person who controls the action. For instance, the agent of the action can be the person denoted by the NP complement, as in the interpretation of "I suggested John to Mary" as 'I suggested to Mary that she choose John to do the work.' However, there must be some intentionally controlled relation between the choice and the action. The suggestee must be able to exert some causal influence on the fact that her choice will be respected when the action takes place. In other terms, the choice may not be reduced to a mental preference with respect to an otherwise uncontrollable process. That is why (9) is odd.

(9)   *Jean ne savait pas qui   il préférait voir   gagner Wimbledon.*
        John did not know whom he preferred to see win   Wimbledon.
        *Je lui   * $^{??}$*ai suggéré Becker*
        I to him   suggested Becker
        (John didn't know who was his preferred possible winner for Wimbledon.
        I suggested Becker to him)

(9) is strange because, under normal circumstances, John has no means to control the issue of the Wimbledon competition. Although he might have personal preferences, they will not affect the result of the tournament in any way. The influence requirement is stored by a black box predicate *influence* in CONSTRAINTS.

     The essential point is that no local information is sufficient to predict the appropriateness of the construction. This is clear for the *influence* predicate in CONSTRAINTS. There are many influence scenarios, which differ, for instance, in which parts of an action are controlled. However, this form of scenario–dependency extends to the **choice** type. The general notion of choice, which is central to the analysis of the construction, has be matched with *situations*, not only with well-defined lexical informations. Given a situation, there is nothing in the representation IV that tells us how to determine whether "*suggérer*" is appropriate or not. We can try to make the representation of the **choose** substructure more accurate in Figure 8.4 simply by substituting Figure 8.5 for it. Figure 8.5 explicitly says that the suggestee must cause the fact that the future action is of type $\rightsquigarrow$ $\boxed{2}$.

     However, this solution just moves the frontier a little farther. In order to determine whether the suggestee is a causal agent of the indicated kind, we still shall have to

$$\begin{bmatrix} \textbf{cause} \\ \text{AGENT} \ .\boxed{3} \\ \text{CAUSED CONT|PRESUPPOSED} : \ \rightsquigarrow \boxed{2} \end{bmatrix}$$

Fig. 8.5.

interpret the situation. For instance, consider the choice situations involved in such different scenarios as selection of abstracts, political vote, commercial decision, intention to support a lobby (by sending money), etc. In all these situations there is a choice and the verb *"suggérer"* would certainly be appropriate. Yet, we lack any representational reliable device that would allow us to tease apart the subsituations where the verb is appropriate. Admittedly, the representation in Figure 8.5 provides important guidelines. It tells us that the suggestee must be a causal agent in the choice situation. However, there are as many ways of being a causal agent as there are possible classes of causal agentivity. The representation does not offer any new insight on that problem, and it is unlikely that more elaborate representations using only predicates in the lexicon (verbs, adjectives, etc.) could do substantially better, because they would have to provide analyses of difficult concepts, like intentionality. Such concepts would have to be decomposed into 'primitives' and/or operational modules that have still to be matched with situations (see Cohen et al., 1990).

This does not imply that a definition of causal agentivity and of *"suggérer"* is not possible. However, any such definition will have to be anchored on nonlexical primitives whose applicability ultimately depends on our ability to classify situations. The problem we face here is different from that which is addressed by Generative Lexicon (Pustejovsky, 1995) or Meaning–Text Theory (Mel'čuk, 1988). Those approaches are concerned with the internal structure of the lexicon and try, wherever this is possible, to analyze predicates as nodes in a network of lexical relations. In the case of *"suggérer,"* it is unclear how we could reduce the interpretation of the verb to a system of purely lexical relations. I return to this question in section (4).

To show that such problems do not originate in a particular class of verbs, I now turn to a different class, which has no semantic relation to that of *"suggérer."*

3.2   The "attendre" Case

The verb *"attendre"* (to wait, to await) is used in some nonproblematic constructions with *"que"*–clauses. *"Attendre que"* P means roughly 'to wait for the state of affairs described by P to become true' and *"s'attendre à ce que"* P roughly 'to expect that P.' However, the verb is also used with nominal complements and its semantics is much less transparent in such configurations. Intuitively, one can distinguish the following cases (see Jayez, 1994).

(10)   a. *J' attends   le   concert*
           I am waiting for the concert
           complement of type **event**
        b. *J' attends   le   bus*
           I am waiting for the bus
           complement of type **mobile**
        c. *J' attends   mon rasoir électrique*
           I am waiting for my   shaver
           complement of type **physical object**
        d. *J' attends   son prochain livre*
           I am waiting for her next   book
           complement of type **physical object**

The interpretation is easy to describe when the complement is of type **event**. The subject of "*attendre*" waits for an event of the type indicated by the NP to begin. The object of the waiting process may only be the *beginning* of the event. (10a) does not mean 'I am waiting for the concert to resume/to finish.' This is not predictable from the general properties of a waiting situation (one can wait for any part of an event to go to its end or to start). So, it must be included in the semantic description of "*attendre*."

For mobile objects such as a bus, a car, or a plane, the most natural interpretation is that one waits for the mobile to arrive. (10b) cannot be interpreted as 'I am waiting for the bus to start.' This is not a predictable result in itself. Because "*attendre*" is always normal with **event** nouns, one could assume that it prefers **event** complements and that other complements must be integrated somehow in an event that constitutes the 'true' complement of "*attendre*." Plausible as it is, this assumption does not explain why the event normally associated with "*bus*," i.e., a transportation, is not considered by "*attendre*." Contrary to what is suggested by a reviewer, "*attendre le bus*" (to wait for the bus) does not entail in any way that the bus will be used as a means of transportation. It is only a strong default preference. In a context where I have to take a picture of a certain bus (because it has a beautiful painting on one of its sides, for instance), (10b) is a quite normal sentence.

For physical artifacts, the intuitive interpretation seems to be that the subject of "*attendre*" waits for taking control over an artifact on which she has no control at the moment of the waiting. However, this interpretation is not available with certain artifacts, e.g., in (11).

(11)   *J' attends   le   ??distributeur de billets*
           I am waiting for the   atm

(11) is strange if somebody is using the atm and I am waiting for my turn. This points to a major difficulty in the description of "*attendre*," namely the definition of the relation of the subject to the object which is 'waited for.' Following,

inter alii, Gruber and Jackendoff, Goldberg proposes that there is a link between physical transfer (carrying an object into the sphere of influence of someone) and transfer of ownership (Goldberg, 1994, pp. 89–100). Obviously, we cannot simply adopt this analysis, because, in many examples with "*attendre*," there is no transfer of ownership. The bus example (10b) is a case in point. However, we can resort to a kindred hypothesis. One observes that, for nonevent complements in (10b) and (10c), the natural uses of "*attendre*" correspond either to a mobile object that is moving, or to a transfer/creation of (temporary) ownership. The common core behind these two seemingly unrelated situations is that the object status *with respect to the subject* (of the verb) is modified in the sense of an increasing control or possibility of use, and that the subject is passive as regards this modification (that she waits for). The process is perceived from the point of view of the subject, not from just any point of view. Note that localization and social control are two major ways of conceiving the status of a thing with respect to another.

"*Attendre*" does not take into account localizations where the subject is not the standpoint. That is why the reconstructed arrivals are always arrivals into the vicinity of the subject. For instance, (10b) cannot mean that I am waiting for the bus to arrive somewhere. The bus must come to the location where I am currently. The requirement that the control of possibility of use be increased explains the impossibility of the departure interpretation in (10b): the departure of the bus can be characterized with respect to myself, if the bus is starting *from* my current location. However, this does not represent an increase in my possibility of using the bus.

Social control is manifest in many situations: becoming the owner of something, controlling (momentarily) the use of an object, etc. However, in the case of "*attendre*," this control must be given to the subject. It is not enough that a common resource becomes free, allowing the subject to use it, as in the case of the atm. The use of the machine must be specifically granted to the subject, which is not the case in queuing up situations, where the status modification is not specifically conceived with respect to the subject. However, this is not true for the bus. A bus I am waiting for does not become 'mine' when it arrives. Observe that the two nonevent cases considered so far (the bus and the shaver) refer to objects that undergo substantial modifications (localization or possession). This preference is perhaps not entirely mysterious. In a sense, when the NP complement is an object rather than an event in a form x "*attend*" y, x literally waits for y (the object), not for an event loosely associated with y.[10] So, we can speculate that, as objects are not events, one of the possible compromises is to find events that are sufficiently 'internal' to the object, hence the requirement on modification.

What about (10d)? On one side, this use is similar to the event-based cases like (10a): the object must be created as the event must take place. (10d) may not mean

---

[10] A similar remark holds for "*commencer*" (to begin) in the analysis proposed in (Godard and Jayez, 1993).

that I am waiting that some person has finished to read a book, only that she has finished to write it. On the other side, (10d) is similar to the control and localization cases. Consider (12).

(12)   *J' attends*   #*son prochain livre pour prendre une décision*
         I am waiting for her next   book to   take   a   decision

Suppose that I am in a situation where I have to wait for my wife to complete a book she started long ago, to vacation with her and that I must then decide where to go. (12) would not be appropriate in such a situation and would sound clumsily metonymic. However, if I am an editor waiting for the critics' reactions to the next book of one of my authors, (12) makes much more sense. Depending on the situation, it can suggest that I intend to read the book but also that I want to know how it will be welcomed, and so forth.

A sentence like (12) is even compatible with situations where reading the book is completely irrelevant. For example, I can wait to know what will be the price policy of the publisher. Will they sell the author's next book at a low or high price? If the price is too low, must I advise the author to find another publisher, and so on. Whatever the interpretation, I am waiting for the book because its completion will allow me to do or to know something, not just because this event coincides with the beginning or the end of other events. This is not the case with event complements, where simple coincidence may be sufficient (*J'attends le début du concert pour partir* = 'I am waiting for the concert to begin to leave'). This not the case either with the arrival sense. For instance, by saying *J'attends Marie* (I am waiting for Mary), I can mean that I am waiting for Mary to come home to leave. Compared with the two previous cases, (12) exhibits the two following properties: (i) there is a modification (the book is created), but it is not defined with respect to the subject, (ii) however, the object which comes into existence pertains to a certain use by the subject.[11]

These two configurations suggest the following representation for "*attendre*" + NP of type **physical object**. To save space, I use a disjunctive notation.

In Figure 8.6, the tags in boldface **a**, **b**, and **c** signal cointerpretation. For instance, the first interpretation of the object NP (**a**), in terms of an event of arrival is correlated with an indeterminate **psoa**. This holds also of the second interpretation (transfer of possession). The last one (the 'creation' sense) is associated with a general **use** predicate, which can apply to the denotation of the complement or to its existence, to the book or to the existence of the book in (12).

The case of "*attendre*" illustrates the two main properties of lexical semantic representations. First, it is not always possible to use general types, which remain relevant across the different semantic classes of predicates. For example, the abstract type **own** is not to be found in the analysis of every verb whose semantics presupposes the reconstruction of some missing structure. It seems to be peculiar to verbs like *attendre* or "to wait." The fact that these two verbs, which are

---

[11] Note that the atm of (11) does not undergo any modification (subject–centered or not).

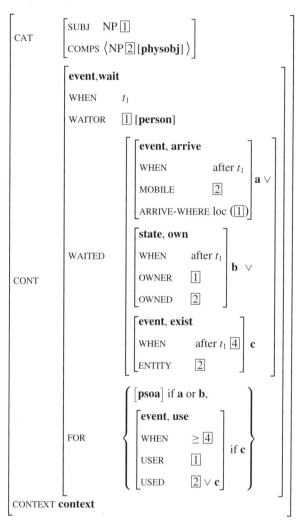

Fig. 8.6.

morphologically unrelated, share most of their interpretation constraints suggest that the **own** interpretation is a reflection of some deeper notion of waiting, which is partly opaque in the analysis I proposed.[12] Another example of nontransferrable type is **modify** proposed by Godard and Jayez (1993) for "*commencer*" (to begin). Assigning this type to certain verbs explains why a sentence like *Les ouvriers ont commencé le mur* (The workers began the wall) can mean, *inter alia*, 'The workers

---

[12] It remains to be seen whether this notion is itself a reflection of the contexts in which some operation/attitude of waiting makes sense. See Resnik (1993) for a discussion of related problems.

began to paint/mend the wall.' In short, *commencer* allows one to interpolate predicates that inherit the **modify** type, which is precisely the case for "*peindre*" (to paint), "*réparer*" (to mend) and other verbs. Now, interpolating the **modify** type with "*attendre*" would incorrectly predict that *J'attends le mur* can mean 'I am waiting for the wall to be painted/repaired.' Actually, this is not the case.

Second, the representation illustrates the hybrid character of the interpretation constraints on "*attendre*" + nonevent NP. There are perfectly standard semantic predicates, such as **arrive** or **exist**, to which it would not be difficult to correlate classes of verbs. To this extent, we can say that the representation is explicit and does not cover hidden complexities. But there is also the **use** predicate whose content remains extremely vague. Clearly, we cannot resort to purely lexical information attached to "book" to interpret sentences like (10d). The only 'constraint' we can assign to the NP y with respect to the interpretation is that the reconstructed predicate (for instance "read," "see how" y "is welcomed," etc.) be compatible with the properties of the book. However, this is not sufficient to promote precise representations, which one could include in the feature structures.[13]

4 Discussion

4.1 Summary

The main findings reported here can be summarized by three points. First, some predicates impose highly underspecified configurations. This was shown by (i) the contextual expectation of "*faire penser à*" evidenced by the "*plutôt*" (rather) test and (ii) by the importance of the shadowy constraint $\leadsto x$ in general. In some cases ("*faire penser à*"), the type $\leadsto x$ is inserted into a very general structure of type **psoa**, which is left unspecified. It is likely that a more detailed analysis could impose further constraints on the appropriate psoa's, decreasing the general level of underspecification. Second, in addition to lexical predicates, whose meaning is relatively stable, I had to use abstract predicates and constraints (**choose**, **use**, *alternative*, etc.), which are very difficult to analyze in a precise way. Third, it seems difficult to predict all and only the correct interpretations by postulating all-purpose types or features. We have to accept that lexical items demand more fine-grained and local representations than those that could be constructed by using a set of predefined features and types. To highlight what the proposed description actually tells us about lexical phenomena, I will link it to the two themes of generativity and vagueness.

---

[13] One could also argue that the predicate **own** is vague, in the indicated sense. For instance, the sentence *J'attends une chambre* (I am waiting for a room) might be used in a situation where I am waiting for the hotel management to assign some room to me. However, surely, this case of ownership is different from legal possession. In fact, we should extend the meaning of **own** so as to cover cases of transient uses of rooms, vehicles, and objects in general.

4.2   *Generativity and Regularity in the Lexicon*

With Generative Lexicon theory (hereafter GL), Pustejovsky (1995) tries to account for what he takes to be one of the central phenomena of language, the ability of human beings to compose linguistic elements in a variety of ways without relying on a fixed, closed, list of co-occurrences. This is the so-called *creative* aspect of language use. GL simulates this ability by hypothesizing that there are four levels of linguistic representation connected by certain generative devices. I cannot list and examine here all the theoretical claims of GL. Instead, I will focus on two points that are directly relevant to the context selection issue.

"Current" theories of lexical semantics are rejected by GL because they assign fixed meanings to words and are subsequently unable to explain the links existing between those meanings. In Pustejovsky's terms, they get caught in the trap of *sense enumeration*. The sense enumeration catch-phrase used over and over in GL writings (see for instance Bouillon and Busa, 1998; Pustejovsky 1991, 1995, 1998; Pustejovsky and Bouillon, 1995) is seriously deceiving. First, it is simply not true that standard semantic descriptions ignore the problem of connections between senses. For example, the French dictionary *Robert Méthodique* (Robert Méthodique 1987, p. 263) proposes a definition of *"commencer"* (to begin), which is quite sensitive to the 'first part of' common core of the different uses.[14] The same remark applies to Godard and Jayez 1993), where it is explicitly assumed that THE sense of *"commencer"* with an **animate** subject denotes a function that returns the first part of an event. There is clearly no 'sense enumeration' here. The spurious character of the label is even more apparent in the *"attendre"* case. In Jayez (1994), it is proposed that the sense of *"attendre"* is described by a highly underspecified Parson-style aspectual formula. In the present representation, it would not be difficult to say that *"attendre"* means something like 'to wait for some eventuality,'[15] so there is no real sense enumeration. To turn to an entirely different style of approach, must we say that Wierzbicka's primitive-based theory of definition (see Wierzbicka, 1996 for a synthesis) is prone to sense enumeration? Certainly not. Wierzbicka's approach gives much importance to the notion of a core meaning, which has enough flexibility to produce various specific senses. However, the description she proposes does not seem to share much with the principles of GL. So, in addition to GL, there are theories of lexical semantics that know better than to enumerate senses and the borderline, which separates those theories from GL must be found elsewhere.

The second aspect worth of comment is the status of **qualia** structure. It is proposed in GL that the semantic information in lexical elements is structured on

---

[14] The *"commencer"* + NP construction with a **person** subject is paraphrased as *faire la première partie d'une chose ou d'une série de choses* (to do/operate the first part of a thing or a series of things). With a **nonperson** subject, it is paraphrased as *"former la première partie de"* (to be/compose/constitute the first part of), etc.

[15] I return to the description of *"attendre"* in the next paragraph.

the basis of four different roles, called **qualia** roles. The qualia structure includes the formal role, which contains the intrinsic properties of entities; the constitutive role, which contains the meronymic information; the telic role, which contains the function of the entity; and the agentive role, that contains the factors that are responsible for the entity's existence. In many cases, the qualia structure allows one to reconstruct missing predicates, as in the overworked example "to begin the book," where the reconstructed interpretations include "to begin to read the book" (*via* the telic role) and "to begin to write the book" (*via* the agentive role). However, (i) it is not clear that other approaches (most notably Mel'čuk's lexical functions, see Melčuk, 1996) would not make similar predictions, (ii) qualia structure is not a panacea. Let me consider the *"attendre"* case under the perspective of qualia structure. Bouillon and Busa (1998) propose that the different semantic values of *"attendre"* are amenable to qualia structure. The idea is to see a construction like *"x attend y pour z"* (*x* is waiting for *y* to *z*) as a correspondence between (i) *z* and the telic role of *"attendre,"* (ii) *y* and the agentive role in the complex structure corresponding to the telic role of *"attendre."* Therefore, the interpretation is roughly: *x* waits for *y* to be true and *y* brings about (agentivity) *z*. This proposal calls for at least four comments.[16]

1.   The notion of telicness[17] the authors appeal to is loose. The process of waiting for a bus can be perceived as a means of being transported. In this and related cases, there is a telic relation between *"attendre"* and *z*. However, consider a sentence like *J'attends la réponse de Marie pour prendre une décision* (I am waiting for Mary's answer to make a decision). Can we say that the function of waiting is to make a decision? This is much less clear than in the bus case. The function of waiting, if any, seems rather to obtain the answer. The answer itself is a means of making a decision and the function of waiting is to delay the decision until the answer is ready. In such cases, the function of waiting is roughly to delay an event until another event takes place.[18]

2.   In GL, the telic role draws its importance from the fact that its stores lexical associates ("read" for "book," etc.) or abstract predicates that help us in the interpretation process. Bouillon and Busa (in this volume) propose, for instance, that for nouns of vehicles the formal part of the telic role contains the information that such entities can serve to transport other entities. This certainly accounts for the default interpretation of *J'attends le bus* (I am waiting for the bus) as 'I am waiting for the bus to take it,' but, as indicated in section 3.2, it has nothing to do with the semantics of *"attendre,"* I can wait for a bus to take a picture of it, say hello to the driver, check whether the bus arrives in due time, and so forth. This problem persists if we change the content of the telic role to incorporate the notion

---

[16]   I do not discuss the intuitive classification of examples, which is quite similar to that of Jayez, (1994).

[17]   I use this term instead of *telicity* to avoid the confusion with the aspectual notion of telicity.

[18]   This is a well-known situation in the theory of concurrent processes *à la* Milner and in planning.

of delay. What is delayed would vary from context to context. There is nothing in the semantics of the verb that *forces* the interpreter to consider the telic role of its object complement. People who wait for buses take them *in general*. That is all there is to the point.[19]

3.   Consider the atm example (11) and compare it with the following situation: a dish full of food is handed around and people help themselves in turn. Here, I can say *J'attends le plat* (I am waiting for the dish). Yet, as in the atm case, I am not the owner of the dish (I have just a transient right of use). It is unclear how we could reflect the difference in terms of qualia structure. Everything seems to be as it should be in terms of telicness: We use the atm and the dish as they should be used. In terms of agentivity, following the proposal of Bouillon and Busa (in this volume), one should incorporate in the representation the precondition for using the object, that is accessing it. Again, there is in principle no problem. So, where does the difference between an atm and a dish come from? Qualia structure is of no avail in this case.

4.   The role of agentivity is unclear. The authors hypothesize that, if an object has no agentive, it may not be denoted by the object complement of "*attendre*." If agentivity is taken to be the mode of production of an object, as in GL, there are two problems with this hypothesis. Event nouns such as "*tremblement de terre*" (earthquake) or "*orage*" (storm) lack agentivity in this sense. Yet, they can be the complement of "*attendre*." For example, if some seer predicted that there will be an earthquake tomorrow, I can say *J'attends le tremblement de terre* (I am waiting for the earthquake). No earthquake is 'produced' or 'brought about' in the same manner as an artifact is. So, the only possibility is to extend the notion of agentivity to include natural phenomena that are produced by natural factors. However, consider now the bus example. I am not waiting for the bus to be produced. So, the authors have to assume that the precondition to the transportation is not the agentive role of the lexical item but a precondition of its use (to get on the bus, for example). In other words, they accept in some cases to dissociate the agentive role of the object complement from the agentive role in the structure for the telic. This casts some doubt on the robustness of the representation and does not allow one to conclude that a lexical item without agentive role is not the complement of "*attendre*," because the agentive role is ignored in some cases.

I do not pretend that the representation I propose for "*attendre*" is unobjectionable, but I seriously doubt that qualia structure would help to improve it. This is not an accident. "*Attendre*" is not specially difficult. The truth is sad and simple. As argued in Jayez & Godard (1995), the lexicon is only *partly* regular. There are

---

[19] In this respect, I agree with the reservations expressed by Fodor and Lepore (1998) on GL. However, this does not cast any doubt on the desirability of a lexical theory which is not a simple reflection of world knowledge. The problem is rather that GL seems to have overestimated the importance of purely lexical constraints.

relatively stable cross-generalizations but also local or regional variations.[20] No system of principles can account for the distribution of lexical items at the level of detail that is considered as desirable in lexical semantics. Further, no magic can spare GL the trouble of dealing with irregularity in the lexicon.

4.3   *Vagueness and Generativity*

The most disputable aspect of my proposal is certainly the intrinsic *vagueness* of some of the abstract predicates used in the representations (RESEMBLE, CHOOSE, USE, the constraints). The analysis of vagueness is reputedly difficult. I will understand here by *vagueness* the fact that, for some given predicate, we are not able to provide a finite list of linguistic predicates that are its possible realizations in various contexts.[21] So, a vague predicate corresponds to an open-ended family of contextual realizations. This is not to say that its meaning is dictated by the context, but rather that it is too general to be characterized by a small family of cases. This situation is not alien to that of similarity-based models such as Case-Based Reasoning or semantic analogy. Insofar as such vague predicates are necessary to classify uses, they introduce a form of nonlocality. In the structure in Figure 8.4, the **choose** relation corresponds to the verb "to choose." So, it cannot be considered as vague at this level of correspondence. However, the observations show that **choose** is not simply the "choose" verb and can only be used in situations where a certain causal relation obtains. It seems impossible to eliminate that relation in an enumerative way, that is by just giving a list of context types.[22] This probably constitutes one of the sources of what is called generativity. In representational structures, vague predicates depend on contextual information to *create* the interpretation, not just to check whether a possible interpretation is adequate. To see the difference, consider again the example of "begin." When "begin" combines with "book" as its complement, we are able (no matter how) to propose interpretations such as "read a book" or "write a book." Obviously, the choice between those interpretations depends on the situation. This is a case where context filters out possible interpretations. However, we do not depend on context to contemplate them. In the present case, we have no special

---

[20] Such variations could perfectly well be *motivated*, in the sense in which metaphors are motivated, that is are not just any random combination of semantic informations. However, as Lakoff and others showed long ago, motivation is not predictability.

[21] This property is only observational. Of course, one could consider it as the symptom of a deeper form of vagueness, namely the impossibility of defining the predicate in a noncircular way, because of its intrinsic fuzziness. I will not consider such issues in this chapter.

[22] However, it might be possible to 'code' the relation in a more precise way, by providing script or case schemas which the appropriate contexts must satisfy, or by translating it into a language equipped with a limited set of abstract primitives (Wierzbicka, 1996). How much is gained by doing so remains to be seen.

interpretation to offer and to test against contextual data. Rather, we have an underspecified structure, which context can fill to favor some given interpretation. Context does not choose, but it participates in the construction of choices. Moreover, the underspecified information is not defeasible. This is why we can say conjointly that the interpretation is nonlocal (we need context) and that it amounts to a selection on contexts (the semantic profile is imposed on contexts, not *by* contexts).

So, the sort of vagueness I am interested in here is not exactly that found in fuzzy predicates or in the sorites-like family of paradoxes. It is rather connected with the Wittgensteinian theme of *rule-following*.[23] A recurrent theme in Wittgenstein's remarks on mathematical or linguistic rules is that rules do not spell out their conditions of application. Our understanding of a rule is richer than what the rule explicitly says. A rule certainly cannot specify in advance each and every circumstance where it can be used. For instance, the representations used in this paper have well-defined formal properties, but they do not say anything substantial about the proper content of the abstract predicates they mention. This is why I have to supplement them with intuitive descriptions of cases. Abstract vague predicates thus work as pointers to families of situations and practices. At this point, we reach the limits of the type of semantic representation used here and in the literature. However, this should not be taken as a special weakness of such representations. In fact, the goal of semantic representations is to package information into distinct areas, not to give a direct access to meaning. No representation can completely replace our intuitions about meaning, but representations can help us to formulate these intuitions and to associate to them more testable constructs.

5   Conclusion

The data presented in this chapter show that the relation between context and interpretation can be conceived in two ways. Either context provides missing information or lexical elements themselves indicate the type of contexts in which they would be maximally appropriate, a general mechanism I labeled context selection. The lexical informations that select contexts are vague. That is, they consist of abstract predicates that cannot be defined by a small family of linguistic predicates. In this respect, lexical semantics relies on intuitive, case-based, script-based, etc., descriptions to substantiate those predicates. Moreover, this vagueness is responsible for the flexibility of meaning, the fact that lexical items are used in multiple different contexts, which obviously cannot be enumerated in advance. This "generativity" is not attributed here to semantic composition, in contrast with GL, but to the human ability to classify contexts. On the contrary, the amount of compositional freedom is limited, because classes of items impose regional constraints that are not amenable to a general semantic form. So, lexical items

---

[23] However, there is some deep connection between the two problems, see Wright (1996).

behave as constructions, in the sense of construction grammars. They are partly idiomatic clusters of semantic and syntactic information and cannot be analyzed by applying only a set of general principles. Summarizing, the traditional division of labor between local semantic information and extraneous contextual data must be reconsidered. In addition to seeing contextual information as the natural complement or substitute of lexical information, we must study seriously the context selection mechanisms inside the lexicon.

References

Asher, N. 1993. *Reference to Abstract Objects in Discourse*. Kluwer Academic Publishers, Dordrecht.

Asher, N., and Lascarides, A. 1995. Lexical Disambiguation in a Discourse Context. *Journal of Semantics* 12: 69–108.

Bonomi, A., and Casalegno, A. 1993. *Only*: Association with Focus in Event Semantics. *Natural Language Semantics* 2: 1–45.

Bouillon, P., and Busa, F. 1998. A Verb Like "attendre": The Point of View of "Generative Lexicon," Unpublished manuscript, ISSCO, Geneva and Brandeis University.

Brown, P., and Levinson, S. C. 1987. *Politeness. Some Universals in Language Use*. Cambridge University Press, Cambridge.

Carpenter, B. 1992. *The Logic of Typed Feature Structures*. Cambridge University Press, Cambridge.

Cohen, P. R., Morgan, J., and Pollack, M. E. (eds.) 1990. *Intentions in Communication*. MIT Press, Cambridge.

Copestake, A., and Briscoe, T. 1995. Semi-productive Polysemy and Sense Extension. *Journal of Semantics* 12: 15–67.

Davis, A. 1996. Lexical Semantics and Linking in the Hierarchical Lexicon, Ph.D. Thesis, Stanford University.

van Deemter, K., and Peters, S. (eds.) 1996. *Semantic Ambiguity and Underspecification*. CSLI Publications, Stanford.

Engdahl, E., and Vallduví, E. 1996. Information Packaging in HPSG. *Edinburgh Working Papers in Cognitive Science* Vol. 12: *Studies in HPSG*, 1–31.

Fauconnier, G. 1997. *Mappings in Thought and Language*. Cambridge University Press, Cambridge.

Fillmore, C. J., Kay, P., and O'Connor, M. C. 1988. Regularity and Idiomaticity in Grammatical Constructions: The Case of *let alone*. *Language* 64: 501–538.

Fodor, J., and Lepore, E. 1998. The Emptiness of the Lexicon: Critical Reflections on James Pustejovsky's "The Generative Lexicon." *Linguistic Inquiry* 29:2, 269–288. Also published in this volume.

French, R. M. (1995). *The Subtlety of Sameness. A Theory and Computer Model of Analogy–Making*. MIT Press, Cambridge.

Godard, D., and Jayez, J. 1993. Towards a Proper Treatment of Coercion Phenomena. *Proc. 6th Conference of the European Chapter of the ACL*, Utrecht University, Utrecht 168–177.

Goldberg, A. E. 1994. *Constructions. A Construction Grammar Approach to Argument Structure*. The University of Chicago Press, Chicago.

Jackendoff, R. 1990. *Semantic Structures*. MIT Press, Cambridge.

Jayez, J. 1994. Significations lexicales et représentations, Unpublished manuscript, EHESS, Paris.

Jayez, J., and Godard, D. 1995. Principles as Lexical Methods. *Proc. AAAI Workshop on Representation and Acquisition of Lexical Knowledge*, Stanford, 57–68.

Jurafsky, D. 1993. A Cognitive Model of Sentence Interpretation: The Construction Grammar Approach, Technical Report TR-93-077, International Computer Science Institute, University of California at Berkeley.

Kaplan, R., and Maxwell III, J. T. 1988. An Algorithm for Functional Uncertainty. *Proc. COLING 88*, Vol. I, 297–302.

Kay, P. 1998. An Informal Sketch of a Formal Architecture for Construction Grammar. In G. Bouma, G.-J. Kruijff, & R. Oehrle (eds). *Proc. FHCG'98*, 175–184.

Krifka, M. 1992. A Framework for Focus–sensitive Quantification, *Proc. Semantics and Linguistic Theory II*. Working Papers in Linguistics 40, Ohio State University.

Lascarides, A., and Copestake, A. 1995. The Pragmatics of Word Meaning. *Proc. Semantics and Linguistic Theory V.*

Lascarides, A., Copestake, A., and Briscoe, T. 1996. Ambiguity and Coherence. *Journal of Semantics* 13: 41–65.

Mel'čuk, I. 1988. *Dependency Syntax: Theory and Practice*. State University of New York Press, Albany.

Mel'čuk, I. 1996. Lexical Functions: A Tool for the Description of Lexical Relations in a Lexicon. In L. Wanner (ed.), *Lexical Functions in Lexicography and Natural Language Processing*, John Benjamins Publishing Company, Amsterdam, 37–102.

Molinier, C. 1984. Etude syntaxique et sémantique des adverbes de manière en *–ment*, Thèse de Doctorat, Université de Toulouse-Le-Mirail, France.

Nølke, H. 1983. Les adverbes paradigmatisants: Fonction et analyse, Etudes Romanes de l'Université de Copenhague, *Revue Romane 23*, special issue.

Pollard, C., and Sag, I. 1994. *Head–Driven Phrase Structure Grammar*. Chicago University Press and CSLI, Chicago and Stanford.

Pulman, S. G. 1997. Higher Order Unification and the Interpretation of Focus. *Linguistics and Philosophy* 20: 73–115.

Pustejovsky, J. 1991. The Generative Lexicon. *Computational Linguistics* 17: 409–441.

Pustejovsky, J. 1995. *The Generative Lexicon*. MIT Press, Cambridge.

Pustejovsky, J. 1998. "Knowledge is Elsewhere": Natural Language Semantics Meets the X–Files. *Linguistic Inquiry* 29:2, 289–310. Also published in this volume.

Pustejovsky, J., and Bouillon, P. 1995. Aspectual Coercion and Logical Polysemy. *Journal of Semantics* 12: 133–162.

Resnik, P. 1993. Selection and Information: A Class–Based Approach to Lexical Relationships, Ph.D. Thesis, University of Pennsylvania.

Reyle, U. 1995. On Reasoning with Ambiguities. *Proc. 7th Conference of the European Chapter of the ACL*, 1–8.

Robert Méthodique. 1987. *Robert Méthodique. Dictionnaire méthodique du français actuel*, Paris: Editions Le Robert.

Rooth, M. 1985. Association with Focus, Ph.D. Thesis, University of Massachusetts at Amherst.

Rooth, M. 1992. A Theory of Focus Interpretation. *Natural Language Semantics* 1: 75–116.

Wierzbicka, A. 1996. *Semantics. Primes and Universals*. Oxford University Press, Oxford.

Wright, C. 1996. Further Reflections on the Sorites Paradox. In R. Keefe & P. Smith, *Vagueness: A Reader*, Cambridge: MIT Press, 204–250.

9   Qualia and the Structuring of Verb Meaning

PIERRETTE BOUILLON AND FEDERICA BUSA

Abstract

This paper focuses on the behavior of the French aspectual verb *"attendre"* (wait). It offers a unified analysis in the theory of *Generative Lexicon* (Pustejovsky, 1995) and briefly hints at how the analysis presented extends to the behavior of the same verb in other languages. We show that, instead of enumerating the various syntactic constructions it enters into, with the different senses that arise, it is possible to give it a rich underspecified semantic representation that acquires its specification in context and will explain both its semantic and syntactic polymorphism.

1   The Polymorphic Behavior of *"attendre"*

In this paper, we focus on issues of verb representation as they bear on the problem of how meaning shifts occur in context. Taking as an example the polymorphic behaviour of the French verb *"attendre"* (wait), we show that its multiple senses can be derived *co-compositionally* from the semantics of the verb and its arguments. Senses need not be enumerated, but can be derived *generatively* from richer representations of words and compositional mechanisms for combining them (Bouillon, 1998; Busa, 1996; Pustejovsky, 1995, 1998b).

The verb *"attendre"* shows interesting polymorphic behaviour (Jayez and Godard, 1995; and Jayez, in this volume), as illustrated in the following examples:

(1)   a. J'attends que tu partes
           'I'm waiting that you leave_subjunctive'
           (I'm waiting for you to leave)
      b. J'attends que tu partes pour travailler
           'I'm waiting that you leave_subjunctive to work'
           (I am waiting for you to leave before I work)
      c. J'attends son prochain livre
           'I'm waiting his next book'
           (I'm waiting for his next book)
      d. J'attends le bus
           'I'm waiting the bus'
           (I'm waiting for the bus)

     e. J'attends le concert
         'I'm waiting the concert'
         (I'm waiting for the concert)
         etc.

In each of the examples in (1), "*attendre*" is associated with a different reading. When the verb subcategorizes for a **clausal complement** (a "*que*"-sentence, S (2a), or a VP (2b)), it means 'to wait for the state of affairs described by the complement to become true.'

(2)   a. J'attends que tu partes.
           'I'm waiting that you leave_subjunctive'
           (I'm waiting for you to leave)
      b. J'attends de savoir la vérité.
           'I'm waiting to know/be told the truth'
           (I am waiting until I know the truth)

When the complement of "*attendre*" is an **NP**, its semantics is less transparent: the verb seems to take a different interpretation in each possible context (Jayez and Godard, 1995):

(3)   a. J'attends le concert
           'I'm waiting the concert'
           (I'm waiting for the concert)
      b. J'attends le bus
           'I'm waiting the bus'
           (I'm waiting for the bus)
      c. J'attends son prochain livre
           'I'm waiting his next book'
           (I'm waiting for his next book)
      d. J'attends mon rasoir
           'I'm waiting my shaver'
           (I'm waiting for my shaver)

In (3a), with an event-denoting noun, "*attendre*" means that the individual is waiting for the event (e.g., "concert") to begin. In (3b)–(3d) where the object of the verb is an individual, the interpretation is different. The sentences mean roughly that the individual is waiting for the objet to exist. As the *mode of existence* differs from noun to noun, the interpretation of the verb is then specific to each one: in (3b), the individual is waiting for the bus to arrive; in (3c), he is waiting for the book to be written/published and in (3d) for the shaver to come into the individual's possession.

Moreover, in all the above examples, the complement of *"attendre"* can also be optionally followed by a **"pour"-VP phrase**, as shown in (4) below:

(4)   a.   J'attends que tu partes pour travailler
'I'm waiting that you leave_subjunctive to work'
(I'm waiting for you to leave before I work)
   b.   J'attends de savoir la vérité pour me mettre en colère
'I'm waiting to know the truth to be angry'
(I'm waiting until I know the truth before I get angry)
   c.   J'attends son nouveau livre pour le critiquer
'I'm waiting his next book to criticize him'
(I'm waiting for his next book to criticize him)

This *"pour"*-VP complement indicates here what event is likely to happen if what is being waited for occurs: *"attendre (que S/de VP1/NP) pour VP2"* (to wait that S/to VP1/NP to VP2) means 'to wait for what is described by S/VP1/NP to become true in order to VP2.'

The data presented so far could be explained within a *monomorphic* approach, such as the one proposed by Godard and Jayez (Godard and Jayez, 1993a, 1993b; and Jayez, in this volume): the information necessary to interpret the complements of *"attendre"* is located in the semantics of the verb. In their account, *"attendre"* is functionally ambiguous: in (2) it takes a clausal complement, in (3) it takes an NP. The verb has therefore two entries that will be linked at the semantic level. In both entries, the verb takes three semantic arguments: the individual who is waiting (WAITOR), the event that the individual expects to take place (the WAITED), and the event that will occur if the WAITED is true (RESULT).

When the complement is clausal, the semantics of the verb are obvious: the *"que"*-sentence or the *"de"*-VP corresponds to the WAITED and the *"pour"*-VP corresponds to the RESULT. However, in case of a nominal complement, the structure of the verb *"attendre"* has also to contain information relative to the predicates that must be interpolated to interpret the different kinds of NPs. For example, if the object is a `vehicle`, the semantics of *"attendre"* indicates that the WAITED is the vehicle's arrival at the location of the WAITOR and the RESULT is that the WAITOR be transported somewhere. In case of `artifact`, the WAITED is its coming into existence or its possession and the RESULT that the individual uses it in some capacity. Finally, in the case of an `event`, what is WAITED is that it begins.

This approach would predict correctly that the two verbs *"attendre"* share the same semantics, despite the different subcategorization properties. However, it fails to take into account the *creative aspect of language*: the examples in (3) can be multiplied, as shown in (5), below:

(5)   a.   J'attends son arrivée
'I'm waiting his arrival'
(I'm waiting for his arrival)

    b. J'attends ma nouvelle voiture
        'I'm waiting my new car'
        (I'm waiting for my new car)

In (5a), "*arrivée*" (arrival) is an event, however the sentence cannot have the interpretation that the subject is waiting for the event to begin, as it is the case with "*concert*," in (3a). Similarly, there are different ways of creating an object: A car (5b) does not come to existence in the same way that a book does (3c). For each kind of new NP, all possible interpretations must therefore be enumerated in the semantics of the verb and it is questionable if this enumeration is possible.

Furthermore, there are restrictions on the kind of NP that is licensed as an object of "*attendre*," as shown in (6), below.

(6)   a. ??J'attends la croyance de P en Z
           'I'm waiting the belief of P in Z'
           (I'm waiting for P's belief in Z)
      b. ??J'attends le ciel
           'I'm waiting the sky'
           (I'm waiting for the sky)

(7)   a. Je commence le livre/un concert, etc.
           (I begin the book/a concert)
      b. ??Je commence le ciel/la croyance de P en Z
           (I begin the sky/P's belief in Z)

It would be clearly unsatisfying to specify such restrictions in the semantics of the verb: They come from the semantic properties of the argument and must be located there. Besides they are manifested with other verbs. For example, somebody can "begin a book" (e.g., 'to publish', agentive), or a "concert" (e.g., 'to play', agentive), but not a "sky" (e.g., 'to produce', agentive or 'to use in some capacity', telic) (7).

Our proposal is to examine the problem from a different perspective: Instead of locating the different interpretations in the semantics of the verb, we show that they can be derived generatively from the semantic properties of the arguments. In the following, we will first describe in very general terms the GL approach, and then present the analysis in more detail.

2   "Attendre" in the Perspective of GL

GL aims at developing underspecified representations that acquire their specification in context (Bouillon, 1998; Busa, 1996; Pustejovsky, 1995). Instead of enumerating the different senses of the words as in a *monomorphic* approach, the theory adopts a *generative* (or semi-polymorphic) point of view (Récanati, 1997). The word has a lexical sense that can be manipulated by a set of generative devices, which derive a potentially infinite number of senses in context.

The lexical sense consists of a set of predicates that define the word. Its description involves three orthogonal levels of representation, as shown in (8): the argument structure (`argstr`), the event structure (`evenstr`), and the qualia structure (`qs`).

$$
(8) \quad
\begin{bmatrix}
\alpha \\
\text{ARGSTR} = \begin{bmatrix} \text{ARG}1 = x : \tau_1 \\ \text{D\_ARG}1 = \text{other nonobligatory participants} \end{bmatrix} \\
\text{EVENSTR} = \begin{bmatrix} \text{D\_E}1 = e_1 : \sigma_1 \\ \text{D\_E}2 = e_2 : \sigma_2 \\ \text{RESTR} = \text{temporal relation between events} \end{bmatrix} \\
\text{QS} = \begin{bmatrix} \text{type-lcp} \\ \text{FORM} = x \\ \text{CONST} = \text{the parts of } x \\ \text{TEL} = \text{the } e_1 \text{ which is purpose or function of } x \\ \text{AG} = \text{the } e_2 \text{ that brings } x \text{ into existence} \end{bmatrix}
\end{bmatrix}
$$

These three levels of semantic description are involved in the representation of all major categories: nouns, verbs, and adjectives. For verbs, the list of arguments distinguishes between *obligatory arguments* (ARG1), which must be syntactically realized, and *default arguments* (D_ARG1), which can be optionally realized in the syntax. The event structure describes the events (`state`, `process`, `transition`) that are involved in the different predicates in the qualia structure and their temporal relation. Qualia structure links arguments and events together and defines their role in the lexical semantics of the word. As the predicates are typed with these different levels of information, the lexical sense can be seen as a kind of *reserve of types*, which allows for different interpretive strategies.

The four qualia roles are interpreted features that provide the basic vocabulary for lexical description, and determine the structuring or clustering of the information associated with a given lexical item (Bouillon, 1998; Busa, 1996; Pustejovsky, 1998a). The FORM(AL) role is the identity function, which provides the most general information about the type of the entity being defined: It links the entity to its broader semantic class. The CONST(ITUTIVE) role provides the mereological part. The TEL(IC) role is interpreted as a modal operator: the event that is encoded in the TELIC is understood as the function or purpose of the entity and it is not required to take place. Conversely, the AG(ENTIVE) is interpreted as the existential quantifier, because the occurrence of the event it expresses is a precondition for every other property of the entity.

In this paper, our treatment of the polymorphism of "*attendre*" can be summarized as follows: Taking advantage of the expressive power of the qualia-based representation for deriving the different senses of the verb and for explaining its restrictions, we consider that, irrespective of the type of the object, the semantics and the syntax of the verb remain the same. What changes is the way in which the verb co-composes with its arguments. As the lexical semantics varies from phrase to phrase, a potentially infinite number of senses can be generated in context.

The semantic type of "*attendre*" is given below:

$$
(9) \quad
\begin{bmatrix}
\textbf{attendre} \\
\text{ARGSTR} =
\begin{bmatrix}
\text{ARG1} = \text{x:ind} \\
\text{D\_ARG1} = [1] \\
\text{D\_ARG2} = [2]
\end{bmatrix} \\
\text{EVENSTR} =
\begin{bmatrix}
\text{E1} = e_0 : \text{state} \\
\text{D\_E3} =
\begin{bmatrix}
\text{D\_E1} = [1] : \text{event} \\
\text{D\_E2} = [2] : \text{event}
\end{bmatrix} \\
\text{RESTR\_1} = e_0 <_{o\alpha} [3] \\
\text{RESTR\_2} = [1] <_{o\alpha} [2]
\end{bmatrix} \\
\text{QS} =
\begin{bmatrix}
\text{attendre-lcp} \\
\text{FORM} = \text{att}(e_0, x, [3]) \\
\text{TEL} = [3]
\begin{bmatrix}
\text{FORM} = \text{P}([2], x) \\
\text{AG} = [1]
\end{bmatrix}
\end{bmatrix}
\end{bmatrix}
$$

In the representation (9), the argument structure specifies that "*attendre*" has three arguments: the waiter (x, typed as `individual`); the event that the individual is waiting for ([1], e.g., the WAITED); and the event that may happen as a result ([2], e.g., the RESULT). Both events are *default-arguments*, because they are optional, as shown in (10).

(10)   a. J'attends depuis longtemps
        'I'm waiting since a long time'
        (I have been waiting for a long time)
    b. J'attends que tu partes
        'I'm waiting that you leave_subjunctive'
        (I'm waiting for you to leave)
    c. J'attends pour travailler
        'I'm waiting to work'
        (I'm waiting to work)

The event structure specifies that "*attendre*" is a state (e_0) and that this state is in an ordered overlap ($<_{o\alpha}$) with the complex event that is waited ([3]). The event [3] involves [1] and [2], which are also ordered by temporal ordered overlap

($<_{o\alpha}$). In (11) for example, the race needs not to be finished so that I can leave.

(11)   J'attends la course pour partir
        'I'm waiting the race to leave'
        (I'm waiting for the race (to start) before I leave)

Finally, the qualia structure relates events and participants: the FORMAL role expresses that the predicate denotes a stative relation (e_0) between an individual (x) and a complex event ([3]), composed of the two subevents [1] and [2]: the individual is waiting for [1] to produce [2]. The TELIC role expresses that the complex event [3] may or may not take place. However, if the subevent [1] occurs, it will be the cause (e.g., AGENTIVE) of [2]. This information is expressed by the TELIC role itself being a complex structure: If we accept that in a qualia structure like (12), β is the cause of α, we can indeed consider that what the individual is waiting for to be true (i.e., [1]) is the necessary condition of the event [2].

(12)
$$\left[\begin{array}{l} \alpha \\ QS = \left[\begin{array}{l} FORM = \alpha \\ AG = \beta \end{array} \right] \end{array} \right]$$

In other words, [1] is understood as the cause (AGENTIVE) of [2] (FORMAL), but it itself has a condition: the individual is waiting for it. [1] is indeed in the scope of the telic role, and hence is likely to occur. One may wait for something that never takes place.

We now show how this structure allows us to explain the different senses of the verb, both with clausal, verbal (*"pour"*-VP), and nominal complements.

3   Clausal Complements and "pour"-VP

Given the qualia structure of *"attendre"* in (9), we can now explain the different interpretations of the clausal and *"pour"*-VP complements.

3.1   *Clausal Complements*

When *"attendre"* takes a clausal complement, the event specifies the semantic component that corresponds to the WAITED. The RESULT is left underspecified: sentences (13) means that 'I'm waiting for you to arrive/ work/ to be drunk' in order to 'do an underspecified event':

(13)   a. J'attends que tu arrives
           'I'm waiting that you arrive_subjunctive'
           (I'm waiting for you to arrive)
        b. J'attends que tu travailles
           'I'm waiting that you work_subjunctive'
           (I'm waiting for you to work)

c. J'attends que tu sois ivre
'I'm waiting that you be_subjunctive drunk'
(I'm waiting for you to be drunk)

Notice that in each case in (13) the interpretation of "*attendre*" changes according to the type of the event of the complement (state, process or transition) that determines the WAITED.

The verb "*travailler*" (to work), in (13b), is a process. As a process it does not refer to a resulting state but corresponds to what comes to existence. We assume that for agentive processes the mode of coming into existence is identified with the FORMAL, as a result, a sentence like (13b) can only mean that 'I'm waiting for the beginning of the process itself' (14).

(14) a.
$$\left[\begin{array}{l} \textbf{j'attends que tu travailles} \\ \text{FORM} = \text{att}(e_0, x:je, [3]) \\ \text{TEL} = [3] \left[\begin{array}{l} \text{FORM} = P([2], x) \\ \text{AG} = [1] = \text{que tu travailles} \end{array} \right] \end{array} \right]$$

b.
$$\left[\begin{array}{l} [1] \\ \text{FORM} = \text{trav\_Act}(e_1, w:tu) \end{array} \right]$$

In (13a), however, "*arriver*" (to arrive) is an achievement. Here, the individual is waiting for the culmination of the event, rather than its commencement. This is explained by the lexical semantics of this type of verb: in GL, achievements are considered as complex events, composed of an initial process ('the act of arriving', AGENTIVE) and a resulting state ('the state of being at some location', FORMAL). With achievement verbs, such as "*arriver*," the resulting state constitutes the *head* of the event structure, namely the most important sub-event in the semantics of the verb (Pustejovsky, 1988; Pustejovsky and Busa, 1995). Given this interpretation of "*arriver*" as a complex object (15b), the interpretation of (13a) becomes explicit: I'm waiting 'for the act of arriving to cause you to have arrived,' in order 'to do something' (15). Here, it is the complex structure of "*arriver*" that is bound to the agentive of the telic of "*attendre*."

(15) a.
$$\left[\begin{array}{l} \textbf{j'attends que tu arrives} \\ \text{FORM} = \text{att}(e_0, x:je, [3]) \\ \text{TEL} = [3] \left[\begin{array}{l} \text{FORM} = P([2], x) \\ \text{AG} = [1] = \text{que tu arrives} \end{array} \right] \end{array} \right]$$

b.
$$\left[\begin{array}{l} [1] \\ \text{FORM} = \text{arr\_Rés}(e_2, w:tu, y:loc) \\ \text{AG} = \text{arr\_Act}(e_1, w:tu) \end{array} \right]$$

Finally, "*être ivre*" (be drunk) is a state and the interpretation is that the waitor is waiting for this state to come into existence. As predicted by this interpretation, states are more natural if they are lexically created, *artifactual* (i.e., *stage-level*), as it is the case for adjectives like "*ivre*" (drunk) (16a) (versus agentive-oriented ones like "*intelligent*" clever for example (16b)) (Bouillon, 1998).

(16)   a. J'attends que tu sois ivre
            'I'm waiting that you are_subjunctive drunk'
            (I'm waiting for you to be drunk)
    b. ??J'attends que tu sois intelligent
            'I'm waiting that you are_subjunctive clever'
            (I'm waiting for you to be clever)

3.2   "*Pour*"-VP

When the verb subcategorizes for a "*pour*"-VP (as shown in the examples in (17)), we have the opposite situation. The event saturates the RESULT directly and it is the element that corresponds to the WAITED that is underspecified:

(17)   a. J'attends pour travailler
            'I'm waiting to work'
            (I'm waiting to begin working)
    b. J'attends pour partir
            'I'm waiting to leave'
            (I'm waiting to leave)

(17a) means that 'I'm waiting before I work':

(18)
$$\left[\begin{array}{l} \textbf{j'attends pour travailler} \\ \text{FORM} = \texttt{att}(e_0, x{:}\texttt{je}, [3]) \\ \text{TEL} = [3] \left[\begin{array}{l} \text{FORM} = [2] = \texttt{travail\_Act}(e_2, x) \\ \text{AG} = [1] \end{array} \right] \end{array} \right]$$

The complex structure of the TELIC in the representation of "*attendre*" also reflects appropriately the control structure of the verb: the complement that corresponds to the RESULT is subject controlled:

(19)   a. J'attends$_i$ que tu$_j$ travailles pour PRO$_i$ partir
            'I'm waiting that you work_subjunctive to leave'
            (I'm waiting for you to work to leave)
    b. *J'attends$_i$ que tu$_j$ travailles pour PRO$_j$ partir
            'I'm waiting that you work_subjunctive to leave'
            (I'm waiting for you to work to leave)

3.3   *Modal Force*

In the treatment of "*attendre*" proposed here, the different complements expressed as "*pour*"-VP and "*que*"-sentence/"*de*"-VP therefore saturate different roles in the qualia structure: the AGENTIVE of the TELIC represents the WAITED; the FORMAL of the TELIC the RESULT:

attendre

$\text{TELIC}_{\text{AGENTIVE}} \longrightarrow$ *"que"*-sentence/ *"de"*-VP, (e.g. WAITED)

$\text{TELIC}_{\text{FORMAL}} \longrightarrow$ *"pour"*-VP, (e.g. RESULT)

This distinction explains quite nicely the different modal force of the complements: clausal complements saturate the AGENTIVE role in the scope of the TELIC role and the existence of the event is asserted. For example, somebody could wait for the week to finish (20).

(20)   J'attends que cette semaine finisse
        'I'm waiting that this week finishes_subjunctive'
        (I'm waiting for this week to finish)

"Pour"-vp, on the other hand, saturates the FORMAL role in the scope of the TELIC: the existence of the event is not asserted since it is dependent on the occurrence of the one expressed by the AGENTIVE. As a result, sentence (21) would be impossible.

(21)   *J'attends pour être en fin de semaine
        'I'm waiting to be at the end of the week'

In the following we extend this analysis to object NP.

4   Metonymic Reconstruction of the Object NP

When *"attendre"* takes an NP, the semantics of the verb does not change. The expression is semantically well-formed if, from the semantics of the noun, it is possible to reconstruct the WAITED and the RESULT. Therefore, an NP may appear as the object of the verb if its semantics is *rich* enough to satisfy such a requirement. In this section, we explore how nominals with a different semantics compose with the verb *"attendre"* to generate a variety of interpretations.

4.1   The NP is a "created" Individual

"Attendre" may compose with nouns denoting a *created* individual, like for example "newspaper," "car," or "symphony" (22), to produce the following interpretation: the individual is waiting for the object to 'be created' (i.e., AGENTIVE) so that he can 'use it in some capacity' (i.e., TELIC).

(22)   a. J'attends le journal du soir
           'I'm waiting the evening newspaper'
           (I'm waiting for the evening newspaper)
        b. J'attends ma (nouvelle) voiture
           'I'm waiting my (new) car'
           (I'm waiting for my (new) car)

c. J'attends la (nouvelle) symphonie de mon ami
   'I'm waiting the new symphony of my friend
   (I'm waiting for the new symphony of my friend)

In (22), the specific way the object is created and used depends on its semantic type. The noun *"journal"* (newspaper), for example, denotes both an organization (for example, "the newspaper fired me") and a printed matter (info.physobj, "I read the newspaper"[1]) as shown in (23), below:

(23)

$$
\begin{bmatrix}
\textbf{journal} \\[4pt]
\text{ARGSTR} =
\begin{bmatrix}
\text{ARG1} = x:\texttt{org} \\
\text{ARG2} = y:\texttt{info.physobj} \\
\text{D-ARG1} = x:\texttt{hum} \\
\text{D-ARG2} = w:\texttt{hum}
\end{bmatrix} \\[30pt]
\text{EVENSTR} =
\begin{bmatrix}
\text{D-E1} = e_1:\texttt{transition} \\
\text{D-E2} = e_2:\texttt{transition}
\end{bmatrix} \\[20pt]
\text{QS} =
\begin{bmatrix}
\texttt{org.info.physobj-lcp} \\
\text{FORM} = y \\
\text{TEL} = \texttt{lire}(e_2,w,y) \\
\text{AG} = \texttt{publier}(e_1,x,y)
\end{bmatrix}
\end{bmatrix}
$$

Because "newspaper" is created by the act of publishing (publier) with the purpose of being read by somebody (lire), the sentence (22a) obtains the lexically driven interpretation in (24): the WAITOR is waiting until 'the newspaper is published' so that 'he can read it.'

(24)

$$
\begin{bmatrix}
\textbf{j'attends le journal} \\[4pt]
\text{FORM} = \texttt{att}(e_0,x:\texttt{je},[3]) \\[6pt]
\text{TEL} = [3]
\begin{bmatrix}
\text{FORM} = [2] = \texttt{lire}(e_2,x,y:\texttt{info.physobj}) \\
\text{AG} = [1] = \texttt{publier}(e_1,w:\texttt{org},y)
\end{bmatrix}
\end{bmatrix}
$$

Similarly, *"voiture"* (car) is an artifact, and *"symphonie"* (symphony) denotes both the music and the process of playing it. As with "newspaper," we can therefore infer *mutadis mutandis* that, in (22b), I'm waiting for the car 'to be constructed' ('repaired' or any other creative_Act) so that 'I can drive it' and in (22c) that I'm waiting for the music 'to be composed' (AGENTIVE), so that 'I can listen to the process of playing it' (TELIC).

---

[1] The notation info.physobj is taken from Pustejovsky (1995), to represent systematically polysemous items such as "newspaper," "book." These nouns denote *complex types*, which simultaneously carry both aspects of meaning (see also Buitelaar, 1997). This, however, does not bear directly on the analysis of *"attendre,"* and for reasons of space we will not discuss the topic of complex types. For the current purposes, it can be taken simply as a way of notating the properties of these types in a *condensed* manner.

Of course, the verb "*attendre*" can take other interpretations with nominals that also denote `physical_object`. In the next section, we explore these additional cases.

4.2   *The NP "is in my possession"*

In examples (25), one of the possible interpretations is that the individual is waiting 'for the object to be in his/her possession of the user' so that 'he/she can use it.'

(25)   a. J'attends mon rasoir
            'I'm waiting my shaver'
            (I'm waiting for my shaver)
        b. J'attends un bonbon
            'I'm waiting a sweet'
            (I'm waiting for a sweet)
        c. J'attends un poumon
            'I'm waiting a lung'
            (I'm waiting for a lung)

The treatment of the TELIC quale as a recursive structure introducing a modal context, namely the event(s) encoded therein may or may not occur, applies to the nominals as well (cf., Bouillon, 1998; Busa, 1996; Pustejovsky, 1996). It is clear that one of the preconditions for the occurrence of the event in the TELIC of the nouns in (25) is that the user possesses the object at the time of reference. For example, the TELIC of "*bonbon*" (sweet) is 'to be eaten' (`manger`) and the necessary condition for that event could be that 'the eater has a sweet' (`avoir`):[2]

$$(26) \quad
\begin{bmatrix}
\textbf{bonbon} \\
\text{ARGSTR} = \begin{bmatrix} \text{ARG1} = \text{x:food} \\ \text{D-ARG2} = \text{y:ind} \end{bmatrix} \\
\text{EVENSTR} = \begin{bmatrix} \text{D-E1} = e_1\text{:state} \\ \text{D-E2} = e_2\text{:event} \end{bmatrix} \\
\text{QS} = \begin{bmatrix} \text{food-lcp} \\ \text{FORM} = \text{x} \\ \text{TEL} = \begin{bmatrix} \text{FORM} = \text{manger}(e_2,\text{y},\text{x}) \\ \text{AG} = \text{avoir}(e_1,\text{y},\text{x}) \end{bmatrix} \end{bmatrix} \\
\text{AG} = \ldots
\end{bmatrix}$$

[2] For illustrative purposes, we have presented the most likely precondition for the occurrence of the event expressed in the TELIC. This could be alternatively represented by means of a contextual variable.

Given a noun with the recursive representation of (27), two interpretations of "*attendre*" are possible as one can possibly wait for any AGENTIVE event to produce another event (e.g, FORMAL). One interpretation is where an individual is waiting for [1] to produce x such that [2] may occur; the other where an individual is waiting for [4] to bring about [5].

$$(27) \quad \begin{bmatrix} \textbf{...-lcp} \\ \text{FORM} = \text{x} \\ \text{TELIC} = [2] \begin{bmatrix} \text{FORM} = [5] \\ \text{AG} = [4] \end{bmatrix} \\ \text{AGENTIVE} = [1] \end{bmatrix}$$

Thus, the two interpretations of sentence (25b) can be derived naturally from the lexical semantics of the verb and the noun, as shown in (27): in (27a), I'm waiting 'for a sweet to be in my possession' (avoir) so that 'I can eat it' (manger); in (27b), I'm waiting 'for the sweet to be produced' so that 'I can eat it'.

$$(28) \quad a. \quad \begin{bmatrix} \textbf{j'attends un bonbon} \\ \text{FORM} = \text{att}(e_0, \text{x}:\text{je}, [3]) \\ \text{TEL} = [3] \begin{bmatrix} \text{FORM} = [5] = \text{manger}(e_2, \text{x}, \text{y}) \\ \text{AG} = [4] = \text{avoir}(e_1, \text{x}, \text{y}) \end{bmatrix} \end{bmatrix}$$

$$b. \quad \begin{bmatrix} \textbf{j'attends un bonbon} \\ \text{FORM} = \text{att}(e_0, \text{x}:\text{je}, [3]) \\ \text{TEL} = [3] \begin{bmatrix} \text{FORM} = [2] = \text{manger}(e_2, \text{x}, \text{y}) \\ \text{AG} = [1] = \text{produire}(e_1, \text{w}, \text{y}) \end{bmatrix} \end{bmatrix}$$

The sentences in (29) illustrate the same range of interpretations with different kinds of nominals, like vehicles:

(29)   a.   J'attends le bus
           'I'm waiting the bus'
           (I'm waiting for the bus)
       b.   J'attends la voiture
           'I'm waiting the car'
           (I'm waiting for the car)

Given the qualia structure of "*bus*" (30), one of the possible lexically driven interpretations of (29a) is as given in (30): I'm waiting 'to get on the bus' (monter_sur) so that 'I can be transported to some other location' (tranport(er)):

(30)

$$
\begin{bmatrix}
\textbf{bus} \\
\text{ARGSTR} = \begin{bmatrix} \text{ARG1} = \text{x:vehicle} \\ \text{D-ARG2} = \text{y:ind} \\ \text{D-ARG3} = \text{z:loc} \\ \text{D-ARG4} = \text{w:loc} \end{bmatrix} \\
\text{EVENSTR} = \begin{bmatrix} \text{D-E1} = e_1 : \text{event} \\ \text{D-E2} = e_2 : \text{event} \end{bmatrix} \\
\text{QS} = \begin{bmatrix} \text{mobile-lcp} \\ \text{FORM} = \text{x} \\ \text{TEL} = \begin{bmatrix} \text{FORM} = \text{transport}(e_2,x,y,z,w) \\ \text{AG} = \text{monter\_sur}(e_1,y,x) \end{bmatrix} \\ \text{AG} = \ldots \end{bmatrix}
\end{bmatrix}
$$

(31)

$$
\begin{bmatrix}
\textbf{j'attends le bus} \\
\text{FORM} = \text{att}(e_0,y:\text{je},[3]) \\
\text{TEL} = [3] \begin{bmatrix} \text{FORM} = [5] = \text{transport}(e_2,x:\text{bus},y,z:\text{loc},w:\text{loc}) \\ \text{AG} = [4] = \text{monter\_sur}(e_1,y,x) \end{bmatrix}
\end{bmatrix}
$$

The other possible interpretation is where the AGENTIVE of the TELIC of the verb is bound to the AGENTIVE of the noun and the result is bound to the TELIC of the noun: I'm waiting 'for the bus to come into existence' so that 'I can use it in whatever capacity.' This last interpretation is less common, but would be perfectly correct in context as: "I'm waiting for the new school bus."

We have shown that in general, with individual nouns, "*attendre*" has two interpretations that are constructed by different bindings of the events provided by the qualia of the noun. This also predicts that different nominals will have different interpretations or degrees of acceptability according to their qualia:

(32)   a. J'attends le livre
              'I'm waiting the book'
              (I'm waiting for the book)
    b. ??J'attends le ciel
              'I'm waiting the sky'
              (I'm waiting for the sky)
    c. ??J'attends la pierre
              'I'm waiting the rock'
              (I'm waiting for the rock)
    d. Le sculpeur attend la pierre
              'the sculptor is waiting the rock'
              (the sculptor is waiting for the rock)

    e. J'attends le ciel bleu
       'I'm waiting the blue sky'
       (I'm waiting for the blue sky)

`Artefacts` like *"livre"* (book) have an AGENTIVE and a TELIC and both interpretations are possible (32a). By contrast, `natural_kinds` like *"ciel"* (sky) or *"pierre"* (rock) have no TELIC or AGENTIVE role specified (e.g., (32b) and (32c)), at least independently of more specific contexts (e.g, (32d)) or where changes in a particular state of the object is expected to take place (e.g., (32e)). Thus, the constraint is that the individual or event denoted by the NP specifies in its type its mode of coming into existence (i.e., the AGENTIVE role) or a function (i.e., the TELIC). In the next section, we examine the different interpretations of *"attendre"* with `event` nominals.

4.3 The NP *"begins"* or *"culminates"*

When the noun is typed as an `event` as in (33), the interpretation of *"attendre"* is the same as with clausal complements and depends on the type of event (state, process, or transition).

    With result nominals such as *"arrivée"* (arrival) or *"départ"* (departure), the individual is waiting for the resulting state, for example the state of 'Pierre having arrived at some location' in (33a), 'having left' in (33b):

(33)   a. J'attends l'arrivée de Pierre
          'I'm waiting the arrival of Pierre'
          (I'm waiting for Pierre's arrival)
    b. J'attends le départ de Pierre
          'I'm waiting the departure of Pierre'
          (I'm waiting for Pierre's departure)

Consider the nominal *"arrivée,"* which has the following representation, involving a process (the initial act of arriving, `arr(iver)_Act`) and a state, namely the result of being at some location, `arr(iver)_Rés`:

(34)

$$
\begin{bmatrix}
\textbf{arrivée} \\[4pt]
\text{ARGSTR} = \begin{bmatrix} \text{D-ARG1} = \text{x:ind} \\ \text{D-ARG2} = \text{y:loc} \end{bmatrix} \\[14pt]
\text{EVENSTR} = \begin{bmatrix} \text{E1} = e_1 : \text{process} \\ \text{E2} = e_2 : \text{state} \\ \text{RESTR} = e_1 <_\alpha e_2 \end{bmatrix} \\[18pt]
\text{QS} = \begin{bmatrix} \text{event-lcp} \\ \text{FORM} = \text{arr\_Rés}(e_2,x,y) \\ \text{AG} = \text{arr\_Act}(e_1,x) \end{bmatrix}
\end{bmatrix}
$$

In composition with "*attendre*," this complex structure saturates the WAITED. (33a) will be then interpreted as 'I'm waiting for Pierre to arrive' in order 'to do something.'

(35)

$$
\begin{bmatrix}
\textbf{j'attends l'arrivée de Pierre} \\
\text{FORM} = \text{att}(e_0, x, [3]) \\
\\
\text{TEL} = [3] \begin{bmatrix} \text{FORM} = [2] \\ \text{AG} = [1] = \text{L'ARR\_DE\_P} \end{bmatrix}
\end{bmatrix}
$$

When the nominal denotes a process like "*voyage*" (trip) in (36a) or "*course*" (race) in (36b), the individual is waiting for the beginning of the action.

(36)   a. J'attends ce voyage
        'I'm waiting this trip'
        (I'm waiting for this trip)
    b. J'attends la course
        'I'm waiting the race'
        (I'm waiting for the race)

With these nominals, the process saturates what comes to existence, as in (37), and the way it is created is left underspecified: The individual is waiting for the existence of the process itself.

(37)

$$
\begin{bmatrix}
\textbf{j'attends ce voyage} \\
\text{FORM} = \text{att}(e_0, x\text{:je}, [3]) \\
\\
\text{TEL} = [3] \begin{bmatrix} \text{FORM} = [2] \\ \text{AG} = [1] = \text{voyage\_Act}(e_1, x)) \end{bmatrix}
\end{bmatrix}
$$

Finally, with nouns denoting states, the result of the composition is ill-formed unless the nominal involves a specification of how it comes about:

(38)   a. ??J'attends la croyance de Pierre en D
        'I'm waiting the belief of Pierre in D'
        (I'm waiting for Pierre's belief in D)
    b. J'attends de nouvelles croyances
        'I'm waiting the new beliefs'
        (I'm waiting for new beliefs)

As shown in (39), "*croyance*" denotes both the particular mental state of holding a belief (for example in "Mary's belief that John is sick") and the complement proposition ("these beliefs are new"). The relationship between the two senses is specified by the qualia structure: the state of believing is the necessary condition (i.e., AGENTIVE) of what is believed:

(39)

$$
\begin{bmatrix}
\textbf{croyance} \\[4pt]
\text{ARGSTR} = \begin{bmatrix} \text{ARG1} = \text{x:prop} \\ \text{D-ARG1} = \text{y:human} \end{bmatrix} \\[10pt]
\text{EVENSTR} = \begin{bmatrix} \text{E1} = e_1 : \text{state} \end{bmatrix} \\[6pt]
\text{QS} = \begin{bmatrix} \text{state.prop-lcp} \\ \text{FORM} = \text{x} \\ \text{AG} = \text{croire}(e_1, \text{y}, \text{x}) \end{bmatrix}
\end{bmatrix}
$$

From (39), the only possible interpretation is that in (38b), which involves the mode of coming into being of the entity: I'm waiting 'for new beliefs to be believed in.'

We extend now the analysis to some puzzling data in Italian.

5   Extending the Analysis

The analysis presented above for the French verb "*attendre*" extends to Italian and accounts for the distinction between two predicates: "*aspettare*" (wait) and "*attendere*" (wait). Although the two verbs are almost synonyms, they differ in their behavior, as shown below:

(40)   a. Marco aspetta che tu parta per lavorare
          'Marco$_i$ is waiting that you$_j$ leave_subjunctive PRO$_i$/??PRO$_j$ to work'
          (Marco is waiting for you to leave before I work)
       b. ??Attendo che tu parta per lavorare
          'Marco$_i$ is waiting that you$_j$ leave_subjunctive *PRO$_i$/?PRO$_j$ to work'
          (Marco is waiting for you to leave to work)
       c. Aspetto la lettera di Mario.
          'I'm waiting the letter of Mario'
          (I am waiting for Mario's letter)
       d. Attendo la lettera di Mario.
          'I'm waiting the letter of Mario'
          (I am waiting for Mario's letter)

The interpretation of (40a) and (40b) are slightly different. In (40a) there is a stronger assumption that the WAITED will take place, and hence the result will follow. In (40b), the speaker is simply waiting for an event to take place, without additional presuppositions. Similarly, both (40c) and (40d) have the common interpretation that 'I am waiting for a letter to reach me.' However, (40c) involves a component that lacks with (40d): someone has already written the letter and I am expecting its arrival.

The contrast is illustrated more clearly in the examples below:

(41)   a. Prima di uscire, devo aspettare la torta.
              'Before I go out, I have to wait for the cake'
              (I can't go out until the cake is ready.)
         b. ??Prima di uscire, devo attendere la torta.
              'Before I go out, I have to wait for the cake'
              (I can't go out until the cake is ready.)

The utterance in (41a), with the verb *"aspettare,"* asserts that there is a cake in the oven, and that the individual is waiting for its completion. In (41b) this interpretation is quite odd, and the sentence can only be interpreted as I am waiting for a cake to be brought to me.

The lack of lexical presuppositions with *"attendere"* is furthemore illustrated in the examples below:

(42)   a. Aspettiamo per partire.
              'We are waiting to leave.'
         b. *Attendiamo per partire.
              'We are waiting to leave.'

The different acceptability of the above examples depends on the presuppositions of the verbs. The oddness of (42b) shows that the event selected by *"attendere"* is not a complex structure, but selects a simple event that is interpreted as the WAITED.

(43)
$$
\begin{bmatrix}
\textbf{attendere} \\
\text{ARGSTR} = \begin{bmatrix} \text{ARG1} = \text{x:ind} \\ \text{D\_ARG1} = [1] \end{bmatrix} \\
\text{EVENSTR} = \begin{bmatrix} \text{E1} = e_0\text{:state} \\ \text{D\_E1} = e_1\text{:event} \\ \text{RESTR\_1} = e_0 <_\alpha [1] \end{bmatrix} \\
\text{QS} = \begin{bmatrix} \text{FORM} = \text{attendere}(e_0,x,[1]) \\ \text{TEL} = [1] = P(e_1,x) \end{bmatrix}
\end{bmatrix}
$$

This short discussion is meant to highlight the usefulness of a linguistic independent vocabulary, such as qualia for purposes of lexical analysis.

6   Conclusion

In this paper, we have claimed that the semantics of *"attendre"* is not functionally ambiguous. The verb always selects for three arguments: the WAITOR (an individual), the WAITED (what the waitor is waiting for to be true), and the RESULT (the event presupposed to happen if what is waited for actually occurs), which map to different surface structures. When *"attendre"* only surfaces with an NP, the nominal must have a rich enough semantics to allow metonymic reconstruction of both the WAITED and the RESULT. We have also shown that this analysis extends to the Italian data, accounting for subtle differences involving the strength of the presuppositions associated to the WAITED.

This analysis opens a number of interesting questions that have not been directly addressed in this paper. In particular, the lexicon provides an anchor onto the discourse. The lexical knowledge, which is associated with nouns, can be viewed as a trigger for a richer set of pragmatically determined interpretations. In particular, we have presented different ways in which the context can specify the possible senses of *"attendre."*

From the perspective of how the lexicon ties to discourse, our treatment is still inadequate. However, while only scraping the surface of what needs to be accounted for in this domain, it opens up exciting research questions.

Acknowledgments

We would like to thank James Pustejovsky, Graham Russell, and Alessandro Lenci for their comments and discussion.

References

Bouillon, P. 1998. *Polymorphie et sémantique lexicale:le cas des adjectifs*, Presse du Septentrion: Lille.

Buitelaar, P. 1998. *CoreLex: Systematic Polysemy and Underspecification*, PhD Thesis, Brandeis University.

Busa, F. 1996. *Compositionality and the Semantics of Nominals*, PhD Thesis, Brandeis University.

Fodor, J.A., and Lepore, L. 1998. The Emptiness of the Lexicon: Critical Reflections on J. Pustejovsky's *The Generative Lexicon*. *Linguistic Inquiry* 29:2, 269–288. Also published in this volume.

Godard, D., and Jayez, J. 1993a. Towards a Proper Treatment of Coercion Phenomena. *Proc. EACL-93*, Utrecht, 167–177.

Godard, D., and Jayez, J. 1993b. Le traitement lexical de la coercion. *Cahiers de linguistique Française 14. Actes du Vème Colloque de pragmatique de Genève*, Genève, 123–149.

Jayez, J., and Godard, D. 1995. Principles as Lexical Methods. *Proc. AAAI workshop on representation and acquisition of lexical knowledge*, Stanford.

Parsons, T. 1990. *Event in the Semantics of English: A Study in Subatomic Semantics*. MIT Press, Cambridge.

Pustejovky, J. 1995. *The Generative Lexicon*. MIT Press, Cambridge.

Pustejovky, J. (1996). *The Quantificational Force of Qualia Structure*, manuscript, Brandeis University.

Pustejovsky, J. 1998a. The Semantics of Lexical Underspecification. *Folia Linguistica* 32: xxx.

Pustejovsky, J. 1998b. Generativity and Explanation in Semantics: A reply to Fodor and Lepore. *Linguistic Inquiry* 29:2, 289–310

Pustejovsky, J., and Boguraev B. (eds). 1996. *Lexical Semantics: The Problem of Polysemy*. Clarendon Paperbacks, Oxford.

Pustejovsky, J., and Bouillon, P. 1995. Logical Polysemy and Aspectual Coercion. *Journal of Semantics* 12: 133–162. (Published also in: Pustejovky and Boguraev, 1996).

Récanati, F. 1997. La polysémie contre le fixisme. *Langue Française* 113: 107–126.

10   Sense Variation and Lexical Semantics Generative Operations

PATRICK SAINT-DIZIER

Abstract

In this paper, we first outline some elements related to sense variation and to sense delimitation within the perspective of the *Generative Lexicon*. We then develop the case of adjectival modification and a few forms of sense variations, metaphors, and metonymies for verbs and show that, in some cases, the Qualia structure can be combined with or replaced by a small number of rules, which seem to capture more adequately the relationships between the predicate and one of its arguments. We focus on the Telic role of the Qualia structure, which seems to be the most productive role to model sense variations.

1   Introduction

Investigations within the generative perspective aim at modeling, by means of a small number of rules, principles and constraints, linguistic phenomena (either morphological, syntactic or semantic) at a high level of abstraction, level that seems to be appropriate for research on multilinguism and language learning. These works, among other things, attempt at modeling a certain form of "creativity" in language: from a limited number of linguistic resources, a potentially infinite set of surface forms can be generated.

Among works within the generative perspective, let us concentrate on the *Generative Lexicon* (Pustejovsky, 1991, 1995), which has settled in the past years one of the most innovative perspective in lexical semantics. This approach introduces an abstract model radically opposed to "flat" sense enumeration lexicons. This approach, which is now well-known, is based (1) on the close cooperation of three lexical semantic structures: the argument structure (including selectional restrictions), the aspectual structure, and the Qualia structure; (2) on a detailed type theory and a type coercion procedure; and (3) on a refined theory of compositionality. The *Generative Lexicon* (GL) investigates the problem of the multiplicity of usages of a sense of a lexeme and shows how these usages can be analyzed in terms of possible type shiftings with respect to the type expected by a usage of that sense defined as the core usage. Type shifting is modeled by a specific inference mechanism: type coercion. The GL shows very clearly the inter-dependence between arguments and predicates.

In our perspective, we are not only interested in deciding whether an expression is an acceptable argument for a predicate and for what reasons, as it is also the case in the GL, but we want to be able to *reconstruct* or to infer the meaning of the proposition from its parts (the predicate and its arguments), and possibly also from the implicit semantics conveyed by the syntactic form (Goldberg, 1994). We assume that the impossibility of building a semantic representation for a proposition entails that it is semantically ill-formed with respect to our grammar, lexicon, and composition rules. This view is very common in formal semantics.

In this paper, the following points are addressed:

- Generative systems require a clear analysis of the notions of word-sense and of sense delimitation. Depending on the strategy adopted (e.g., large number of narrow senses for a lexeme as in WordNet, or very few but large senses as in many AI works), the nature and the scope of generative operations may be very different. For delimiting senses, convergences, and differences between conceptual and lexicographic analysis are briefly investigated in this paper.
- The Qualia structure is a complex structure, quite difficult to describe. Recent works have shown evidences for the existence, in particular of the Telic role, (explored for example in the EuroWordNet project, the European WordNet). Qualias are well-designed and useful for nouns, but look more artificial for other lexical categories. We show in addition that it is the telic role of nouns that is the most useful, and how the internal structure of this role can (1) be made more precise and its use more reliable and accurate by means of types and (2) be partitioned by means of types into ontological domains for modeling some forms of metaphors. This restriction on the Telic role makes it easier to use and specify Qualia structures.
- Types are not sufficiently *constrained* to account for the constraints holding, for each predicate, on the different sense/usage variations they may be subject to. We show that an underspecified *Lexical Conceptual Structure* (LCS) (Jackendoff, 1990), where conceptual variables are typed, is more appropriate because of its ability to represent the polymorphism of senses in the GL.
- Elements of the Qualia structure can be incorporated into semantic composition rules to make explicit the semantics of the combination predicate-argument, instead of developing lexical redundancy rules.
- We contrast a rule-based approach (also used by other authors such as Copestake and Briscoe, 1995; Nunberg and Zaenen, 1992; Ostler and Atkins, 1992) with the Qualia-based approach to deal with sense shiftings and in particular selective binding, metaphors (which the GL cannot resolve a priori), and metonymies. Rules seem to be more precise via

the specification of constraints, whereas type shifting is a general, highly abstract operation. Rules can also be activated at different levels in the parsing process (at lexical insertion level or in semantic composition rules), whereas type coercion occurs only at a certain point, when parsing the item. Another view is presented in Jackendoff (1997) with the *principle of enriched composition*, which is in fact quite close to our view, but restricted to a few specific coercion situations (aspectual, mass-count, picture, begin-enjoy).

- The rules for type shifting we present here are not lexical rules, as in Copestake and Briscoe (1995), but they are part of the semantic composition system, which makes them more general.

- As shown in Pustejovsky (1995) and Copestake and Briscoe (1995), type coercion is not a process internal to the verb, but it operates at the level of the proposition, allowing a sentence such as:

$$\textit{Mary enjoys } [_{object} \textit{ the film] and } [_{event} \textit{ eating ice-cream].}$$

However, this type of sentence is problematic for unification because the verb must bear two types for the first object, syntactically an NP and a proposition (S-bar), and semantically a physical object and an event. We show that a constraint-based approach, which allows domains to be assigned to variables (the variable representing the semantics/syntax of the object) would be a good solution.

   To illustrate this study, we first survey the different senses and sense variations of one of the most polysemic French adjectives: *"bon"* (good), which covers most of the main sense variation situations that adjectives may undergo. Additional adjectives, often cited in the GL literature as *"rapide,"* *"triste,"* or *"facile"* (fast, sad, easy), behave similarly. In fact, we observed many behavior similarities within semantic families of adjectives (e.g., evaluative, locational, aspectual adjectives). Next, we present for verbs and VPs the case of sense variation and the treatment of some forms of metaphors and metonymies related to the use and to actions on objects. To give more strength to our study, we focus on a few verbs while showing that the results extend to the verbs of the same semantic class.

2   The Problem of Sense Delimitation

2.1   *Preliminaries*

Sense delimitation is a very delicate, but crucial, problem. It has been studied at length by many authors and in many projects.

   Let us say very informally that, in our perspective, we assume that a sense (more or less large and constrained) of a lexeme has a basic form and basic expressions also called basic usage(s) (a surface form reflecting the basic sense). For example, let us assume that for the verb "devour," meaning roughly 'eat fast and much,' the basic sense has an animal as subject and an edible object, dead or alive, as its object. Then "Fido devours meat" is a basic usage. The basic sense expects some types of arguments but it may also originate derived usages (via the above generative operations), which are more or less constrained and limited. Next, we have "John devours books," where both the subject and the object are metaphorical. Because we can only observe linguistic realizations of these derived usages, sense delimitation is then defining sets of usages sharing the same semantic "root," and identifying that root. Meaning is then assigned to linguistic expressions from the meaning of their constituents and by taking into account the semantic shifts introduced by the generative operations involved.

This perspective may be felt to be somewhat naive and archaic: (1) examples abound where it is not possible to identify a root among usages, and (2) usages are not necessarily derived from a more or less unique root but may result from complex interactions among derived usages. Nevertheless, we can say that:

- Our perspective is workable for utterances from relatively standard texts. It is of course always possible to find counter-examples, but then their occurence rate may be very low and should be evaluated.
- There exist formal and practical tools to "soften" the notion of semantic root, e.g., polymorphic types, or complex systems for semantic representations.
- Our approach is incremental, allowing the adjunction, step by step, of new usages.
- Semi-fixed forms and fixed forms are treated apart, and we believe that a number of counter-examples to our approach could fall in this class.

Sense delimitation is largely an open problem. It is indeed almost impossible to state precise and general principles that characterize the boundaries of different senses of a lexeme and what a sense exactly is. To make our approach workable, let us assume that senses exist independently of linguistic realizations, whatever they are called (e.g., concepts), and that it is possible to formally represent them. Sense delimitation largely depends on the theoretical and practical perspectives and, to a large extent, on intuition. The difficulty is then to elaborate a coherent system of sense delimitation and of sense/usage variation. Extreme solutions have been proposed, which are not totally satisfactory. For example WordNet (Fellbaum, 1993) tends to introduce one sense per usage, where a usage is characterized by the semantic features of the arguments. For example, WordNet has 27 different senses for the verb "give." Distinctions between senses are often very subtle and somewhat hard to represent in a formal semantic representation. This approach is very useful in the sense that it provides a very detailed description of the usages of a large number of words in English, but we think it lacks generalizations about language, which are often useful for NLP systems to work efficiently. On the other extreme, there are AI systems that tend to postulate a unique sense for a lexeme and very complex derivation procedures, involving complex logical systems, to produce different sub-senses. This may be explained by the fact that most AI approaches are not concerned with usages in language but just by meaning representation.

Our perspective is in-between these extremes. We think that the different usages of a word should be organized around a small, relatively generic, number of senses. From these senses, similarly to the GL, generative procedures should produce or recognize derived usages, with possible slight changes in meaning. Some elements for delimiting senses in adjectives are given in Saint-Dizier (1998).

A second problem is the definition of the nature and the form of constraints related to sense delimitation. For example, there are meaning components within a given sense that can be more or less constrained or opened. Within a given sense, modalities, which are often more peripheral, such as manner, means, goals, existence of an effect or telicity, may be left unconstrained whereas elements such as the type of agent, the existence of a cause, or the type of the first object (e.g., physical object or not, as in "*vendre un objet*" = to sell versus "*vendre quelqu'un*" = to denounce) may be much more constrained.

Then, given a set of usages assumed to be related to a unique sense, on what basis should the basic usage(s) and, therefore, the basic sense be defined? We think, from our experiments, that it is often the most usual usage that is the most primitive, probably the most concrete one, often one of the most widely used, and also possibly historically and ontogenetically the oldest (Mari, 1997). The semantic properties and representation of the basic usage must then be able to allow and possibly to explain the derived usages.

2.2   *Semantic Representations of Senses: A Psycho-linguistics Perspective*

These questions inevitably raise the problem of the semantic representation. Even if it is not comprehensive, it turns out, from our experiments on different semantic classes of verbs, that the LCS is a relatively adequate framework (possibly associated with a few attribute-value pairs for some properties) to represent the semantics of the expressions subject to the sense variations we have identified, and to allow for the implementation of the generative operations advocated in the previous section (see also B. Dorr's work on LCS forms for verb classes in English in Dorr et al., 1995). The different, hierarchically organized, elements at stake in the LCS seem to correspond, in general, to the variation factors that we have identified and to be sufficiently fine-grained.

It turns out that, in the LCS, the primitive constituents and some basic formulae correspond to different steps of the categorization procedure when learning a language. It will then be possible to modify or replace autonomous and often elementary parts of the LCS by others when representing sense variations, in a way similar to the human categorization and learning procedures that modify the structure of concepts. Notice that operations of composition within the

LCS are simply the embedding and the concatenation of LCS formula within others.

On a psycho-linguistic level, Dubois and Saint-Dizier (1996) has shown, for the possession verb family, elements of meaning that organize this family around prototypical kernels. For example, verbs such as "*racheter*" and "*facturer*" aggregates very early in language developement stages to the kernel verb "*acheter*" (buy). Then, verbs such as "*indemniser*," "*payer*," "*rembourser*," "*rémunérer*," "*dédommager*" (indemnify, pay, refund, bill) come later. With each of these levels can be associated well-formed fragments of LCS, which can be combined with the kernel's representation and can make the meaning of these verbs more precise and distinct from the kernel (Dubois and Saint-Dizier, 1996).

The generative operations we present operate on types and on LCS fragments, that they modify via substitution or concatenation to take into account sense variations. To allow for flexible substitutions and for the monotonicity of semantic composition rules, some LCS fragments will be represented apart, e.g., as default representations or as underspecified representations. Generativity, in a certain sense, is directly related to the evolution of the language activity. This statement looks trivial, but it has some immediate consequences on the type of structural element necessary to implement generative operations.

3   A Conceptual Analysis of the Polysemic Behavior of Adjectives

In this section, we investigate the semantics of adjectives and their polysemic behavior within a GL perspective. A model based on rules and on underspecified LCS forms is given, and various forms of metaphors and metonymies are studied. We focus on the adjective "*bon*" (good), which is one of the most polysemic adjectives in French. The study of adjectives such as "*rapide*," "*difficile*," and "*triste*" (fast, difficult, sad), which appear quite frequently in the GL litterature, shows many similarities and confirm the hypothesis presented here.

The syntax and the semantics of a number of adjectives has been investigated in Bouillon (1996, 1997), in a relatively strict GL framework. Our approach is more independent from the GL technical elements (e.g., the exact contents of the Qualia structure) and investigates in more depth the computation of the semantic representation of the compound adjective + noun. We also explore the modeling of metonymies and selection, and develop some sense variation rules.

3.1   *Elements for Delimiting Senses for Adjectives*

The GL approach requires a conceptual analysis of adjectives in order to focus on a relatively small number of senses. The idea is to isolate conceptual "behaviors," while taking also into account the constraints of linguistic realizations as in the lexicographic approach.

For sense delimitation, the following guidelines can be considered (see also the EEC DELIS project, for syntax and morphology):

1. if an adjective can be combined with two nouns with very different semantic types, then two different senses are involved, or there is a single sense, but a metaphor or a metonymy is involved;
2. opposites or antonyms should have a good proportion of similar conceptual behaviors, but with opposite meanings;
3. adjectives that are synonyms or that belong to the same family should share a large set of common conceptual behaviors, more specialized adjectives have in general narrower usages;
4. in terms of semantic representation (i.e., LCS), different senses of an adjective should have different semantic representations (assuming that the representation system is accurate enough);
5. it is difficult, in most cases, to coordinate different senses, for example *bon billet et repas* (*a valid ticket and meal).

3.2   Meanings of "bon"

Let us consider the adjective "*bon*," which is one of the most polysemic adjective: 25 senses identified in WordNet (e.g., Fellbaum, 1993). In fact, "*bon*" can be combined with almost any noun (except color names) in French, and as (Katz, 1966) pointed out, "good" would need as many different readings as there are functions for objects.

We have identified the following senses and sense variations (metaphors and metonymies in particular, expressed as in Lakoff and Johnson, 1980), for which we give some examples:

1. Idea of a good working of a concrete object with respect to what it has been designed for: *un bon tournevis, de bons yeux* (good screw-driver, good eyes). Metaphors abound: e.g., 'communication acts as tools': *une bonne plaisanterie/mise au point* (a good joke/explanation), 'function for tool' (*un bon odorat*), 'paths as tools' ("a good road"). Metonymies are rather unusual because if X is a part of Y, a good X does not a priori entail a good Y.[1]
2. Positive evaluation of moral, psychological, physical, or intellectual qualities in humans: *bonne personne, bon musicien* (good person, good musician). The basic sense concerns professions and related activites or humans as a whole: It is the ability of someone to realize something for professions, and for humans in general the high level of their moral

---

[1] This needs refinements: there are some weak forms of upward inheritance in the part-of relation: e.g., if the body of a car is red, then the car is said to be red.

qualities (qualities are more global in that case). This second sense could be viewed as a large metaphor of the first, with a structure-preserving transposition to a different ontology: from tools to professional or moral skills.

There are some *light* metaphors such as: 'social positions or ranks as professions' ("a good boss/father/friend/citizen"), and a large number of metonymies: 'image for person, image being a part of a person' ("a good reputation"), 'tool for profession' ("a good scalpel"), 'place for profession' ("a good restaurant"). These metaphors, which are identical for French and English, have a good degree of systematicity.

3. Intensifier of one or more properties of the noun, producing an idea of pleasure and satisfaction (this is different for sense 5):[2]

    - noun(+edible): "good meal/dish/taste" = tasty, with metonymies such as 'container for container' ("a good bottle/glass");
    - noun(+fine-art): "good film/book/painting" = valuable, with metonymies such as 'physical support for contents' ("good CD");
    - noun(+smelling): "good odor" (this is less frequent for other senses);
    - noun(+psycho): "good relation/experience";
    - noun(+human relations): "good neighbours".

    Note that *"bon"* can only be used with neutral or positive nouns, we indeed do not have in French "*good ennemies," "*good humidity" with the sense outlined here.

4. Quantification applied to measures or to quantities: "a good meter," "a good liter," "a good amount/salary," "a good wind." In this case, "good" means a slightly more than the unit/measure indicated or above the average (for terms that are not measure units, such as wind or salary). This sense being quite different because it is basically a quantifier, it won't be studied hereafter.

5. Idea of exactness, accuracy, correctness, validity, freshness, etc.: *un bon raisonnement/calcul* = exact, accurate (a good deduction/computation), "good note/ticket" = valid, "a good meat" = fresh or eatable, "a good use" = appropriate, "good knowledge" = efficient, large, and of good quality. The meaning of *"bon"* is therefore underdetermined. Depending on the noun, the semantics of *"bon"* is slightly different, this is not really a case of co-composition. It is the semantic type of the noun and that of the selected predicate in the telic role of the noun which determine the meaning of the adjective in this particular NP. We call this phenomenon, by comparison with selective binding, **selective projection**, because the meaning is projected from the telic role.

---

[2] Norms are being defined for about 600 top-most nodes of a general purpose ontology in different projects and research groups (e.g., NMSU, ISI, Eagles EEC project), they will be used as soon as available.

In addition to these senses, *"bon"* appears in a large number of fixed or semi-fixed forms such as: *le bon goût, le bon sens, le bon temps, une bonne gifle.*

Almost the same behavior is observed for all evaluative adjectives, such as "excellent," "terrific," "bad," or "lousy" in French. For example, for *"mauvais"* (bad), senses 1, 2, and 3 are identical, sense 4 is only applicable to amounts (*mauvais salaire*, low salary), not to units and sense 5 is almost identical, it conveys the idea of erroneous deduction, invalid ticket, bad use, and rotting meat. Note that in WordNet, "bad" has only 14 senses, whereas "good" has 25 senses, with no clear justification.

3.3   *Generative Devices and Semantic Composition*

Let us now analyze from a GL point of view the meanings of the adjective *"bon."*

In Pustejovsky (1995), to deal with the compound adjective+noun, a predicate in the telic of the noun is considered. For example, "fast," modifying a noun such as "typist," is represented as follows:

$$\lambda e \ [type'(e, x) \ \wedge \ fast(e)]$$

where e denotes an event. This formula says that the event of typing is fast. A similar representation is given for "long," in "a long record." This approach is appropriate to represent temporal notions in a coarse-grained way, i.e., the event is said to be fast (with potential inferences on its expected duration) or long. However, this approach is not viable for *"bon,"* and many other adjectives with little or no temporal dimension. In:

$$\lambda e \ [type'(e, x) \ \wedge \ good(e)]$$

it is not the typing event that is "good" but the way the typing has been performed (certainly fast, but also with no typos, good layout, etc.). A precise event should not be considered in isolation, but the representation should express that, in general, someone types well, allowing exceptions (some average or bad typing events). This involves a quantification, more or less explicit, over typing events of x. Finally, *"bon"* being polysemous, a single representation is not sufficient to accommodate all the senses.

The semantic representation framework we consider here is the LCS, it has some obvious limitations, but seems to be appropriate for our current purpose. It is associated with a typed λ-calculus.

Sense 1: "Bon" = that works well

This first sense applies to any noun of type tool, machine or technique: "a good car," "a good screw-driver." The semantic representation of *"bon"* requires a predicate from the telic role of the Qualia structure of the noun. It is the set (potentially infinite) of those predicates that characterizes the polymorphism. We have here a typical situation of *selective binding* (Pustejovsky, 1991), where the representation of the adjective is a priori largely underspecified. Let us assume that any noun that can be modified by "*bon*" has a telic role in which the main function(s) of the object is described (e.g., execute programmes for a computer, run for a car[3]), then the semantics of the compound adjective + noun can be defined as follows:

Let N be a noun of semantic type α, and of Qualia: [..., Telic: T, ...] where T denotes the set of predicates associated with the telic role of the noun N. Let Y be the variable associated with N and let us assume that T is a list of predicates of the form $F_i(\_, \_)$. Then the LCS-based representation of "*bon*" is:

$$\lambda Y : \alpha, \; \lambda F_i, \; [_{state} \; BE_{+char,+ident}([_{thing} \; Y],$$
$$[_{+prop} \; ABILITY\text{--}TO(F_i(Y, \_)) = high])]$$

which means that the entity denoted by the noun works well, expressed by the evaluation function ABILITY-TO and the value "high." This type of low-level function abounds in the LCS, this principle is introduced in Jackendoff (1997). Note that the second argument of the predicate F_i does not need to be explicit (we use the Prolog notation "_" for these positions).

The Qualia allows us to introduce in a direct way **a pragmatic or interpretative dimension** via the instanciation of $F_i(\_, \_)$.

The constant "high" can be replaced by a more accurate representation, (e.g., "above average"), but the problem of evaluating a functionality remains open. Note also that instead of quantifying over events, "*bon*" is described as a state: The functionalities of the object remain good, even when it is not used effectively. If several functionalities are at stake, we may have a conjunction or a more complex combination of functions F_i.

From a compositional point of view, the combination Adjective+Noun is treated as follows, where R is the semantic representation of the adjective, T, the contents of the telic role of the Qualia of the noun N of type α, τ, a particular element of T and Y, the variable associated with the noun:

$$\text{sem-composition}(Adj(R), Noun(Qualia(T)))$$
$$= \lambda Y : \alpha, \; \exists F_i(Y, \_) \in T, \; (N(Y) \; \wedge \; R(Y)(F_i(Y, \_))).$$

The open position in R(Y) is instanciated by β-reduction. The selection of F_i is simple: For basic tools, there is probably only one predicate in the Qualia (screwdriver $\rightarrow$ screw), for more complex nouns, there is an ambiguity that is reflected by the nondeterministic choice of F_i, but probably organized with preferences, which should be added in the Qualia. It is the constraint on the type of Y that restricts the

---

[3] Less prototypical predicates can also be considered (e.g., comfort or security for a car), which are properties probably described in the constitutive role of the Qualia of car.

application of that semantic composition rule. This notation is particularly simple and convenient.

Metaphors are treated in a direct way: the constraint on the type of Y can be enlarged to:

$$\lambda Y : \beta \; \wedge \; metaphor(\beta, \alpha)$$

and the remainder of the semantic composition rule and semantic formula remains unchanged. We have, for example:

> *metaphor(communication–act, tool)* (joke).
>
> *metaphor(communication–path, tool)* (road).

The function F_i selected is again a predicate in the telic of the noun, with no interpolation toward a more normalized terms, as done in the GL for type shifting (e.g., we use: make-laugh(X,Y) for "joke" and drive-on(X,Y) for "road").

We have evaluated that, in French, there are about twelve frequent forms of metaphors for this sense. The study of this first sense suggests that the introduction of a hierarchy of preferences would be a useful extension to the Telic role, reflecting forms of prototypicality among predicates.

Sense 2: *"Bon" restricted to cognitive or moral qualities*

Another sense of *"bon"* modifies nouns of type profession or human. The treatment is the same as in the above section, but the selection of the predicate(s) $\tau = F_i(X, Y)$ in the telic of the noun's qualia must be restricted to properties related to the moral behavior (makes-charity, has-compassion, has-integrity) when the noun is a person, or to some psychological attitudes and cognitive capabilities when the noun denotes a profession (e.g., "a good composer"). Alternatively, some of these properties could be found in the constitutive role (approximately the part-of relation), if properties can be parts of entities.

The typing of the predicates in the Qualia roles can be done in two ways: (1) by means of labels identifying the different facets of a role, as in Bergler (1991) for report verbs, but these facets are often quite ad hoc and hard to define, or (2) by means of types directly associated with each predicate. These types can, for example, directly reflect different verb semantic classes as those defined in Levin (1993) or Saint-Dizier (1996) on a syntactic basis, or the major ontological classes of WordNet and their subdivisions. This solution is preferable, because it does not involve any additional development of the Telic role, but simply the adjunction of types from a separate, pre-defined ontology.

An LCS representation for this sense of *"bon"* is, assuming the following types for F_i:

$$\lambda Y : human, \; \lambda F_i : action\text{--}related\text{--}to\text{--}profession \; \vee \; moral\text{--}behavior$$
$$[_{state} \; BE_{+char,+ident}([_{thing} \; Y], \; [_{+prop} \; ABILITY\text{--}TO(F_i(Y, \_)) = high])].$$

When several predicates are at stake, a set of $F_i(Y, \_)$ can be considered in the representation, or the statement is ambiguous.

Metonymies such as "a good scalpel" are resolved by the general rule: 'tools for professions.' This information could be in a knowledge base or, alternatively, it can be infered from the Telic role of the tool: any instrument has a predicate in its telic role that describes its use – the type of the first argument of the predicate is directly related to the profession that uses it. For example, scalpel has in its telic role:

$$cut(X : surgeon \lor biologist, \ Y : body).$$

When the profession is identified, the standard procedure for determining the meaning of the compound can be applied. Metonymies using the part-of relation are quite simple to resolve using the constitutive role, as in the GL.

If this sense is viewed as **a metaphor of the first sense** (i.e., cognitive capabilities as practical/professional capabilities), then we can have here a **direct modeling of metaphors**, as fomulated in Lakoff and Johnson (1980): a transposition of the current meaning to a distinct, but compatible, ontology. We can assume that structured parts of qualia roles in the Qualia structure correspond to different ontologies and to actions related to different ontological domains. These parts that structure a role (mainly the formal and telic ones), as advocated above, can be identified by means of types, such as those associated with the WordNet verb classes (and subclasses). Then, switching from one part of a role to another is a switch from an ontological domain to another. Very briefly, the telic role of a tool (sense 1) is of the form:

```
tool: Qualia: [..., Telic: P(X,Y): technical-action, ...].
```

The type technical-action is, for example, a subtype of the WordNet verb class; "verbs of creation, destruction and use." Then, a profession and a person (sense 2) have the following generic Qualia elements of interest to us:

```
profession: [..., Telic: ... P(X,Y): technical-action, ...].
    human: [..., Telic: ..., P1(X,Y): psy-verb, ...].
```

We have here a direct transposition from the Telic of a tool (1) to the telic of a profession (different ontological domains are considered because the two lexical entries, tool and profession, belong to two different domains) and where a predicate $P(X,Y)$ of the same type is considered, or (2) to the telic of a human, where a predicate of another ontology (human psychology) is considered. In this latter case, the difference in ontological domains is characterized by both the type of the lexical entry and the type of the predicate in the Qualia roles considered. The predicate is no longer P but P1. This behavior cannot be made systematic. Such shiftings need to be explicitly specified, but it is nevertheless of much interest to use the descriptive power of the Qualia roles to model some metaphors.

Sense 3: "Bon" as an intensifier

Another main role of "*bon*" is to emphasize a quality of the object denoted by the noun. As shown in section 2, there is a certain action associated with the telic of the modified noun that produces a certain pleasure. For example, watching a good film entails a certain pleasure.

Let us consider again a noun N of type α (e.g., edible object) associated with the variable Y. The entity (human) undergoing the pleasure is not explicit in the NP, it is represented by X, and included in the scope of a λ-abstraction. Let $F_i(X, Y)$ be the predicate selected in the telic role of N. The LCS representation is then:

$$\lambda X : human, Y : \alpha, \ F_i(X, Y)$$
$$[_{event} \ CAUSE([_{event} \ F_i(X, Y)],$$
$$[_{state} \ BE_{+psy}([_{thing} \ X],$$
$$[_{place} \ AT_{+psy}([_{+place} \ pleasure])])])].$$

We have here another form of representation for "*bon*," where F_i is a CAUSE.

The term "pleasure" is an element of an ontology describing (e.g., mental attitudes and feelings). It is relatively generic and can be replaced by a more precise term, via *selective projection* (see below for sense 5), depending on the nature of the pleasure.

An alternative representation describes a path toward the value "pleasure," giving an idea of progression:

$$\lambda X : human, Y : \alpha, \ F_i(X, Y)$$
$$[_{event} \ CAUSE([_{event} \ F_i(X, Y)],$$
$$[_{event} \ GO_{+psy}([_{thing} \ X],$$
$$[_{path} \ TOWARDS_{+psy}([_{+place} \ pleasure])])])].$$

Notice that this sense of "*bon*" does not imply an idea of quantity: A good meal does not entail that the meal is big, a good temperature does not entail that the temperature is high, but rather mild. The semantic composition rule is similar as in 3.1.

The metonymy 'container for containee' ("a good bottle") is resolved by a type shifting on Y. Y may be of type β iff:

$$\exists Z : \alpha, \ Y : container \ \wedge \ container\text{-}for(Y, Z).$$

Inferences are identical (e.g., "a good CD").

3.4   *Long-distance Compositionality*

The NP "a good meat" is related to senses 2 or 5, it therefore includes in its domain of meanings structures presented in sections 2.2 and 2.4. Instead of choosing one solution (a generate and test strategy), a set can be provided (as in constraint programming, see section 6). Now, if we have an NP of the form: *une viande bonne à consommer* (a meat good to eat), then the parsing of *"consommer"* will provoque the selection of sense 5 (and subsense 'fresh/consumable' via selective projection) because of the type of *"consommer."* If, conversely, we have *une viande bonne à déguster* (a meat good to savour), then, because *"déguster"* is of type *eat.enjoy* (a dotted type in the GL), sense 2 is selected. The space of meanings is restricted when additional information is found.

A second case involves default reasoning (as in Pernelle, 1998). In *un bon couteau pour sculpter* (a good knife to carve), by default, the action that the knife performs well is that protypically found in its telic role. However, if a less proto-typical action is found explicitly in the sentence, then this latter is preferred and incorporated into the semantic representation instead of the default case. Indeed, the telic role describes prototypical actions, because the others are often unpre-dictable. The default meaning of *"bon"* is kept and *frozen* until the whole sentence has been parsed. If there is no contradiction with that sense, then it is assigned to the adjective, otherwise, it is discarded in favor of the sense explicitly found in the sentence.

Finally, we consider the expressions "Y makes a good X, Y is a good X" as collocations where "good" is not fully treated compositionally.

4   Selection and Dimensions of Interpretation for Verbs

Selection is directly related to the problem of sense delimitation because it is more or less complex depending on the "breadth" of a sense. The larger a sense is, the more complex is this phenomenon. It also well illustrates the use of LCS and how the meaning of a proposition is computed from the fundamental structure and semantics of the verb, its arguments, and the taking into account of usage variations.

We hypothesize that a verb sense receives a single LCS representation, possibly largely underspecified, and possibly a list of (partial) instanciations constrained by the nature of the arguments and also possibly by pragmatic factors. This *polymor-phic* representation is the representation of the verb. Usage variations entailed by metaphors or metonymies do not alter the meaning of the verb, but they are pro-voked by the juxtaposition of a verb and an argument. It is therefore the meaning of the VP or of the proposition which is not "standard." In a selection situation, the verb meaning becomes more specialized (a definition of subsumption in LCS is given in Dubois and Saint-Dizier, 1996). In the Generative Lexicon (Pustejovsky, 1991, 1995), selection is treated by selective binding, which is an operation en-tirely based on type concordance and type subsumption. No attempt seems to be made to construct a meaning representation, which is not in fact the main goal of the GL.

Let us now present a few examples. Note that the verb classes considered here are those we defined for French (Saint-Dizier, 1996), they do not necessarily overlap with those defined in Levin (1993) or with those of WordNet.

4.1   *The Case of Construction Verbs*

The construction verb class includes verbs like *"construire,"* *"bâtir,"* *"édifier,"* *"réaliser,"* *"composer"* (build, construct, realize, compose), etc. Let us concentrate on the verb *"construire,"* which includes usages such as:

Construire une maison/un cercle/un projet/une relation (to build a house/a circle/a project/a relation).

The sense variation goes from a central meaning with a concrete, physical object to an abstract object. The general representation of this verb is:

$$\lambda J, I, [_{event} CAUSE([_{thing} I],$$
$$[_{event} GO_{+char,+ident}([_{path} TOWARD_{+char,+ident}([_{state} EXIST]),$$
$$FROM_{+char,+ident}(part\text{-}of(J)),$$
$$VIA_{+char,+ident}(definition\text{-}constitutive(J))])]).$$

which describes the coming into being of J. Two functions, related to lexical data, are used: part-of(J) that gets the parts of J, and definition-constitutive(J) that gets the definition of J (e.g., a circle is a set of points equidistant from a particular point: the center). If this definition is not available in the lexical entry corresponding to the lexeme J, then the function remains as it is, just stating that J has a certain constitutive definition.

4.2   *The Sell Verbs*

The sell verb class introduces a simple default representation. Let us consider the verb *"vendre"* (sell), generic element of the class. Its basic argument is a physical object (which has an intrinsic value). Besides this usage, we have slightly more metaphorical ones, such as:

Vendre des rêves/des illusions (to sell dreams/illusions).

If we assume that, in this latter case, a dream has no intrinsic value, it is its association with *"vendre,"* which gives rise to the idea of value via the expectations on the argument. We also have expressions like *"vendre quelqu'un"* = to betray someone. These usages define the possible sense variations of the verb "sell." We can then say that these objects, in association with verbs of the "sell" class (and a few other classes as well) get (e.g., a fictive value), represented by the function: FICTIVE-VALUE(J), and there is also a type shifting on J.

The basic representation of "sell" is the following:

$$\lambda I, J, K, [_{event} CAUSE([_{thing} I],$$
$$[_{event} GO_{+poss}([_{thing} J],$$
$$[_{path} FROM_{+poss}([_{thing} I]), TO_{+poss}([_{thing} K])]),$$
$$GO_{+poss}([_{thing} P],$$
$$[_{path} FROM_{+poss}([_{thing} K]), TO_{+poss}([_{thing} I])])])]$$
$$\wedge DEFAULT(P, VALUE\text{–}OF(J), J,$$
$$TYPE(J) = physical\text{–}object, COERCED\text{–}TYPE(J) = none).$$

where P is the anchoring point for the default, activated when J, the variable concerned, is of type physical-object. In this case, which is the standard one, J need not be coerced to any other type. The default representation represents the basic usage, for the other cases, this default is not used and other types of representations are anchored at P.

The general form of a default is then:

DEFAULT(anchor, representation, variable concerned, expected type for argument, coerced type if appropriate).

When the type is not physical object, then a different value is anchored to the position P, as explained above. The other possible values may equivalently (1) be specified in the representation of the verb, similarly to the default, but not with the status of a representation by default, and associated with constraints of use, or (2) by means of a rule. If the first case is chosen (with constraints on the type of the object), then it has the following form:

OTHER-REPT(P, FICTIVE-VALUE(J), J, TYPE(J)

= abstract artefact, COERCED-TYPE(J) = physical-object).

4.3   A Few Cognition Verbs

Cognition verbs are not very easy to represent with the standard LCS primitives. Additional primitives can be defined, but, for the sake of simplicity, let us here work with the primitives defined in the LCS literature.

The verb *"concevoir"* (conceive) has some similarities with the verb *"construire"* studied above: it is also the coming into being, but, in general by means of a mental operation. A simple LCS representation is the following:

$$[_{event} CAUSE([_{thing} I], [_{event} GO_{+epist}([_{thing} J],$$
$$[_{path} TOWARDS_{+epist}([_{state} EXIST(J)])],$$
$$[_{means} BY\text{–}MEANS\text{–}OF_{+epist}([QR(agentif, epist)])])])]$$

where QR(Role, Constraints) extracts one or more predicate in the role called Role from the Qualia structure, via the constraints given in the variable Constraints (in the example any predicate of type epistemic).

If we want to avoid the notion EXIST(J), then, *"concevoir"* can also be represented as follows:

$$[_{event} \ CAUSE([_{thing} \ I], \ [_{event} \ GO_{+epist}([_{thing} \ J],$$
$$[_{path} \ TOWARDS_{+epist}([_{prop} \ QR(agentif, \ epist)])])])].$$

Then, for example, in "conceive a house," J = house and QR(agentive, epist) = draw(I, house), compute(I, characteristics, house), evaluate(I, costs, house), and so forth. However, this agentive role is not necessarily as rich as one may wish. However, at the level of a lexical representation, the two forms given above should suffice.

In metaphorical uses of *"concevoir,"* the semantic field epist may change and become *loc* or *psy* ("conceive a child"). This verb shows a way LCS and elements from the GL can be combined to produce a detailed semantic representation of an utterance.

The same approach is also valid for a psychological and cognition verb such as *"contrôler"* (control). In this example, it is interesting to note how and to what extent the semantic representations of the different senses are different.

A first sense of *"contrôler"* is to check for or have knowledge of some properties of objects or persons. The simplest LCS form is:

$$[_{event} \ CAUSE([_{thing} \ I], \ [_{event} \ GO_{+epist}([_{thing \ \lor \ prop}$$
$$STATUS(QR(telique, prop, \ J))],$$
$$[_{path} \ TOWARDS_{+epist}([_{place} \ I])])])].$$

In the function QR, we have added the specification of the argument, J here, to avoid any confusions. This representation is simple and direct if J is an NP or a PP, but if it is a proposition, then it must be represented in J.

If *"contrôler"* introduces, in addition, an idea of iterativity, then a manner, REPEATINGLY, must be added:

$$[_{event} \ CAUSE([_{thing} \ I], \ [_{event} \ GO_{+epist}([_{thing \ \lor \ prop}$$
$$STATUS(QR(telique, prop, \ J)],$$
$$[_{path} \ TOWARDS_{+epist}([_{place} \ I])],$$
$$[_{manner} \ REPEATINGLY])])])].$$

The predicates extracted from the telic role must be very prototypical of the argument: usually *norms* are the elements that are regularly controlled.

Finally, *"contrôler"* also has the sense of *dominate* meaning have control on the actions of someone. This sense being more remote than the two first ones, it has a representation that is quite different:

$$[_{state} BE_{+epist \lor +psy}([_{thing} J],$$
$$[_{event} CAUSE([_{thing} I], [_{event} QR(telique, actions, J)])])].$$

We have here a state where J is in the state where I is the cause of a number of its actions, given in particular in its telic role.

Similar observations have been made for other types of cognition verbs such as "*chercher*," "*comprendre*," "*dériver*," "*éclaicir*" (search, understand, derive, enlighten). Other verb classes, such as communication verbs and cooking verbs, are also based on this approach. In these examples, it is also interesting to note the level and the nature of underspecified elements: They are usually of a low level in the representation and are in general semantic fields, basic ontological functions or GL Qualia predicates. No variable is added and no primitive is changed by sense variations.

5 Metonymies Related to Uses and to Actions on Objects

Let us now investigate, for several classes of verbs, metonymies related to uses and to actions on objects, as introduced in section 2. The elements used to treat these metonymies could be close to those found in the telic and agentive roles of the Qualia structure, they may be more vague and may also have a larger scope. This entails that the distinction between the agentive and the telic roles is weakened (e.g., the bringing about or creation, destruction [also in the Formal role], and the use of an object may overlap). By the implicit focus imposed by the semantics of the verb on a certain property of the argument, this property imposes its type to the argument, producing a kind of type shifting.

The observations we made tend to show that there are several regularities in argument shiftings, over sets of verbs, often over verb semantic classes as those constructed for English in WordNet or in Levin (1993) or for French, as those we have defined in Saint-Dizier (1996). However, there are several restrictions, in particular those naturally imposed by each verb on their arguments. There are also idiosyncrasies, and cases where argument shiftings are more or less acceptable in NL utterances.

A recurrent problem is the description of the properties of the objects in the lexicon. Although there are emerging trends toward a normalization of lexical descriptions and the use of ontologies,[4] there are still many significant differences in the nature of the representations and in their granularity. The lexical data we use here are made as precise and concrete as possible, but it is clear that they need a reformulation to be consistent with a particular lexical system.

---

[4] Norms are being defined for about 600 top-most nodes of a general purpose ontology in different projects and research groups (e.g., NMSU, ISI, Eagles EEC project).

5.1   The "object to event" Metonymy

Let us consider first the treatment of famous cases of the GL where a type "object" is coerced into an event (e.g., the famous "begin a book"). If we have a general common-sense rule that says that *any physical object has been created, may be used or deleted*, then the type *alternation object → event* can be accounted for directly. Besides physical objects, we also have products of the human activity such as projects, debates, ideas, and so forth, which can become events. They are in general elements with a certain idea of duration and of production of a result.

Thus, in the sentence:

"To begin a novel,"

a "novel" is a physical object. The verb "begin" selects an object of type event. The type shifting rule *physical–object → event* can be applied. The ambiguity of the sentence is left unresolved. In fact, many types of events can be associated with this construction, such as: "read," "write," "summarize," "classify," "index," "analyze," "edit," "copyedit," "cover," and so on. These interpretations may be felt to be part of a pragmatic component. Similarly to adjectives, preferences among predicates can be given.

Besides the verb "begin," the above common-sense rule is also used for most verbs specifying actions: starting, creation, realization, fabrication, completion, destruction, maintenance verb semantic classes. Most verbs of creation, consumption, and destruction in WordNet also accept this argument shifting:

"To industrialize a product" = to industrialize the manufacturing of a product,

where industrialize selects an object of type "procedure" (a property of a product is that it is for example produced or manufactured).

From these examples, we can somewhat generalize the above rule as follows:

physical–object ∨ *intellectual–activity → event*

This rule is valid for object arguments of the verb classes mentioned above. For the subject argument phenomena are different and somewhat more restricted. There are, in particular, many metonymies. There are, of course, other semantic types of objects, not presented here, which can undergo this type shifting.

5.2   The Metonymy: Objects for Their Value

We now introduce type shifting operations on other properties of objects, which are not metaphors in the constructions we consider. These properties seem to be often measurable, such as the monetary value, the intensity of a smelling, and so forth.

If a common-sense rule states that any physical object may have a certain monetary value, we then have the type shifting:

$$physical–object \rightarrow monetary–value,$$

as in:

Payer une maison (to pay a house) = to pay the value of the house

since "pay" selects an object of type *monetary value* (as in "to pay a salary").

Another set of properties are those related to measures: *augmenter, monter/ baisser une note, une action* (increase/decrease a mark, a share) = to increase the value of a mark, of a share (a mark has the property of being characterized by a value of type real or integer), or related to odors, as in:

Sentir une fleur (to smell a flower) = to smell the perfume of a flower.

For this latter example, we have a shifting rule of the form:

$$object(+has–smell) \rightarrow smelling,$$

and the verb "to smell" selects an object of type smelling/odor. We think that the odor of a plant may not be in the constitutive of the word "plant," because it is not a real part.

5.3   *Metonymies Related to Functionalities or to the Use of an Object*

Argument shifting related to the functionalities or to the use of an object goes beyond the alternation *object* → *event* presented above, while remaining in the same spirit. Some general and relatively frequent metonymies are related to the functions, to the use, to the emergence, to the transformation, or to the access of/to the object. We have, for example, the following cases, where, besides introducing a rule modeling the metonymy, we give a list of some of the most prominent verbs that accept this type shifting on their object argument. These examples need, obviously, to be further analyzed and categorized, but they nevertheless give a good view of what the type shiftings is:

- *Automatiser/amorcer une procédure* (to automate/start a procedure) = to automate the running of a procedure, assuming that "*automatiser*" selects an object of type *process*. Most "starting" verbs may be subject to this type shifting.

  The rule is then, roughly:

  $$phys–object(+procedure) \rightarrow process.$$

- *Arrêter/hater/accélérer/activer/ajourner/retarder/repousser/un projet - un modèle de voiture* (to start, ..., a project - a car model) = to stop the course of the production of a car model, the course of a project. Verbs like "*arrêter*" and in fact most "aspectual verbs," select an object of type *event* and may undergo the above type shifting, characterized roughly by the following shifting rule:

$$phys\text{-}object(+artefact) \rightarrow process.$$

The use of the term "process" is still approximate and it may be necessary to define a more precise typology of events. Below, events will be made more precise by means of feature, this is a temporary notation.

- *Annoncer/communiquer/rapporter/révéler un secret - de la neige* (to announce ... snow) = to announce the creation, the existence, the coming into being, the arrival, or the end of something. These communication or report verbs select an object of type *event*. The general shifting rule is, roughly:

$$phys\text{-}object \rightarrow event(+coming\text{-}into\text{-}being).$$

- *Défendre/interdire/autoriser un jeu - un jouet - un lieu - une sortie - un spectacle* (to forbid ... a game, a toy, a place, a show) = to forbid/ allow the access to a place, the use of a toy, the attendance to a show. The "allow/forbid" verb class selects objects of type *event* expressing uses, accesses, attendance, movement, etc. The general shifting rule is, roughly:

$$phys\text{-}object(place \lor toy \lor \ldots) \rightarrow event(+\,use \lor +\,access \lor \ldots).$$

The argument shifting phenomena on the subject are slightly different and seem to be less complex:

- *Jean amuse/charme/captive/divertit/plaît/déplaît* ... (John amuses ...) = the actions or the behavior(+verbal $\lor$ + physical) of John amuses. Most of the verbs of the "amuse" class are subject to this shifting, which we can summarize as follows:

$$human \rightarrow event(+behavior \lor +actions).$$

- Similarly, but on a larger scale, we have: *Les syndicats influencent la stratégie de l'entreprise* (the trade unions influence the company's strategy) = the behavior(+verbal $\lor$ +physical) of the trade-unions (of type *human-organization*) influences the company's strategy. Most verbs of the transformation class in French undergo this shifting, such as: "*changer*," "*métamorphoser*," "*transformer*," "*affermir*," "*amoindrir*," "*améliorer*," "*redresser*," etc. (approximately: change, transform, transform [again], reduce, improve, restore), with their own additional, more or less idiosyncratic constraints on the subject. Other subjects related to natural or to mechanical activities are also subject to this shifting. It is interesting to note that this construction corresponds to a context (nb. 151, equivalent to a syntactic alternation) in French (Saint-Dizier, 1996). About 9.6% of the French verbs may undergo it, and are quite diverse.

The general form of a type shifting rule is then, roughly, the following:

$$< Verb\ class >,\ < argument\ involved >,\ < constraints >,$$
$$Type1\ \to\ Type2.$$

In forthcoming work, we will see that the syntactic form is part of the constraints of application, because some syntactic forms block type shifting.

The examples above show a quite good systematicity, and let us say that there is sufficient evidence, in spite of necessary exceptions, to motivate a treatement at this level. The Qualia structure turns out not to be necessary to determine acceptability of the sentences. The Qualia is useful to interpret them, but this interpretation is rather pragmatic, and we think that the ambiguity should be left unresolved.

6   Computational Aspects: Toward Constraint-based Systems

From a computational perspective, we think that programming languages based on unification and the generate and test strategy may be too weak to handle the problem of polysemy in general. We indeed need languages which support the idea of, for example, conveying sets (disjunctions) of potential solutions. Constraint-based approaches handle domains of potential assignments for variables; domains become restricted as soon as constraints are formulated on them, via dedicated constraint resolution mechanisms.

Constraint logic programming (e.g., Benhamou and Colmerauer, 1993) is one such paradigm where logical implication has been paired with other mechanisms for handling various forms of constraints, in particular on finite domains. In that case, more or less complex algorithms have been developed and integrated into logic programmes. These algorithms basically handle classical operations on sets (e.g., intersection).

For example, in sentences such as:

"John knows$_{+wh,-Wh}$ [that whales are mammals]$_{-wh}$ and [whether they have lungs or not]$_{+wh}$."
"Mary enjoys [the film]$_{object}$ and [eating ice-cream]$_{event}$."

the verbs "know" and "enjoy" must select two a priori incompatible types, syntactic or semantic. For the latter sentence, a rule of the following form, in DCG associated with constraints can be used:

```
vp --> v(Sel-restr), sentence(Sem),
    {domain(X,Sel-restr), domain(Y,Sem),
    included-into(Y,X)}.

sentence(Sem) -->
    sentence(Sem1), [and], sentence(Sem2),
    {domain(X,Sem), domain(Y,Sem1),
    domain(Z,Sem2),
    included-into(Y,X), included-into(Z,X)}.
```

Between brackets are the constraints, which are not interpreted as Prolog terms, but as predicates related to set manipulations. The predicates `domain` and `included-into` express constraints, they are therefore not evaluated to true or false.

The same approach can be used to handle type coercion in the GL, where a domain for a variable can be the (finite) set of all the types the entity denoted by the variable can be coerced to. The domain then expresses the generative expansion of the entity. No commitment to any particular derived type is made a priori.

7   Conclusion

In this paper, we have presented an analysis of adjectival modification and several cases of selective binding and metonymies on semantic classes of verbs withing the GL perspective. We have proposed several extensions to the Telic role to be able to account for the representation of the different forms of sense variations. In particular, we have shown how types can be added, and how predicates from the telic participate to the construction of the semantic representation of the compound noun + adjective and in the verb-argument relation. We have also shown how Telic roles contribute to the modeling of metaphors.

Coercions and the treatment of metaphors and metonymies are generally assumed to be general principles, however, they are in fact more specialized than they seem at first glance (e.g., *une bonne toque/plume* = a good cook/writer is quite specific, or very constrained). It is probably necessary to introduce narrower selectional restrictions on their use. Finally, of much interest is to know how much these rules are subject to linguistic variation.

Acknowledgments

I would like to thank Alda Mari for working jointly with me on preliminary studies from which this work emerged. I also thank James Pustejovsky, Federica Busa, Mouna Kamel, and Françoise Gayral for discussions that greatly helped improving this work. Finally, I thank Pierrette Bouillon for a detailed and accurate revision of this text and for her useful remarks and questions on its contents.

References

Benhamou, F., and Colmerauer, A. (eds.) 1993. *Constraint Logic Programming*. MIT Press, Cambridge.

Bouillon, P. 1996. Mental State Adjectives: the Perspective of Generative Lexicon. *Proc. Coling'96*, Copenhague.

Bouillon, P. 1997. *Polymorphie et sémantique lexicale*, Thèse de troisième cycle, Université de Paris VII.

Copestake, A., and Briscoe, T. 1995. Semi-Productive Polysemy and Sense Extension. *Journal of Semantics* 12:1, 273–302.

Dorr, B. J., Garman, J., and Weinberg, A. 1995. From Syntactic Encodings to Thematic Roles: Building Lexical Entries for Interlingual MT. *Machine Translation* 9: 71–100.

Dubois, D., and Saint-Dizier, P. 1996. Construction et representation de classes sémantiques de verbes: une coopération entre syntaxe et cognition. *Proc. RFIA96*, Rennes, France.

Fellbaum, C. 1993. English Verbs as Semantic Net. *Journal of Lexicography* 3(4): 278–301.

Goldberg, A. 1994. *Constructions: A Construction Grammar Approach to Argument Structure*. University of Chicago Press, Chicago.

Jackendoff, R. 1990. *Semantic Structures*. MIT Press, Cambridge.

Jackendoff, R. (1997). *The Architecture of the Language Faculty*. MIT Press, Cambridge.

Katz, G. 1966. *The Philosophy of Language*. Harper and Row, New-York.

Lakoff, G., and Johnson, M. (1980). *Metaphors We Live By*. University of Chicago Press, Chicago.

Levin, B. 1993. *English Verb Classes and Alternations: A Preliminary Investigation*. Chicago Univ. Press, Chicago.

Mari, A. 1997. *Une analyse de la générativité en sémantique lexicale utilisant la structure lexicale conceptuelle*. Research report, Université de Lausanne and IRIT.

Nunberg, G. D., and Zaenen, A. (1992). Systematic Polysemy in Lexicology and Lexicography. *Proc. Euralex92*, Tampere, Finland.

Ostler, N., and Atkins, S. 1992. Predictable Meaning Shifts: Some Lexical Properties of Lexical Implication Rules. In J. Pustejovsky and S. Bergler (eds.), *Lexical Semantics and Knowledge Representation*. Springer-Verlag, Berlin.

Pernelle, N. 1998. *Raisonnement par défaut et lexique génératif*, PhD dissertation, LIPN, Paris.

Pinker, S. 1993. *Learnability and Cognition*. MIT Press, Cambridge.

Pustejovsky, J. 1991. The Generative Lexicon. *Computational Linguistics* 17:4.

Pustejovsky, J. 1995. *The Generative Lexicon*. MIT Press, Cambridge.

Saint-Dizier, P. 1996. Verb Semantic Classes Based on 'Alternations' and on WordNet-like Semantic Criteria: A Powerful Convergence. *Proc. Predicative Forms in Natural Language and in Lexical Knowledge Bases*, IRIT, Toulouse, to appear in early 1999 in a volume with same title, Kluwer Academic (P. Saint-Dizier, ed.).

Saint-Dizier, P. 1998. A Generative Lexicon Perspective for Adjectival Modification. *Proc. COLING98*, Montréal.

11   Individuation by Partitive Constructions in Spanish

SALVADOR CLIMENT

Abstract

Because partitive constructions ("a grain of rice," "a cup of coffee") are one of the ways of individuating referents in many languages, there is a need to establish the mechanisms to obtain appropriate representations for such compounds by composing partitive nouns and noun phrases that denote a whole of reference. Furthermore, some partitives are nouns that show a polymorphic behavior. Namely, depending on the context, they may be interpreted either as object referents or as partitives (e.g., "cup," container vs. cointainee interpretations). This work discusses these and other related issues and posits representations intended to account for such phenomena in Spanish.[1] The main claim is that the semantics of partitives largely depends on constitutive information. More specifically, the semantics of portions seems to be grounded on a generalized construal of any entity as being *made of* some stuff.

1   Introduction

A semiotic need, which probably any existing or conceivable language has to satisfy, is the capability of referring to entities as discrete individual units. The mechanism by which languages *extract* individuals from a continuum of reference is usually called *individuation* (cf., e.g., Lyons, 1977).

Languages have different mechanisms to convey information about individuation. English uses deictic reference ("this"), pronouns ("him"), or a range of noun-headed constructions ("two trees," "a branch," "many cups of coffee," "this team," "a group of people," "a head of cattle"). Euskera[2] marks nouns when referring to discrete specific entities by means of either singular or plural suffixes (1a,b), while when they denote an indefinite genericity they are not marked (1c) (cf. Sagüés, 1989). In the latter case they are described as bearing the so-called number of *mugagabe* ("without boundaries").

---

[1] Nevertheless, for ease of explanation, and given the fact that partitive constructions are quite similar in structure and conceptualization in both languages, examples of English are generally used throughout the work.

[2] A language spoken in Euskadi, a country in the North of Spain.

(1)   a. etxe-a [house-SINGULAR] = the house (definite)
       b. bi etxe-ak [two house-PLURAL] = the two houses (definite)
       c. bi etxe [two house-MUGAGABE] = two houses (non definite)

Classifier Languages, such as Japanese, Chinese, or Thai individuate, in many cases, by means of classifier constructions. In (2a,b), the noun or its specifier are affixed or combined with a morpheme that, apart from denoting *individual entity*, sets different kinds of formal specifications on (i.e., they *classify*) the entity thus construed: type, shape, collection, animacy, consistency, size, arrangement, quantity, etc. (cf. Allan, 1977). In absence of the noun, classifiers may also be used, in deictic constructions or anaphorically (2c,d).[3]

(2)   a. khru· lâ·j khon [teacher three person] = three teachers
       b. os-tehk te [three-plant tree] = three trees
       c. tua nán [body this] = this (animal, object, etc.)
       d. sì· tua [four body] = four (animals, objects, etc.)

Bunt (1981, cf. Vossen, 1994) posits that there are two basic manners of referring to entities: discrete and cumulative, which largely correspond to the notions of bounded and unbounded concepts (Jackendoff, 1991; Langacker, 1991). Roughly, an amount of a discrete entity is representable as a set of individuals. Unbounded concepts are representable as an undifferentiated mass, such that portions of it are conceived as different amounts of the same stuff. Boundaries of concepts which are referred to cumulatively (i.e., *unbounded*) are not in view or of concern.

English, Spanish, French, and related languages place no overt marker on lexemes that could help distinguishing between kinds of entities. Therefore, differences must be induced from their grammatical behavior (e.g., alternations "much"/ "many" and the such, namely countability). On the contrary, in Euskera and Classifier Languages all nouns are in principle *unbounded*, thus needing combination to some morpheme to bound them.

In short, there seems to be two general language independent principles related to this question. First, there are two fundamental ways of conceptualizing things: either as individuals or as *stuff*. Second, communication requires that languages have means of expressing individuation. Languages, such as Euskera or Classifier Languages, show that lexicalization of discreteness is ... a sort of universal objective default for many kinds of entities (e.g., houses, teachers, trees) – in fact, in such languages the apparent default is the opposite.

Similarly, it must be noticed that the very same entity can be referred to by means of nouns inherently denoting either *bounded* or *unbounded* concepts. Depending on the speaker's perspective or on pragmatic constraints, a song can be called "noise" (compare (3a) and (3b)); a cigarette can be called "tobacco"; a stick, "wood" ((3c) → (3d)), a fight, "violence"; a gown, "cloth"; or a herd, "animals" ((3e) → (3f)) – or even "meat" (3g). In other words, it seems that identical entities can be

---

[3] (2a,c,d) are data from Thai (Allan, 1977); (2b) is Chinese (Lyons, 1977).

alternatively referred to either as individuals or as the stuff they are conceived as being *made of*.

(3) a. Qué maravillosa canción! [what beautiful song] = what a beautiful song!
   b. Vaya ruido espantoso! [what noise horrible] = what a horrible noise!
   c. Trae aquí ese palo. [bring here that stick] = give me that stick
   d. Trae aquí esa madera. [bring here that wood] = give me that piece of wood
   e. Esos rebaños son del Rey. [those herds are of-the King] = those herds belong to the King
   f. Esos animales son del Rey. [those animals are of-the King] = those animals belong to the King
   g. Toda esa carne es del Rey. [all that meat is of-the King] = all that meat belongs to the King

Alternatively, the same word form can be used in many cases to express either *bounded* or *unbounded* construals of an entity. The obvious example in English (4a,b) or Spanish (4c,d) is that of mass-count alternations, but it is not the only one. In Spanish, the singular form of typically countable individuals can be used to refer to indefinite plurality (4e), although the use of the plural form (4f) is the usual procedure. In cases like (4e), politician (singular) is seen in the same way as, for instance, "rice"; that is, individual units (grains of rice, individual politicians) are outside the conceptual scope – the cumulation is what really matters.

(4) a. I need more coffee.
   b. I need another coffee.
   c. Voy a comer arroz. [I-go to eat rice] = I'm going to eat rice
   d. Voy a comerme un arroz. [I-go to eat-DATIVE a rice] = I'm going to eat a (dish of) rice
   e. Hay mucho político corrupto. [there-is much politician corrupt] = there are a lot of corrupt politicians
   f. Hay muchos políticos corruptos. [there-are many politicians corrupt] = there are a lot of corrupt politicians

The phenomenon illustrated in (4e) is somewhat similar to that of *grinding* (cf. Jackendoff, 1991). The difference is that in the case of grinding ((5a) → (5b), (5c) → (5d)), the derived singular forms (5b,d) stand for a slightly different kind of entity: the *stuff* the original individual is (conceived as being) made of. Therefore, *grinding* sense extensions are analogous to alternations such as "song"/"noise" or "stick"/"wood," mentioned above in (3).

(5) a. The car ran over a dog.
   b. There was dog all over the street.

    c. Pon un tomate en la ensalada. [you-put a tomato in the salad] ("tomato" = an individual vegetable)

    d. Pon tomate en la pizza. [you-put tomato in the pizza] ("tomato" = tomato-derived sauce)

At least in Spanish, all the examples in (3), (4) and (5) systematically involve *bounded/unbounded* alternations. On the one hand, the same entity can be alternatively referred by means of either bounded or unbounded grammatical units (e.g., a song: (3a,b); a cup of coffee: (4a,b); a plurality of politicians: (4e,f). On the other hand, a word form – such as "coffee" (4a,b), "*arroz*" (4c,d), "dog" (5a,b) or "*tomate*" (5c,d) – can alternatively refer to either individuals or stuff.

    Moreover, all these alternations seem to rely on a general principle of construal: any individual entity (no matter if abstract or physical) is *made of* some kind of stuff. For example, [a coffee] is made of [coffee]; [a dog] is made of [dog/flesh]; [a song] is made of [sound/noise]; a [bottle] is made of [glass]; [a piece of information] is made of [information]; [a sheet of paper] is made of [paper].

    Nevertheless, it is obvious that not every possible alternative interpretation of a lexeme necessarily bears a similar, balanced, linguistic status. For instance, in Spanish or English, some words ("tomato," "politician," "dog," "song") typically denote individuals while other ("coffee," "noise," "rice," "wood") typically denote stuff. That is, in spite of the fact that given the appropriate linguistic context nouns can be forced to adopt the alternative denotation, the speaker's intuition is that, in some cases, the *individual* denotation is the basic one, and the *mass* reading is derivative. In other cases the opposite holds.

    Note that this phenomenon does not depend on *how things really are* but on how they are conceptualized. There is no objective difference between [rice] and [lentils], which explains why the first lexical concept is typically cumulative and the second is discrete. Furthermore, the same concept may be typically cumulative in one language but typically discrete in another one; for instance, [furniture] is cumulative in English but discrete in Spanish. In English a discrete item is "a piece of furniture," while in Spanish a discrete item is a "*mueble*" (singular) and a multiplicity, "*mueble-s*" (plural).

2   Lexicalization of Individual Entities

Several kinds of things, apart from typical individuals (6a,b) can be referred to in a discrete way, for instance, a number, set or plurality of things (6c,d,e); a quantity of a mass (6f,g,h); a part, portion or element of a discrete entity (6i,j,k,l).

(6)   a. un árbol [a tree] = a tree

        b. un palo [a stick] = a stick

        c. una jauría de lobos [a pack of wolves] = a pack of wolves

        d. un equipo [a team] = a team

        e. ganado, animales [cattle, animals] = cattle, animals

    f.   un vaso de vino, un vino [a glass of wine, a wine] = a glass of wine
    g.   una madera, una barra de madera [a wood, a bar of wood] = a piece of wood, a bar of wood
    h.   un arroz, un plato de arroz [a rice, a dish of rice] = a dish of rice
    i.   una rama [a branch] = a branch
    j.   la cima de una montaña [the top of a mountain] = the top of a mountain
    k.   una cabeza de ganado [a head of cattle] = a head of cattle
    l.   uno del equipo [one of-the team] = one of the team

Moreover, it is also a fact that not every individual entity happens to be lexicalized in a given language. Some entities are referred to by means of a single lexeme (6a,b,d). Others are not lexicalized, so they are referred by means of partitive phrases (6c,j). Finally, others can be expressed by means of both, depending on certain properties such as shape, container, and so forth (6f,g,h).

The consequence for the semantic representation of nominals is that in many cases referential nouns and partitive constructions (i.e., phrases [*PartitiveNoun* "of" *NounPhrase*]) are denotationally equivalent, because both denote discrete entities. Therefore, semantic representations for both referential nouns and partitive constructions must be somewhat equivalent. For instance, the semantic composition of "head" + "of" + "cattle" must produce a representation roughly equivalent to that of "animal"; or the composition of "bar" + "of" + "wood," to that of "stick."

From a *Generative Lexicon* (henceforth GL) perspective this also means that formal representations of partitive constructions must behave in composition analogously to nouns. That is, they must bear a QUALIA STRUCTURE able to act compositionally in the same way as the QUALIA STRUCTURE of nouns does. Consider the examples in (7).

(7)   a.   bake the cake
          b.   *bake the slice of cake
          c.   enjoy the cake
          d.   enjoy the slice of cake
          e.   eat a cake
          f.   eat a slice of cake

Pustejovsky (1995) describes (7a) as a typical case of co-composition, where composition is triggered by the identitity of the AGENTIVE ROLE of the verb, "bake," and that of the complement, "the cake." This composition must be blocked in (7b), because the AGENTIVE ROLE of "slice of cake" is not a process of baking, but a process of slicing. Besides, (7c) is explained as a case of type coercion (a predicate coercing an argument to shift to the type requested by its selectional restrictions). "Enjoy" in (7c) selects for a complement typed **event**, a type that is obtained from the TELIC ROLE of "cake," **eat**; such a mechanism must also be at work with (7d), given that in this case the TELIC ROLE of "slice of cake" is also **eat**.

Another crucial semantic aspect to be accounted for is the regular selection of arguments by verbs. For instance, a verb such as "eat" selects for arguments of type **food**, such as "cake" in (7e). Consequently, "slice of cake" in (7f) must also be typed **food** – not for instance **portion**, as it could be expected from the type of the syntactic head of the partitive construction, "slice."

We conclude from this section that it is important for the framework to account for the composition between a partitive noun (henceforth, PN) and its NP-complement, in order to provide the mechanisms that give raise to the appropriate structure for the full partitive phrase [PN "of" NP].

3   General Properties of Partitive Nouns and Partitive Constructions

An important property of partitive constructions is that the position of the PN can be filled either by typical PNs ("piece," "slice," or the such), or by common nouns in a partitive function. The latter type are subject to linguistic creativity, because most of them are metaphorical extensions. Consider (8):

(8)   a. a labyrinth of streets
       b. una lluvia de insultos [a rain of insults] ≅ a shower of abuse
       c. una montaña de documentos [a mountain of documents]

As usual in language, there are also in-between cases. The most relevant are those of nouns that can systematically occur either as referential (common) nouns or as relational partitives, as it is the case of containers ("break the cup" vs. "drink a cup of coffee").

A crucial goal within GL is to account for this and any other case of logical polysemy in a way that avoids enumerating separate senses in the lexicon. The way to proceed is to posit underspecified lexical entries bearing the following properties: On the one hand, they should subsume and account for either senses of the word; on the other, they should express the systematic relationship that holds between them.

In this work, I will only consider the semantics of pure partitives, and I will develop a formal representation for portions and containers. The former are taken as typical examples of partitives, and the latter as the paradigmatic case of nouns that are logically polysemous between partitives and objects. The case of those regular common nouns that are occasionally re-classified as partitives, such as "labyrinth," "rain," or "mountain" in (8), is not addressed in this work, because the case has to be framed within a broader account, including the treatment of metaphoric sense extensions.

There are several notionally different kinds of partitive nouns. At first sight we may distinguish between *grouping* ("group," "pack," "team") and *extracting* partitives (portions of a mass, elements of a collection). A third main kind to be considered is that of topological parts, such as "end," "tip," or "surface." A classification of partitives is developed in §4 attending to the different kinds of terms they can combine with. Nevertheless, all partitives share a number of the following common characteristics:

- Partitives are nouns that cannot be referential in isolation.[4] They always need a complement to build complete reference to an entity, hence they are logically relational.
- A partitive construction (e.g., "cup of coffee") always denotes an individual, even in the case the NP-complement of reference (e.g., "coffee") denotes a mass; therefore, composition of partitives with NPs is a mechanism of individuation.
- Partitives usually have a multiple semantic function. They are relative quantifiers of their complement nominal, because they specify a quantity in relation to the entity of reference (cf. Langacker, 1991). In addition, most of them behave as adjectives because they predicate different kinds of properties of the entity, e.g., shape ("bar," "sheed"), means of bringing about ("slice"), structure ("grain"), and so forth.
- Partitives act as functors that take the entity denoted by the NP as an argument; as a result they are subject to selectional restrictions. §4 below discusses this point in some detail.

Partitives denoting portions typically select for cumulative complements: either a mass or a plural (that is also a cumulation, in this case a cumulation of individuals). Nevertheless, there are also cases, as in (9), in which the complement is, at least on the surface, not a cumulative but an individual.

(9)   a. un trozo de silla [a portion-fragment of chair]
        b. una rodaja de tomate [a round-slice of tomato]

In cases like (9), the individual usually surfaces bearing the grammatical features of cumulative reference, namely zero-determination. This can suggest that some effect of mass-re-classification of individuals might take part in the process. A solution to deal with this problem is presented in §5.

In spite of being the syntactic head of partitive constructions, partitives do not seem to be the semantic head. Recall the example (7f) in the previous section, or other analogous examples, such as "drink a cup of coffee" or "read a mountain of documents." "Drink" selects for arguments of type **liquid_food**, therefore "cup of coffee" must also be typed **liquid_food**, and not **container**. Analogously, because "read" selects for arguments of type **text**, "mountain of documents" must be of type **text**, not **mountain**.

With respect to the syntactic aspect of composition, I will treat partitive phrases not as an N/PP constituent, but as a nominal compound, PN/NP. This follows the analysis of Chomsky (1981) for similar cases, which argues that the preposition in

---

[4] Notice that some of them can, for instance containers as in "break the cup"; but in this case "cup" doesn't refer to a portion but to the object. §6 below is devoted to discuss this kind of polysemy.

this kind of structures is a mere surface case marker lacking semantic content. This analysis is supported in Spanish by the possibility of ellipsis – usually occurring in spoken performance – of the preposition *"de"* (of) in phrases such as (10a); something that, on the other hand, is not possible in the case of semantic contentful prepositions (10b).

(10) a. un vaso vino [a glass wine] (= Un vaso de̲ vino, a glass of̲ wine)
  b. *Vengo Barcelona. [*I come Barcelona] (= Vengo de̲ Barcelona, I come from̲ Barcelona)

The consequence is that, unlike what happens with head nouns taking PP complements, in the case of partitive constructions the semantics of both the partitive and the NP contributes in a balanced way to that of the resulting compound, thus allowing to obtain representations, which account for problematic cases of verb-partitive phrase compositions such as those in (7) above.

4   Selectional Restrictions and Subtypes of Partitives

In order to outline the rules of composition of partitives, in §5 I will discuss the case of portions denoting either shapes ("ingot," "bar") or fragments detached from a solid mass ("fragment," "slice"), which are typically described as selecting arguments denoting homogeneous mass entities. Notwithstanding, partitive nouns or pronouns can also select for a variety of other types of entities. For instance, in Spanish: groups (11a), aggregates (11b), determined (11c) or undetermined (11d) plurals, nongrinded individuals (11e), or granular masses (11f).

(11) a. uno/un miembro del equipo (one/a member of the team)
  b. algo/un montón/un camión de ganado [some/a lot/a truck of cattle]
  c. uno de los aristócratas (one of the aristocrats)
  d. un montón/saco/kilo de patatas (a lot/sack/kilo of potatoes)
  e. la cúspide de la montaña (the top of the mountain)
  f. un copo de nieve ([a flake of snow], a snowflake)

In order to account for such a range of selectable types, a generalization can be made using the insights of Jackendoff (1991) about boundedness and internal structure of lexical concepts.

In that framework, features $+/-$B(ounded) and $+/-$I(nternal_structure) are used to account for a range of phenomena involving both entities and events. Boundedness has been described in §1; Internal_structure accounts for concepts internally composed by a series of elements of one type – e.g., "team": members; "the light flashed all night": a series of single flashes.

For entities this feature system can be represented as a type sortal, as in Figure 11.1.

Moreover, bare plurals are assumed to be $-$B$+$I concepts, therefore they are assimilated to aggregates. For instance, "lambs" is regarded as an (unbounded)

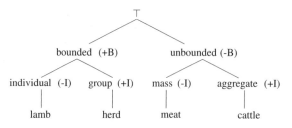

Fig. 11.1. Type lattice.

aggregation of elements of type **lamb**, thus it is denotationally equivalent to "cattle" – compare (12c) and (12a) below. It can be further assumed that determination of a plural places boundaries on the set thus defined; therefore a determined plural, e.g., "the lambs," is assimilable to a group – compare (12d) and (12b).

These notions are straightforwardly represented in a GL framework by using the types in Figure 11.1 to encode entailments about boundedness, +/−I features as CONSTITUTIVE (namely, Part-Whole) information, specifically a member-set relationship (cf. Winston et al., 1987), as in (12).

(12) a.
$$\begin{bmatrix} \textbf{cattle} \\ \text{ARG1} = \text{x} : \textbf{aggregate} \leq \textbf{unbounded} \\ \text{CONST} = \texttt{member\_of}\,(\text{x}, \text{y} : \textbf{animal}) \end{bmatrix}$$

b.
$$\begin{bmatrix} \textbf{herd} \\ \text{ARG1} = \text{x} : \textbf{group} \leq \textbf{bounded} \\ \text{CONST} = \texttt{member\_of}\,(\text{x}, \text{y} : \textbf{animal}) \end{bmatrix}$$

c.
$$\begin{bmatrix} \textbf{lambs} \\ \text{ARG1} = \text{x} : \textbf{unbounded} \\ \text{CONST} = \texttt{member\_of}\,(\text{x}, \text{y} : \textbf{lamb}) \end{bmatrix}$$

d.
$$\begin{bmatrix} \textbf{the lambs} \\ \text{ARG1} = \text{x} : \textbf{bounded} \\ \text{CONST} = \texttt{member\_of}\,(\text{x}, \text{y} : \textbf{lamb}) \end{bmatrix}$$

Given this, Spanish partitive nouns and pronouns can be sorted according to their selectional restrictions as shown in Table 11.1.

Beyond this general classification any specific partitive can bear its own subtype restrictions (e.g., "flock": birds). In some cases, restrictions are so constraining that the phrase has to be considered more a collocation than a partitive construction, e.g., "a pride of lions."

5   Formalization Within the GL Framework

In this section, I will consider the semantics of portions as a kind of paradigmatic case of partitives. Other kinds of partitives can be handled following the guidelines

Table 11.1. *Classification of partitives according to their selectional restrictions*

- **Selecting bounded (+B) concepts (individuals, groups and determined plurals)**
  - **Selecting +B + I (groups and determined plurals)**
    - Element-extracting pronouns
      "*uno*" (one), "*alguno*" (someone), etc.
      e.g., *uno del equipo* (one of the team)
      - **Specifically selecting groups**
        - Element-extracting partitive nouns
          "*miembro*" (member), "*elemento*" (element), etc.
          e.g., *un miembro del equipo* (a member of the team)
  - **Selecting +B – I (individuals)**
    - Nouns of boundaries and other parts of individuals
      "*punta*" (tip), "*superficie*" (surface), "*parte*" (part), etc.
      e.g., *la punta de la lengua* (the tip of the tongue)
- **Selecting unbounded (–B) concepts (masses, aggregates and bare plurals)**
  - Containers
    "*botella*" (bottle), "*cesto*" (basket), "*camión*"(truck)
    e.g., *una botella de vino* (a bottle of wine), *un cesto de naranjas* (a basket of oranges), *un camión de ganado* (a truck of cattle)
  - Metrics
    "*litro*" (litre), "*kilo*"
    e.g., *un litro de vino* (one litre of wine), *un kilo de naranjas* (one kilo of oranges), *un kilómetro cuadrado de bosque* (one square kilometer of forest)
    - **Selecting –B in singular (masses and aggregates)**
      - Mass quantifying pronouns
        "*algo*" (some), "*poco*" (a little bit), etc.
        e.g., *un poco de pan* (a little bit of bread)
    - **Selecting –B + I (aggregates and bare plurals)**
      - Groups
        "*grupo*" (group), "*hilera*" (row), "*bandada*" (flock)
        e.g., *un grupo de gente* (a group of people)
    - **Selecting –B – I (masses)**
      - **Selecting homogeneous solid masses**
        - Portions
          "*rebanada*" (slice), "*lámina*" (sheet)
          e.g., *una rebanada de pan* (a slice of bread)
      - **Selecting granular masses**
        - Elements
          "*grano*" (grain), "*copo*" (flake)
          e.g., *un grano de arena* (a grain of sand)

---

discussed here, in addition to their specificities, such as selectional restrictions or kind of constitutive information (see §4 above), among others.

As said above, the relational nature of partitives arises from the fact that they are nouns that can only achieve complete reference to some entity by relation to another noun. Therefore, just as other kinds of relational predicates such as "brother"

(13a,b) need to have in scope a related argument, partitives, when appearing in isolation, need a context from where to retrieve, either overtly or by means of anaphor or ellipsis, another argument of reference ((13c,d,e) and (13f,g,h)).

(13)   a. *John es hermano. = *John is brother
        b. John es hermano de Jane. [John is brother of Jane] = John is a brother of Jane's
        c. ?? I ate a big slice.
        d. I ate a big slice of cake.
        e. It was a delicious cake. I ate a big slice.
        f. ?? Dame dos manojos. [give-me two bunch-PLURAL] = ??Give me two bunches
        g. Qué rosas tan bonitas. Dame dos manojos. = What beautiful roses. Give me two bunches
        h. Dame dos manojos de rosas. = Give me two bunches of roses

The semantic representation of relational nouns in Pustejovsky (op.cit.) assumes the existence of a so-called *default argument* (defined as a parameter that participates in the logical expressions of the qualia, but that is not necessarily expressed syntactically). Default arguments are subject to existential closure and are related to the true argument in the FORMAL role of the *qualia structure*, e.g., consider "brother" in (14).

$$
(14) \quad
\begin{bmatrix}
\textbf{brother} \\[4pt]
\text{ARGSTR} =
\begin{bmatrix}
\text{ARG1} = x : \textbf{human} \\
\text{D\_ARG1} = y : \textbf{human}
\end{bmatrix} \\[10pt]
\text{QUALIA} = \begin{bmatrix} \text{FORMAL} = \texttt{brother\_of}(x, y) \end{bmatrix}
\end{bmatrix}
$$

Analogously, a PN such as "slice" must bear a structure such as that of (15), thus accounting for both its relational nature and its individuative function. The latter property is reflected in the representation by the fact that the resulting type of the portion (**x**), is always **individual**, independently of the type of the complement (the default argument, **y**).

$$
(15) \quad
\begin{bmatrix}
\textbf{slice} \\[4pt]
\text{ARGSTR} =
\begin{bmatrix}
\text{ARG1} = x : \textbf{individual} \\
\text{D\_ARG1} = y
\end{bmatrix} \\[10pt]
\text{QUALIA} = \begin{bmatrix} \text{FORMAL} = \texttt{slice\_of}(x, y) \end{bmatrix}
\end{bmatrix}
$$

As shown in (9) above, portion partitives can select for individuals. Nevertheless, let us assume (following Copestake and Briscoe, 1995; Sinclair, 1990) that the default value for the complement of a partitive is an entity of type **mass**, thus considering selection of individuals as a sort of exception that must be treated specifically. Therefore, let us start from a representation such as (16).

$$(16) \quad \begin{bmatrix} \textbf{portion} \\ \text{ARGSTR} = \begin{bmatrix} \text{ARG1} = x : \textbf{individual} \\ \text{D\_ARG1} = y : \textbf{mass} \end{bmatrix} \end{bmatrix}$$

One of the basic characteristics of mass entities is that their properties still hold even when undergoing a partition – a cup of coffee is still coffee, a portion of cake is still cake, and so on. Consequently it must be expected that their general purpose or function, namely their TELIC ROLE, must not change when portioned. Thus, assuming that the TELIC ROLE for "coffee" and "cake" is, respectively, "drink" and "eat," the same values must hold for "cup of coffee" and "slice of cake." This is represented by coreference of the TELIC values of both the complement and the portion in (17).

$$(17) \quad \begin{bmatrix} \textbf{portion} \\ \text{ARGSTR} = \begin{bmatrix} \text{ARG1} = x : \textbf{individual} \\ \text{D\_ARG1} = y : \begin{bmatrix} \textbf{mass} \\ \text{TELIC} = \texttt{[1]} \end{bmatrix} \end{bmatrix} \\ \text{QUALIA} = \begin{bmatrix} \text{TELIC} = \texttt{[1]} \end{bmatrix} \end{bmatrix}$$

On the other hand, it seems obvious that, because the whole always preexists the portion, the way in which the portion is obtained out of the whole is a kind of information that cannot be contributed by the semantics of the noun denoting the whole, but by the semantics of the partitive. In GL terms, the AGENTIVE ROLE of a partitive construction, if relevant, must carry a value that does not depend on the QUALIA of the complement, but on that of the partitive: e.g., cake: AGENTIVE = "bake_act"; but slice_of_cake: AGENTIVE = "slice_act", as shown in (18).

$$(18) \quad \begin{bmatrix} \textbf{portion} \\ \text{ARGSTR} = \begin{bmatrix} \text{ARG1} = x : \textbf{individual} \\ \text{D\_ARG1} = y : \begin{bmatrix} \textbf{mass} \\ \text{TELIC} = \texttt{[1]} \\ \text{AGENTIVE} = \texttt{mass-agentive} \end{bmatrix} \end{bmatrix} \\ \text{QUALIA} = \begin{bmatrix} \text{TELIC} = \texttt{[1]} \\ \text{AGENTIVE} = \texttt{portion-agentive} \end{bmatrix} \end{bmatrix}$$

Another point is that, if every portion is made of the very same substance than the whole it has been extracted from, then portions stand in a constitutive relation to its whole of reference. This kind of relationship, namely *made_of*, has been traditionally analyzed as one of the several Part-Whole relationships that can hold between lexical concepts (cf. Winston et al., 1987).[5] In the GL

---

5   In Climent (1998), I argue that any kind of merological linguistic information emerges from one of the following three basic schemata: component-entity (an entity composed of parts of different type), element-multiplicity (an entity composed of parts of the same type), and stuff-entity. Further subclassifications can be traced out from either the types of the part or the whole (e.g., member-group vs. member-aggregate; part-object vs. locative inclussion) or the number of merologic relations that hold (e.g., stuff-entity vs. ingredient-entity).

framework, information about Part-Whole relationships is encoded in the CONSTI-
TUTIVE quale.

It must be noticed that different Part-Whole relations can hold for the same lexical concept. For instance, a [dog], simultaneously, has component-parts [head],
[legs], etc.; it is made of [flesh], [blood], etc.; and it can be member of a [pack]. To
the extent that different types of Part-Whole information could affect the behavior
of a word, it might be necessary for the CONSTITUTIVE to incorporate such relationships, which are different in nature. This can be represented by assuming the
existence of sub-quales within the CONSTITUTIVE ROLE, as it is the general procedure in LKB (a GL-based knowledge representation formalism; Busa et al., 1998;
Copestake, 1992), where QUALIA features do not necessarily bear single values but
a series of typed Attribute-Value sub-quales. Under this view, the representation
for "dog" can be seen as in (19):

$$(19) \quad \begin{bmatrix} \textbf{dog} \\ \\ \text{CONSTITUTIVE} = \begin{bmatrix} \text{MADE\_OF} = \textbf{flesh, blood, ...} \\ \text{HAS\_PARTS} = \textbf{head, legs, ...} \\ \text{MEMBER\_OF} = \textbf{pack} \end{bmatrix} \end{bmatrix}$$

For ease of exposition, I will not explicitly subclassify CONSTITUTIVE roles
throughout the rest of this work if not necessary. Therefore, a representation such
as [CONST = MADE_OF = flesh(x)] will be simply noted [CONST = flesh(x)].

From this point of view, the semantics for "portion" will be represented as in
(20), thus accounting for the fact that every portion is made of the same stuff than
its whole of reference.

$$(20) \quad \begin{bmatrix} \textbf{portion} \\ \\ \text{ARGSTR} = \begin{bmatrix} \text{ARG1} = x : \textbf{individual} \\ \text{D\_ARG1} = y : \textbf{mass} \end{bmatrix} \\ \\ \text{QUALIA} = \begin{bmatrix} \text{CONST} = y \end{bmatrix} \end{bmatrix}$$

Summing up, we can define a portion (as a typical example of a partitive) as in
(21):

$$(21) \quad \begin{bmatrix} \textbf{portion} \\ \\ \text{ARGSTR} = \begin{bmatrix} \text{ARG1} = x : \textbf{individual} \\ \text{D\_ARG1} = y : \begin{bmatrix} \textbf{mass} \\ \text{TELIC} = [1] \end{bmatrix} \end{bmatrix} \\ \\ \text{QUALIA} = \begin{bmatrix} \text{FORMAL} = \text{portion\_of}(x, y) \\ \text{CONST} = y \\ \text{TELIC} = [1] \\ \text{AGENTIVE} = R(...x...) \end{bmatrix} \end{bmatrix}$$

That is, a portion is an individual entity extracted from some mass, to which
it bears a constitutive relation and preserves its basic functionality. The portion

also carries other kinds of idiosyncratic pieces of semantic information, such as AGENTIVE (means of obtention of the portion) or others. Specifically, many partitives carry information about formal properties of the resulting entity. For instance, shape – "*barra*" (bar), "*lámina*" (sheed); magnitude – "*mole*" (huge mass); disposition – "*rollo*" (roll); consistency "*zurullo*" (chubby mass); etc.[6] This information can be explicity encoded in knowledge representation formalisms such as LKB as in (22a). Nevertheless, from a pure GL point of view, it is enough to assume, as I will do here, that both kinds of semantic information, namely something being a portion and being long-shaped, are embedded in the content of the same FORMAL predicate (22b).

(22) a. $\begin{bmatrix} \textbf{bar} \\ \text{FORMAL} = \text{SHAPE} = \textbf{long} \end{bmatrix}$

 b. $\begin{bmatrix} \textbf{bar} \\ \text{FORMAL} = \texttt{bar\_of}\,(\texttt{x, y}) \end{bmatrix}$

Let us consider now the composition of a typical case of a partitive construction in Spanish, "*trozo de pan*" (piece-portion of bread). The representation of "*trozo*" (piece, detached portion) – possibly the most typical portion noun in Spanish – must be that in (23):

(23)
$$\begin{bmatrix} \textbf{trozo} \\ \text{ARGSTR} = \begin{bmatrix} \text{ARG1} = \text{x} : \textbf{individual} \\ \text{D\_ARG1} = \text{y} : \begin{bmatrix} \textbf{mass} \\ \text{TELIC} = [1] \end{bmatrix} \end{bmatrix} \\ \text{QUALIA} = \begin{bmatrix} \text{FORMAL} = trozo\_de\,(x,\,y) \\ \text{CONST} = \text{y} \\ \text{TELIC} = \textbf{[1]} \\ \text{AGENTIVE} = dividir(\texttt{e, z, y, x})\,(dividir \cong \texttt{to portion}) \end{bmatrix} \end{bmatrix}$$

For "*pan*" (bread), I assume the mass-reading representation (24), considering for the time being that *packaged* readings of typical masses ("one coffee," "one cake," "one bread") are derived sense-extensions.

(24)
$$\begin{bmatrix} \textbf{pan} \\ \text{ARGSTR} = \begin{bmatrix} \text{ARG1} = \text{x} : \textbf{mass} \end{bmatrix} \\ \text{QUALIA} = \begin{bmatrix} \text{FORMAL} = pan\,(\texttt{x}) \\ \text{TELIC} = comer(\texttt{e, y, x})\,(comer = \textbf{to eat}) \end{bmatrix} \end{bmatrix}$$

By feature unification, both structures contribute to the composition of the partitive construction, thus resulting in the co-composition in (25):

---

[6] By analogy with classifiers, a classification of semantic information conflated within partitives might be found in Allan (1977).

(25)

$$\begin{bmatrix} \textbf{trozo de pan} \\ \text{ARGSTR} = \begin{bmatrix} \text{ARG1} = x : \textbf{individual} \\ \text{D\_ARG1} = y : \textbf{pan} \leq \textbf{mass} \end{bmatrix} \\ \text{QUALIA} = \begin{bmatrix} \text{FORMAL} = trozo\_de(x, y) \\ \text{CONST} = pan(y) \\ \text{TELIC} = comer(e, z, y) \\ \text{AGENTIVE} = dividir(e', w, y, x) \end{bmatrix} \end{bmatrix}$$

Once composed this way, the partitive construction is outfitted to undergo further desirable operations of composition predicted by GL. For instance, recall the problematic cases involving "slice of cake" (7), which I presented at the end of §2.[7] They are solved in the following way:

- "*Bake a slice of cake" is blocked because the AGENTIVE ROLE of "slice of cake" is no longer a "bake_act" but a "slice_act," contributed to the compound by the partitive.
- In sentences such as "enjoy the slice of cake" the verb can coerce the type of the partitive phrase to **event** via its TELIC ROLE, **eat**, in the same way that it does in "enjoy the cake."
- Verbal selection of arguments referred by partitive phrases is allowed via the CONSTITUTIVE quale, as a new case of type coercion. This way, "eat" can select "slice of cake" by picking **cake ≤ food** in the CONSTITUTIVE role of the compound.

Furthermore, selectional restrictions of verbs involving formal properties of the nominal are achieved by regular selection of the main argument (**x**) of the partitive phrase, which is specified by the predicate in the FORMAL quale. For instance, a verb such as "*quebrar*" (break) selects for elongated objects; "*desenrollar*" (unroll, unwind) for rolled things; or "*doblar*" (fold) for thin entities. So, partitive phrases such as *una barra de madera* (a bar of wood), *un rollo de cuerda* (a coil of rope), or *una lámina de hierro* (a sheet of iron) will be selectable for such verbs via their respective FORMAL roles ("bar," "coil," "sheet") – and not by type coercion involving their CONSTITUTIVE roles ("wood," "rope," "iron").

5.1   *Portions Selecting Individuals*

Let us consider now the case of composition of partitives with individuals. I have adopted the standard view that partitives, or at least their typical example, portions, select for entities of type **mass**. Nevertheless, counterexamples are constantly found in language, as in *un trozo de silla* (a portion-fragment of chair), where "*silla*" is obviously **individual**.

---

[7] For ease of exposition, I use here those examples in English; the representation of "slice of cake" is analogous to that of Spanish "*trozo de pan*."

Notwithstanding, as suggested above, it has to be noticed that *"silla"* in the example, although in principle referring to an individual object, bears the surface grammatical features of mass entitites. Namely, although being in singular, it is zero-determinated. The observation might suggest that perhaps some kind of mass-re-classification of the term has occurred. I will explore this intuition below.

Given the semantic representation of the partitive *"trozo"* set in (23), we find two main problems when trying to compose it with *"silla"*:

(i)   *"Trozo"* selects for masses, but *"silla"* is an individual

(ii) The representation of *"trozo"* forces the TELIC role of the partitive construction to be co-indexed to that of the syntactic complement, but although the obvious function of a chair is to sit on it, this cannot be held for a fragment of a chair.

The second point is related to the fact that the portioning of an individual destroys or dismembers it. Therefore, in general, it cannot be expected for portions of individuals to preserve their TELIC roles, but see below the case of "a chapter of a book."

I will treat this kind of composition as a case of type coercion. Intuitively, it seems that the application of a portion partitive on the individual forces to its reclassification to mass. The reason is that portioning an individual object results on a new kind of object, which is no longer the previous individual but something made of the same stuff as it. A fragment of a chair is no longer a chair, but simply something that is made of the same material than the original chair. Namely, if a chair is made of wood, a fragment of a chair is nothing but a piece of wood.

As discussed in §1, any object is made of some material – for example, chairs are made of wood, bottles are made of glass – and it is generally possible to conceive of it as either an individual object or the stuff it is made of. Within an appropriate context, chairs can be called "wood," bottles "glass," and so on.

The possibility of deriving mass readings out of individuals, namely *grinding*, is something that Copestake and Briscoe (1995) have proposed to manage using Lexical Rules, which shift the type of the nominal. Specifically, they posit Lexical Rules to deal with animal-food alternations (e.g., lamb-animal → lamb-food), but also to deal with less systematic cases, such as "dog" in (5b), repeated below in (26).

(26)   There was dog all over the street.

Pustejovsky (1995) has suggested that animal-food logical polysemies can be managed by using Lexical Conceptual Paradigms (LCPs), which are represented using *dotted types* (**x•y**). Roughly, a LCP is a type constructor that allows for the availability of three diferent but related types of a word: for example, for "door," the physical object, the aperture, and the so-called *dotted types*, **phys_obj•aperture**, which encompasses both of them. So, entries represented by means of LCPs, e.g., "haddock" in (27), are underspecified representations in which lexical units share properties of two types, thus allowing for picking the appropriate reading depending on the context.

(27)

$$
\begin{bmatrix}
\textbf{haddock} \\[4pt]
\text{ARGSTR} = \begin{bmatrix} \text{ARG1} = x : \textbf{ind\_animal} \\ \text{ARG2} = y : \textbf{food\_stuff} \end{bmatrix} \\[12pt]
\text{QUALIA} = \begin{bmatrix} \textbf{ind\_animal} \bullet \textbf{food\_lcp} \\ \text{FORMAL} = \text{R}(x, y) \\ \text{TELIC} = \text{eat}(e, w, y) \end{bmatrix}
\end{bmatrix}
$$

Both solutions, Lexical Rules and LCP representations, seem to have problems with systematicity. Sentences such as (28a) and also (28b) below suggest that *grinding* is generally applicable, provided the appropriate context.

(28)   a. Mole is eaten in many parts of Africa.

       b. The cannibals were eating stewed explorer.

Therefore, one solution is to type **animal** – possibly including humans – to account for (28b) as an **animal•food_lcp** and let all hyponyms to inherit such a specification. However, this will result in a number of weird typing statements. Analogously, an unrestricted *grinding* Lexical Rule will result in sense over-generation. The other solution is to decide case by case which animals should be typed **animal•food**, or be allowed to undergo the Lexical Rule. In this case, because edibility is strongly culture-dependent, some possible cases will fall out of account.

To deal with this problem, Copestake and Briscoe (1995) propose to associate frequency information to the Lexical Rules that are applicable to an entry, thus modeling the conditional probability that a word form will be used in a specific sense.

As GL is not a probabilistic model, the solution I propose is to represent systematically the general knowledge that every individual is *made of* some stuff. This kind of knowledge is the background for sentences such as (26), (28), (5d), (9); alternations such as those in (3); and, in general, any *grinding* derivation.

As discussed above, "made_of" information can be encoded in the CONSTITUTIVE quale. So for instance, consider the representation of "*silla*" (chair) in (29).

(29)

$$
\begin{bmatrix}
\textbf{silla} \\[4pt]
\text{ARGSTR} = \begin{bmatrix} \text{ARG1} = x : \textbf{individual} \end{bmatrix} \\[12pt]
\text{QUALIA} = \begin{bmatrix} \text{FORMAL} = silla(x) \\ \text{TELIC} = sentarse(e, z, x)\, (sentarse = \text{sit on}) \\ \text{CONST} = silla\_\text{stuff}\ (y : \textbf{mass}) \end{bmatrix}
\end{bmatrix}
$$

The assumption of a representation such as (29) for individuals is equivalent to the existence of an unrestricted *grinding* rule, which will stay latent until the context triggers its application (e.g., the word falling under the scope of a **mass**–selecting predicate. Other examples for individual entities can be considered in (30).[8]

---

[8] This solution will still pose problems (in English) for dealing with food readings such as those of (28). Consider "lamb" (30a). Because **lamb_stuff** stands for some flesh/meat concept, there is no precise "food" information in its CONST predicate. Therefore, selectional restrictions of verbs like

(30) a.
$$\begin{bmatrix} \textbf{lamb} \\ \text{CONST} = \texttt{lamb\_stuff(y)} \end{bmatrix}$$

b.
$$\begin{bmatrix} \textbf{bottle} \\ \text{CONST} = \texttt{glass(y)} \end{bmatrix}$$

c.
$$\begin{bmatrix} \textbf{dog} \\ \text{CONST} = \texttt{dog\_stuff(y)} \end{bmatrix}$$

This way, the composition of *"trozo"* (23) and *"silla"* (29) will result in (31) by application of type coercion. Regular composition cannot be achieved because selectional restrictions of the partitive (mass) are not satisfied by the type of the complement (individual); but the availability of a mass-type predicate in the CONSTITUTIVE quale of silla allows for the operation of type coercion, therefore typing requirements of the partitive are satisfied.

(31)
$$\begin{bmatrix} \textbf{trozo de silla} \\ \text{ARGSTR} = \begin{bmatrix} \text{ARG1} = x : \textbf{individual} \\ \text{D\_ARG1} = y : \textit{silla\_stuff} \leq \textbf{mass} \end{bmatrix} \\ \text{QUALIA} = \begin{bmatrix} \text{FORMAL} = \textit{trozo\_de}(x, y) \\ \text{TELIC} = \text{TELIC}(y) \\ \text{CONST} = y \end{bmatrix} \end{bmatrix}$$

The representation in (31) accounts for a fragment of a chair to be an object that is made of the material chairs are made of (e.g., wood). The same way, constructions such as *un trozo de cordero* (a portion of lamb) or *un trozo de botella* (a fragment of a bottle) will be composed from *"trozo"* (23) and, respectively, *"cordero"* and *"botella"* (30a,b), to produce (32):

(32) a.
$$\begin{bmatrix} \textbf{trozo de cordero} \\ \text{ARGSTR} = \begin{bmatrix} \text{ARG1} = x : \textbf{individual} \\ \text{D\_ARG1} = y : \textit{carne} \end{bmatrix} \\ \text{CONST} = \textit{carne} \end{bmatrix}$$

b.
$$\begin{bmatrix} \textbf{trozo de botella} \\ \text{ARGSTR} = \begin{bmatrix} \text{ARG1} = x : \textbf{individual} \\ \text{D\_ARG1} = y : \textbf{glass} \end{bmatrix} \\ \text{CONST} = \textbf{glass} \end{bmatrix}$$

The other effect of these compositions is that the TELIC roles of the original individuals, for example, chair-object: TELIC = sit_on(e,z,x:**ind**), are no longer at reach of the semantics of the partitive construction. The underlying consequence is that, as expressed in (31), the TELIC of the partitive construction, if relevant, is

"to eat" are still not strictly fit. This is not a problem in Spanish, because one single word, *"carne,"* subsumes both senses – flesh and meat. Moreover, it is conventional in Spanish to regard any *carne* as potentially edible. Therefore, *"cordero"* (lamb) and any other animal term will be selectable by "eating" verbs via their CONSTITUTIVE role.

nothing but that of the material the original individual is made of. Namely, the TELIC of *un trozo de cordero* is that of *"carne,"* (i.e., eat see footnote #9).

Nevertheless, this latter effect is not desirable when composing for instance "a chapter of a book" because, apart from the constitutive information (a chapter of a book being a part of a book) one would expect from "a chapter of a book" a QUALIA STRUCTURE similar to that of "a book," that is, AGENTIVE = **write** and TELIC = **read**, so that a phrase such as "begin a chapter of a book" could reach via type coercion the same interpretation than "begin a book" – begin to read/write a book.

The intuition to be formalized is that, although "a book" being an individual, its portioning by application of "chapter" does not result (as it did when portioning "chair") in the destruction or dismembering of the original individual, thus consequently in the loss of their properties. Instead, it seems that "chapter" selects for some *mass*-related aspect of "book" (namely its contents) thus preserving its properties in that respect, as with regular portioning of masses.

Pustejovsky (1995) conceives "book" as a noun that is systematicaly polysemous between [object] and [information] ([text]); therefore it is represented as a dot object of type **information•phys_obj_lcp** where, roughly, properties of both physical objects and information are simultaneously available via inheritance. Consider its semantics in (33):

$$
(33) \quad
\begin{bmatrix}
\textbf{a book} \\[4pt]
\text{ARGSTR} = \begin{bmatrix} \text{ARG1} = x : \textbf{text} \\ \text{ARG2} = y : \textbf{phys\_obj} \end{bmatrix} \\[12pt]
\text{QUALIA} = \begin{bmatrix} \text{FORMAL} = \mathtt{hold(x,y)} \\ \text{TELIC} = \mathtt{read(e,w,x)} \\ \text{AGENTIVE} = \mathtt{write(e',z,x)} \end{bmatrix}
\end{bmatrix}
$$

"Chapter" is to be represented as usual portions (i.e., (21) above, more specifically as a (more informative) subtype (34) that bears the added property of being non-AGENTIVE). In general, portions are non-TELIC; that is, they do not specify a function of their own but they retain that of the mass of reference. The representational consequence is that the TELIC role of the portion is co-indexed with that of its deep argument. Besides, unlike partitives such as "slice," "chapter" does not entail any specific means of obtention of the portion out of the whole. Therefore, in the case of "chapter," in addition to the TELIC, the AGENTIVE is also co-indexed with that of the complement.

$$
(34) \quad
\begin{bmatrix}
\textbf{chapter} \\[4pt]
\text{ARGSTR} = \begin{bmatrix} \text{ARG1} = x : \textbf{individual} \\ \text{D\_ARG1} = y : \begin{bmatrix} \textbf{mass} \\ \text{TELIC} = [1] \\ \text{AGENTIVE} = [2] \end{bmatrix} \end{bmatrix} \\[18pt]
\text{QUALIA} = \begin{bmatrix} \text{FORMAL} = \mathtt{chapter\_of(x,y)} \\ \text{TELIC} = [1] \\ \text{AGENTIVE} = [2] \end{bmatrix}
\end{bmatrix}
$$

The *dotted typing* of "book" gives access by inheritance to its **mass** typing (35a) (cf. Pustejovsky, 1995, §8.3), thus allowing for regular unification and resulting in the desired structure for "chapter of a book" (35b).

(35)   a.   **book ≤ info • phys_obj ≤ info ≤ mass**

$$
\text{b.} \quad
\begin{bmatrix}
\text{chapter of a book} \\[2pt]
\text{ARGSTR} =
\begin{bmatrix}
\text{ARG1} = \text{x} : \textbf{individual} \\[2pt]
\text{D\_ARG1} = \text{y} :
\begin{bmatrix}
\textbf{book} \\
\text{TELIC} = \textbf{read} = [2] \\
\text{AGENTIVE} = \textbf{write} = [1]
\end{bmatrix}
\end{bmatrix} \\[2pt]
\text{QUALIA} =
\begin{bmatrix}
\text{FORMAL} = \texttt{chapter\_of}(\text{x, y}) \\
\text{TELIC} = [2] \\
\text{AGENTIVE} = [1]
\end{bmatrix}
\end{bmatrix}
$$

Notice in (33) that the variable that is bound in both the TELIC and the AGENTIVE ROLEs of "book" is that standing for "text" – not that standing for object. Consequently, in "chapter of a book," the TELIC and AGENTIVE ROLEs also refer to text/information. Thus, type coercion operations that apply to "a book" ("begin a book" = begin to read/write a book-text) will also apply to "a chapter of a book."

Representation of partitives other than portions can be set following the guidelines posed in this section, plus attending to specificities relative to selection of the type of the deep argument (see §4), and others. For instance, for group-element alternations: nonpreservation of the TELIC role, and a different subtype of CONSTITUTIVE relation – *member_of* instead of *made_of*. I will not discuss such cases here, now turning to the more special case of nouns that are systematically polysemous between objects and partitives (e.g., containers).

6   The Case of Containers

Nouns of containers are systematically polysemous between two readings: the object (container) and the portion possibly contained in it (containee). In the cases where the noun is noncomplemented but it is portion-denoting it must be assumed, as it is the rule with any partitive noun, that either the complement is ellipsed (because such information is retrievable from the context) or the partitive noun is referring anaphorically to the containee of reference. Let us consider the examples in (36).

(36)   a.   Toma, una copa. [grasp/take/have-IMPERATIVE, a glass]
       b.   Rompe la copa. [break the glass]
       c.   Rompe la copa de vino. [break the glass of wine] ≅ break the glass of wine /"break the wine glass")
       d.   Un trozo de copa. [a portion-fragment of glass]
       e.   Se derramó la copa. [IMPERSONAL-PASSIVE spill-PAST the glass]
       f.   Se derramó la copa de vino. [IMPERS-PASSIVE spill-PAST the glass of wine]

    g. Termina la copa. [finish-IMPERATIVE the glass] ≅ finish your drink)
    h. Disfruta de la copa. [enjoy of the glass] ≅ enjoy the drink)

(36a) is ambiguous between an object or a drink, while the rest of examples can only have one of the alternative readings, which is forced by the verb. So, "*romper*" (to break) in (36b,c) imposes to "*copa*" the *object* reading, regardless of whether or not it is complemented or not. In fact, "*copa de vino*" in (36c) is also ambiguous in another way: It may refer either to *a glass filled with wine*, or to *a glass usually used to contain wine*. The former is the usual case of partitive construction; in the latter case "*copa de vino*" is another kind of compound. But in both cases – more remarkably, concerning the issues discussed here, in the former – "*copa*" can only have an *object* reading. Last, "*trozo*" in (36d) also forces "*copa*" to an *object* interpretation because such partitive, as discussed above, is a predicate that selects for solid masses.

    The other way round, "*derramar*" (to spill) selects for liquids, therefore "*copa*" in (36e) and "*copa de vino*" in (36f) refer unambiguously to the containee, which is explicit in (36f) but implicit in (36e).

    Finally, verbs in (36g,h) also force "*copa*" to some *containee* interpretation, but with a remarkable implication: both "*terminar*" (to finish) and "*disfrutar*" (to enjoy), as discussed in Pustejovsky (1995) and pointed out in previous sections, select for event internal arguments; therefore in such cases "*copa*" must receive a *containee* – TELIC interpretation, namely *to drink the glass (of wine)*.

    Regular polysemies are formally represented in the GL framework by using LCPs (see §5). Using such a mechanism, I will represent containers as a **container•containee_lcp**, as in (37), thus resulting in an underspecified lexical entry in whose ARGUMENT STRUCTURE arguments of both the physical object and the contained stuff are represented. Consider the representation of *copa* in (37).

$$(37) \quad \begin{bmatrix} \textbf{copa} \\[4pt] \text{ARGSTR} = \begin{bmatrix} \text{ARG1} = x : \textbf{object} \\[4pt] \text{ARG2} = y : \begin{bmatrix} \textbf{unbounded} \\ \text{TELIC} = [1] \end{bmatrix} \end{bmatrix} \\[20pt] \text{QUALIA} = \begin{bmatrix} \textbf{container•containee\_lcp} \\ \text{FORMAL} = \texttt{contains(x, y)} \\ \text{CONST} = \texttt{glass(w)} \\ \text{TELIC} = \textbf{[1]} \end{bmatrix} \end{bmatrix}$$

    Both arguments are related in the FORMAL quale by a containment predicate, which accounts for both the relational facet of **copa** and its relative – quantifier function – a "glass of something" is the quantity of **y** contained in the object **x**.

    Its CONSTITUTIVE role is that of the object – the stuff the object is made of. In this case, a reference to the containee (compare the representation for portions in §5) is not necessary because such kind of information is straightforwardly available from ARG2. This is due to the fact that containers are *dot objects* (both types are simultaneously available) not just monomorphic relational predicates as pure partitives of type portion are – where only one type, **portion ≤ individual**, is the true argument.

Finally, as well as in portions, the TELIC role is co-indexed to that of the mass of reference.[9]

So now consider the lexical entry for "*vino*" ("wine") in (38), which is the usual for mass nouns as described in §3:

(38)
$$\begin{bmatrix} \textbf{vino} \\ \text{ARGSTR} = \begin{bmatrix} \text{ARG1} = \text{x} : \textbf{mass} \end{bmatrix} \\ \text{QUALIA} = \begin{bmatrix} \text{FORMAL} = \texttt{vino(x)} \\ \text{TELIC} = \texttt{drink(..,x,..)} \end{bmatrix} \end{bmatrix}$$

Co-composition of both (37) and (38) results in the representation for "*copa de vino*" (glass of wine) in (39):

(39)
$$\begin{bmatrix} \textbf{copa de vino} \\ \text{ARGSTR} = \begin{bmatrix} \text{ARG1} = \text{x} : \textbf{object} \\ \text{ARG2} = \text{y} : \begin{bmatrix} \textbf{vino} \\ \text{TELIC} = \textbf{drink} = [1] \end{bmatrix} \end{bmatrix} \\ \text{QUALIA} = \begin{bmatrix} \text{FORMAL} = \texttt{contains(x, y)} \\ \text{CONST} = \texttt{glass(w)} \\ \text{TELIC} = \texttt{drink(..,y,..)} = [1] \end{bmatrix} \end{bmatrix}$$

The effect is that structures (37) and (39) account for the cases in (36) in the following way:

- Selectional requirements of "*romper*" (break, (36b,c)) on the one hand, and "*derramar*" (spill; (36e,f)) on the other, are accomplished by respectively selecting ARG1 (the object) or ARG2 (the containee) in (37) or (39). In the case of (36e), the substance that is spilled is not overtly specified but existentially closed:

  $\exists x \exists y spill(e, y) \land unbounded(y)[\ldots \land glass(x) \land contains(x, y) \ldots]$

- In the case of "*trozo*" (36d), the composition will proceed as explained in §5, that is by selecting the CONSTITUTIVE predicate, which is relative to the object, thus accounting for a fragment of a glass (object) to be a piece of glass (substance).
- Selectional restrictions of "*terminar*" (finish) and "*disfrutar*" (enjoy) (36g,h) are satisfied by type coercion of the type of the complement to that of its TELIC role: **drink**.

---

[9] Indeed the object itself, e.g., "cup," have a built-in function, that of containing something. Nevertheless this sort of information seems not to be relevant for compositional purposes; consequently, I only consider the TELIC role relative to the containee.

- Last, the ambiguity of (36a) resides in the ambiguity of the verb, "*tomar*," which can be alternatively equivalent to "grasp" or "ingest." In any case, the corresponding sense will select for the appropriate argument of the complement: ARG1 (object), or ARG2 (the containee).

7   Final Remarks

In Spanish and many other languages, individual entities can be referred not only by means of regular noun-headed phrases but also by partitive constructions. The latter show a range of semantic properties that differ in many ways from those of the former. Specifically, some of their compositional properties appear to be dependent not on the semantics of the head (the partitive) but on that of the complement (the noun denoting the whole of reference).

To account for that, in this work, the semantic representation of partitive constructions has been built by co-composition. Therefore, both the partitive and its NP-complement contribute in a balanced way to create a lexical structure for the compound that will be appropriate for further compositional operations in the same way than regular NPs do.

Moreover, the case of nouns that are systematically polysemous between referential nouns and relational partitives is also accounted for, using containers as the typical case. Such nouns are treated as LCPs, thus providing a single under-specified representation able to account in any case for the appropriate sense of the word in a range of possible contexts.

A crucial aspect in this account is the relevance of the role played by the constitutional quale. Partitive constructions set a merological relation to the entitiy denoted by the embedded NP-complement (the "whole"); a relation that is entailed by the kind of partitive noun heading the phrase. Furthermore, the merological relationships of the whole itself is in many cases critical for the compositional process.

In the cases that have been worked out as typical examples (i.e., portions, such a constitutive relation is of type entity-stuff, namely, "made of"). This relation stands for the assumption that most entities are or can be conceptualized by speakers as being made of some stuff. Besides, the classification of partitive nouns and pronouns that is provided in §4 above suggests that also the rest of basic merological schemata can be involved in the process. For instance, an element-multiplex relation should play a role in constructions such as "one of the Xs" or "a group of Xs." A complete account of the semantic properties of the rest of the types of partitives will be developed in further research.

Acknowledgments

I am grateful to Toni Martí for her comments and constant help and advice; and also to Joaquim Moré and Gabriel Oreggioni for their contributions to this paper. This work has been partially supported by the Project PB 94-0831 of the DGICYT.

References

Allan, K. 1977. Classifiers. *Language* 53: 285–312.

Bunt, H. C. 1981. *The Formal Semantics of Mass Terms.* Ph.D. Thesis, University of Amsterdam.

Busa, F., Lenci, A., Calzolari, N., and Pustejovsky, J. 1998. Building a Semantic Lexicon: Structuring and Generating Concepts. *Proc. Conference on Computational Semantics,* Tilburg.

Chomsky, N. 1981. *Lectures on Government and Binding.* Foris, Dordrecht.

Climent, S. 1998. *Individuación y relaciones parte-todo. Representación para el procesamiento computacional del lenguaje.* Ph.D. Thesis, Universitat de Barcelona.

Copestake, A. 1992. *The Representation of Lexical Semantic Information.* PhD Thesis, University of Sussex.

Copestake, A., and Briscoe, T. 1995. Semi-Productive Polysemy and Sense Extension. *Journal of Semantics* 12: 15–68.

Jackendoff, R. 1991. Parts and Boundaries. In B. Levin and St. Pinker (eds.), *Lexical and Conceptual Semantics.* Elsevier Science Publishers, Amsterdam.

Langacker, R. 1991. *Foundations of Cognitive Grammar. Vol II. Descriptive Application.* Stanford University Press, Stanford.

Lyons, J. 1977. *Semantics.* Cambridge University Press, Cambridge.

Pustejovsky, J. 1995. *The Generative Lexicon.* MIT Press, Cambridge, MA.

Sagüés, M. 1989. *Gramática elemental vasca.* Txertoa, San Sebastián.

Sinclair, J. 1990. *COLLINS COBUILD English Grammar.* Collins, London.

Vossen, P. 1994. A Functional Approach to the Grammatical and Conceptual Individuation of First-order Nouns. *Proc. Functional Grammar Conference,* York.

Winston, M. E., Chaffin, R., and Hermann, D. 1987. A Taxonomy of Part-Whole Relations. *Cognitive Science* 11: 417–444.

12   Event Coreference in Causal Discourses

LAURENCE DANLOS

Abstract

This study concerns the causal discourses that express a *direct causation*. With the help of the extended event structure for causative verbs proposed in Pustejovsky (1995), I will show that they involve an event coreference relation when the result is expressed by a causative verb in its transitive use. Then I will define two types of event coreference: generalization and particularization. Next, I will show that discourses expressing a direct causation with a resultative rhetorical relation involve a generalization relation (which explains their awkward behavior), while those discourses with an explanation rhetorical relation involve a particularization relation (which accounts for their normal behavior). Finally, I will study discourses in which the result is expressed with an unaccusative form of a causative verb. This study leads to question the extended event structure for unaccusatives proposed in Pustejovsky (1995).

1   Direct Causation and Event Coreference

1.1   The Notion of Direct Causation

It is well known that causal relations can be of different kinds. Among them, the direct causal relation is often mentioned in the literature and among others, by Fodor (1970) and Schank (1975). In the line of these works, I define the notion of a direct causation on conceptual grounds as follows: the result is a physical change of state for an object Y,[1] the cause is an action performed by a human agent X, the action is the direct cause of the change of state.

On linguistic grounds, the result of a direct causation can be expressed in a sentence built around a causative verb, first studied in its transitive use. The cause can be expressed in a sentence juxtaposed to the sentence expressing the result (other means exist apart from this paratactic structure: they will be presented in Section 2.6). If the cause precedes the result, a *resultative* rhetorical relation is observed, (1a); an *explanation* rhetorical relation is observed when the order of the sentences is reversed, (1b).

---

[1] I will leave aside psychological changes of state because psych-verbs possess specific properties.

216

(1)   a. Fred hit the carafe against the sink. He cracked it.
       b. Fred cracked the carafe. He hit it against the sink.

Both (1a) and (1b) have a natural causal interpretation in which the action of hitting the carafe directly caused its crack(s).

Similarly, (2a) and (2b) have a natural causal interpretation in which Fred's jumping off the plane without a parachute directly caused his death.

(2)   a. Fred jumped off the plane without a parachute. He killed himself.
       b. Fred killed himself. He jumped off the plane without a parachute.

On the other hand, (3a) and (3b) express an indirect causation: forgetting (mental act) cannot directly cause a fatal outcome. (3a) or (3b) is an elliptical form of a longer causal chain: Fred's jumping off a plane (without a parachute) is not explicitly expressed.

(3)   a. Fred forgot his parachute. He killed himself.
       b. Fred killed himself. He forgot his parachute.

Finally, (4) and (5) do not have the interpretation of a direct causation.

(4)   a. Fred was angry with Mary. He broke the carafe.
       b. Fred broke the carafe. He was angry with Mary.
(5)   a. Fred hit the carafe against the sink. John cracked it.
       b. John cracked the carafe. Fred hit it against the sink.

(4a) and (4b) have a *motivation* interpretation, and (5a) and (5b), where the agents are not coreferent, have a motivation or *narration* interpretation.

Intuitively, the notion of direct causation relies on a *small* distance between the cause and the result. However, it is well known that the distance between the cause and the result is hard to evaluate, because a causal relation can be broken down in an arbitrarily long cause-result chain. This is the reason why I am going to delimit the notion of direct causation with the help of linguistic notions.

In this chapter, only causal discourses in which the result is expressed by a causative verb will be examined, in Sections 1 and 2 in its transitive use, in Section 3 in the unaccusative one.[2]

Adopting the extended event structure of Pustejovsky (1995) for causative verbs, I am going to show that the discourses that express a direct causation differ from other causal discourses by the fact that they involve an event[3] coreference relation.

Causative verbs are generally analyzed as complex predicates involving a causing sub-event (e_1), which brings about a new state (e_2) (see Chierchia, 1989;

---

[2] Therefore, the discourses in which the result is expressed in a stative construction (e.g., "The carafe is cracked") or in a periphrastic construction (e.g., "Fred made the carafe crack") will not be examined.

[3] The term "event" should be read as *eventuality*: it covers both static and dynamic situations and is represented by the symbol e.

Dowty, 1979; Levin and Rappaport, 1995; Moens and Steedman, 1988, among others). With Pustejovsky's extended event structure, the (informal) analysis of "Fred cracked the carafe" is given in (6): e_1 is a cracking act of Fred (f) on the carafe (c), e_2 is the cracked state of the carafe, e_1 precedes ($<_\alpha$) e_2, and the head (*) is on the causing sub-event e_1.

(6)

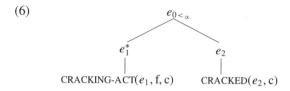

Let us now analyze (1a). The fact that the first sentence describes the direct cause of the result described in the second sentence can be expressed in the following terms: the first sentence describes an event (Fred's hitting the carafe), which is in an event coreference relation with the causing sub-event of the result (Fred's cracking act on the carafe). This event coreference relation is made explicit in diagram (7) in which the hitting event is represented by e_1 as is the cracking act. The two occurrences of e_1 are linked by a coreference relation, the second occurrence of e_1 is linked to the resulting state e_2 by a (direct) causal relation.

(7)   *Fred hit the carafe against the sink.*   *He cracked it.*

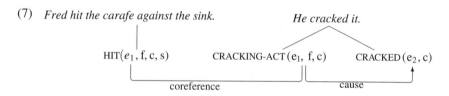

Therefore, linguistic means exist to delimit the notion of direct causation involved in a resultative discourse such as (1a). These linguistic means can be used *mutatis mutandis* for the direct causal relation involved in an explanation discourse such as (1b). The analysis of (1b) is shown in diagram (8), which is based on the same principles as (7).

(8)   *Fred cracked the carafe.*   *He hit it against the sink.*

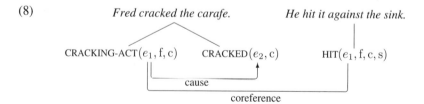

This analysis is also valid for (2a) and (2b): the cause sentence describes an event that can be interpreted as coreferent with the causing sub-event of the result sentence. This is not the case in (3a) and (3b), because the act of forgetting cannot be coreferent with the killing act. Similarly in (4a) and (4b): an angry state cannot be coreferent with a breaking act. Finally, in (5a) and (5b), the event described in the cause and the causing sub-event cannot be coreferent because their agents are not coreferent.

Notations and Conventions

The discourses studied in the next sections have a S_a. S_c. or S_c. S_a. structure in which:

- the symbol S_c represents a sentence built around a causative verb in its transitive use. In the active, S_c is informally equal to X V_c Y W, in which V_c denotes a causative verb and W a possibly empty sequence of adjuncts.
- the symbol S_a represents a sentence that describes an action achieved by the same human being X on the object Y. In the active, S_a is informally equal to X V_a $W1$ Y $W2$, in which V_a denotes an action verb and $W1$ and $W2$ possibly empty sequences of arguments or adjuncts.

In this paper, any variation on verb tenses will be ignored: V_a and V_c will always be in the simple past.[4]

So far, I have shown that a S_a. S_c. or S_c. S_a. discourse expresses a direct causation when the event described in S_a is coreferent with the causing sub-event in S_c. No difference between S_a. S_c. and S_c. S_a. discourses has been noted yet. However, subsequent sections present differences between these two kinds of discourses, in particular, when S_c comprises an adjunct. These differences will be explained by the fact that the **type** of event coreference relation involved is not the same in S_a. S_c. and S_c. S_a. discourses. Before presenting two types of event coreference, it is worth examining the different types of sub-causing events.

1.2 Unspecified Versus Specified Sub-causing Event

It has long been noted that, among causative verbs, some specify the resulting state but leave the causing event unspecified (e.g., "crack," "sink," "kill"), while others such as "slice" and "wax" specify both the resulting state and something about the event leading up to it (see Levin and Rappaport, 1995). The former are found in the S_c of a direct causation discourse, (1a) or (1b) with "crack," while the latter are not.

---

[4] If the simple past is translated in French as a "passé composé," the acceptability of the French discourses is the same as that of the English ones (Danlos, 1996). However, if the simple past is translated as a "passé simple," the acceptability changes (Amsili & Rossari, 1998).

When attempting to form a direct causation discourse with a causative verb that specifies its causing sub-event (e.g., "slice"), we obtain a discourse with another interpretation. For example, a discourse such as (9a) can only be understood as an *enablement*: the event described in the first sentence allows but does not cause the event described in the second sentence. Fred still has to perform some action with the knife in order to get the baguette sliced. This action can only be described in "Fred sliced/cut the baguette with a knife." However, (9b) is a *particularizing discourse* (see next section) and not a causal one.

(9)   a.   Fred took a knife. He sliced the baguette.
       b.   Fred cut the baguette with a knife. He sliced it.

Hence, I propose the following hypothesis:

> *The existence of a $S_a. S_c.$ or $S_c. S_a.$ discourse with an interpretation of direct causation is a linguistic proof that the causative verb in S_c does not specify the causing sub-event.*

In the event structure of a causative verb V_c, I represent the predicate of the causing sub-event as a variable indicated by the ? sign if left unspecified, for example, ?-CRACKING-ACT(e_1, x, y), and as a constant otherwise, e.g., SLICING-ACT(e_1, x, y). When the predicate of a causing sub-event is a variable, it can be bound by the predicate of a S_a sentence: a discourse with an interpretation of direct causation is then obtained. Most of the causative verbs where the causing sub-event is unspecified detransitivize into unaccusative forms (Levin and Rappaport, 1995).[5] The variants of $S_a. S_c.$ and $S_c. S_a.$ discourses in which the causative verb is in an unaccusative form will be studied in Section 3.

1.3   Types of Event Coreference

An event coreference relation is to be found between two successive descriptions D_1 and D_2 of the same event. The description of an event can be either linguistically realized or not. When it is linguistically realized, it is as a (pro)nominal phrase or a sentence. It is not linguistically realized for a sub-event, which can only get a conceptual representation, such as ?-CRACKING-ACT(e_1, x, y).

Event coreference has mainly been studied when D_2 is a (pro)nominal phrase, which refers to an event in a coreference relation with a sentence, $D_1 = S_1$ (see, among others, Webber, 1988). In Danlos (1999a), I have studied event coreference between two sentences. In this paper, I concentrate on the event coreference relations observed in $S_a. S_c.$ and $S_c. S_a.$ discourses that express a direct causation:

---

[5] The causing sub-event, whose predicate is a variable, is then shadowed. On the other hand, let me informally advance the hypothesis that a causing sub-event, whose predicate is a constant, cannot be shadowed. The unaccusative form would lose one part of the semantics of the verb, namely the information given by the predicate of the sub-causing event. This could explain why "slice" or "wax" cannot detransitivize into unaccusative forms.

They are coreference relations between the description of an event linguistically realized as a sentence and the description of the same event that is not linguistically realized.

Two types of event coreference, *particularization* (noted as PART) and *generalization* (noted as GEN), can be defined as follows.

> Two descriptions D_1 and D_2 of the same event e are in a particularization relation with $D_2 = PART(D_1)$ if D_2 conveys some new information about e when compared to the information known from D_1.

> Two descriptions D_1 and D_2 of the same event e are in a generalization relation with $D_2 = GEN(D_1)$ if D_2 does not bring any new information about e.

To illustrate these two types of event coreference, let us consider the well known case in which D_2 is a (pro)nominal phrase and D_1 a sentence:

(10)   a. Fred arrived at midnight. This woke up Mary.
        b. Fred arrived at midnight. This unforeseen arrival surprised Mary.

In (10a), $D_2 = $ "this," $D_1 = S_1$, and $D_2 = GEN(D_1)$ because a pronoun does not bring new information. In (10b), $D_2 = $ "this unforeseen arrival," $D_1 = S_1$, and $D_2 = PART(D_1)$ because D_2 brings the information that Fred's arrival was unforeseen.

When D_1 and D_2 are both sentences, a particularization relation is observed in *particularizing discourses* such as (11), and a generalization relation is observed in *generalizing restatement discourses* such as (12). In (11a), $S_2 = PART(S_1)$ because it specifies that the damage was a stain and the garment was a shirt.

(11)   a. Fred damaged a garment yesterday. He stained a shirt.
        b. Fred told Mary that she is pretty. He complimented her at noon.

(12)   Fred stained a shirt yesterday. Therefore, he damaged a garment.

In (11b), $S_2 = PART(S_1)$ because "at noon" brings new temporal information, while "X compliment Y" re-describes (without bringing new information) "X tell Y that Y is pretty". In (12), $S_2 = GEN(S_1)$ and S_2 is introduced by "therefore" with an epistemic value (Rossari and Jayez, 1996). In the next section, it will be shown that some S_a. S_c. discourses may look as causal, but are in fact particularizing or restatement discourses.

In section 2, I will present the hypothesis that the event coreference relation is a generalization for S_a. S_c. discourses and a particularization for S_c. S_a. discourses. This hypothesis explains contrasts such as the one observed between (13a) with a S_a. S_c. structure and (13b) with a S_c. S_a. structure. In these discourses, S_c comprises a time adjunct ("at noon"). (13b) has a natural interpretation of direct causation, whereas (13a) does not have this interpretation.

(13)   a. ?Fred hit the carafe against the sink. He cracked it at noon.
        b. Fred cracked the carafe at noon. He hit it against the sink.

In support of this last point, consider a connective such as "therefore" or "as a consequence."

(14)   a.   Fred hit the carafe against the sink. Therefore, he cracked it.
         b.   *Fred hit the carafe against the sink. Therefore, he cracked it at noon.

The connective "therefore" is used to explicitly indicate a resultative rhetorical relation: (14a), which is obtained from (1a) after insertion of "therefore," is stylistically unfelicitous, but it is a paraphrase of (1a). On the other hand, (14b), which is obtained from (13a) after insertion of "therefore," is meaningless (hence the * sign in front of it). (13a) might just possibly be understood as a *narration* (Asher, 1993), although this interpretation is better expressed in "Fred hit the carafe against the sink at 11 am. He cracked it at noon." In conclusion, (13a) has no natural interpretation, hence the ? sign in front of it.

Before presenting my hypothesis, I will examine other interpretations of S_a. S_c. discourses.

1.4   Interpretations of S_a. S_c. Discourses

In (15) with a S_a. S_c. structure, the change of state (i.e., the death of the rabbit) is a new piece of information, which cannot (or should not) be inferred from S_a, because the rabbit could have been safe and sound, or simply wounded.

(15)   Fred fired a shot at the rabbit. He killed it.

It is this type of discourses I am interested in: The interpretation is a direct causation with a resultative rhetorical relation. However, discourses with a S_a. S_c. structure may have other interpretations. This is the case when the change of state is not a new piece of information, either because it can be inferred from S_a or because it is *available* from S_a, or because it is known from a prior context, as shown in the three subsections below, respectively. I will establish that some adjuncts may or may not be inserted in S_c depending on the interpretation of a S_a. S_c. discourse.

S_a. S_c. Discourses as Particularizing Discourses

Consider the following discourses:

(16)   a.   ?Fred cut the throat of the rabbit. He killed it.
         b.   Fred cut the throat of the rabbit. He killed it at noon.
         c.   Fred cut the throat of the rabbit. He did it at noon.
         d.   Fred cut the throat of the rabbit. More precisely, he killed it at noon.

When the action described in S_a obligatorily implies the change of state described in S_c, a S_a. S_c. discourse without any adjunct in S_c sounds poor because it is redundant, (16a). This redundancy disappears if S_c comprises an adjunct: (16b) is natural. The point is that (16b) is not a resultative causal discourse in which S_c describes the result of S_a: It is a particularizing discourse in which both sentences describe the same event. The second sentence brings a new temporal information through "at noon." "X kill Y" re-describes – without bringing new information – "X cut the throat of Y." [6] This analysis of (16b) is confirmed by the fact that it is paraphrased by (16c) with the pronominal form "did it." (16b) is also paraphrased by (16d) in which the connective *more precisely* explicitly (although unfelicitously) indicates a particularization relation between the two sentences.

It is worth underlining the contrast in the acceptability of S_a. S_c. discourses related to the possibility or impossibility to infer the change of state from S_a.

(17)   a.   Fred fired a shot at the rabbit. He killed it.
       b.   ?Fred fired a shot at the rabbit. He killed it at noon.
       c.   Fred fired a shot at the rabbit. He did so at noon.
       d.   Fred fired a shot at the rabbit. therefore, he killed it.

(17a) (= (15)) without an adjunct in S_c is natural, whereas (16a) is redundant. (17b) with an adjunct in S_c does not have any natural interpretation, whereas (16b) is natural with a particularization interpretation. (17c) is not in a paraphrastic relation with (17b), whereas (16c) paraphrases (16b). (17d) with the connective "therefore" (unfelicitously) paraphrases (17a), whereas (16d) with the connective "more precisely" (unfelicitously) paraphrases (16b).

In conclusion, an extralinguistic factor (i.e., can the change of state be inferred from S_a?) is crucial for the acceptability and the interpretation of S_a. S_c. discourses. Of course, this extralinguistic factor, as any other extralinguistic factor, is subjective, depending on the speaker's view of the world.

To illustrate the consequences of this point, consider the pair in (18) with $V_c =$ "crack" in (18a) and $V_c =$ "break" in (18b).

(18)   a.   ?Fred hit the carafe against the sink. He cracked it at noon.
       b.   ?Fred hit the carafe against the sink. He broke it at noon.

I have presented this pair to a number of speakers. Speakers agree that (18a), which repeats (13a), is deviant. On the other hand, opinion differs for (18b): Some speakers (including me) consider that this discourse is as deviant as (18a), while other speakers consider it natural.

In (18a), the cracked state of the carafe is plausible, but nobody can infer it from the cause. The speakers who consider (18b) natural have a view of the world in which the broken state of the carafe is an ineluctable consequence of the cause

---

[6] In (16b), each sentence is built around a causative verbal form. The event coreference relation between the two sentences relies on coreference and inference relations between their sub-events. Their causing sub-events are interpreted as coreferent with CUTTING-THROAT(e_1, f, r), which specifies ?-KILLING-ACT(e_1, f, r). Their resulting states stand in an inference relation: DEAD(e_2', r) can be inferred from CUT-THROAT(e_2, r).

(they activate the rule: when a carafe is hit against a sink, it is broken). Therefore, they interpret (18b) as (16b) (i.e., with a particularization relation between the two sentences). The speakers who do not consider that a carafe hit against a sink is a broken carafe cannot interpret (18b) with a particularization relation, and therefore judge (18b) as deviant as (18a).

S_a. S_c. Discourses as Achieved-Goal Discourses

Another subtle issue concerning the newness of the change of state in S_a. S_c. discourses is the fact that the S_a cause sentence describes or allows to infer a goal. For example, the S_a sentences in (19) indicate explicitly or implicitly that Fred's goal is Mary's death. In my view of the world, (19a) should not be perceived as redundant because Fred may fire a shot at Mary inadvertently (without a goal, for example, while cleaning his rifle) or with the goal of wounding her.

(19)   a.   Fred fired a shot at Mary to kill her.
          b.   Fred fired a shot at Mary carefully aiming for her heart.

It is normal to continue a S_a sentence as in (19) with a sentence that indicates whether or not the goal is achieved, as in (20).

(20)   a.   Fred fired a shot at Mary to kill her. He succeeded.
          b.   Fred fired a shot at Mary carefully aiming at her heart. However, he missed her.

If the goal is achieved, no connective is needed, (20a). If it is not, the use of a connective such as "however" is preferable, (20b). This contrast between (20a) and (20b) means that the default outcome of S_a is "success."

The discourse relation in (20a) is obviously not a causal resultative relation. Let us call it an *achieved-goal* relation. Consider now the discourses in (21) and (22) that have a S_a. S_c. structure.

(21)   a.   Fred fired a shot at Mary to kill her. He killed her at noon.
          b.   Fred fired a shot at Mary carefully aiming at her heart. He killed her at noon.

(22)   a.   ?Fred fired a shot at Mary to kill her. He killed her.
          b.   ?Fred fired a shot at Mary carefully aiming at her heart. He killed her.

The discourses in (21) with an adjunct in S_c are natural, while the discourses in (22) without any adjunct in S_c sound poor. None of these discourses have a causal resultative interpretation (the insertion of "therefore" is totally forbidden). The discourses in (21) receive a natural achieved-goal interpretation: S_c brings the information that Fred achieved his goal and that it happened at noon. The discourses in (22) sound poor, probably because "success" is the default outcome of S_a. In (21) (or (22)), the change of state (Mary's death) is not a brand-new piece of information because it is already *available* through the goal phrase in S_a.[7]

When S_a does not include a goal adjunct, the ability to infer one from its content may vary from one speaker to another. Consider the pair in (23). Speakers agree that (23a) with V_c = "wound" is deviant. On the other hand, opinion is divided for (23b) with V_c = "kill" (which repeats (17b)). Some speakers (but not me) consider it natural with an achieved-goal relation. For them, the change of state (Mary's death) is made available by S_a because they activate the rule: when an individual fires a shot at another individual, the purpose of the former is of killing the latter.[8]

(23)   a.   ?Fred fired a shot at Mary. He wounded her at noon.
       b.   ?Fred fired a shot at Mary. He killed her at noon.

S_a. S_c. *Discourses as Restatement Discourses*

Discourse (24a) in which S_c comprises an agent-oriented adjunct is poor (the interpretations as a direct causation and as a narration are not naturally available). However, if it is inserted in a context where Mary's death is already known, the whole discourse becomes acceptable, (24b).

(24)   a.   ?Fred fired a shot at Mary. He killed her deliberately.
       b.   After the discovery of Mary's body, the police arrested her lover, Fred. He made a full confession. They had an argument. Fred picked up his rifle. **He fired a shot at Mary.** Therefore, **he killed her deliberately.**

In the last sentence of (24b), which is introduced by "therefore" with an epistemic value, the speaker draws her conclusions: What happened to Mary was a murder and not an accident. In other words, the speaker makes a restatement. A restatement interpretation has nothing to do with a causal one. A causal discourse stands at the informational level and both the cause and the result are new information for the hearer. On the other hand, a restatement stands at the intentional level and does not bring any new information.

Summary

A discourse with a S_a. S_c. structure can receive (at least) four interpretations:

- a causal resultative interpretation when the change of state is a brand-new piece of information,
- a particularization interpretation when the change of state can be inferred from S_a,

---

[7] On the other hand, in (i), in which S_a includes a goal adjunct, the cracked state of the carafe is a brand-new information because it has nothing to do with the goal.
(i) Fred hit the carafe against the sink to draw Mary's attention. He cracked it.
[8] The "cracked" and "broken" states for a carafe can be compared respectively to the "wounded" and "dead" states for an animate object.

- a achieved-goal interpretation when the change of state is made available by S_a,
- a restatement interpretation when the change of state is known from a prior context.

I have shown that some adjuncts may or may not be inserted in S_c depending on the interpretation that can be given to a S_a. S_c. discourse. If one wants to say anything relevant about the insertion of adjuncts in S_c, it is thus crucial to stick to a given interpretation. In the rest of this paper, only S_a. S_c. discourses in which the change of state is (interpreted as) a brand-new piece of information will be examined. These discourses should receive a causal resultative interpretation. The question is to determine under which conditions they receive this interpretation. For example, how can the contrast between (1a) without adjunct in S_c and (13a) with a time adjunct in S_c be explained? My answer to this question is the (H1) hypothesis presented below.

2   (H1) Generalization Hypothesis for S_a. S_c Discourses and (H2) Particularization Hypothesis for S_c. S_a Discourses

I am going to defend the following hypothesis:

(H1)   *A S_a. S_c. discourse, in which the change of state is a brand-new infor-mation, has a natural interpretation of direct causation if and only if the description of the causing sub-event in S_c is a **generalization** of the description of the event in S_a.*

(H2)   *A S_c. S_a. discourse has a natural interpretation of direct causation if and only if the description of the event in S_a is a **particularization** of the description of the causing sub-event in S_c.*

Let us briefly show that (H1) is valid when S_c does not comprise any adjunct. The description of the causing sub-event in S_c is an unspecified act achieved by X on Y. Hence, it does not bring any new information compared to the description of that event in S_a in which this act is lexically specified. By the inverse principle, the S_c. S_a. discourses illustrated so far involve a particularization relation. In other words, the diagrams in (7) and (8), in which the coreference relation is nontyped (so nonoriented), ought to be replaced respectively by the diagrams in (25) and (26), in which the coreference relation is typed (and oriented).

(25)   *Fred hit the carafe against the sink.*   *He cracked it.*

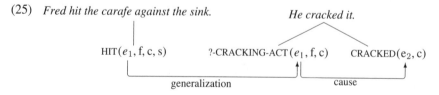

(26)

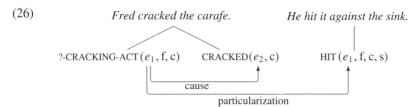

In this section, a S_a. S_c. or S_c. S_a. discourse, which has a natural interpretation of direct causation, will be qualified as *acceptable*. It will be qualified as *unacceptable* otherwise, and will be annotated by the # sign.

2.1   Method

To show the validity of (H1), it must be shown that a S_a. S_c. discourse is acceptable only if the description of the causing sub-event in S_c generalizes S_a, (i.e., it does not bring new information compared to what is known from S_a). The following method will be used. Starting with an acceptable S_a. S_c. discourse without any adjunct in S_c, different types of adjuncts are inserted in S_c.[9]

Surprisingly, differences in acceptability are observed. They correlate with the differences of scope of the adjuncts modifying the causative verb. More precisely, if an adjunct modifies the causing sub-event, the discourse is unacceptable. Otherwise, it is acceptable. If an adjunct modifies the causing sub-event, the description of the causing sub-event in S_c does not generalize S_a. Otherwise, it does. This method is illustrated in the following paragraph with time and quantifier adjuncts inserted in (1a).

Note that the interpretation of direct causation is lost when a time adjunct is inserted in S_c, as in (13a) repeated in (27a). On the other hand, when a quantifier adjunct is inserted in S_c, the interpretation of direct causation is maintained, (27b).

(27)   a.   #Fred hit the carafe against the sink. He cracked it at noon.
        b.   Fred hit the carafe against the sink. He cracked it badly.

The contrast between (27a) and (27b) correlates with the difference of scope between time and quantifier adjuncts (modifying a causative verb). A time adjunct modifies the causing sub-event (and the final state),[10] while a quantifier adjunct modifies only the final state. Therefore, the description of the causing sub-event

---

[9] Only adjuncts which can be inserted in S_c in isolation will be examined.

[10] Although (Pustejovsky and Busa, 1995) state that a time adjunct modifies only the headed event, here the causing sub-event, the inappropriateness of (i) shows that a time adjunct modifies also the final state. In "Fred killed Mary at noon," both Fred's killing act and Mary's death occur around noon.

(i) *Fred killed Mary at noon and she died at 2 pm.

in (27a) is ?-CRACKING-ACT$(e_1, f, c) \wedge$ at-noon(e_1) This description does not generalize S_a: it brings new temporal information, which is not available in S_a, because S_a does not include a time adjunct.[11] The description of the final state in (27b) is CRACKED$(e_2, c) \wedge$ badly(e_2). The description of the causing sub-event is ?-CRACKING-ACT(e_1, f, c), and it does generalize S_a.

In other words, (H1) predicts that any S_a. S_c. discourse in which S_c comprises an adjunct that modifies the causing sub-event has no natural interpretation of direct causation (i.e., is unacceptable). In the next sections, this prediction will be confirmed, as well as other predictions made by (H1) or (H2).

2.2   Adjuncts That Modify the Causing Sub-event

More about Time Adjuncts

Three cases are going to be examined: discourses with (i) only one time adjunct either in S_a or S_c, (ii) one time adjunct in S_a and another one in S_c which refers to a posterior time, (iii) one time adjunct in S_a and a more specific one in S_c.

I have shown above that a S_a. S_c. discourse in which S_c (but not S_a) comprises a time adjunct is unacceptable, (27a). This unacceptability is explained by (H1). On the other hand, a time adjunct can be inserted in S_a: (28) is acceptable, which is explained by (H1) because the description of the causing sub-event in S_c generalizes S_a.

More generally, as the reader can verify, any adjunct that can be inserted in S_a in isolation can be inserted in S_a in the context of a S_a. S_c. discourse, while maintaining an interpretation of direct causation. The description of the sub-causing event in S_c remains a generalization of S_a. Therefore, in the rest of this paper, only the insertion of adjuncts in S_c will be examined for S_a. S_c. discourses.

(28)   Fred hit the carafe against the sink at noon. He cracked it.

For S_c. S_a. discourses, a time adjunct can be inserted either in S_c, (29a), or in S_a, (29b). The acceptability of these discourses conforms to (H2) because S_a particularizes the description of the causing sub-event in S_c: It brings new information by specifying the cracking act which is left unspecified in S_a.

(29)   a. Fred cracked the carafe at noon. He hit it against the sink.
         b. Fred cracked the carafe. He hit it against the sink at noon.

Let us now examine the discourses obtained with a time adjunct in S_a and another one in S_c, which refers to a posterior time. Both S_a. S_c. and S_c. S_a. discourses are unacceptable, (30a) and (30b).

---

[11] The discourses in which both S_a and S_c comprise a time adjunct will be examined in the next section.

(30) a. #Fred fired a shot at Mary on Sunday. He killed her on Monday.
      b. #Fred killed Mary on Monday. He (had) fired a shot at her on Sunday.

Recall the famous example in Fodor (1970): "*Fred killed Mary on Monday by shooting her on Sunday."[12] From the observation that this example is almost meaningless, Fodor (and most linguists after him) claims the following: A causative verb in its transitive form cannot be used to express an indirect causation. I argue that this claim does not correspond to the right analysis of the data. (30) and Fodor's example do not involve a direct causation because the causing sub-event in S_c does not corefer to the event described in S_a because they do not occur at the same time.[13] This is not because a transitive verb cannot be used when an indirect causation is expressed. Indeed, a transitive causative verb can be used when an indirect causation is involved, (31) with an indirect causation between Fred's shooting and Mary's death.

(31) Fred killed Mary. He fired a shot at her on Sunday. She had an hemmorhage. She died on Monday.

(31), in which it is impossible to modify "kill" by a time adjunct specifying the day, will be discussed again in Section 3 on unaccusatives.

The last case to be examined deals with one time adjunct in S_a ("yesterday") and a more specific one in S_c ("at noon"). Only S_a. S_c discourses will be examined. A contrast is then observed depending whether S_a describes a single action, (32a), or an iteration of actions, (32b) in which "bomb" means 'send a bunch of bombs at' with a durative aspect.

(32) a. #Yesterday, the enemy sent a bomb at the boat. They sank it at noon.
      b. Yesterday, the enemy bombed the boat. They sank it at noon.

(32a) is not acceptable, which is explained by (H1): "at noon" brings a new piece of information on the causing event. On the other hand, (32b) is natural. Does it falsify (H1)? Let us check whether (32b) does have an interpretation of direct

---

[12] Fodor's example does not have a paratactic structure contrarily to (30). However, it will be shown in Section 2.6 that there is no difference between paratactic and nonparatactic structures for the data examined here. Another difference between Fodor's example and (30) is the use of "fire a shot at" instead of "shoot." This is because "Fred shot Mary" implies compulsorily Mary's death, a case that has been put aside in Section 1.4

[13] There is no difference of acceptability between (30a) with a S_a. S_c. structure and (30b) with a S_c. S_a. structure. This is because what is at stake is the lack of an event coreference relation. The type of event coreference relation involved, generalization or particularization, which accounts for differences between S_a. S_c. and S_c. S_a. discourses, is therefore irrelevant. The unacceptability of (30) should be compared to that of (i) with "two seconds later" or (ii) with "two seconds before." (i) and (ii) are unacceptable because the causing sub-event in S_c does not corefer to the event described in S_a because they do not occur at the same time.

(i) # Fred fired a shot at Mary. Two seconds later, he killed her.

(ii) # Fred killed Mary. Two seconds before, he (had) fired a shot at her.

causation. Strictly speaking, the bombing of the boat does not cause its sinking. It is the fact that at least one of the bombs hit the boat, let's say at time t, before noon. Before t, all the sending of bombs that did not hit the boat are not in a causal relation with the sinking. It is thus impossible to postulate a coreference relation between the bombing and the causing sub-event of the sinking. Moreover, the interpretation of (32b) involves an achieved-goal relation (Section 1.4), as shown in (33), which glosses (32b).

(33)   Yesterday, the enemy started to bomb the boat and they continued to bomb it until they reach their goal, sinking it. They achieved their goal at noon.

This gloss calls for comments on extralinguistic grounds. A person may perform a single action without having any specific goal. It does not seem to be the case for an iteration of actions: a (normal) person is not expected to perform the same action several times without having a goal. On linguistic grounds, this goal may be inferable from a sentence describing the type of action achieved and repeated. For example, in (32b), the goal of the enemy is inferable from S_a. In S_c, it is indicated that the enemy achieved its goal and that it happened at noon. In conclusion, this interpretation of (32b), in which the bombing does not corefer to the sinking act (see above), does not exhibit a direct causation. Therefore, (32b) does not falsify (H1).

In the rest of this paper, the S_a. S_c. or S_c. S_a discourses in which S_a describes an iteration of actions or a durative action will be put aside.[14]

Let us now briefly examine the other adjuncts that modify the causing event. The S_c. S_a. discourses will not be systematically presented. They behave as expected: Each adjunct that is licensed in S_c in isolation (or in S_a) is licensed in S_c. S_a. discourses, while maintaining an interpretation of direct causation. This normal behavior is explained by the (H2) particularization hypothesis.

Locative Adjuncts

In the carafe example, the agent and the patient are in the same place. It is impossible to specify this place in S_c, (34).

(34)   #Fred hit the carafe against the sink. He cracked it at Mary's.

In the boat example, the agent and the patient are not in the same place. It is impossible to specify in S_c either the place of the agent, (35a), or that of the patient, (35b).

---

[14] Let me just add however that a frame adjunct can be inserted in S_c when S_a describes an iteration of actions, (i), while this is not possible when S_a describes a single action, (ii). The unacceptability of (ii) is explained by (H1). A frame adjunct indicates the temporal distance between the onset of the causing sub-event and the occurrence of the resulting state (Pustejovsky, 1991). It brings thus information on the duration of the causing sub-event.
  (i) The enemy bombed the boat. They sank it in two hours.
  (ii) # The enemy sent a bomb at the boat. They sank it in a fraction of a second.

(35) a. #The enemy sent a bomb at the boat. They sank it from Buru.

b. #The enemy sent a bomb at the boat. They sank it near Brest.[15]

These data on S_a. S_c. discourses conform to (H1). The reader can verify the validity of (H1) and (H2) when there are two locative adjuncts, one in S_a, another one in S_c, these two locative adjuncts referring either to two different places or to one place included in the other one.

Agent-Oriented Adjuncts

A sentence with an agent admits adverbial phrases (adverbs, prepositional phrases, or subordinate clauses) directed toward the agent, (36). The verb "break" is used instead of "crack" because a sentence such as "Fred cracked the carafe in a spirit of vengeance." sounds poor, because of the basically unintentional nature of "crack."

(36) Fred broke the carafe (casually + in a casual way + in a spirit of vengeance + while dreaming of his fiancée + while washing it + to draw Mary's attention).

However, in S_a. S_c. discourses, these adverbial phrases cannot appear within S_c: (37) cannot be interpreted as causal discourses (the insertion of "therefore" is totally forbidden). On the other hand, some speakers interpret (37) as particularizing discourses (Section 1.4) because they consider that the broken state of the carafe can be inferred from S_a.

(37) #Fred hit the carafe against the sink. He broke it (casually + in a casual way + in a spirit of vengeance + while dreaming of his fiancée + while washing it + to draw Mary's attention).

An agent-oriented adjunct modifying a causative verb brings new information about either the causing sub-event e_1 or the agent while achieving e_1. For example, in "Fred broke the carafe casually," "casually" modifies the manner in which e_1 was achieved (Pustejovsky, 1991), while in "Fred broke the carafe in a spirit of vengeance," the adjunct indicates the state of mind of Fred while achieving e_1. Therefore, the unacceptability of (37) is explained by (H1).[16]

Adjuncts that indicate the speaker's judgment on the agent cannot be inserted in S_c, (38).

(38) #Fred fired a shot at the rabbit. Cruelly, he killed it.

[15] This discourse becomes acceptable if S_a describes an iteration of actions, see (i), which seems to imply that the boat was sailing.
(i) The enemy bombed the boat. They sank it near Brest.

[16] Instrumental adjuncts are considered as agent-oriented adjuncts: (i) cannot be given a causal interpretation (the insertion of "therefore" is forbidden). Some speakers give (i) an achieved-goal interpretation because they activate the following rule: If someone fires a shot at a rabbit (an animate object), it is with the goal of killing it.
(i) #Fred fired a shot at the rabbit. He killed it with a rifle.

The unacceptability of (38) is explained by the fact that the presence of "cruelly" implies that Fred wanted the rabbit to be dead (Molinier, 1990), information which is not brought by S_a. See a similar argumentation for (41b) in Section 2.4.

Having examined all the types of adjuncts that modify the causing sub-events, we will now ponder over the adjuncts that do not modify the causing sub-event.

2.3   Adjuncts That Do Not Modify the Causing Sub-event

Recall that for S_a. S_c. discourses (see Section 2.1) a quantifier adjunct that modifies the final state can be inserted in S_c, (27b).

Among temporal adjuncts, the only ones left aside so far are the durative adjuncts like "for two hours" or "forever." When they are admitted in S_c in isolation, they indicate the duration of the final state (Pustejovsky, 1995). In S_a. S_c. discourses, they can be inserted in S_c, (39). For a permanent state as "sunk," only a durative adjunct like "forever" can be inserted.

(39)   a.   Fred delivered a punch straight to Mary's stomach. He knocked her out for two minutes.

        b.   The enemy sent a bomb at the boat. They sank it forever.

A speaker-oriented adjunct such as "unfortunately" or "naturally" can be inserted in S_c, (40a). It indicates the speaker's judgment on the whole event, as shown in (40c) which paraphrases (40b). Therefore, it does not bring new information on the causing sub-event.

(40)   a.   Fred hit the carafe against the sink. Unfortunately, he cracked it.

        b.   Unfortunately, Fred cracked the carafe.

        c.   Fred cracked the carafe and (I think) it is unfortunate.

All the types of adjuncts that can modify a sentence built around a causative verb have now been examined, and this study has shown that the (H1) generalization hypothesis is valid for S_a. S_c. discourses and the (H2) particularization hypothesis is valid for S_c. S_a. discourses. The last issues to be examined are the nature of the causative verb with respect to the intentionality of the agent, and the presence and nature of the arguments.

2.4   Nature of the Causative Verb in S_c

In S_a. S_c. discourses, S_c cannot be built around a causative verb that intrinsically contains the notion of a goal. Contrast (41a) with "kill" and (41b) with "murder." Only (41a) is acceptable when Mary's death is not known from a prior context (see Section 1.4 and Danlos, 1987).[17]

---

[17] A discourse such as (i) is a particularizing discourse, see Section 1.4

    (i) Fred stabbed Mary. He murdered her at noon.

(41) a. Fred fired a shot at Mary. He killed her.
      b. #Fred fired a shot at Mary. He murdered her.

The semantics of "X murder Y" is roughly 'X kill Y by deliberately acting with the goal of Y being dead.'[18] In (41b), S_c brings thus a new information on the causing event: It was goal-oriented and the goal was the death of Mary. This information is not given in S_a because Fred may have fired a shot at Mary inadvertently (without a goal) or with the goal of wounding her. So the (H1) hypothesis explains the unacceptability of (41b). On the other hand, when S_a conveys the information that the action was performed in the purpose of killing Y, Y's death is made available by S_a and an achieved-goal discourse can be built with "murder" or "kill," (42) ((42b) repeats (21b)).

(42) a. Fred fired a shot at Mary carefully aiming at her heart. He murdered her at noon.
      b. Fred fired a shot at Mary carefully aiming at her heart. He killed her at noon.

In S_c. S_a. discourses, S_c can be built around a causative verb that intrinsically contains the notion of a goal, (43). The acceptability of (43) conforms to (H2).

(43) Fred murdered Mary. He fired a shot at her.

2.5   Arguments

So far, we have examined only S_a. S_c. discourses in which (i) the agent and the patient in S_c are expressed by pronominal anaphora of the NPs expressing the agent and the patient in S_a, (ii) both S_a and S_c are in the active form.

Consider first S_a. S_c. discourses in which the agent in S_c is expressed by a definite NP in an anaphoric relation with the NP expressing the agent in S_a, (44).

(44) a. Fred fired a shot at the rabbit. The hunter, who had a rifle, killed it.
      b. Fred fired a shot at the rabbit. The hunter, who is blue eyed, killed it.
      c. Fred hit the carafe against the sink. This idiot cracked it.

The discourses in (44) are acceptable, and so appear to be counter-examples to (H1) because the subject in S_c brings new information on X. However, this new information concerns X in itself and not X as being a participant in the causing sub-event. This claim may sound *ad hoc*, especially for (44a). However, it is supported by data observed in particularizing discourses (see Danlos, 1999a and Section 1.3). The discourses in (45) are all particularizing discourses: In each one, both

---

[18] In the line of note 5, this semantics of "murder" could explain why this verb does not detransitivize into an unaccusative. Its causing sub-event, i.e., ?-KILLING-ACT$(e_1, x, y) \wedge$ GOAL(e_1, e_2) with DEAD(e_2, y), cannot be shadowed. The unaccusative form would lose the information given in GOAL(e_1, e_2).

sentences refer to the same event and "at noon" brings new temporal information on the event involved. Yet, the presence of "at noon" is obligatory: the discourses in (46) are meaningless.

(45)   a. Fred killed the rabbit. The hunter, who had a rifle, killed it at noon.
       b. Fred killed the rabbit. The hunter, who is blue eyed, killed it at noon.
       c. Fred cracked the carafe. This idiot cracked it at noon.

(46)   a. *Fred killed the rabbit. The hunter, who had a rifle, killed it.
       b. *Fred killed the rabbit. The hunter, who is blue eyed, killed it.
       c. *Fred cracked the carafe. This idiot cracked it.

In other words, for (46a) and (46b), whatever the information conveyed by the relative clause may be, it cannot be interpreted as information on the agent X as a participant in the killing event: It is interpreted as information on X in itself. Because there is no reason for the interpretation conveyed by a relative clause to change between causal and particularizing discourses, it can be stated that, in (44a) or (44b), the relative clause brings new information on X in itself but not on X as being a participant in the causing sub-event. Therefore, these discourses are not counter-examples to (H1). The same is true of (44c).

Let us now look at variations on diathesis in S_a. S_c. discourses. When S_c is in the active, S_a can be in the passive with an agent, (47a), but cannot be in the passive without an agent, (47b). When S_c is in the passive with an agent,[19] the paradigm is given in (48).

(47)   a. The carafe was hit against the sink by Fred. He cracked it.
       b. #The carafe was hit against the sink. Fred cracked it.

(48)   a. Fred hit the carafe against the sink. It was cracked by this idiot.
       b. The carafe was hit against the sink by Fred. It was cracked by this idiot.
       c. #The carafe was hit against the sink. It was cracked by Fred.

The unacceptability of (47a) and (48c) is explained by (H1): The agent is not mentioned in S_a, but it is in S_c. So S_c brings new information on the causing sub-event (who is the agent).

---

[19] The cases where S_c is in the passive without an agent, (i), are left aside because the sentence "It was cracked," is better understood with a stative reading, which gives a motivation interpretation to (i).
(i) Fred hit the carafe against the sink. It was cracked.
However, when translating a simple past as a passé composé, the French translation of (i) has an interpretation of direct causation which conforms to (H1), (ii).
(ii) Fred a heurté la carafe contre l'évier. Elle a été fêlée.
In (iii), the agent is not mentioned in any sentence, but it is understood that it is the same person in S_a and in S_c.
(iii) La carafe a été heurtée contre l'évier. Elle a été félée.
(The carafe was hit against the sink. It was cracked.)

2.6   Concluding Remarks on S_a. S_c. and S_c. S_a. Discourses

In S_a. S_c discourses, all the parameters in S_c (adjuncts, verb, and arguments) have been examined, and this exhaustive study leads to the following conclusion: The (H1) generalization hypothesis is valid. This hypothesis accounts for the awkward behavior of these discourses. The S_c. S_a. discourses have not been examined in such an exhaustive way, but the reader can check that the (H2) particularization hypothesis explains their normal behavior.

In addition, only the S_a. S_c. and S_c. S_a. discourses with a parataxic structure have been examined. However, other structures made up of a single sentence can express a direct causation. For example, a present participle, (49a), a coordination, (49b), or a *narrative relative*, (49c), can express a direct causation with a rhetorical resultative relation.

(49)   a. Fred hit the carafe against the sink, cracking it.
        b. Fred fired a shot at Mary and (he) killed her.
        c. The carafe was hit against the sink by Fred who cracked it.

These structures are not always appropriate, but this topic will not be discussed here (Bouayad, 1997; Danlos, 1988). When they are, they behave exactly as S_a. S_c. discourses, as shown in (50).

(50)   a. #Fred hit the carafe against the sink, cracking it at noon.
        b. Fred hit the carafe against the sink, cracking it badly.
        c. #The carafe was hit against the sink by Fred who broke it to draw Mary's attention.
        d. #Fred fired a shot at Mary and (he) murdered her.

A direct causation can also be expressed in a single sentence with an explanation rhetorical relation, (51). These discourses behave normally, as S_c. S_a. discourses do.

(51)   a. Fred cracked the carafe by hitting it against the sink.
        b. The carafe was cracked by Fred who hit it against the sink.

3   Causal Discourses with an Unaccusative Form

If the unaccusative form of V_c is substituted to its transitive form in an acceptable S_a. S_c. discourse, a natural discourse is obtained with (apparently) the same interpretation, (52).

(52)   a. Fred hit the carafe against the sink. It cracked (badly).
        b. Fred fired a shot at the rabbit. It died (unfortunately).[20]
        c. The enemy sent a bomb at the boat. It sunk (for ever).

---

[20] Although "die" is not morphologically related to "kill," I consider, for the sake of simplification, that "die" is the unaccusative form of "kill."

In extended event structures (Pustejovsky, 1995), unaccusatives are differentiated from transitives only by the fact that the former are right headed while the latter are left headed. Therefore, (52) could be analyzed as the equivalent S_a. S_c. discourses (i.e., with a generalization relation between the first sentence and the causing sub-event in the second one). However, neither Pustejovsky's event structure for unaccusatives nor the analysis of (52) as involving a generalization relation are satisfactory.

Although Pustejovsky considers that the causing sub-event is the same in a transitive and unaccusative form, namely an action performed by an agent on the patient,[21] it has long been noted in the literature[22] that an unaccusative is better understood as an eventuality that occurs *spontaneously, without the intervention of an animate agent, under a natural force, with the unique control of the patient engaged in the change of state.* In other words, the causing sub-event for an unaccusative should be an (unspecified) internal process in the patient, and not an (unspecified) external action performed by an agent. This position is confirmed by three phenomena observed with causal discourses.

a) If the unaccusative form of V_c is substituted to its transitive form in an acceptable S_c. S_a. discourse, a nonnatural discourse is obtained, (53).

(53)   a. ?The carafe cracked. Fred hit it against the sink.
         b. ?The rabbit died. Fred fired a shot at it.
         c. ?The boat sunk. The enemy sent a bomb at it.

The inappropriateness of (53) can be explained as follows: The first unaccusative sentence leads the reader to infer that the eventuality described occurs *by itself*, whereas the second sentence invalidates this inference in describing the intervention of an agent.

b) A S_a. S_c. discourse is unacceptable when it includes two different time adjuncts, (30a) repeated in (54a). On the other hand, the equivalent of (54a) with an unaccusative is natural with a causal interpretation, (54b).

(54)   a. #Fred fired a shot at Mary on Sunday. He killed her on Monday.
         b. Fred fired a shot at Mary on Sunday. She died on Monday.

(54b) expresses an indirect causation. Fred's shooting triggered off an internal process within Mary (e.g., an hemmorhage), which led to her death. This internal process can be explicitly expressed as in (55). It is this internal process that can be considered as the direct cause of Mary's death (i.e., interpreted as coreferent to the sub-causing event of the unaccusative).

(55)   a. Fred fired a shot at Mary on Sunday. She had an hemmorhage. She died on Monday.

---

[21] The agent is unknown for an unaccusative.
[22] See among others Boons et al., 1976; Labelle, 1990, 1992; Ruwet, 1972 for French; and Haspelmath, 1993; Levin and Rappaport, 1995; Smith, 1970 for English.

    b. Fred fired a shot at Mary on Sunday. She died from an hemmorhage on Monday.

c) A S_a. S_c. discourse with X = Y is acceptable if X is proto-agent (Dowty, 1991) in S_a, (56a)–(56c), and unacceptable if X is proto-patient, (56d)–(56f) (see Danlos, 1999b for more details on this paradigm). On the other hand, the equivalents of (56) with an unaccusative form are all natural with a causal meaning, (57).

(56)   a.   Fred took an overdose of cocaine. He killed himself.
          b.   Fred fell in a ravine. He killed himself.
          c.   Fred threw himself in a ravine. He killed himself.
          d. #Fred was thrown in a ravine. He killed himself.
          e. #Fred got hit by a begonia pot. He killed himself.
          f. #Fred got pneumonia. He killed himself.

(57)   a.   Fred took an overdose of cocaine. He died.
          b.   Fred fell in a ravine. He died.
          c.   Fred threw himself in a ravine. He died.
          d.   Fred was thrown in a ravine. He died.
          e.   Fred got hit by a begonia pot. He died.
          f.   Fred got pneumonia. He died.

The lack of event coreference in (56d)–(56f) explains the unacceptability of these discourses: The event described in S_a, in which X is not a (proto)agent, cannot corefer to the causing sub-event in S_c, in which X is (proto)agent. For (57d)–(57f), it would be awkward to state that the sub-causing event is an action performed by an agent because there is no agent involved. On the other hand, if it is stated that the sub-causing event is an internal process in the patient, the (indirect) causal meaning of (57d)–(57f) is explained as follows: the first sentence describes an eventuality that X underwent as a patient; this eventuality triggered off an internal process within X (e.g., X had pneumonia in (57e)), which led to a fatal outcome.

Discourses such as (52) (or (57a)–(57c)) should now be reconsidered. Do they have really the same interpretation as the equivalent S_a. S_c. discourses? For example, do (58a) and (58b) have the same interpretation?

(58)   a.   Fred fired a shot at Mary (on Sunday). He killed her.
          b.   Fred fired a shot at Mary (on Sunday). She died.

(58b) can be viewed in two ways. The first one consists in stating that (58b) has the same interpretation as (58a), the only difference being a pragmatic factor, i.e., namely emphasis on Fred's agentivity in (58a) but not in (58b). The second one consists in stating that (58b) is an under-specified variant of a discourse such as (54b). (58b) can be used to describe the same situation as that described in (54b) or a similar discourse: It just leaves the temporal information unspecified. The first interpretation involves a direct causation as in (58a). It implies that one considers (as Pustejovsky does) that the sub-causing event is an action performed by an agent on the patient. It is the only case that supports this position. The second interpretation involves an indirect causation as in (54b). It implies that one considers that the sub-causing event is an internal process within the patient. This position is supported by numerous linguistic works on unaccusatives (see note 22) and by the three phenomena specific to causal discourses, which have just been described. The conclusion is imperative: The second interpretation is more linguistically justified than the first one. In other words, the sub-causing event in an unaccusative is an internal process within the patient, and (58b) does not involve a direct causation with an event coreference between S_a and the sub-causing event in the unaccusative.

This conclusion, however, is not totally satisfying. First, with two different types of causing sub-event for transitives and unaccusatives, one of the important features of Pustejovsky's proposal is lost, namely the fact that transitives and unaccusatives have the same representation *modulo* headedness. One way to keep the same representation for transitives and unaccusatives, while differentiating the nature of the causing sub-event, is to use a complex event structure as shown in (59). The realization of a transitive occurs by heading e_1, that of an unaccusative by heading e_2.[23]

(59)

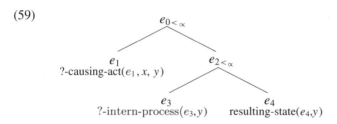

I cannot start here a discussion about this complex event structure, and examine how to project syntax from it. However, the following points are worth mentioning. With this complex event structure, the event representation of (31) is given in (60).[24]

---

[23] The topology and the nonterminal nodes of the event structure in (59) are identical to those of the event structure proposed in Pustejovsky (1995, p. 220) for periphrastic causative constructions, (i).
(i) Fred's shooting Mary on Sunday caused her to die on Monday.
Pustejovsky argues that a verb that encodes lexically causation does not have the same behavior as the periphrastic causative construction, therefore that their event representation should be differentiated. I agree: the leaves in my (59) and his (93) are different.

[24] With the usual two leave tree structure for transitives and unaccusatives, the event representation of (31) leads to the stupid following question: does Mary die from Fred's shooting or from an hemmorhage? This question does not arise in (60). However, even with my complex event structure, the following question arises: what is the event representation of a discourse longer than (31), in which several eventualities between the sentences expressing Mary's hemmorhage and her death on Monday would be described (e.g., "She got a surgery. The surgeon tried to ...").

(60)   Fred killed Mary.
          $\text{kill}(e_0, f, m) \wedge \text{dead}(e_4, m)$
          He fired at her on Sunday.
          $\text{firing-a-shot}(e_1, f, m) \wedge \text{on-Sunday}(e_1)$
          She had an hemmorhage.
          $\text{hemmorhage}(e_3, m)$
          She died on Monday.
          $\text{on-Monday}(e_2)$

In (59), it is understood that a time adjunct takes scope over both e_1 and e_2 in the transitive form (see note 10), and only over e_2 in the unaccusative form. This scope explains why it is not possible to insert a time adjunct specifying the day in the first sentence of (60): e_1 and e_2 did not occur on the same day. It also explains why (54a) is not acceptable while (54b) is.

Finally, this complex event structure explains why (58b) can be given both an interpretation close to (58a) (with just a change of head) and an interpretation close to (54b) (with just a lacking temporal adjunct). This is more satisfactory than making a decision in favor of the second interpretation, as one is led to make it with the usual two leave tree structure for causative verbs (see above).

4   Conclusion

Any study on causality is inevitably dangerous: Causality implies dealing with extralinguistic knowledge that is hard to formalize. Nevertheless, this chapter has presented a rigorous linguistic study of some causal discourses. Rigor has been possible thanks to the use of linguistic notions (i.e., event coreference and type of event coreference).[25] This discourse study relies on lexical semantic works (concerned mainly with sentences in isolation). Conversely, it has shown that discourse considerations can shed a light on lexical semantics.

I would like to conclude by saying that the data have been presented for English, but that they are also valid for French (Danlos, 1996), Korean (Pak, 1997), Italian (Fiammetta Namer, personal communication), and very likely for many other languages.[26]

---

[25] Rigor has also been obtained thanks to the help of some extralinguistic precautions, e.g., the result is not an ineluctable consequence of the cause (Section 1.4), and the cause describes a single (nondurative) action and not an iteration of actions (Section 2.2).

[26] Some graduate students are looking at the data in Arabic, Hebrew, Russian, Chinese, and Japanese. Their research has not falsified the present hypotheses up to now. However, further and more careful work is still necessary. I thank them for their feedback, which was essential.

Acknowledgments

I would like to thank Pierrette Bouillon, Patrick Caudal, Michel Cosse, Bertrand Gaiffe, James Pustejovsky, Anne Reboul, Laurent Roussarie, as well as an anonymous reviewer. Their comments were essential.

References

Asher, N. 1993. *Reference to Abstract Objects in Discourse*. Kluwer, Dordrecht.

Amsili, P., and Rossari, C. 1998. Tense and Connective Constraints on the Expression of Causality. *Proc. 36th Annual Meeting of the ACL and 17th International COLING, COLING-ACL'98*, Montréal, 48–54.

Boons, J.-P., Guillet, A., and Leclère, Ch. (1976). *La structure des phrases simples en français: constructions intransitives*. Droz, Genève.

Bouayad, N. 1997. *Les relatives narratives: formalisation en vue de la génération de textes*. Mémoire de DEA de Linguistique Informatique, Université Paris 7.

Chierchia, G. 1989. *A Semantics for Unaccusatives and its Syntactic Consequences*, Manuscript, Cornell University, Ithaca.

Danlos, L. 1987. *The Linguistic Basis of Text Generation*. Cambridge University Press, Cambridge.

Danlos, L. 1988. Connecteurs et relations causales. *Langue Française 77*, Paris: Larousse, 92–127.

Danlos, L. 1996. Relations causales directes: discours, structure événementielle et coréférence événementielle. In L. Emirkanian and L. Bouchard (eds), *Traitement automatique du français écrit*, Les Cahiers Scientifiques, ACFAS, Montréal, 1–70.

Danlos, L. (1999a). Event Coreference Between Two Sentences. *Proceedings of the International Workshop on Computational Semantics, IWCS'99*, Tilburg.

Danlos, L. 1999b. Formes pronominales réfléchies et rôles thématiques. In M. Plénat (ed.), *Volume en hommage à Andrée Borillo*. Presses Universitaires de Toulouse, Toulouse.

Dowty, D. 1979. *Word Meaning and Montague Grammar*. Reidel, Dordrecht.

Dowty, D. 1991. Thematic Proto-Roles and Argument Selection. *Languages* 67: 547–619.

Fodor, J. 1970. Three Reasons for Not Deriving *kill* from *cause to die*. *Linguistic Inquiry* 1: 429–438.

Haspelmath, M. 1993. More on the Typology of Inchoative/causative Verb Alternations. In B. Comrie and M. Polinsky (eds). *Causatives and Transitivity*. John Benjamins, Amsterdam.

Labelle, M. 1990. Unaccusatives and Pseudo-Unaccusatives in French. *Proc. NELS 20*, GSLA, Amherst.

Labelle, M. 1992. Change of State and Valency. *Journal of Linguistics* 28: 375–414.

Levin, B., and Rappaport, M. 1995. *Unaccusativity: At the Syntax-Lexical Semantics Interface*, MIT Press, Cambridge, MA.

Moens, M., and Steedman, M. 1988. Temporal Ontology and Temporal Reference. *Computational Linguistics* 14:15–28.

Molinier, C. 1990. *Une classification des adverbes en -ment. Langue Française* 88, Larousse.

Pak, M. 1997. Les relations causales directes en français et en coréen. *LingvisticæInvestigationes* XXI(1): 139–162.

Pustejovsky, J. 1991. The Syntax of Event Structure. In B. Levin and S. Pinker (eds.), *Lexical and Conceptual Semantics*. Elsevier Science Publishers, Amsterdam, 47–81.

Pustejovsky, J. 1995. *The Generative Lexicon*, MIT Press, Cambridge, MA.

Pustejovsky, J., and Busa, F. 1995. Unaccusativity and Event Composition. In P. M. Bertinetto, V. Binachi, J. Higginbotham, and M. Squartini (eds.), *Temporal Reference: Aspect and Actionality*. Rosenberg and Sellier, Turin, 159–178.

Rossari, C., and Jayez, J. 1996. *Donc* et les consécutifs; des systèmes de contraintes référentielles. *LingvisticæInvestigationes* XX(1): 117–143.

Ruwet, N. 1972. *Théorie syntaxique et syntaxe du français*. Le Seuil, Paris.

Schank, R. 1975. *Conceptual Information Processing*. North Holland, Amsterdam.

Smith, C. S. 1970. Jespersen's Move and Change's Class and Causative verbs in English. *Linguistics and Literary Studies in Honor of A. A. Hill*, Vol. 2. Mouton, The Hague.

Webber, B. L. 1988. Discourse deixis: Reference to Discourse Segments. *Proc. 26th Annual Meeting of the Association for Computational Linguistics (ACL'88)*, Buffalo, NY, 113–123.

PART III

Interfacing the Lexicon

13   Introduction

FEDERICA BUSA AND PIERRETTE BOUILLON

The common thread that connects the first three papers is that, contrary to a wide-held view, metonymy and metaphor can be studied systematically. The contributors present and analyze various data sets that are taken to fall outside of the traditional areas of knowledge investigated in contemporary linguistic research. Our goal is to show that a subset of phenomena that have been labeled lexical idiosyncrasies (sense shift phenomena) and world/pragmatic knowledge effects (metonymy and metaphor) actually constitute a privileged window on the nature of lexical knowledge.

The papers by Julius Moravcsik and by Nicholas Asher and Alex Lascarides present detailed studies of metaphorical expressions. Their arguments are presented in such a way that it makes it clear how a particular data set may significantly affect the methodology for carrying out the study of the mental lexicon. In particular, while the lexicon can provide the key to understanding metaphor, in turn, this use of language represents actual evidence for determining the structuring of lexical information.

The paper by Jerry Hobbs extends, in an interesting and possibly controversial manner, the range of phenomena that are thought as metonymy: He makes us reconsider the relation between syntax and semantics. For example, as surprising as may be his treatment of extraposition as an instance of metonymy, we are forced to acknowledge the role of interpretive strategies when grammar alone fails to make sense of certain structures. In focusing on the role of abduction as a key element for explaining metonymic phenomena, Hobbs does not address the internal structure of words. In this sense his contribution differs from a number of others in the volume, in that Hobbs does not acknowledge the semantic constitution of words as a key to explain certain syntactic mappings and to differentiate between different types of meaning shifts. Drawing such a distinction between the contribution of lexical semantics from commonsense reasoning could actually strengthen the role of abduction in the interpretive process.

The last paper by Adam Kilgarriff is meant to present a radically different view, which challenges the contribution of the generative line of research in lexical semantics. Kilgariff's conclusion is not too dissimilar from that of Jayez: Contextual variations are too large and unpredictable for a model of individual lexical structures to be viable. Drawing on a set of "experimental results" based on corpus data on "nonstandard" uses of words, Kilgarriff claims to evaluate the Generative Lexicon framework. By "nonstandard" use, Kilgarriff refers to cases where the meaning of a word is not found in a dictionary definition of that word. Is this a satisfactory characterization of "nonstandard" use or even a ground for establishing distinctions between literal and nonliteral meanings? We argue that it is not, especially because many dictionaries do list metonymic and metaphorical senses. Because the latter are arguably "nonliteral" meanings, then, according to Kilgrariff's argument, they must be different from "nonstandard" meanings. As a result, the analysis of "nonstandard" has nothing to do with GL, because the framework is concerned with the systematic shifts that occur in the cases of metonymic extensions, co-compositional phenomena as well as certain metaphorical uses of words (see, Moravcskik, and Asher and Lascarides in this volume). All of these can be found in dictionary definitions.

There is, however, a lesson that can be learnt from Kilgarriff's paper: When faced with an actual corpus and real use of words, there is an even greater need for a framework for lexical semantics with an actual theoretical vocabulary, an actual set of compositional rules, and an actual methodology. In absence of this, any statement is just rethoric.

14 Metaphor, Creative Understanding, and the Generative Lexicon

JULIUS M. MORAVCSIK

1 Introduction

Metaphor, and the distinction between the figurative and the literal uses of language, have puzzled philosophers and linguists at least since Aristotle. The puzzle can be stated in the following, rough, form: How can words in certain configurations mean something different from what they mean in their literal use, prescribed by the rules of the language, and at the same time convey significant insights into what we, in a given context, take as parts of reality? In order to appreciate the force of the question we must separate the metaphorical meanings from the new literal meanings that an individual, or a group, might introduce into a language, such as parenting, or critiquing. Such innovations are extensions of literal language, not metaphors. Metaphors rest on rules of language, but also violate them. They do not describe reality directly. Thus, the true/false dichotomy does not apply to them without qualifications. An adequate theory of metaphor should explain this unique position of metaphoric meaning. To expand on this a little, this essay proposes that a theory of metaphoric meaning should account for the following list of facts or intuitions.

(i) Metaphors give us new meanings and a deepened understanding of the objects of our descriptions or reasoning.
(ii) Metaphors can have aesthetic value.
(iii) At some stage, a subjective element enters into the interpretation of metaphors. This element is creative insofar as it goes beyond what is given by the rules of language but it presupposes and rests on such rules.
(iv) Constructing and interpreting metaphors requires mastery of a natural language. In order to achieve adequate results, however, it requires also the use of imagination, aesthetic sensitivity, and creative reconceptualizations.
(v) Metaphors are about the world, in the ordinary sense of this phrase. At the same time, their descriptive power differs from that of literal uses.

An adequate theory of metaphor should specify how metaphoric meaning differs from literal meaning. In order to understand a metaphor, we must know what the words involved mean in ordinary uses. At the same time, we must relate the metaphoric to the literal meaning in terms other than just to identify, entailment, or overlap of meanings.

These preliminary reflections suggest moving to a framework that differs from the standard decompositional semantics – as, for example, that of Fodor and Katz (Katz and Fodor, 1963) – and also from the standard formal semantics used by logicians, within which meanings are related either by identity, or overlap, or containment.[1] Philosophical semantics operates with the notions of synonymy (identity of meaning), or homonymy (distinctness, ambiguity), or containment (entailment). The relation between literal and metaphoric meanings, as well as some of the compositional structures of metaphors, do not fall into these categories. Nor does it help to try to employ notions already utilized by linguists, such as metonymy. Within that use one element (e.g., "scepter") stands by fiat for another ("authority"). But metaphor is not, as we shall see, such conventional legislation.

It has been suggested in the past by many writers that metaphorical meaning or force depends on associations that the reader brings to the text. This view can be given a clearer formulation by the addition that in the successful cases the associations are matters of communal rather than mere individual understanding. In other words, a certain linguistic and cultural community will have, in addition to associations that vary among individuals, certain associations with certain words or expressions that either everyone or at least a critical mass shares.

Still, even in this form the proposal faces formidable difficulties. Associations are psychological elements related to our fears, pleasures, past connections of events, and so forth. These may add to how one reacts to words, but they do not change meaning. However, according to our theory, metaphor does change meaning. Its development is not merely a psychological matter. It is also a semantic process in which the ordinary meaning undergoes change. As we shall see, the theory to be proposed in the following does satisfy this condition. Furthermore, the proposal suggests ways in which metaphor plays important roles in diachronic processes as well.

2   Productive Lexical Semantics and Figurative Language

Linguists and philosophers work a lot with conjoining or decomposing linguistic elements. Lexical meanings are decomposed into a collection of conjuncts and in logic functions are decomposed into more specific ones. Within the lexical semantics adopted for this essay, meanings are not analyzed solely into a conjunction of smaller parts, but as productive, generating new items according to rules based on a more rich internal lexical semantic structure.

Earlier work in semantics already recognized the limitations of mere conjunctive analysis. Adverbs provide obvious examples. "John swims slowly" cannot be decomposed into "John swims" and "John slowly." (Or more idiomatically: "John is slow.") An adequate analysis must show how according to the initial sentence,

---

[1] For example, see R. Carnap (1956).

John's swimming is slow, by whatever standard the context specifies, while leaving open the possibilities that John is fast in other ways. The adverb modifies the verb that denotes swimming. Thus, the whole is more than a mere sum of parts. Grammatical structure as well as this semantic sketch supports treating adverbs as modifiers. However, there is also another way of interpreting the initial sentence as involving a holistic semantic complex. One could interpret the meaning as 'John is slow in a swimmingish way.' Thus, John is slow in this way but not others. Both analyses support the claim that "swims slowly" does not behave like "red table," which indicates simply the overlap between two semantic units. We can apply the idea of holistic semantic units also in other areas. This insight underlies the semantic theories of Pustejovsky (Pustejovsky, 1995) and Moravcsik (Moravcsik, 1990), which stress the common ground rather than difference in detail. We shall utilize these theories in our analysis of metaphor.

In Moravcsik's AFT analysis lexical meaning has the following fundamental fourfold structure:

m-factor: specifying constituency; e.g., abstract, temporal, physical, etc.

s-factor: specifying both a generic domain of application, as well as distinguishing properties that separate the denotation from the rest of the genus. This factor must also include the principles of individuation and persistence contained in the lexical meaning under analysis. In more contemporary terms; understanding the meaning of a descriptive word must involve understanding of complexes in which the word is combined with quantifiers. These principles help also in specifying the basic argument structures of verbs.

a-factor: specifying conceptually linked causal origins and powers (e.g., artifact, or biological, and cleansing, burning, etc.).

f-factor: specifying the functional element in the meaning. (e.g., what artifacts are by their own nature to be used for, the function of flying for birds, etc.).

In this scheme, the factors are not merely conjoined, but form a holistic unit, just as the factors of adverbials do. For example, the m-factor restricts the types of structures that the s-factors can contain. If the m-factor is the property of being abstract, than in the s-factors physical individuation or persistence principles cannot be contained. Furthermore, only the m- and s-factors are obligatory elements in every lexical meaning. Words standing for abstract entities like numbers do not have an a-factor. Again, the f-factor limits the possible m-factors. What we use to sleep on cannot have just any kind of constituency (e.g., abstract). The proper specification of lexical meaning is: R(m,s,a,f) where "R" stands for that unique relation that ties the elements of meaning into a holistic unit. (This aspect of *real* definitions was noticed already by Aristotle who insisted on their holistic nature.) This proposal has psychological implications. For example, it shows that understanding a word is more than just giving it definitions in terms of conjuncts.

We will use this terminology. It corresponds, roughly, to the *qualia structure* of Pustejovsky's lexical representation.[2]

One of the great advantages of this analysis is that we can compare lexical meaning on more subtle ways than the mere synonymy-homonymy relations offered by the standard lexical semantics. The qualia structure represents an internal anatomy of lexical meaning that underlies the explication of polysemy, and other relations showing what is semantically common between certain syntactically different expressions.

The elements of qualia structure are described as constitutive, formal, agentive, and telic. One can see intuitively how these roughly correspond to the fourfold anatomy of the AFT system.

Using the qualia structure (or AFT) helps us see how widespread the phenomenon of underspecification is, and how one can bring out its productive potential. It has been noticed that the semantics of verbs like "use" or "take" is *light* (Grimshaw, 1990). Pustejovsky describes this aspect of these words as being *underspecified*.[3] The following example should clarify this. In various applications "use" carries different entailments, for example, it is different to use a person, a car, a phrase, mathematics, and so on. Yet we do not want to construe the resulting semantic units as different lexical items.

We can show that a much larger portion of the lexicon can be construed as having an underspecified aspect than the standard examples given traditionally. Let us consider "emergency" and take it to mean: 'a state of appropriately impending disaster of appropriate magnitude, requiring in appropriate ways appropriately immediate response.' The occurrences of "appropriate" in this account are merely place-holders, to be filled in differently within the contexts of the indefinite variety of types of emergency, thus ending up with different entailments. What counts as immediate in naval warfare is very different from what counts as immediate response in the case of a bee-sting. What counts as an emergency in the case of operation is very different from what counts as a "state of emergency" declared by a country at war. It would be absurd to list all of these types of emergency as a separate lexical items. It might occur to someone to represent the situation as involving many species under one genus. However, the following example should show that the structures involved are more like in the case of adverbials, where not only can the same person be slow in some ways and not in other, but the same swimming that can be slow for an Olympic champion, and fast for a recreational swimmer. Likewise, the same state of affairs can be an emergency for the secretary working at her desk, but not for the academic department for which she works. So the same swim can be slow and not slow, the same state an emergency and not an emergency. These situations could not arise within genus-species classifications. Thus, we should give "emergency" the kind of general

---

[2] Pustejovsky (1995), p. 76 and pp. 85–86.

[3] Pustejovsky (1995), p. 87.

account sketched above; made more precise by formulating it within the qualia or AFT structures, and construe the lexical meaning as not a fixed set of necessary and sufficient conditions, but as a set of structural conditions with the potential of indefinite expansions and specifications.

The same phenomena can be illustrated in the case of "walk." This term too is under-specified. What is a walk for an infant is not a walk for an adult, and recuperating patients are given standards for what counts as a walk by their nurses. Again, the point is not simply that there are many kinds of walks, but that the same sequence is a walk if viewed from the position of a patient recuperating from a serious operation, and is not a walk when viewed from the perspective of healthy young adults.

The examples show that the phenomenon under consideration applies to all achievement verbs and those standing for concepts of growth and development. In the case of "he used the car to get to the station," we understand that the use of the car was to drive it, and not to, for example, sell it. In the case of the secretary, to respond to the emergency might involve calling the mechanic who fixes the word processor, while in the case of the admiral, it would involved sending the fighter planes off the deck of the carrier. We shall see how an analysis of metaphor can rely on this productivity in the lexicon.

3   Idioms

We shall turn, briefly, to the analysis of idioms, as an introduction to the semantics of figurative language. In the analysis of the figurative aspects of idiomatic meaning, we shall rely on qualia structure and productivity. The analysis will distinguish idioms from both metaphors and similes. With the help of the lexical theory sketched above, we shall point to important differences among these types of figurative speech, as well as to the underlying common ground. The account to be given rests on some of the key insights of the treatment of idioms by Sag and Wasow.[4] The main concerns of their essay differ considerably from those of this paper. Their effort centers on examining what roles, if any, citing idiomatic structure should pay in attempts by syntactic arguments to show the superiority of one grammatical theory over another. Among their claims, however, one is very relevant to the results of this essay. This is their showing that one cannot construe all idioms as syntactic and semantic islands. Many idioms are partly decomposable. For example, "he kicked the bucket" – meaning 'he died' – is an island. Interpreting it does not involve semantic or syntactic decomposition. The connections is between the idiom and the corresponding literal expression, and it is a semantic *fiat*, or purely conventional identification.

In contrast, an idiom like "he spilled the beans" can be partly decomposed. This articulation shows some of the elements to have figurative meaning. In the

---

[4] Sag and Wasow (1994), pp. 491–538.

terminology of Sag and Wasow, these are "idiomatically combining expressions" (Sag and Wasow, 1994). Thus, this idiom differs from the ones like "he kicked the bucket" ('he died') or "she shoots the breeze" ('she chats') where the idiom is assigned a semantic equivalent to a literal expression, without being decomposable into distinct parts. Such *islandish* idioms can convey more than their literal counterparts. For example, these may evoke attitudes, stimulate the imagination with their picturesque modes of expression. However, knowing the meaning of such idioms is not a matter of knowing the lexical meanings and rules of compositionality of the natural language in which the idiom is embedded. In the case of "he spilled the beans," however, we start applying the compositional rules and assign the relevant components the meaning that these have in literal use.

Many other idioms, such as "was thrown to the wolves" or "she was pulling strings for him" exhibit the same phenomena. The Sag-Wasow paper is a goldmine for illustrations. The metaphor links, somehow, spilling the beans to disclosing, either intentionally or in a state of having weak will, information that was meant to be kept confidential. This example might tempt someone to suppose that in the case of idioms we go typically from a materialistic or physical base to something abstract. This can be shown to be false by examples like "having second thoughts" or describing inanimate things in animate terms, like the raging storm or the smiling sun. Natural languages do not have built in materialistic prejudices.

Let us look at one case in detail. How does the metaphor "she spilled the beans" end up as describing in a new way the unintentional or character-flawed release of information that was meant to be kept secret? The key elements of the idiom are: "spilled" and "beans." The second element needs to refer to either a mass (in this case abstract) or a countable collection with very small units. This semantic constraint, however, does not select the linguistic item in question. It could have been "peas," "lentils," or any other such item. Hence, the relation between "beans" and what *bits of information* denote is arbitrary and purely conventional. The other part, "spill," is, however, metaphorical. We can see this by first considering its AFT (or squalia) analysis.

m-factor: temporal (being an activity) physical process (what we spill has weight, whether it be milk or peanuts).

s-factor: features distinguishing careless release of appropriate material from an appropriate container from other physical processes, adding also principles of individuation and persistence (encoding what counts as one act of spilling and what counts over time as the same act.) This information is the basis of the minimal essential argument structure of the verb.

a-factor: essential causal agent: animate; essential consequent: the resulting transfer of some substance to an unwanted place. ("spill" is an achievement verb).

f-factor: null element (This may seem strange with an achievement verb, but unlike in the case of "cooked the meal" where admissible processes are determined largely by the result, that does not hold in this case. Only a specific physical process counts as achieving the result specified by the a-factor; the "spilling way." In this respect "spill" contrasts also with such functionally defined words as "chair."

In order to derive the metaphoric meaning, we start with removing the constraint of physicality from the s-factor, and hence also from the m-factor. The result is an underspecified concept, namely the concept of carelessly letting out of appropriate material from appropriate container. In this context, we take *material* and *container* in their most general sense: in this sense a sentence can contain a verb. The justification for regarding the resulting meaning underspecified, and not a generic term with species, is that once we removed the m-factor of the literal meaning the term became transcategorical. It can be applied to contexts such as arguments containing premises as well as to kegs containing beer. Spilling bean was a specification of the underspecified notion. The new specification, unlike the one just mentioned, is not derived by the rules of the language. It is the kind of spilling that can involved the release of information. One might say that it is a "spillingish" release of information. This specification is the product of creative imagination, and not the application of the semantic rules of English. It gives us a fresh feel for what this kind of information revealing can be. It starts as a subjective conception, but if successful it becomes intersubjective.

Let us now spell out the relations between the literal bean spilling, the idiomatic one including the metaphorical part, and the case of the literal meaning of "carelessly releasing information." The literal bean spilling has as m-factor the concrete, while the metaphorical part of the idiom shifts the m-factor, and changes partly the semantic content of the whole, leaving a part up to imagination to fill. Thus, as far as the rules of language are concerned, the output is complete.

In the literal case, we can ask such questions as: 'how much of the beans were spilled?' 'How clumsily was it done?' In the idiomatic, partly decomposable case the analogous detailed questions are left up to the imagination, individual, and, hopefully, communal. In the case of literature, this can remain a satisfactory outcome. In the case of scientific uses of metaphor, the researchers are spurred on to find a theoretically adequate and interpreter-invariant filling, or specification. Thus, the metaphor becomes a new literal expression, with the standard semantic rules of language extended to it. In the case of the literal "he released information carelessly (or as a result of weak will)" the meaning gives us an understanding of the result of an action, with rather general constraints on the mode of performance. However, further questions can be asked, concerning specific details. The rules of language offer guidelines for how to find answers to these. In contrast, the idiomatic version contains a part that remains open as far as the rules of language are concerned, and needs filling by creative imagination, pointing to ways in which the release is "spillingish."

The need for creativity is also stressed by an earlier account of Nogales.[5] However, in her account the general categorization is already a matter of creative imagination. Within her account we create new categories within which to accommodate the new description. Once we have the qualia structure/AFT articulation of the lexical meanings, we can derive the category by looking at literal meanings and going back to an underspecified concept, thus leaving creativity as such to the new speculation, though, to be sure, going to an appropriate or apt underspecified meaning also requires imagination. These comparisons should facilitate our ability to apply the account given to other expressions containing metaphoric content such as "pulling strings," "being thrown to the wolves," and so forth. In the latter case, the shift in m-factor is not from concrete to abstract, but from mere physical action to the psychological.

This analysis of idioms introduces us to a kind of non-literal semantic analysis that helps us to see also why idioms play an important role in natural languages, and are not of mere ornamental significance. It is easy to imagine various contexts in which the kind of creative and imaginative new specification of meanings is desirable. It points to new ways of thinking and talking, without saddling the language with myriads of ambiguities. Idioms are not just *pretty*. They lead us to new ways of seeing some aspects of reality.

4   Metaphor

The theory of metaphor that was already illustrated in the previous section has to take a stand and give an explanation to the following claims:

(i)   Interpretation of metaphor requires the mastery of literal uses of language.

(ii) An adequate interpretation of metaphor requires awareness of the productivity of the lexicon, and the holistic nature of the understanding of lexical meaning that cannot be analyzed as merely the sum of parts.[6]

(iii) Understanding a metaphor requires lifting out of a literal sense a layer of meaning that constitutes an underspecified concept.

Claim (i) states what is a conceptual truth. Metaphorical use is related to literal use in the same way in which counterfeit money is related to genuine money.[7] There could be no country in which only counterfeit money existed, without there ever having been a genuine one. There may be a historical stage in which the earlier genuine money disappeared and only the counterfeit is left. However, without

---

[5] Nogales (1993), Chapter 3. Most of Nogales' work was completed before the appearance of the books by Moravcsik and Pustejovsky. Her insights are hopefully preserved in this proposal, and embedded within the productive lexical theory.

[6] In Moravcsik (1998), Chapter 5, there is a detailed explication of this kind of understanding.

[7] This example was given by Gilbert Ryle in his seminars.

there having been at one point genuine currency, it makes no sense to talk about counterfeit. Something being counterfeit depends on, and is derivative from the notion of the genuine. In the same way, metaphorical meaning depends on there being, or having been, some literal meanings of some expressions.

Instead of surveying the many philosophical attempts of past to present to offer an adequate account of metaphor,[8] we shall give illustrations and explications of the theory of this essay.

Let us start with a case of simple subject-predicate form, with a literal subject, and a metaphorical predicate. In "Juliet is the sun," the subject is literally "Juliet." The proper name here is, of course, not like a postal stamp, glued onto an element of reality, but an expression with a determinate syntactic role, and an essential count noun (e.g., being a woman) attached to the name so as to provide for its application principles of individuation and persistence. These principles are derived from the concept human under which the bearer of "Juliet" in this context is subsumed.[9] Without such a characterization of the subject, the specification of the literal meanings of the parts of the sentence and the reconstruction of relevant underspecified concept and its new specification would be impossible.

The following is the literal semantic analysis of the key term in the predicate, "sun."

m-factor: concrete, physical.
s-factor: large, warmth and life giving/enabling heavenly body. Principle of individuation and persistence is the same as for other heavenly bodies.
a-factor: natural body, enters into casual interactions.
f-factor: radiates whatever is assumed to be a key ingredient for living.

Viewed in this way, Juliet cannot be a (the?) sun. We can abstract, however, from the characterization just given an underspecified concept: 'being in an appropriate way the source of what is taken to be essential to the life and persistence of the appropriate entities.' This description of the underspecified meaning makes it possible for the meaning of "sun" to be a specification. The underspecified concept is transcategorial in the same sense as illustrated earlier, for it cuts now across the inanimate/animate distinction.

We turn now to the analysis of the specification given by the metaphorical application to Juliet. The context of the drama reveals a person's deep love for another person. Various aspects of the love are involved. It is central and most important to the lover of Juliet, its "life" and development depends on what Juliet radiates toward the lover, intensity ("heat"), and so on.

The choice of metaphor suggests either the conviction of the speaker that there is no current literal description that would capture what is intended, or that there are indefinitely many ways of capturing it, but because of the huge number of partial

---

[8] For a fine critical review of previous philosophical theories, see Nogales (1993), Chapters 1 and 2.
[9] Stressed repeatedly by Chomsky in recent publications.

descriptions, a summary of literally ascribable attributes is out of the question. In other words, ineffability, or too much complexity. Thus, the new specification is not a product of applying the rules of language, nor is it an arbitrary and purely subjective picture presented. There are no semantic criteria in the language as of now as to what counts as one person's life revolving in a loving way around the another person in a loving way. Hence, the creative and imaginative leap of specification, unique to nonliteral use. Understanding it is to understand the rules of language, and to establish a cognitive and imaginative link to the specification the speaker points to.

In contrast with this positive illustration we can consider for the same context, "Juliet is a refrigerator." To be sure, Juliet and a refrigerator have some properties in common. Being complex, being a physical entity, being difficult to deal with are plausible candidates. However, the essentially cooling function of the refrigerator, and the passion in which Juliet is both object and subject are diametrically opposed to each other. One might consider a less clear case, such as "Turandot is a refrigerator." On the surface, this does not work for reasons similar as those given in the case above. Turandot engenders intense affection, the refrigerator cools things off, and yet, the purported metaphor is not completely inept. Turandot does stand – in the opera – for coldness and cruelty. Yet the metaphor will not be really successful, because inside Turandot is full of intense (hot?) feelings and passion. The refrigerator does not capture this, unless we strain things and think of the electricity required to run the refrigerator as being symbolized here. (Do we construct special metaphors for refrigerator repair men?)

Our analysis explains also how metaphor can have aesthetic value. As we saw, metaphors can lead to new ways of conceptualizing parts of reality. Metaphor enables us to relate what are on the surface very different entities. This helps us in seeing that there is some flexibility in what are regarded at a given time as our basic categories. Cognitive categories play a key role in our making sense of things, or understanding things. That is the fundamental element in our cognitive life, not mere information processing. Any human notion is *conceptually dense* (i.e., admits of an indefinite enumber of different articulations). At some time this class of such articulations makes sense, at another time, another subset. Metaphor helps to make previously unilluminating articulations illuminating, or at least intelligible. Thus, it enriches our conceptual realm, and with that our ability to see beauty in complexes of symbols, previously not considered as candidates for aesthetic appreciation. Like music or painting, metaphor too makes a conceptual or perceptual complex constantly open to new interpretations.

What we said about the role of the metaphoric for diachronic phenomena in connection with idioms can now be seen on a larger scale. Given the productive aspects of the lexicon and metaphor as a special case of this, we see new specifications not yet within the rules of language presenting themselves as candidates for later enriching the literal, thus paving the way also for new metaphors.

We shall turn now to the analysis of a complex metaphor within which metaphoric iteration is also exemplified. Our example is:

"The flash of a neon light . . . touched the sound of silence."

The complexity of the metaphor requires a segmentation of the text, so that our method of analysis can apply to it. The following is the proposed structure:

The flash of a neon light (touched (the sound of (silence))).

The first and last elements retain their literal meanings. These function as se-mantic anchors providing the pillars for the metaphorical constructions.

The justification for the segmentation is that light touching something must be metaphoric, because the m-factors for "light" and "touch" are different. However, one cannot determine the metaphoric meaning of "touch" if we do not know the entities involved in the touching. The situation is analogous to trying to interpret the meaning of "tall" in a context in which we do not know whether the discussion is about tall humans or tall stories. Thus, we start with the innermost element of the segmented sentence, namely silence. The four meaning factors for "silence" are:

m-factor: time, and more specifically state (vs. process, etc.)
 s-factor: stretch of time experienced as containing nothing audible. (one might wonder whether there need be contrast-dependency; i.e., can there be an experienced silence for those who never (cannot) experience anything audible? We cannot go into this here.).
 a-factor: null element, because none of the psychological elements that silence can evoke in various humans is essentially related to it.
 f-factor: the achieving in humans of the contrast between audible and inaudible.

We turn now to "sound," ignoring the undoubtedly interesting contrast between "sound" and "noise." The difference is not relevant to our investigation. The fol-lowing is the four factor analysis of "sound."

m-factor: time, more specifically: state (as above).
 s-factor: experience of the audible in most general terms (ignoring sound/noise. distinction) with temporal continuity as the principle of persistence, and spatio-temporal as the principle of individuation.
 a-factor: null.
 f-factor: the potential to evoke feelings from humans and be the foundation of the phonological aspect of languages.

Having laid out the analysis of the literal meanings of "silence" and "sound," we shall now sketch the metaphoric meaning of "sound of silence." This case differs from "Juliet is the sun," for there we have two different m-factors, while in the case under analysis the two items have the same m-factor. What makes the complex in spite of this not interpretable in literal ways is the contrast and incompatibility of "sound" and "silence" in their ordinary conceptualization. We therefore employ the same procedure we used before on metaphor. First, we move to an appropriate underlying underspecified concept that embraces both "sound" and "silence." It will have to contain the audible and the intervals of there not being anything audible. Hence, it will range over all sound and silence complexes as well as distinct periods of sound and silence. The fact that there is no name for this underspecified concept in English currently is irrelevant to the investigation. Having placed sound and silence under this wider notion, we can understand in this context the metaphorical use of "sound" as the audial experience of the lack of audible. What is this experience like? The rules of language do not say. Creative imaginative specification has to provide the answer. An answer might be that amidst the noises, and sounds (in the ordinary sense) we can experience something audible that is the opposite of what we call ordinary "sound." This calls for a psychological and not physical/scientific reflection. The metaphor, the new imaginative specification of an underspecified concept that we rarely call to consciousness, directs us to experiences containing what the ear processes as both partly audible and partly inaudible. Then it focuses on what we hear as the inaudible part. This reconceptualization does not provide a mechanism for filling in all relevant details. These need to emerge in the mind of the audience, and may be to an extent interpreter-relative.

Poets refer to hearing silence occasionally. One example is provided by the poem *Winter Night* by Jozsef Attila,[10] an East European poet. The exact relevant language in that poem is "hearing the silence," but it is natural to interpret that as an abbreviated version of hearing the sound of silence. Having specified the complex object, containing a metaphorical element, for "touch" we shall look at the AFT analysis of this verb.

m-factor: time, physical event.
s-factor: the process of two elements ending up in contact. Spatio-temporal distinctness specifies individuation and persistence.
a-factor: both entities involved need be physical.
f-factor: resulting common boundaries.

This characterization does not allow light to touch something, because – in the nonscientific sense – it is not a physical object. Thus, we move to the underspecified concept of the appropriate entity establishing in an appropriate way a common boundary with an appropriate object. Given the rules of language, we could introduce the notion light touching darkness (i.e., having a common boundary). However, we need to move even one step further from such an expansion. "Light"

---

[10] Attila Jozsef, *Winter Night*, my own translation.

and "dark" are in the same conceptual sphere; "light" and "sound" are not. To present a specification in which light and the sound of silence are the element touching each other, we need to move to the creative imaginative specification that we have talked about already. The rules of language back this only insofar as these allowed us to form the underspecified concept. The imaginative leap, then calls for the intersubjective understanding of how the mood the line expresses includes seeing light and the sound of silence as partners in a common boundary situation. There are other examples of this in poetry, for example, "grass whispered a touched sound."[11] Thus, imagination can go beyond categories and establish common boundaries in a transcategorial way. Transcategoriality is in other contexts already an aesthetic tool. For example, we can talk of dark sound, loud colors, and heavy sounds.[12] This account of meaning and metaphor might seem to be in conflict with *realistic* formal semantics, but this need not be the case. Formal semantics is *realistic* only to the extent of assuming some way of connecting some parts of language with some parts of reality. It does not specify whether the reality is abstract or spatio-temporal, and whether the links established are within the boundaries of current science. We should represent the phenomenological human date as it is. Trying to keep it within the boundaries of current science is to put the cart before the horse. As to formalizability, this theory leaves it open what formal means one might find to represent metaphorical content. We analyzed iterated metaphor here. This shows how partly indeterminate statements can enter into higher levels of indeterminacy in metaphorical constructions. This is human creativity at its best.

5   The Place of Metaphor in Theories of Language

Let us see now how the theory just presented accounts for the claims listed at the outset of the introduction. First, our theory entails that metaphor interpretation requires mastery of the rules of literal language, because our selecting the appropriate underspecified concept for the generation of the imaginative leap is based on knowing what literal use provides. Secondly, our theory rests on the productivity of the lexicon, because the relation between the underspecified concept and the new specification is theoretically analogous to the specification of the meaning of a word like "want." The construction of the imaginative leap shows where subjective and thus unique creative elements enter the cognitive generating process. The same construction shows also how we rely on literal use, and how we go also beyond it. Finally, metaphors as analyzed above are about reality, even though their descriptive power differs somewhat from that of literal use.

Because the specifications given in the previous section are merely an application of the general criteria given at the outset, we can see that these more specific

---

[11] Hooper (1965), p. 83.
[12] Transcategorical links are discussed at length in the aesthetic theory of the late D.W. Prall.

conditions are also met. The theory presented provides an explanatory account of metaphor, provided we do not have positivist conceptions of explanation in mind within which explanation amounts to some sort of reductionism. The theory presents an account of how conceptualization, mastery of the rules of natural languages, and creative imaginative moves combine in metaphor constructing or interpretation. The structure of the account is analogous to Chomsky's account of creativity in ordinary language understanding. Chomsky leaves the phenomenon irreducible, and locates it within the larger frame of syntactic competence and other human cognitive capacities.

It follows from our theory that a complete literal paraphrase of metaphor is impossible, because the final specification of the underlying underspecified concept is not governed by the semantic rules of literal use. This general sketch of the theory leaves various interesting questions open. So far, we posited the ability of selecting appropriate underspecified categories, and the capacity to construct imaginative specifications not covered by standard semantic rules as the basic cognitive requirements for metaphor interpretation, to apply cross-linguistically. However, one might expect many other cross-linguistic constraints. For example, are there crosscultural *laws of imagination* that place restrictions on what, for a given context, can count as an appropriate underspecified concept? Are there general constraints on what will count, psychologically, as an illuminating new imaginative specification? Answering these questions is an interesting task for future research. As of now, this theory offers itself as the basic background within which such work could become fruitful.

We distinguished in the theory so far idiom, metaphor, and literal use. Creativity emerges on different levels. There is some creativity in forging a new purely conventional semantic rule, such as the one that represents in the idiom we studied the use of "beans" as referring to information. There are other forms of creativity, such as the one that enables us to go from "parent" to "parenting" or from "critique" to "critiquing," in each case changing some of the meaning while leaving many layers stable. We should not see the new metaphoric conception of a specification of something general as creativity emerging from semantic processing, without any *relatives*.

We shall complete the picture by the proposal to treat simile as a literal statement. Such statements say that some element $\underline{x}$ (literally described) is similar to another element $\underline{y}$ (also literally described). Because logic shows that any two entities have an infinite number of predicates in common, and hence are – in some way – similar, so far we have not said anything really informative. Similes become successful, however, when the common property they point to turns out to be, for the purposes described contextually, salient (psychologically) and explanatory. In Plato's famous simile, a cave and our progress out of it is likened to the Platonically ideal educational process. The success of the simile depends on the common elements between release from perceptual and cognitive lack of sound judgment and the common elements between lack of vision and lack of self-knowledge being illuminated by the juxtaposition. According to this analysis simile is *between* metaphor and ordinary literal use. It is similar to literal use in that it can be judged true or false. However, it is like metaphor insofar as we ultimately evaluate it as explanatory and insightful or not.

Both simile and metaphor can lead to new meanings being forged either in science or in ordinary discourse. For example, "force" has first a specific literal meaning, then one can see crosscategorical connections that enables it to be reconstructed as having metaphoric meaning, and eventually the new reference can develop into a scientifically precise notion. Thus, metaphor or simile can be vehicles for meaning change.

As we saw, this account of metaphor evolves out of Pustejovsky's new analysis of polysemy. Polysemy is a vital element in a natural language, for it comes between synonymy and ambiguity. If, for all polysemous readings, we would have to introduce new semantic entries and hence ambiguity, we would burden the lexicon and the language learner excessively, and lose the productivity and flexibility of our language uses. The flexibility is needed, because at any given stage a language may not mark out each meaning sharply. Polysemy can leave things in an incomplete state out of which productive devices generate literal or metaphoric new alternatives to cope with novel experience.

References

Carnap, R. 1956. *Meaning and Necessity*. University of Chicago Press, Chicago.

Grimshaw, J. 1990. *Argument Structure*. MIT Press, Cambridge.

Hooper, P. 1965. Reach of Touch. *Quarterly Review of Literature* 14: 130–146.

Katz J., and Fodor, J. 1963. The Structure of a Semantic Theory. *Language* 39: 170–210.

Moravcsik, J. 1990. *Thought and Language*. Routledge, London.

Moravcsik, J. 1998. *Creativity, Meaning, and the Partial Inscrutability of the Human Mind*, CSLI Publications, Standford.

Nogales, P. 1993. *A Philosophical Examination of Metaphor*. Doctoral Dissertation, Stanford University.

Pustejovsky, J. 1995. *The Generative Lexicon*. MIT Press, Cambridge.

Sag, I., and Wasow, T. 1994. Idiom. *Language* 70: 491–538.

15   Metaphor in Discourse

NICHOLAS ASHER AND ALEX LASCARIDES

Abstract

In this paper, we offer a novel analysis of metaphor, which attempts to capture both their conventional constraints on their meaning, and the ways in which information in the discourse context contributes to their interpretation in context. We make use of lexical rules in a constraint-based grammar to do the former task, and a formal semantics of discourse, where coherence constraints are defined in terms of discourse structure, to do the latter task. The two frameworks are linked together, to produce an analysis of metaphor that both defines what's linguistically possible and accounts for the ways in which pragmatic clues from domain knowledge and rhetorical structure influence the meaning of metaphor in context.

1   Introduction

This paper focuses on metaphor and the interpretation of metaphor in a discourse setting. We propose constraints on their interpretation in terms of linguistic structures. Specifically, the constraints are based on a particular conception of the lexicon, where lexical entries have rich internal structure, and derivational processes or productivity between word senses are captured in a formal, systematic way (e.g., Copestake and Briscoe, 1995; Pustejovsky, 1995). By constraining metaphor in terms of these linguistic structures, we show that their interpretation is not purely a psychological association problem (cf. Lakoff and Johnson, 1980), or purely subjective (e.g., Davidson, 1984). Recent accounts of metaphor within philosophy have not given systematic accounts of this sort (e.g., Black, 1962; Hesse, 1966; Searle, 1979). We leave open the question of whether their insights are compatible with the theory proposed here.

Many have thought that the principles of metaphorical interpretation cannot be formally specified (e.g., Davidson, 1984). We will attack this position with two claims. The first is that some aspects of metaphor are productive, and this productivity can be captured effectively by encoding generalizations that limit metaphorical interpretation in a constraint-based framework for defining lexical semantics. This patterns in a loose sense with Lakoff and Johnson's (1980) view that the metaphor is productive. However, whereas they view the productivity as based in psychological concepts, we demonstrate that the productivity is essentially linguistic in nature. Indeed, from a methodological perspective, we would claim

262

that the productive aspects of metaphor can give the linguist clues about how to represent semantic information in lexical entries.

Moreover, it is well known that domain knowledge and the way people structure fundamental concepts such as time and orientation influence metaphorical interpretation (Lakoff and Johnson, 1980, and others). Our second claim takes this further, and we argue that *rhetorical relations* – such as *Elaboration, Contrast*, and *Parallel*, among others – that connect the meanings of segments of text together, can also influence the meaning of metaphor when they are presented in multisentence discourse, or even poetry. Through studying metaphor in discourse, we learn how to link lexical processing to discourse processing in a formal framework. We will give some preliminary accounts of how this link between words and discourse determines metaphor.

2   Metaphor in the Lexicon

First, we consider some examples of metaphoric productivity (cf. Moravscik, this volume). Lakoff and Johnson (1980) cite many examples of the phenomena, and argue that they are based on the conceptual system we live by. For example, they describe a CONDUIT metaphor, where ideas are treated as objects and language is viewed as a container:

(1)   a. I gave you that idea.
         b. It's difficult to put my ideas into words
         c. When you have a good idea, try to capture it immediately in words.

But there are limits to the productivity, which must be captured. We must explain why (2a) are acceptable, but (2b) are odd, for example:

(2)   a. Don't force your ideas into the student's head/onto the proletariat.
         b. ?Don't force your ideas into the chairman/into the proletariat.

(1) and (2) provide evidence that phrases that denote linguistic expressions (e.g., "words") and phrases that denote the cerebral parts of humans (e.g., "student's head") can act as containers of ideas; hence the preposition "into" in these metaphors are acceptable (but "onto" would be odd). On the other hand, phrases that denote people (e.g., "chairman," "proletariat") cannot behave as containers (note that "onto the proletariat" is better than "into the proletariat" in (2). Why is this so?

There is also productivity in the way the class of "throw"-verbs combine with an abstract object such as abuse, as illustrated in (3a). However, (3b) shows that this metaphorical phenomena is *semi*-productive.

(3)   a. John threw/hurled/lobbed/flung/tossed abuse at Mary.
         b. ??John batted/slapped/punted/tipped/flipped abuse at Mary.

An adequate theory of metaphor must describe how "hurl abuse" is semantically distinct from "throw abuse," and also specify constraints on metaphorical interpretation that predict that (3a) are acceptable and (3b) are not. Similar semi-productivity is illustrated in the class of "get"-verbs when combined with an abstract argument such as "new lease of life" in (4):

(4)   a.   John acquired/got/earned/gained/procured/stole/won a new lease of life.
       b.   ??John hired/rented/ordered/fetched/gathered a new lease of life.

A further source of productivity, and one which we will examine in detail in this paper, concerns the 'normal' versus the metaphorical use of verbs describing change of location (CoL) in English and in French:

(5)   a.   Jean est entré en crise.
       b.   Jean est passé de l'autre côté de la loi.
       c.   He entered a blue funk/ came out of his blue funk.
       d.   Sam crossed the line of permissible behavior.
       e.   He deviated from the norm.
       f.   He skirted over the holes in the argument.
       g.   She stayed right on target.
       h.   You have now entered the Twilight Zone.
       i.   Jean est à la guerre.
       j.   He is outside (within) the law.
       k.   He is on top of the situation.
       l.   He was way off base.

(5a–h) employ verbs of motion or motion complexes, that in the typology described in Asher and Sablayrolles (1995) describe changes of location (CoL). (5i–l) employ complexes describing a position of the subject; these have a metaphorical behavior very similar to the behavior of CoL complexes, and so we will loosely refer to these as CoL verbs too for the purposes of this paper.

These verbs conventionally apply to spatial locations. And yet the arguments to the verbs aren't of this type in (5). Following Lakoff and Johnson (1980), we don't treat the sentences in (5) as evidence that these verbs have a vague semantic sense, thereby increasing the burden on pragmatics to compute the specific senses in context, where one of these specific senses takes spatial locations as arguments. If we adopted this strategy, then we would lose a lot of information about how the conventional semantics of these verbs are constrained, and we would lose linguistic generalizations about the kinds of spatial arguments that the various CoL verbs can take. Rather, we assume that the CoL verbs in (5) are not being used in their conventional sense, but rather in some metaphorical one.

However, there is a systematic relationship between the conventional sense of these verbs and their metaphorical senses. We agree with Lakoff and Johnson (1980), that conventional versus metaphorical ambiguity is not homonymous, but rather there is a predictable relationship between the two senses. In particular, Asher and Sablayrolles (1995) describe a taxonomy for French CoL verbs, which places restrictions on the kinds of movement that the CoL verb describes. For example, "*entrer*" takes the interior of some location or object *l* as an argument, and it describes an event of moving from some location near *l* to inside *l*.[1]

On the other hand, "*arriver*" is similar to "*entrer*" in that it takes the interior of some object or place *l* as an argument and describes an event of moving inside *l*, but it is also different in that it starts at a point *outside* the contextually defined "nearby zone" of *l*. In essence, the source of movement for "*arriver*" is 'further away' from the goal than it is for "*entrer*," but the goals in each case are the same.[2] With this in mind, the sentences in (5) expose a lexical generalization, that should be represented in a formal and computationally tractable manner. The lexical generalization is this: The essential structure of the path described by CoL verbs – that is the type of change of location from a source to a goal via an intermediate path – is preserved in the metaphorical meaning. In other words, what distinguishes a particular CoL verb from other kinds of verbs in the conventional use, also distinguishes it from those verbs in their metaphorical use.

In particular, because the conventional use of "*entrer*" requires the interior of some physical location *l* as an argument, and it describes movement from near *l* to inside *l*, the metaphorical use of "*entrer*" requires an argument that needn't be some physical location, but it must have *extension*, so that we can talk about its interior. A bad mood or blue funk (mauvaise humeur) is such an example: It can be conceived of as having extension, because it is a state which extends in time. Hence, (5c) is acceptable, and means that John 'transformed' from being in a good mood to being in a bad mood. If these predictions are correct, then just as conventional "*entrer*" is restricted in use (e.g., "?John entered the line" is odd), its metaphorical interpretation will be restricted also. And this prediction is borne out, because it is possible to create incoherent examples. It is difficult to conceive of a line of permissible behavior as having extension. The consequence is that you can cross it but not enter it, as shown in (6):

(6)   a.   John crossed the line of permissible behavior.
       b.   ??John entered the line of permissible behavior.

Furthermore, it is difficult to conceive of a disturbing conclusion as having a "nearby zone," either spatial or otherwise. Further, this predicts that (7a) is

---

[1] Note that the words 'interior' and 'inside' are used loosely here, in the sense that *l* needn't be a container. Rather, any spatial zone that has some (at least two-dimensional) spatial extent has an interior or inside. So *entrer en France* or *entrer dans l'espace* are acceptable uses of "*entrer*" because both "*France*" and "*l'espace*" have interiors, and they are conventional uses since both "*France*" and "*l'espace*" are spatial zones.

[2] It is important to stress that the English "arrive" and "enter" have slightly different interpretations to their French counterparts. In particular, the difference between "arrive" and "enter" seems to depend in part on the functional or telic role of the spatial argument. We forego a detailed discussion of this here.

acceptable, but (7b) is odd:

(7)   a. We have arrived at a disturbing conclusion.   .
        b. ??We have entered a disturbing conclusion.

Intuitively, the examples (3) and (4) follow these generalizations too, because these generalizations can explain the difference in acceptability between the a. and b. sentences. For example, what distinguishes "hire" from other "get"-verbs is that a contract is involved and the arrangement is temporary. According to our lexical generalization, these things that distinguish "hire" from other "get"-verbs in the conventional sense also form the basis for distinguishing these verbs in their metaphorical senses. However, it is difficult to conceive of a contract, metaphorically or otherwise, that underlies gaining a new lease of life.

In this paper, we will suggest how to exploit Asher and Sablayrolles (1995) classification of CoL verbs in French to explain these examples. We will encode the semantic information in a computational lexicon described within a typed feature structure framework, where other forms of productivity and polysemy have been studied extensively (e.g., Boguraev and Pustejovsky, 1990; Briscoe et al., 1990; Copestake and Briscoe, 1995; Lascarides et al., 1996; Pustejovsky, 1991, 1995; and others). This framework is compatible with constraint-based grammars such as HPSG (Pollard and Sag, 1994), and one can characterize certain types of productivity via lexical rules. We will propose a lexical rule called the Metaphor Lexical Rule, which encodes directly in the lexicon the restrictions on the metaphorical interpretation of words. Simply put, this rule will ensure that although the types of arguments of a verb can change in a metaphorical setting, the characteristics that differentiate it from other verbs in its class cannot. Therefore, because *"entrer"* describes physical movement from nearby to inside a physical space in its conventional setting, it must describe some transition or movement from nearby to inside something that needn't be a physical space (e.g., it could be a state or mood), in its metaphorical setting. Thus, the Metaphor Lexical Rule places *linguistic* constraints on the possible range of metaphorical interpretations of a particular word. This rule forms the basis for distinguishing between the acceptable and incoherent metaphors in (1–5).

Moravscik (this volume) argues that metaphorical senses are unspecific. This is supported in our theory by the fact that the Metaphor Lexical Rule won't always fully determine the interpretation of a metaphorical use of a word in a particular context; it simply limits the possibilities. However, the discourse context can influence the interpretation of metaphor, and in particular it can refine the unspecific senses that are determined by lexical information. We claim that some aspects of this influence of discourse on metaphor can be determined by computing how the metaphorical phrase is rhetorically connected to its discourse context. We will model this information flow between rhetorical relations and metaphor in a formal theory of discourse structure known as SDRT (Asher, 1993), which is distinctive in that it supplies an account of how rhetorical relations in discourse can affect semantic content of the propositions it connect. In some cases, this added semantic content will specify the nature of the metaphor.

3   The Semantics of CoL Verbs in French

Asher and Sablayrolles (1995) describe a taxonomy of French CoL verbs, which groups them into ten classes. These classes are distinguished in terms of the seven zones that are depicted in Figure 15.1. The Z-inner-halo is typically defined to be the reference location provided by the complement to the verb (e.g., the object denoted in the PP); or this location may be contextually defined by the discourse context. The Z-outer-halo is space that is near to this location, and this is determined contextually, as is the 'far away' space Z-outer-most.

The ten classes stipulate which boundaries of these seven zones the movement described by the verb must cross, and the direction of this movement. These classes are depicted schematically in Figure 15.2. The boundaries of the zones that the movement described by the CoL verb must cross determines the kinds of arguments that the verb takes. All CoL verbs have a reference location l as one of their arguments, but their meaning differs in how this reference location is exploited in constraints on the source, goal, and intermediate path of the eventuality described. We have already described in words the restrictions on the movements described by "*entrer*" and "*arriver.*" The verb "*sortir*" resembles "*entrer*" in that it describes a motion involving l and a point in the near outside of l, but the movement goes in the opposite direction; l is the source of this movement and the point in the neighborhood is the goal.

The kind of information depicted in Figure 15.2 can be represented in a typed feature structure (TFS) framework for representing lexical semantic information.

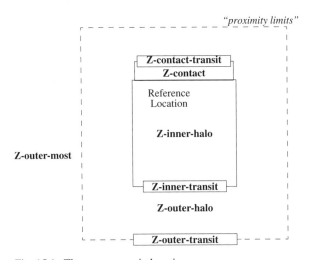

Fig. 15.1. The seven generic locations.

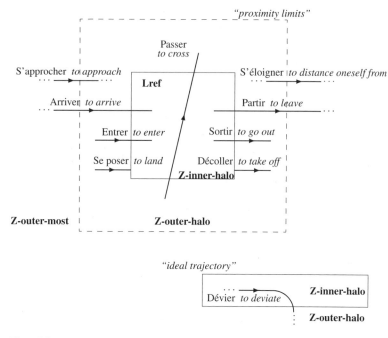

Fig. 15.2. The 10 groups of verbs of **Change of Location.**

Through doing this, one can integrate the information about paths in the semantic component with other syntagmatic information provided in a constraint-based grammar such as HPSG (Pollard and Sag, 1994), so as to produce a compositional semantics for phrases and sentences involving CoL verbs. Using a constraint-based formalism also enables us to restrict the types of arguments that a verb can take, via the typing system that accompanies the TFSs.

HPSG is specially designed to capture the linking between syntactic structure and predicate argument structure in logical form. For example, the type **tverb** (standing for transitive verb) receives the type constraint given in Figure 15.3, and the type **dans-PPverb** (standing for a verb that takes a "*dans*"-PP) is given in Figure 15.4.

$$
\begin{bmatrix}
\textbf{tverb} \\
\text{ORTH} : \textbf{string} \\
\text{SYN} : \begin{bmatrix} \text{CAT} : \textbf{v} \\ \text{SUBJ} : \textbf{NP}_{\boxed{x}} \\ \text{SUBCAT} : \textbf{NP}_{\boxed{y}} \rangle \end{bmatrix} \\
\text{SEM} : \begin{bmatrix} \text{INDEX} : \boxed{e} \\ \text{LISZT} : \left\langle \begin{bmatrix} \textbf{rel} \\ \text{EVENT} : \boxed{e} \\ \text{ARG1} : \boxed{x} \\ \text{ARG2} : \boxed{y} \end{bmatrix} \right\rangle \end{bmatrix}
\end{bmatrix}
$$

Fig. 15.3. The type constraint for **tverb.**

$$
\begin{bmatrix}
\textbf{dans-PPverb} \\
\text{ORTH : } \textbf{string} \\
\text{SYN : } \begin{bmatrix} \text{CAT : } \textbf{v} \\ \text{SUBJ : } \textbf{NP}_{\boxed{x}} \\ \text{SUBCAT : } \textbf{PP}[\textit{dans} \ \textbf{NP}_{\boxed{\text{lref}}} \ ] \end{bmatrix} \\
\text{SEM : } \begin{bmatrix} \text{INDEX : } \boxed{e} \\ \text{LISZT : } \left\langle \begin{bmatrix} \textbf{rel} \\ \text{EVENT : } \boxed{e} \\ \text{ARG1 : } \boxed{x} \\ \text{ARG2 : } \boxed{\text{lref}} \end{bmatrix} \right\rangle \end{bmatrix}
\end{bmatrix}
$$

Fig. 15.4. The type constraint for **dans-PPverb**.

We can exploit these generalizations in building lexical entries of verbs, because any verb of type **tverb** (e.g., *"traverser"*) or **dans-PPverb** (e.g., *"entrer"*) will inherit the linking given in Figures 15.3 and 15.4, respectively, and so we do not have to encode this information explicitly in each lexical entry. This is a model of lexical processing that has been suggested by many computational linguists (e.g., Copestake, 1992) and in previous work, we have suggested how such a model can be linked to a theory of discourse processing, to handle disambiguation (Asher and Lascarides, 1995a; Asher and Sablayrolles, 1995) metonymy (Lascarides, 1995; Lascarides and Copestake, 1998) and zeugma (Lascarides et al., 1996). We will use it here to model metaphor.

Given the way we have classified CoL verbs, the semantics of each lexical entry will include information about the path of movement – from source through strict intermediate path (SIP) to goal – and various values that differentiate the different CoL verb classes. To capture these generalizations in a constraint-based formalism, we introduce more information about the semantics of the word than is standardly represented in HPSG, in a similar manner to that adopted in Copestake and Briscoe (1995) and Pustejovsky (1991, 1995). In particular, information about the type of event described by *"aller"* is given at the INDEX, via the *qualia structure*. A qualia structure for a given lexical entry provides information about the kind of object or event referred to by the word, along several dimensions. It reflects the fact that real world knowledge and word meaning are not necessarily distinct on this view of the lexicon (cf. Moravscik, 1990). Instead, lexical semantic information is a strictly limited fragment of world knowledge: This fragment interacts with knowledge of language and so is conventionalized in various ways. For example, a *qualia structure* for a word that denotes an object may include certain information about its appearance and its purpose. One dimension of description in the qualia structure is of special importance here. The FML dimension (standing for *formal*, and also known as *differentiae*) stipulates properties of the object or event being described, which distinguish it from other objects/events in a larger domain. We demarcate this information in the feature structure, so that we can define in the lexicon the generalization that this information is preserved when the verb is interpreted metaphorically, as we will shortly see. It should be stressed, however, that the value of the FML feature may not include *all* real world knowledge that's

$$\begin{bmatrix} \textbf{CoL-verb} \\ \text{ORTH : } \textbf{string} \\ \\ \text{SEM :} \begin{bmatrix} \text{INDEX:QUALIA:FML :} \begin{bmatrix} \text{SOURCE:ARG1 : } \boxed{\text{x}} \\ \text{SIP:ARG1 : } \boxed{\text{x}} \\ \text{GOAL:ARG1 : } \boxed{\text{x}} \end{bmatrix} \\ \text{LISZT:ARG1 : } \boxed{\text{x}} \end{bmatrix} \end{bmatrix}$$

Fig. 15.5. Type constraints for **CoL-verb**.

relevant to distinguishing objects or events from each other. Information in the *qualia*, although closely connected with real world knowledge, does not subsume it. It includes only a limited subset, for which there must be syntagmatic evidence that the information is part of the conventional meaning.

In the case of CoL verbs, the differentiae describe the properties of the source, intermediate path, and goal of the movement described by the verb. Indeed, the fact that these properties constrain the syntax of their conventional use (and their metaphorical use), as shown in (6), provides evidence that they are part of the conventional meaning of the verbs. To encapsulate these properties of movement in the lexical entries for verbs, we first place constraints on the type **CoL-verb**, which ensure that each **CoL-verb** has features that define the source, SIP, and goal of the path, and ensure that the object that is defined to be at the source, SIP, and goal of the movement is the thing denoted by the first argument in the semantic structure; which in turn is the subject of the sentence given the linking provided by the type constraints on verbs discussed above. This is given in Figure 15.5.

Second, we must ensure that the spatial zones, which will ultimately be introduced as arguments to the source, SIP and goal of the path in any given lexical entry for a CoL verb, are defined by the complement when it exists (for note that the value of SEM:LISZT:ARG2 may be contextually defined). We represent these as implicative constraints. In words, (8) stipulates: if a TFS has some path π with value **Z-inner-halo**, then this value is computed as a (contextually defined) function f_{ih} of the value **l**, which is the second argument in the predicate argument structure in logical form. Similarly for **Z-outer-halo** and **Z-outer-most**.

(8)   a. $\langle \pi \rangle = $ **Z-inner-halo** $\rightarrow$
           (**Z-inner-halo** $= f_{ih}(\mathbf{l}) \wedge$
           $\langle$SEM:LISZT:ARG2$\rangle \mathbf{l}$)
       b. $\langle \pi \rangle = $ **Z-inner-halo** $\rightarrow$
           (**Z-outer-halo** $= f_{oh}(\mathbf{l}) \wedge$
           $\langle$SEM:LISZT:ARG2$\rangle \mathbf{l}$)
       c. $\langle \pi \rangle = $ **Z-outer-most** $\rightarrow$
           (**Z-inner-halo** $= f_{om}(\mathbf{l}) \wedge$
           $\langle$SEM:LISZT:ARG2$\rangle \mathbf{l}$)

Finally, we must encode the fact that when a CoL verb is used conventionally, the first argument in the semantic structure must be a mobile object, and the second one must be a physical space, so that we guarantee that the CoL verb describes an event where a mobile object moves in physical space in some way. We assume that this selectional restriction on the arguments to the conventional sense of a CoL verb are encoded via type constraints on the value of SEM:INDEX for this verb. So we assume that, at least in their conventional setting, CoL verbs invoke an event e in semantics that is of type **CoL-event**, and this type has constraints on it, which restrict the types of the other arguments in the semantic structure: the first argument must be a **mobile-object** and the second one must be a **physical-space**. This is specified in the implicative constraint (9):

(9)   ⟨SEM:INDEX⟩**CoL-event** →

(⟨SEM:LISZT:ARG1⟩**mobile-object**∧

⟨SEM:LISZT:ARG2⟩**physical-space**   )

We encode these selectional restrictions on this 'semantic' type **CoL-event**, rather than via the type constraints on **CoL-verb**, for two reasons. First, many have argued that selectional restrictions must be semantically, rather than syntactically, determined. Second, as we have shown, **CoL-verb**s need not be used conventionally; they can be used metaphorically. In such cases, the syntax remains the same but the types of the arguments in the semantic structure change. We can represent this preservation of syntax but change in selectional restrictions if we keep constraints on syntax and selectional restrictions separate in this way.

For example, the CoL verb *"entrer"* is a **CoL-dans-PPverb**, which is a subtype of **CoL-verb** and **dans-PPverb**. Consequently, *"entrer"* inherits the constraints from both these types. In particular, it inherits the linking constraints on **dans-PPverb** provided in Figure 15.4, and the constraints given in Figure 15.5. So the specification of the lexical entry for the conventional use *"entrer"* is given in Figure 15.6.

Note that in this TFS, the event is typed to be **CoL-event**. Therefore, the subject and object are restricted to be of types **mobile-object** and **physical-space**, respectively via the implicative constraint (9). Taking this and the type constraints

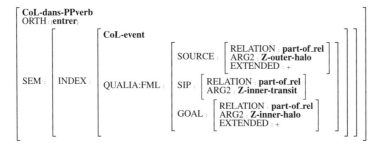

Fig. 15.6. The TFS for *"entrer."*

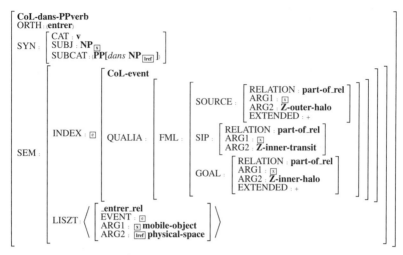

Fig. 15.7. The Expanded Feature Structure, derived from the conventional lexical entry for "*entrer*."

on **dans-PPverb** and **CoL-verb** into account, the expanded version of the lexical entry for (the conventional use of) "*entrer*" is given in Figure 15.7. Note that by (8), the values for **Z-inner-halo** and **Z-outer-halo** in this TFS must be contextually defined via the reference location given by the complement, and that these values must be extended. In contrast, the **Z-inner-transit** need not be extended. This reflects the fact that this zone need not be contextually defined for "*entrer*" to be used coherently. However, if it can be defined (e.g., as the door of the room, for *Jean est entré dans la salle*, or customs for *Jean est entré en France*), then the lexical structure of "*entrer*" predicts that Jean entered through this zone, (i.e., through the door or through customs).[3]

So the verb "*entrer*" (and other verbs grouped with "*entrer*") describe a motion of an object ⊠, which by the semantic constraints on **CoL-event** must be a **mobile-object**, and this object goes from a place outside of, but near to, the inside of a location of reference (given by the complement PP if it exists), where this location must be **physical-space**, to the inside of that location of reference, via an inner-transit zone, if it can be defined. So, the TFS for the phrase "*entrer en ville*" is given in Figure 15.8. For the sake of brevity, we have omitted the syntactic component. For the purposes of this paper, we also treat "*en*" as indistinguishable from "*dans le*."

---

[3] This aspect of the meaning of *Jean est entré dans la salle* can be overridden in sufficiently rich discourse contexts, and so it provides a good candidate for the use of lexical defaults, in the style of Lascarides and Copestake (1998, 1999). We forego a discussion of that here, because it will divert us from the main purpose of this chapter.

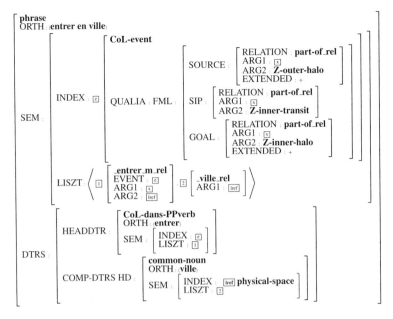

Fig. 15.8. The TFS for "*entrer en ville.*"

4   Lexical Restrictions on Metaphor

All lexical entries for the conventional sense of CoL verbs are encoded so that the type of event on SEM:INDEX is **CoL-event**. Consequently, by the type constraints given in (9), [lref] must be a physical space. The argument [lref] may be picked up from a syntactic complement in the sentence, such as a PP, or it may be specified through contextual information in the preceding discourse. It is ultimately used, via the implicative constraints in (8), to define the properties of the movement described by the CoL verb, which appear in the SEM:QUALIA:FML component of the lexical entry.

Because the argument [lref] is restricted to be physical-space, all the lexical entries for the conventional sense of CoL verbs cannot be the ones that are used to represent the sentences in (5). Attempting to compose the TFSs in these cases within the grammar will fail, because the relevant argument that fills the [lref] slot doesn't have the appropriate type on the path SEM:INDEX in its lexical entry. In particular, if we consider the example (5a), where the argument which fills in [lref] is "*crise*" or *crisis*, there is a type clash triggered by the type constraints on **CoL-event**: this requires the semantic index of [lref] to be **physical-space**, but filling [lref] with the PP complement "*crise*" makes it **non-physical-state**, as shown in the lexical entry for "*crise*" given in Figure 15.9. In words, this TFS

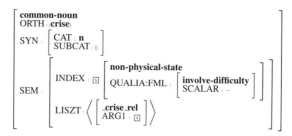

Fig. 15.9. The feature structure for *"crise."*

defines *"crise"* to be a nonphysical state, and what differentiates it from other nonphysical states in its subclasses and superclasses is that it is nonscalar and involves difficulty.

As we have mentioned, the sentences in (3), (4), and (5) expose a lexical generalization: What distinguishes a word from other kinds of words in the conventional use, also distinguishes it from those words in their metaphorical use. Therefore, in particular, the metaphorical senses of CoL verbs preserve the properties of the path, which describes the motion, from the source to a goal via an intermediate path.

Ideally, we should capture this constraint as a generalization in the lexicon: The lexicon should predict which aspects of a lexical entry can vary in metaphorical interpretation, and which cannot. We have demarcated the semantic properties of words that distinguish it from other words in a larger domain in the feature SEM:INDEX:QUALIA:FML (cf. Pustejovsky, 1991, 1995). Because of this, we can capture the constraint that the value on this path is preserved in a metaphorical setting. We specify this constraint in a *lexical rule*, which we represent as a function between TFSs in the spirit of Briscoe and Copestake (1999). The relevant rule is given in Figure 15.10.

The Metaphor Lexical Rule constrains the metaphorical senses of words. The left hand side (LHS) TFS constrains which words can have metaphorical senses, and the RHS TFS constrains the metaphorical senses in the following ways: orthography, syntax, the linking constraints given by the root type, and the differentiae for the

$$
\begin{bmatrix}
\textbf{type} \\
\text{ORTH} : \boxed{1} \\
\text{SYN} : \begin{bmatrix} \text{CAT} : v \lor n \lor adj \lor adv \lor prep \end{bmatrix} \\
\text{SEM} : \begin{bmatrix} \text{INDEX} : \begin{bmatrix} \text{QUALIA:FML} : \boxed{2} \end{bmatrix} \end{bmatrix}
\end{bmatrix}
\longmapsto
\begin{bmatrix}
\textbf{type} \\
\text{ORTH} : \boxed{1} \\
\text{SEM} : \begin{bmatrix} \text{INDEX} : {}^{\flat}T \begin{bmatrix} \text{QUALIA:FML} : \boxed{2} \end{bmatrix} \end{bmatrix}
\end{bmatrix}
$$

Fig. 15.10. The Metaphor Lexical Rule.

conventional senses of words are preserved in the metaphorical senses.[4] However, regardless of the (semantic) type of the index of the conventional sense of the word, it can be anything in the metaphorical sense. This latter piece of information is captured by the value $^{\flat}\top$ on the path SEM:INDEX in the RHS TFS. In line with Mereurs (1995), we use the notation $^{\flat}\top$ to indicate that the type $\top$ doesn't unify with the input TFS to the lexical rule, but rather $\top$ *replaces* it.

From a formal perspective, these properties arise from the way inputs and outputs to the rule are computed. One uses unification and default unification respectively (e.g., Briscoe and Copestake, 1999). First, a TFS can be input to the rule only if it is unifiable with the LHS TFS in that rule. So, because of the value given on SYN:CAT in the LHS TFS, the Metaphor Lexical Rule will take as input only words that are verbs, nouns, adjectives, prepositions, and adverbials. However, it predicts that quantifiers (e.g., "all"), auxilliaries (e.g., "do") and connectives (e.g., "but," "and") don't have metaphorical senses.

Default unification implements the requirement that information in the input should carry over to the output of the lexical rule, provided that it is consistent with the output type defined by the rule, and any further constraints specified in the rule. Reentrancies as well as matching types in the lexical rule across the LHS and RHS TFSs capture equivalences between the conventional and metaphorical senses.[5] To compute the output of the rule, given the input, one replaces the reentrancies and matching types (e.g., the root type **type** in the Metaphor Lexical Rule) in the RHS TFS with the values on these paths given by the input TFS. This is then treated as indefeasible information. So, for example, if the input to the rule is the lexical entry *"entrer"* given in Figure 15.6, then the indefeasible information that's used to compute the output to the rule has root type **CoL-dans-PPverb** (and so the output will inherit the linking constraints associated with verbs of this type); the value ⟨**entrer**⟩ on ORTH; the same value on SEM:INDEX:QUALIA:FML as that given in Figure 15.6, and the value $^{\flat}\top$ on SEM:INDEX (the $\flat$ sign indicating that $\top$ will replace any value given on this path by the input TFS, rather than unify with it, as we mentioned before). The input TFS is then taken to be persistent default information, and

---

[4] This account assumes that all the information in the differentiae is preserved in the metaphorical meaning. This may seem like a strong claim. However, as we have mentioned, the differentiae don't include all of the real world knowledge that people recruit to distinguish between objects and events; it only includes that information for which there is evidence that it affects linguistic structures. So preserving all aspects of the differentiae is a weaker restriction than one might expect.

[5] Note that in line with Copestake and Briscoe (1995), this rule can be glossed as a single feature structure typed **metaphor-lexical-rule**, where the TFS on the LHS of $\longmapsto$ is the value of the feature INPUT or 1, and the TFS on the RHS is the value of the feature OUTPUT or 0. Thus, the reentrancies in this rule can be assigned the standard semantics. Treating lexical rules as TFSs in this way allows us to specify a subtype of this lexical rule, which could restrict the metaphorical interpretation of subclasses of the class of words that can be interpreted metaphorically even further. Such rules would inherit from the TFS typed **metaphor-lexical-rule** the constraint that the differentiae must be preserved. However, these subtypes of the rule could specify further constraints in addition to this one.

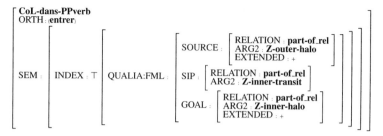

Fig. 15.11. The output of the Metaphor Lexical Rule for "*entrer.*"

the output of the rule is computed by default unifying these things together, as described in Lascarides and Copestake (1999) (cf. the definition of lexical rules given in Briscoe and Copestake, 1999). We take the default information to be persistent, so that any qualia information that survives in the metaphorical sense because it was consistent with the indefeasible information (e.g., the value of the differentiae) remains marked as default. As shown in Lascarides and Copestake (1999), it could therefore subsequently be overridden, when it is combined with incompatible (indefeasible) qualia information from other lexical entries in the phrase. However, because the differentiae in the metaphorical senses of words contain indefeasible information, this information cannot be overridden by incompatible information in other lexical entries in the phrase.

For example, the output of the Metaphor Lexical rule for the TFS in Figure 15.6 is given in Figure 15.11. Thus, the metaphorical entry for "*entrer*" is the same as the conventional entry, save that **CoL-event** is replaced with ⊤ (note that ⊤ replaces **CoL-event** rather than default unifies with it, as explained earlier). Therefore, the type constraints on **CoL-dans-PPverb** apply to the metaphorical sense of "*entrer.*" In contrast, the type constraints on **CoL-event**, which applied to the conventional sense, do not apply to the metaphorical sense, because this type has been replaced with ⊤. Thus, the TFS representing the metaphorical entry for "*entrer,*" once it is expanded out via inheritance with the relevant type constraints, looks exactly like the entry given in Figure 15.7, save that: **CoL-event** is replaced with **event** (it must be **event** because of the type constraints on **dans-PPverb**); **mobile-object** and **physical-space** no longer feature at all; and **_entrer_rel** is replaced with **rel**. Moreover, were we to add any other features of "*entrer*" to the conventional entry in Figure 15.6, such as a telic role under SEM:INDEX:QUALIA, then these would survive as persistent defaults in the metaphorical entry. That is, they would appear by default and marked as default in the TFS for the metaphorical sense of "*entrer.*"

The consequence of changing the type on SEM:INDEX is that the denotation of the metaphorical sense of the word is potentially of a different kind from the denotation of its conventional sense. Moreover, as we have mentioned in the case of "*entrer,*" any constraints produced by this type in the conventional entry do not

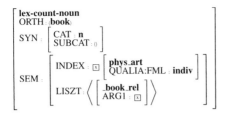

Fig. 15.12. The Typed Feature Structure for "book".

survive in the metaphorical entry. For CoL verbs in general, this means that their metaphorical senses can have subjects and complements that are not mobile objects or physical spaces, respectively. Similarly, given the lexical entry for a noun like "book" given in Copestake and Briscoe (1995), as shown in Figure 15.12, "book" is still a lexical count noun when it is used metaphorically – and so has the syntax-semantics linking associated with this type – and it still refers to an individuated object (because this is the value on the FML path), but it need not be a physical artefact, because the type on SEM:INDEX changes from **phys_art** to ⊤.

Note also, that because the Metaphor Lexical Rule will ensure that any qualia information apart from the value on FML survives in the metaphorical entry only by default, the kinds of words that metaphorical senses can combine with is different (and in general a larger set) than the ones that the conventional sense can combine with. For example, QUALIA:CST defines the stuff that an object is made up of (Pustejovsky, 1991, 1995). The Metaphor Lexical Rule ensures that the value of this on the metaphorical sense of a word is marked as default. So consider "cloud," for example. In its conventional sense, the value on QUALIA:CST is marked to be of type **physical-cum** (so clouds are made up of a physical cumulation of stuff; cf. Copestake and Briscoe, 1995, Lascarides et al., 1996). So this value survives in the metaphorical entry for "cloud." However, it is marked as default, and can be overridden by incompatible information in other lexical entries in the phrase, or by pragmatic information in the discourse context (Lascarides and Copestake, 1998). This happens in "cloud of suspicion": this refers to something made up of (nonphysical) suspicion, rather than something physical.

It should be stressed that the Metaphor Lexical Rule will not determine the interpretation of a metaphorical use of a word on its own. This is because, as is standard in constraint-based approaches to lexical semantics, several of the values in the representation of the lexical entry are underspecified in some sense. In particular, the value on SEM:INDEX is ⊤ – the most general type of all. We have utilized this underspecification in order to capture the fact that the metaphorical uses of words are in general less determinate than their conventional counterparts, about the semantic types of words that they can combine with to form phrases (cf. Moravscik, this volume). However, it is not completely unconstrained. The Metaphor Lexical Rule captures linguistic restrictions: orthography, linking and the differentiae must all be preserved. This constrains the possible senses of metaphorical uses, and pragmatic information must be used to compute the preferred interpretation in the given discourse context from this range of possibilities. So, in general, one cannot compute the metaphorical interpretation of a word in context in the absence of open-ended, nonmonotonic pragmatic reasoning. We will examine how pragmatic information aids the interpretation of metaphor in section 5. At any rate, the Metaphor Lexical Rule serves to restrict the possibilities *monotonically* in the lexicon.

In the case of CoL verbs, the Metaphor Lexical Rule will capture the fact that the distinctions among the CoL verbs and verb complexes, described in Asher and Sablayrolles (1995), are preserved in the metaphorical sense extensions. As we have seen, we assume the *differentiae* of CoL verbs stipulate the constraints on the source, goal, and intermediate path that distinguishes it from other verbs. Further, the Metaphor Lexical Rule ensures these constraints are maintained in the metaphorical senses, but the types of the arguments the verbs take won't be constrained to be **mobile-object** and **physical-space** anymore.

As an illustrative example, let's examine how the Metaphor Lexical Rule contributes to the analysis of (5a) in the monotonic component of the grammar. As we have already mentioned, the TFSs for the conventional senses of *"entrer"* and *"crise"* given in Figures 15.7 and 15.9 cannot be unified. Indeed, the same holds for all the examples we have seen in (5). However, we can use the Metaphor Lexical Rule to produce TFSs that will unify. There are three alternatives. First, we can create a metaphorical sense for *"entrer"* via the Metaphor Lexical Rule which will unify successfully with the TFS for *"crise"* given in Figure 15.9. Second, we could allow *"crise"* to be input to the Metaphor Lexical Rule rather than *"entrer"*; or third, we allow both *"entrer"* and *"crise"* to be input. Allowing both to be input would result in more work for the pragmatic component, because more information would be removed from the TFSs by the Metaphor Lexical Rule. On the other hand, preserving the TFS for *"entrer"* and allowing *"crise"* to undergo the mapping defined by the Metaphor Lexical Rule would mean that *"crise"* would have to be interpreted as a **physical-space** (because the conventional sense of *"entrer"* would constrain it to this), which is differentiated from other physical spaces in that it involves difficulties (because the output of the Metaphor Lexical Rule on *"crise"* would preserve the differentiae). This interpretation of *"crise"* as a physical space would have to be pragmatically determined, and it is unclear how one could conceive of a physical space involving difficulty. Therefore, we will examine in detail here the analysis produced by allowing *"entrer"* to undergo the mapping, and *"crise"* to stay as it is. With this assumption, and using the TFSs given in Figures 15.11 and 15.9, the TFS for the phrase *entrer en crise* is given in Figure 15.13 (for the sake of simplicity, we have again omitted syntactic information).

There is more work to be done. The arguments to CoL verbs in their metaphorical use must be interpretable as locations in some qualitative space, so that the

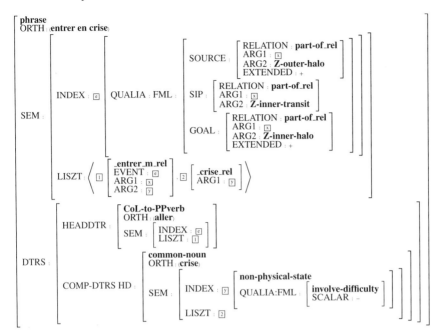

Fig. 15.13. The TFS for the phrase *"entrer en crise."*

zones Z-outer-halo, Z-inner-halo and possible Z-inner-transit, which feature in the *differentiae* of the verb, can be computed in line with the implicative constraints given in (8). This computation will determine the (nonspatial) path given by the metaphorical phrase. That is, we must (contextually) compute the zones need in the differentaie from *"crise,"* so that we can compute the source, intermediate path and goal of the (nonspatial) path.

There are two strategies we could adopt at this point. The first is to define lexical rules that produce sense extensions of nouns that allow them to be interpreted as locations in some qualitative space. Indeed, these lexical rules could be subtypes of the Metaphor Lexical Rule and inherit from that rule the fact that the value on QUALIA:FML must be preserved. The second is to assume that these locations are contextually determined, rather than assuming that they are computed in the lexicon itself. We adopt the latter strategy for two main reasons. First, the lexical rule strategy would proliferate senses of nouns in an unnecessary manner. There is no *prima facie* reason for assuming that *"crise"* as it is used in (5a) is a different sense from *"crise"* as it is used in (10), for example.

(10)   La crise a commencé en Septembre 1939.

Second, even outer most zones and nearby neighborhoods for spatial locations such as *"l'école"* are contextually determined, and so assuming that the zones are contextually determined for nonspatial nouns as well produces a more uniform analysis. Therefore, we need to formally represent generalizations in the pragmatic component, which enable one to compute the necessary zones of qualitative space for nonspatial nouns.

We are on less certain ground when interpreting nouns as locations in qualitative space, because we have not made an exhaustive study of them. However, we tentatively propose two generalizations. First, we claim that any nonscalar common noun or NP α that has an antonym β allows us to construct locations in qualitative space as follows: the Z-inner-halo is α itself, and the Z-outer-halo is the antonym. This rule is formally defined in Zones for Non-Scalar Nouns:

- Zones for Non-Scalar Nouns:
  $(noun(\alpha) \land antonym(\alpha, \beta)) \rightarrow (Z\text{-}inner\text{-}halo(\alpha, \alpha) \land Z\text{-}outer\text{-}halo(\alpha, \beta))$

It is important to stress that this rule doesn't enable us to compute outermost zones (or Z-outer-most) for nonscalar nouns. If we cannot determine what the zones are, we must assume they have no extension; they can be thought of as absent.

The second generalization for computing zones involves scalar nouns: for example *bad mood*. If α is part of a *scalar* system (e.g., good, bad, better, worse), then we claim that the outermost zone is the antonym, and the *near* neighborhoods of the qualitative space can be constructed via the α-like objects γ in the scale. This rule is given in Zones for Scalar Nouns:

- Zones for Scalar Nouns:
  $(noun(\alpha) \land antonym(\alpha, \beta) \land scalar(\alpha) \land scale(\alpha, \gamma)) \rightarrow$
  $(Z\text{-}inner\text{-}halo(\alpha, \alpha) \land Z\text{-}outer\text{-}halo(\alpha, \gamma) \land Z\text{-}outer\text{-}most(\alpha, \beta))$

So, for example, for the NP *bad mood*, the Z-inner-halo is the bad mood, the Z-outer-most is a good mood, and the near neighborhoods γ are moods that go progressively from good to bad, as one goes from the Z-outer-most towards the Z-inner-halo.

These two rules enable us to compute zones for the verb's arguments, when the lexical entry of the verb produces a logical form that requires such an interpretation. However, it should be stressed that we do not consider these generalizations to form part of the lexicon. Rather, these rules are viewed as pragmatic information on how one can compute locations in qualitative space from nouns, as and when they are required for interpreting a phrase.

As an example of how these generalizations contribute to the metaphorical interpretation of CoL phrases, consider example (5a) again. *"Crise"* is a nonscalar noun with an antonym, and therefore the rule Zones for Non-scalar Nouns applies, whereas Zones for Scalar Nouns does not. Thus, we can infer that the Z-inner-halo is a state of crisis, the Z-outer-halo is a state of 'equilibrium,' but the outermost zones aren't computable at all. Luckily, the FML feature on *"entrer"* doesn't require this zone to have extent, and so there is no anomaly. Thus, we predict that (5a) is acceptable, and it means that Jean was first in a state of equilibrium, and then at some point after he was in a state of crisis. Similarly, *entrer dans une nouvelle crise* and *sortir de la crise* are also acceptable.

Moreover, this theory predicts that any CoL verb that requires that the source or goal be a Z-outermost cannot combine with a nonscalar noun such as "*crise*" to produce an acceptable metaphor. This is supported by the linguistic data. For example, the CoL verb "*aller*" requires the source of the movement to be the **Z-outermost**, as shown in Figure 15.2. So the metaphorical interpretation of "*aller*" is lexically restricted by the Metaphor Lexical Rule to require the source to be this region. Thus, we predict, correctly, that "*aller en crise*" and "*aller à une crise*" are both odd, contrasted with "*aller en ville*" and "*aller à la ville*," which are both acceptable. This is because the source of the metaphorical movement, which is lexically constrained to be **Z-outermost**, cannot be computed from "*crise*."

The Metaphor Lexical Rule combined with our observations about the ontological status of certain locations also predicts that (5d) is fine, while (11) is not.

(5)   d.   Sam crossed the line of permissible behavior.

(11)   *Sam has entered the line of permissible behavior.

A line, even one in a qualitative space defined by possible behaviors (a scalar concept again), is something that can be crossed but that cannot be entered, since lines in our commonsense geometry have no extension (for a discussion see Aurnague and Vieu, 1993). Thus, the lexicon will fail to provide TFSs that can combine in the monotonic component of the grammar to produce an acceptable representation of (11).

By studying certain aspects of metaphorical productivity, we have learned about the kinds of features that we need in the semantics: representing *differentiae* would be useful for capturing lexical constraints on the degree of variation permitted in metaphorical interpretation.

As a further example, consider "hit"-verbs such as "hammer." The metaphorical sentences (12a) are acceptable, whereas (12b) is odd:

(12)   a.   John hit/hammered/flattened/crushed Mary with abuse.
           b.   *John tapped Mary with abuse.

Our lexical restriction on metaphor can predict this. The conventional sense of "tap" is distinct from "hit," "hammer," "flatten," and "crush," in that it describes an action that (by default) does not affect the essential characteristics – such as shape – of the patient. This difference between "tap" and other verbs in its class is represented in its SEM:INDEX:QUALIA:FML value. Assuming that "abuse" is coherently used only if the patient is affected in some essential way, the Metaphorical Lexical Rule predicts the difference in acceptability between (12a), where such an affect can be computed via the differentiae of the metaphorical senses of the verb (which are the same as in their conventional senses), and (12b) where no such affect can be computed because the metaphorical sense of "tap" fails to provide it.

A further example of metaphorical productivity comes from Ortony (1979): adjectives that apply to physical objects, can be applied in a metaphorical sense to humans: "straight," "bent," "soft," "hard," "narrow," "broad," and so on. The licensing of these metaphorical uses of adjectives can be represented via a lexical rule, which is a more specific version of the Metaphor Lexical Rule, in that it instantiates the argument that the adjective modifies to be of type **human** (rather than ⊤). However, this lexical rule would not specify the semantics of the metaphorical sense in any detail. Pragmatics will be needed to compute this.

Having captured this lexical generalization, we can capture a further one: That physical objects can apply as predicates to humans, and they receive a metaphorical interpretation where the adjectives that apply to the physical object are now applied in their metaphorical sense to the human. So, for example, the lexical rule would predict that "rock" can take an argument of type **human**, and that in this metaphorical use, the adjectives that apply to the original **physical-object** meaning of "rock," now apply in their metaphorically shifted sense to the **human**. So (13) is interpreted as "John is solid, heavy, hard to move," and so forth.

(13)   John is a rock.

It must be stressed, however, that because the metaphorical senses of the adjectives are underspecified in the lexicon, then so is the metaphorical sense of "rock." The lexical rule licenses the predicate argument structure in (13), but gives few clues about the resulting meaning. Pragmatics reasoning is needed for this task. This is why although the interpretation of (13) is relatively clear (because this is a fairly well-used, and therefore according to Searle (1979), it is arguably an established use of "rock"), the metaphorical meaning of (14) is unclear, without further pragmatic information, even though the predicate-argument structure of the sentence is licensed by the grammar:

(14)   ?Sam is a pebble.

We now turn to the task of modeling how pragmatics influences metaphorical interpretation, given the confines of metaphor specified by the Metaphor Lexical Rule (and its subtypes of lexical rules).

5   Metaphor in Context

The Metaphor Lexical Rule delimits the possibilities for metaphorical interpretation, but as is standard in constraint-based approaches to lexical semantics, it leaves the meanings of words underspecified. On some occasions (e.g., in (5a)) the semantic types of the arguments with which the words combine can serve to resolve some of this underspecification. However, in general, pragmatic reasoning is required to flesh out the interpretation of metaphor in a discourse context. It is well-known that pragmatic information, such as domain knowledge, influences metaphorical interpretation (e.g., Lakoff and Johnson, 1980). We take this further, and claim that *rhetorical relations* such as *Narration* and *Contrast* also influence the meaning of metaphor.

Let's consider a particular example where discourse structure (as defined by rhetorical relations) and pragmatics influence the interpretation of metaphor. We observed in section 4 that the meaning of (14) in isolation of any discourse context is hard to compute. But it is acceptable in (15):

(14)   ?Sam is a pebble.

(15)   a.   John is a rock.
           b.   But (compared to John) Sam is a pebble.

We think that the *Contrast* relation in (15) provides the information we need in order to calculate the metaphorical meaning of "pebble" at the discourse level. Note that it cannot simply be domain information about pebbles and rocks, because this was available for the interpretation of (14) and failed by itself to yield a coherent interpretation. Rather, the clue lies in the *juxtaposition* of (15a) and (15b), and the fact that (15b) *Contrasts* with (15a).

To see how the *Contrast* relation determines metaphor in (15), we will link the lexical reasoning described above, to the semantics of *Contrast* in SDRT (Asher, 1993). First, we must build the logical forms of the two sentences compositional via the grammar. Because of the type clash in constructing the compositional semantics from the conventional lexical entries for (15a), we are forced to a metaphorical interpretation of "rock" using the more specific lexical metaphorical rule concerning **physical-objects**. For the sake of simplicity, we assume (15a) is simply represented by the logical form $\alpha(j)$, where α represents the semantic content of the metaphorical interpretation of the predicate "rock."

We have argued that the metaphorical interpretation of "rock" is established, and therefore we assume here that α is computed to be *reliable*. However, the Metaphor Lexical Rule gives us further information. The value of SEM:INDEX:QUALIA:FML, or in other words, the *differentiae*, is preserved in the lexical entry for the (metaphorical use of) "rock."

Before we discuss the value of the differentiae for "rock," let us produce the syntagmatic representation of (15b). After doing that, we must reason about how it attaches to the constituent $\alpha(j)$ with a rhetorical relation. As with (15a), the grammar fails to build the syntagmatic representation of (15b) out of the conventional lexical entries because of type clashes in the TFSs. We must use a metaphorical interpretation of "pebble." In contrast to the semantic content of the first constituent $\alpha(j)$, however, we fail this time to obtain enough information in this process to get an informative constituent $\beta'(s)$.

Using the techniques described in Lascarides and Asher (1991, 1993) and elsewhere, we must attach the constituent $\beta'(s)$ through attaching this constituent with a rhetorical relation to the discourse context. In general, computing the rhetorical relation involves nonmonotonic reasoning on the reader's background knowledge. However, in this case, the rhetorical relation must be *Contrast*, as indicated by the cue word "but." Therefore, we must check the coherence of the *Contrast* relation in (15), by ensuring that the discourse constituents, which are the DRSs that represent the two sentences being connected together, are isomorphic both structurally and semantically, and that there is a contrasting theme between them. There is a default heuristic that one aims for as much structural and semantic isomorphism as possible. Maximum isomorphism is achieved, if "rock" is associated with "pebble" in the structural mapping between the constituents, and the semantics of these items contrast with each other.

In SDRT computing a rhetorical relation between constituents can trigger modifications to the semantics of the constituents themselves (Asher, 1993; Asher and Lascarides, 1994, 1995). Intuitively, this process corresponds to accommodating the information that's necessary to ensure discourse coherence is maintained (cf. Stalnaker, 1978). It captures the intuition that speakers expect hearers to infer information that's not explicitly said during discourse processing. Each rhetorical relation imposes coherence constraints in terms of the semantic relation between the constituents being attached. If the necessary information isn't already there, then it can be added in a constrained manner. Therefore, because we successfully interpret the metaphorical use of "rock" in (15a), we can use the coherence constraints on *Contrast* to infer further semantic content for the interpretation of "pebble" in this context. "Pebble" will mean whatever produces the maximally contrasting theme, given the conventional constraints defined by the Metaphor Lexical Rule.

Now, we assume the conventional sense of "rock" has a value for SEM:QUALIA: FML, which distinguishes it from other objects in the same semantic class (e.g., the conventional senses of "boulder," "pebble," and so on). So, the conventional sense of "rock" specifies in SEM:QUALIA:FML that rocks are bigger than pebbles, but smaller than boulders. Similarly, the value of SEM:QUALIA:FML in the (conventional sense of) "pebble" contains the information that pebbles are smaller than rocks. So, given that the Metaphor Lexical Rule ensures that the values of SEM:QUALIA:FML (i.e., the differentiae) survive in metaphorical interpretation, these differentiae provide us with a scale with which we can compare (the metaphorical senses of) "pebble" and "rock." The partial order of sizes between pebbles and rocks given in the differentiae becomes a scale of reliability, because we know "rock" means *reliable* in (15a). Because "pebble" precedes "rock" on this partial order, "pebble" means *less reliable*. Moreover, to maximize the contrast as dictated by the rhetorical relation *Contrast* between (15a) and (15b), *"pebble"* doesn't just mean *less reliable*; it means *unreliable* in this discourse context. On the other hand, "boulder" in (15a,c) means *more reliable*.

(15)   c. But (compared to John) Sam is a boulder.
        d. ?But (compared to John) Sam is a stone.

Because "stone" is not specified according to size in the differentiae of the conventional entries, it doesn't feature in the partial order, and so one cannot compute the degree of reliability that "stone" is supposed to mean in (15a,d). In this case, the *Contrast* relation doesn't help us further specify the metaphorical meaning of "stone." Therefore, our theory correctly predicts that (15a,d) is anomalous.

SDRT's strategy of accommodation comes into play in cases like these. The need for discourse coherence triggered a modification of the truth conditional content of the representation $\beta'(s)$ of the meaning of (15b) (again, for details see Asher, 1993), so that we obtain the necessary contrasting theme. Indeed, according to this revision technique as it is defined in Asher (1993), we replace $\beta'(s)$ with $\neg\alpha(s) \wedge \beta'(s)$.[6] This gives us the right intuitive results: namely, that (15b) in this context means that Sam is a pebble, and not a rock. A similar inference holds for (15a,c).

We now consider an example where the discourse context actually triggers a metaphorical interpretation. Sentence (16), in the absence of information to the contrary, means that I (conventionally) climbed a (**physical-space**) greasy pole.

(16)   I have climbed to the top of that greasy pole.

There is no reason to believe that the sentence is metaphorical, because the grammar permits the conventional sense of the CoL verb "climb" and the **physical-space** "greasy pole" to combine successfully. However, in (17) – which is a slightly expanded example from Searle (1979), that he attributes to Disraeli – the *Contrast* relation again helps us to determine the metaphorical interpretation of (17b). However, further and in contrast with (15), the relation, together with the proposition expressed by the first sentence, *trigger* the metaphor in the first place.

(17)   a. I have always despised politics.
        b. But I have climbed to the top of that greasy pole.

Again using the techniques in SDRT, one must check the coherence of the *Contrast* relation, and aim for maximum structural and semantic isomorphism between the constituents. Furthermore, the anaphoric expression "that greasy pole" must be resolved to an available antecedent from the discourse context. Given the discourse context, SDRT predicts there is only one candidate antecedent: "politics." However, the type hierarchy in the constraint-based grammar prevents "that greasy pole" from being identified with "politics," unless it undergoes type coercion. Therefore, using a principle of Charity familiar from philosophical work on metaphor (Black, 1962, 1979; Searle, 1979), we learn that "that greasy pole" is to be interpreted metaphorically, and is identified with politics (and so "greasy" is assigned a metaphorical interpretation, which is ascribed to politics). Thus, through calculating the anaphora resolution, with the aid of the discourse structure, we have triggered a metaphorical interpretation of "that greasy pole."

However, now, the conventional CoL verb "climb" cannot combine with "that greasy pole" anymore, because the CoL verb "climb" requires an argument of type **physical-space**, and the TFS we must use to represent "that greasy pole," which in

---

[6] Note that given that β' is so underspecified, this conjunction is satisfiable. If it weren't satisfiable, then the *Contrast* relation would be incoherent.

turn has been chosen on the basis of constraints on anaphoric links in the discourse, is not of this type. Therefore, using the principle of Charity again, "climb" must be interpreted in a different way.

The constraints described in the Metaphor Lexical Rule, ensure respectively that the differentiae component is definitely preserved, and furthermore, that as many properties as possible, in addition to the *differentiae* of conventional "climb," are preserved in the metaphorical interpretation. The former property means that all the properties of the source, intermediate path and goal of "climb" in (17b) – save that they are of type **physical-space** – are preserved. This is similar for the phrase "to the top." So, Disraeli starts at the bottom of politics, and climbs to the top. We must therefore assign "politics" a qualitative scale: The career hierarchy (clerk to prime minister) is a plausible candidate, and under this interpretation, (17b) means that Disraeli worked his way up the career hierarchy. Note that the way we view the orientation of the career hierarchy is itself an example of metaphor, which is determined in part by the fundamental values in our culture (Lakoff and Johnson, 1980). Thinking of clerk as at the bottom and prime minister as at the top is a coherent metaphorical interpretation of the concept of career, whereas the opposite orientation, with the clerk at the top and prime minister at the bottom, would be incoherent.

A particularly compelling metaphor uses a combination of world knowledge and discourse structure. Arguably, this occurs in Romeo's metaphor for Juliet:

(18)   a.   What light through yonder window breaks?
        b.   It is the East, and Juliet is the sun!

William Shakespeare, *Romeo and Juliet, Act II, Scene 2*

Because (18a) is a question, by the constraints in SDRT it must form part of a question answer pair (*QAP*) (Asher and Lascarides, 1995). An answer to this question is a proposition that asserts what the light is. Indeed, as we will see, (18b) gives us an answer, but not a direct one; we have to infer what the direct answer is.

One task is to resolve the anaphor "it" in (18b). Just as in (17), the discourse context constrains this to be identified with either the window or the light. Both invoke type violations (for neither light nor windows can be the East, although they can be "in" the East), and will force a metaphorical interpretation. The identification of the anaphor with "window" is more plausible, because the mass term "light" doesn't determine a physical location to the extent that "window" does. So we have determined that the physical window is the metaphorical East. The second clause of (18b) informs us that Juliet is the metaphorical sun. This is computed along the same lines as the analysis of sentence (13), because we are associating a human with a natural object. Therefore, Juliet is ascribed with the adjectives, metaphorically interpreted, that conventionally apply to the sun, such as light and radiance. Typically, these are connected with beauty, and so we infer from the second clause of (18b) that Juliet is beautiful. However, we still have to determine how (18b) answers the question in (18a). Using the world knowledge that the sun rises in the East, one can assume that the metaphorical interpretation of (18b) is also one where the metaphorical sun rises in the metaphorical East. Because the metaphorical East is, physically, the window, and the metaphorical sun is Juliet, this information places Juliet at the window. Having learned that Juliet, who is the sun, is at the window, the question in (18a) is answered: Juliet is the light breaking at the window. One could infer further content, using world knowledge of the sort Shakespeare might have assumed his audience would have at their disposal (like a roughly Ptolomaic view of the universe); for example, as Juliet is the metaphorical sun, she is at the center of Romeo's world.

6   Conclusion

We have shown how to compute metaphorical interpretations from a combination of two mechanisms: lexical rules, which specify the range of possible meaning shifts of classes of words; and a theory of discourse structure, which provides mechanisms for adding truth conditional content to metaphorically interpreted constituents, relative to the context in which they are uttered. We showed how this can explain data concerning: verbs involving change of location; the metaphorical shift of meaning of words that refer to kinds of physical objects when they are predicated of persons; and the dependence of metaphorical interpretation upon discourse structure. What we have done, of course, is very far from a comprehensive theory of metaphor. At best we have offered a proof of concept of an approach. But by using the modern logical tools of formal pragmatics and semantics, we hope that we and others can make progress on this difficult subject and that in turn a better understanding of metaphor will enhance our understanding of lexical meaning and lexical processes.

7   Acknowledgments

This paper was presented at the 1995 AAAI Spring Symposium Workshop entitled *Representation and Acquisition of Lexical Knowledge: Polysemy, Ambiguity and Generativity*. We would like to thank the participants of this workshop for their useful comments. In addition, we would like to thank Julius Moravscik for his comments on an earlier draft of this paper.

References

Asher, N. 1993. *Reference to Abstract Objects in Discourse*. Kluwer Academic Publishers, Dordrecht.

Asher, N., and Lascarides, A. 1994. Intentions and Information in Discourse. *Proc. 32nd Annual Meeting of the Association for Computational Linguistics*, Las Cruces, pp. 34–41.

288   *Nicholas Asher and Alex Lascarides*

Asher, N., and Lascarides, A. 1995. Lexical Disambiguation in a Discourse Context. *Journal of Semantics* 12: 69–108.

Asher, N., and Lascarides, A. 1998. Questions in Dialogue. *Linguistics and Philosophy* 23.3: 237–309.

Asher, N., and Sablayrolles, P. 1995. A Typology and Discourse Semantics for Motion Verbs and Spatial PPs in French. *Journal of Semantics* 12: 163–209.

Aurnague, M., and Vieu, L. 1993. Towards a Formal Representation of Space in Language: A Commonsense Reasoning Approach. *Proc. IJCAI93 Workshop on Spatial Reasoning*, Chambery, France.

Black, M. 1962. *Models and Metaphors*. Cornell University Press, Cornell, NY.

Black, M. 1979. More About Metaphor. In A. Ortony, *Metaphor and Thought*. Cambridge University Press, Cambridge, pp. 19–45.

Boguraev, B., and Pustejovsky, J. 1990. Lexical Ambiguity and the Role of Knowledge Representation in Lexicon Design. *Proc. 13th International Conference on Computational Linguistics (COLING90)*, Helsinki, pp. 36–42.

Briscoe, E.J., and Copestake, A. 1999. Lexical Rules in Constraint-based Grammars *Computational Linguistics* 25.4: 487–526.

Briscoe, E.J., Copestake, A., and Boguraev, B. 1990. Enjoy the Paper: Lexical Semantics via Lexicology. *Proc. 13th International Conference on Computational Linguistics (COLING90)*, Helsinki, pp. 42–47.

Copestake, A. 1992. *The Representation of Lexical Semantic Information*, PhD dissertation, University of Sussex, Brighton, England.

Copestake, A., and Briscoe, E.J. 1995. Semi-Productive Polysemy and Sense Extension. *Journal of Semantics* 12: 15–67.

Davidson, D. 1984. What Metaphors Mean. In D. Davidson, *Inquiries into Truth and Interpretation*. Clarendon Press, Oxford, UK, pp. 245–264.

Evans, R., and Gazdar, G. 1989a. Inference in DATR. *Proc. 4th Conference of the European Chapter of the Association for Computational Linguistics (EACL89)*, Manchester, England, pp. 66–71.

Hesse, M. (1966). *Models and Analogies in Science*. University of Notre Dame Press, Notre Dame, IN.

Lakoff, G., and Johnson, M. 1980. *Metaphors We live By*. The University of Chicago Press, Chicago.

Lascarides, A., and Asher, N. 1991. Discourse Relations and Defeasible Knowledge. *Proc. 29th Annual Meeting of the Association of Computational Linguistics (ACL91)*, Berkeley USA, June 1991, pp. 55–63.

Lascarides, A., and Asher, N. 1993. Temporal Interpretation, Discourse Relations, and Commonsense Entailment. *Linguistics and Philosophy* 16: 437–493.

Lascarides, A., Briscoe, E. J., Asher, N., and Copestake, A. 1996. Order Independent and Persistent Default Unification. *Linguistics and Philosophy* 19: 1–89.

Lascarides, A. 1995. The Pragmatics of Word Meaning. *Proc.* AAAI *Spring Symposium Series: Representation and Acquisition of Lexical Knowledge: Polysemy, Ambiguity and Generativity*, Stanford, Ca, pp. 75–80.

Lascarides, A., and Copestake, A. 1998. The Pragmatics of Word Meaning. *Journal of Linguistics* 34.2: 387–414.

Lascarides, A., and Copestake, A. 1999. Default Representation in Constraint-based Frameworks. *Computational Linguistics* 25: 55–105.

Lascarides, A., Copestake, A., and Briscoe, E.JJ. 1996. Ambiguity and Coherence. *Journal of Semantics* 13: 41–65.

Mereurs, D. 1995. Towards a Semantics for Lexical Rules as Used in HPSG. *Proc. ACQUILEX Workshop on Lexical Rules*, University of Cambridge, Cambridge.

Moravscik, J.M. 1990. *Thought and Language*. Routledge, London.

Ortony, A. 1979. *Metaphor and Thought*. Cambridge University Press, Cambridge.

Pollard, C., and Sag, I.A. 1994. *Head-Driven Phrase Structure Grammar*, CSLI, University of Chicago Press, Chicago and London.

Pustejovsky, J. 1991. The Generative Lexicon. *Computational Linguistics* 17: 409–441.

Pustejovsky, J. 1995. *The Generative Lexicon*. MIT Press, Cambridge MA.

Searle, J. 1979. Metaphor. In A. Ortony (ed.), *Metaphor and Thought*. Cambridge University Press, Cambridge, pp. 92–123.

Stalnaker, R. 1978. Assertion. In P. Cole (ed.), *Syntax and Semantics, volume 9: Pragmatics*. Academic Press, Oxford, UK.

16   Syntax and Metonymy

JERRY HOBBS

Abstract

Metonymy is refering to one entity by describing a functionally related entity. When this is formalized in an *Interpretation as Abduction* framework, it can be seen that an isomorphic process solves a number of problems that have hitherto been viewed as syntactic. In these cases, the coercion function associated with the metonymy comes from material that is explicit in the sentence. For example, in "John smokes an occasional cigarette," it is the smoking rather than the explicit argument of "occasional," the cigarette, that is occasional; there is a coercion from the cigarette to the smoking event, where the coercion relation is provided by the "smokes" predication itself. Other phenomena analyzed in this manner are extraposed modifiers, container nouns, the collective-distributive ambiguity for some plural noun phrases, small clauses in disguise such as "This country needs literate citizens," and the assertion of grammatically presupposed material. These examples lie on the boundaries between syntax, semantics, and pragmatics, and illustrate the utility of a framework in which the three areas are modeled in a uniform fashion.

1   Metonymy

Metonymy is the linguistic device by which an entity is referred to by refering to a functionally related entity. For example, when we say "John reads Proust" we really mean "John reads the novels by Proust." We may say that "Proust" has been *coerced* into "the novels by Proust." Alternatively, we may say that "read" has been *coerced* into "read the novels by."

Thus, there are two ways to characterize metonymy. Metonymy occurs when an explicit predication $P(X)$ is conveyed by a fragment of text and the intended interpretation is $P(F(X))$ for some function F. This can be viewed as X being coerced into $F(X)$; this corresponds to the usual characterization of metonymy as an entity being coerced into something functionally related to it. Or it can be viewed as the predicate P being coerced into the predicate $P \circ F$, or P composed with F. Nunberg (1995) refers to the first case as *deferred ostension* and to the second case as *predicate transfer*. He argues that the former occurs only in actual cases of ostension, as when a parking attendent holds up a key and says "This is parked out back." In nonostensive cases, including the vast majority of examples that occur in discourse, he argues that the metonymies should be thought of as

290

instances of predicate transfer. His arguments rest primarily on the availability of entities for subsequent pronominal reference and occurrence within elliptical constructions. In the following examples, the first two illustrate deferred ostension, the second two predicate transfer:

> This [holding up key] is parked out back and may not start.
> *This [holding up key] is parked out back and fits only the left front door.
> John is parked out back and has been waiting fifteen minutes.
> *John is parked out back and may not start.

In the first two examples the key X is coerced into the car $F(X)$ and the latter becomes the only possible subject for the second clause. In the last two examples, John X remains the same and is the only possible subject for the second clause; the predicate

$$\lambda X[X \text{ is parked out back}]$$

is coerced into something like

$$\lambda X[\text{the car belonging to } X \text{ is parked out back}]$$

In section 2 of this paper, I briefly introduce the framework of *Interpretation as Abduction*. In this framework, it is straightforward to formalize both varieties of metonymic coercion, and this is done in section 3. Sections 4 through 8 present a range of examples of phenomena that have previously been viewed as syntactic that can in fact be viewed as a special kind of metonymy, where the coercion relation is provided by the explicit content of the sentence itself. The phenomena considered are extraposed modifiers, ataxis, container nouns, the distinction between distributive and collective readings of plurals, and what may be called "small clauses in disguise." There are cases where grammatically subordinated material in sentences functions as the main assertional claim of the sentence, and in section 9 these are similarly analyzed as examples of metonymy where the coercion relation is provided by the explicit content of the rest of the sentence.

2   Background: Interpretation as Abduction

The framework adopted in this chapter is that of *Interpretation as Abduction* (henceforth, IA) (Hobbs et al., 1993). In this framework, the interpretation of a sentence is the least-cost abductive proof of the logical form of the sentence. That is, to interpret a sentence one tries to prove the logical form by using the most salient axioms and other information, exploiting the natural redundancy of discourse to minimize the size of the proof, and allowing the minimal number of consistent and plausible assumptions necessary to make the proof go through. Anaphora are resolved and predications are pragmatically strengthened as a by-product of this process.

More generally in the IA framework, the job of an agent is to interpret the environment by proving abductively, or explaining, the observables in the environment, thereby establishing that the agent is in a coherent situation. This perspective is expanded upon in section 9 below.

The representational conventions used in this chapter are those of Hobbs (1983, 1985, and 1995). The chief features relevant to this chapter are the use of eventualities and the use of typical elements of sets to represent information about pluralities. The latter is described in section 7. Here, eventualities will be explicated briefly.

Corresponding to every predication $p(x)$ there is a predication $p'(e, x)$ which says that e is the eventuality of p being true of x. Existential quantification in this notation is over a Platonic universe of possible individuals. The actual truth or existence of e in the real world is asserted by a separate predication $Rexists(e)$. The relation between the primed and unprimed predicates is given by the following axiom schema:

$$(\forall x)[p(x) \equiv (\exists e)[p'(e, x) \wedge Rexists(e)]]$$

That is, p is true of x if and only if there is an eventuality e of p being true of x and e exists or obtains in the real world.

Eventualities are posited not just for events, such as flying to someplace – $fly'(e, x, y)$ – and activities, such as reading – $read'(e, x, y)$ – but also for stable conditions, such as being a cigarette – $cigarette'(e, x)$ – and even having a particular proper name – $John'(e, x)$. For economy, in the examples below eventualities will only be introduced where they are material to what is being illustrated, primarily when they appear as arguments in other predications. Otherwise, the unprimed predicates will be used.

Using these notational devices, the logical form of sentences is an existentially quantified conjunction of atomic predications. The translations of several specific grammatical constructions into this logical form are given in the examples in the rest of this chapter. In general, instead of writing

$$(\exists \dots, x, \dots)[\dots \wedge p(x) \wedge \dots]$$

I will simply write

$$\dots \wedge p(x) \wedge \dots$$

Knowledge in this framework is expressed in (generally defeasible) axioms of the form

$$(\forall x, y)[p(x, y) \supset (\exists z)q(x, z)]$$

These will be abbreviated to expressions of the form

$$p(x, y) \supset q(x, z)$$

The focus of the interpretation process is to make explicit the information conveyed by the text in context, rather than, for example, to determine its truth conditions.

In the IA framework, syntax, semantics, and pragmatics are thoroughly integrated, through the observation that the task of an agent in explaining an utterance by another agent is normally to show that it is a *grammatical, interpretable* sentence whose content is somehow involved in the *goals* of the speaker. It has already been said that a sentence is *interpretable* insofar as its logical form can be proved abductively. The linkage with *goals* is described in section 9. A set of syntactic and lexical axioms characterize *grammaticality* and yield the logical form of sentences.

In Hobbs (1998) an extensive subset of English grammar is described in detail, largely following Pollard and Sag's (1994) *Head-Driven Phrase Structure Grammar* but cast into the uniform IA framework. In this treatment, the predicate *Syn* is used to express the relation between a string of words and the eventuality it conveys. Certain axioms involving *Syn*, the "composition axioms," describe how the eventuality conveyed emerges from the concatenation of strings. Other axioms, the "lexical axioms," link *Syn* predications about words with the corresponding logical-form fragments. There are also "transformation axioms," which alter the places in the string of words predicates find their arguments.

In this chapter, a simplified version of the predicate *Syn* will be used. We will take *Syn* to be a predicate of seven arguments.

$$Syn(w, e, f, x, a, y, b)$$

w is a string of words. e is the eventuality described by this string. f is the category of the head of the phrase w. If the string w contains the logical subject of the head, then the arguments x and a are the empty symbol "$-$". Otherwise, x is a variable referring to the logical subject and a is its category. Similarly, y is either the empty symbol or a variable referring to the logical object, and b is either the empty symbol or the category of the logical object. For example,

$$Syn(\text{``reads a novel''}, e, \mathbf{v}, x, \mathbf{n}, -, -)$$

says that the string of words "reads a novel" is a phrase describing an eventuality e and has a head of category verb. Its logical object "a novel" is in the string itself, so the last two arguments are the empty symbol. Its logical subject is not part of the string, so the fourth argument is the variable x standing for the logical subject and the fifth argument specifies that the phrase describing it must have a noun as its head. In Hobbs (1998) the full *Syn* predicate contains argument positions for further complements and filler-gap information, and the category arguments can record syntactic features as well.

Two of the most important composition axioms are the following:

$$Syn(w_1, x, a, -, -, -, -) \wedge Syn(w_2, e, f, x, a, -, -)$$
$$\supset Syn(w_1 w_2, e, f, -, -, -, -)$$
$$Syn(w_1, e, f, x, a, y, b) \wedge Syn(w_2, y, b, -, -, -, -)$$
$$\supset Syn(w_1 w_2, e, f, x, a, -, -)$$

The first axiom corresponds to the traditional "S → NP VP" rule. It says that if w_1 is a string describing an entity x and headed by a word of category a and w_2 is a string describing eventuality e, headed by a word of category f, and lacking a logical subject x of category a, then the concatenation $w_1 w_2$ is a string describing eventuality e and headed by a word of category f. The second axiom corresponds to the traditional "VP → V NP" rule. It says that if w_1 is a string describing eventuality e, headed by a word of category f, and lacking a logical subject x of category a and a logical object y of category b and w_2 is a string describing an entity y and headed by a word of category b, then the concatenation $w_1 w_2$ is a string describing eventuality e, headed by a word of category f, and lacking a logical subject x of category a, but not lacking a logical object.

A typical lexical axiom is the following:

$$read'(e, x, y) \wedge person(x) \wedge text(y) \supset Syn(\text{"read"}, e, \mathbf{v}, x, \mathbf{n}, y, \mathbf{n})$$

That is, if e is the eventuality of a person x reading a text y, then the verb "read" can be used to describe e provided noun phrases describing x and y are found in the appropriate places, as specified by composition axioms. Lexical axioms thus encode the logical form fragment corresponding to a word ($read'(e, x, y)$), selectional constraints ($person(x)$ and $text(y)$), the spelling (or in a more detailed account, the phonology) of the word ("read"), its category (verb), and the syntactic constraints on its complements (that x and y must come from noun phrases). The lexical axioms constitute the interface between syntax and world knowledge; knowledge about reading is encoded in axioms involving the predicate $read'$, whereas knowledge of syntax is encoded in axioms involving Syn, and these two are linked here. In the course of proving that a string of words is a grammatical, interpretable sentence, the interpretation process backchains through composition axioms to lexical axioms (the syntactic processing) and then is left with the logical form of the sentence to be proved. A proof of this logical form was the original IA characterization of the interpretation of a sentence.

The proof graph of the syntactic part of the interpretation of "John read *Ulysses*" is shown in Figure 16.1. Note that knowledge that John is a person and "Ulysses" is a text is used to establish the selectional constraints associated with "read."

There are systematic alternations because of which the arguments of predicates are not found in the canonical locations specified by the lexical axioms. Transformation axioms accommodate these alternations. The (somewhat simplified) rule for passivation illustrates this.

$$Syn(w, e, \mathbf{v.en}, x, a, y, \mathbf{n}) \supset Syn(w, e, \mathbf{pred}, y, \mathbf{n}, -, -)$$

If w is the past participle of a verb that takes a subject x of category a and an NP object y, then w can function as a predicate complement, taking an NP subject refering to y.

Metonymy can also be characterized by transformation axioms.

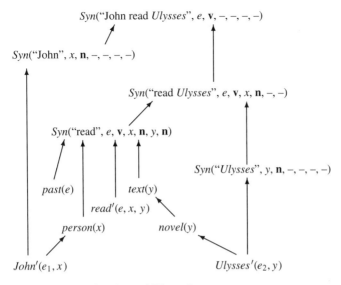

Fig. 16.1. Parse of "John read *Ulysses*".

3   Axioms for Metonymy

Both varieties of metonymic transfer can be easily captured in the present frame-work by means of transformation axioms. The coercion from X to $F(X)$ is a matter of substituting for the leading argument (or eventuality) variable in the *Syn* predication another variable representing a functionally related entity.

(1) $Syn(w, e, f, x, a, y, b) \land rel(e_0, e) \supset Syn(w, e_0, f, x, a, y, b)$

Here, e plays the role of X and e plays the role of $F(X)$. Viewed from the perspective of interpretation, this says that the phrase w is being used in the embedding context as though it referred to or described one entity or eventuality e_0 but in fact w, by itself, refers to or describes a related entity or eventuality e. From the perspective of generation, it says that if you want to refer to or describe an entity or eventuality e_0, you can do so by referring to or describing a related entity or eventuality e.

The coercion from P to $P \circ F$ is a matter of substituting for one of the x or y arguments in the *Syn* predication another variable representing a functionally related entity. Two axioms are required, one for each argument position. The first is

(2) $Syn(w, e, f, x_0, a, y, b) \land rel(x_0, x) \supset Syn(w, e, f, x, a, y, b)$

The effect of this axiom in interpretation is as follows: The axiom is applied to the predicate or head word w in the proof graph below the point at which it links up with its argument x. Above the application of this axiom, the argument is the variable x and refers to the explicit, uncoerced argument. The axiom introduces the coercion relation $rel(x_0, x)$. Below the application of the axiom, the argument is x_0, the implicit, coerced argument. It is this that becomes the argument of the predication associated with w and to which the selectional constraints are applied. The NP describing x then really does refer to x and is thus available for subsequent pronominalization.

The other "predicate transfer" axiom is

(3) $Syn(w, e, f, x, a, y_0, b) \wedge rel(y_0, y) \supset Syn(w, e, f, x, a, y, b)$

Figure 16.2 illustrates the use of Axiom (3) on the sentence

John read Proust.

in conjunction with axioms that say that Proust wrote novels, which are texts, and that the writing relation is a possible coercion.

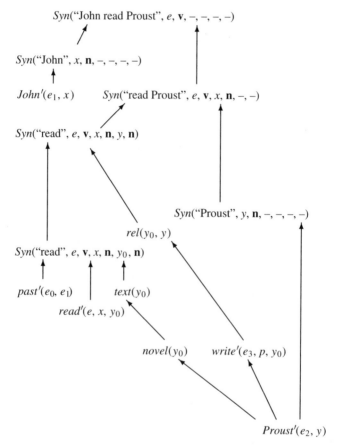

Fig. 16.2. Parse of "John read Proust" using Axiom (3).

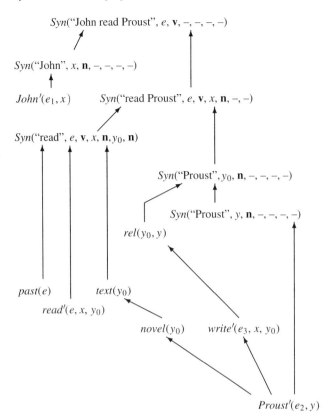

Fig. 16.3. Parse of "John read Proust" using Axiom (1).

The coercion occurs on the word "read," changing its logical object from Proust to the novels of Proust. This in effect "transfers" the predicate "read" into the predicate "read the novels of." Note that the phrase "Proust" is still and only an NP referring to the man Proust and not his works. This is what restricts the possibilities for subsequent pronominal reference.

By contrast, if this example were to be handled with Axiom (1), as a coercion from Proust to the novels of Proust, the interpretation would be as illustrated in Figure 16.3.

In this chapter, Nunberg's (1995) lead will be followed, and cases of metonymy will be treated as instances of predicate transfer, thus involving axioms (2) and (3).

I will not attempt here to determine possible constraints on metonymic coercions. Here the coercion relation *rel* will be axiomatized in the loosest possible way. It is symmetric and transitive:

$$(\forall x, y) rel(x, y) \supset rel(y, x)$$
$$(\forall x, y, z) rel(x, y) \wedge rel(y, z) \supset rel(x, z)$$

For the purposes of this chapter, any relation will be taken to be a possible coercion relation. This is captured by the axiom schema

(4) $(\forall \ldots, x, \ldots, y, \ldots)[p'(\ldots, x, \ldots, y, \ldots) \supset rel(x, y)]$

That is, any two arguments of the same predication are related to each other. Any predication can function as a coercion relation between any two of its arguments, including its eventuality argument.

Of the possible coercion relations, the most salient will be selected by the abductive interpretation process. Among the most salient relations between entities are those conveyed explicitly in the text itself. A number of seemingly disparate phenomena that are normally thought of as syntactic can be analyzed as examples of metonymy, where the coercion relation is provided by the explicit content of the sentence itself. Six such cases will be examined here – extraposed modifiers of the subject, ataxis, container nouns, distributive readings, small clauses in disguise, and the assertion of grammatically subordinated information.

4   Extraposed Modifiers

Consider the sentences

Mary saw Denver flying to Chicago.
A jolly old man arrived with an armload of presents.
The man arrived whom John had invited to dinner.

Neither the seeing nor Denver was flying to Chicago, but Mary. It was the old man who had an armload of presents, not the arriving event. John had invited to dinner the man and not the arriving event. In each of these cases what seems as though it should be a right modifier to the subject NP is extraposed to the end of the sentence.

It is possible to interpret these cases as examples of metonymy, where the coercion relation is provided by the predication associated with the head verb. That is, normal syntactic processing would attach the postmodifier to the verb, and then that would be coerced to the subject, using the predication of the verb itself as the coercion relation. Thus, by normal syntactic processing, the seeing is flying to Chicago, the arriving event is with an armload of presents, and John had invited the arriving event to dinner. These interpretations will not satisfy the selectional constraints associated with "fly," "with," and "invite," respectively. Applications of axioms (2) and (3) thus coerce each of these arguments to the subject of the sentence. In the first sentence

$see'(e, m, d)$

coerces from the seeing e to Mary m, and in the second and third sentences

$arrive'(e, m)$

coerces from the arriving e to the man m.

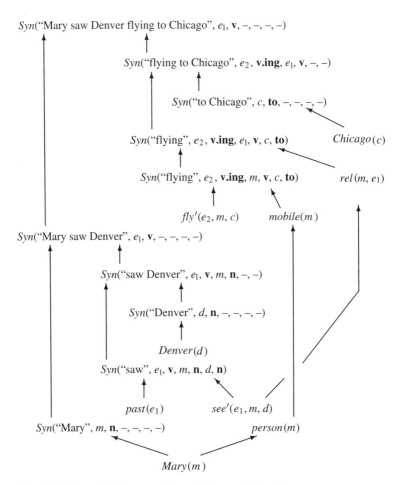

Fig. 16.4. Parse of "Mary saw Denver flying to Chicago"'s.

Figure 16.4 illustrates this with the sentence "Mary saw Denver flying to Chicago." Here the preposition "to" is viewed as making the NP "Chicago" available as a "to" complement, and the reader can deduce the composition axiom for sentence-level adverbials from the top branch of the proof graph.

A similar analysis can be used to correct for incorrect prepositional phrase attachments. In

I saw the man in the park with the telescope.

if the park is incorrectly identified as the logical subject of "with," the *in* and *see* relations can be used to coerce it to the seeing event. Instead of the park being with the telescope, the seeing event by me of a man in the park is with the telescope.

Preposed right modifiers of nouns can be handled in the same way. In

> Of all the options mentioned, several are viable.

the preposed PP "Of all the options mentioned" is first attached as a modifier to "viable." Metonymic interpretation then uses the viability relation itself to coerce the attachment onto "several." More precisely, suppose the logical form includes the predication *viable' (e, x)*, where *x* is the typical example of the several options. The explicit logical subject of the predicate "of" is first *e*. The predication *viable' (e, x)* is then used as a coercion relation to coerce the logical subject of "of" from *e* to *x*.

Sometimes, the complement of an adjective used prenominally appears as the noun complement, as in

> a similar book to that.

This can also be viewed as an example of metonymy. The complement "to that" is taken first as a property of the book *b*.

$$Syn(\text{"to that"}, e, \mathbf{p}, b, \mathbf{n}, y, \mathbf{n})$$

This is then decomposed by the metonymy axiom (2) into

$$Syn(\text{"to that"}, e, \mathbf{p}, e_1, \mathbf{n}, y_1, \mathbf{n}) \wedge rel(e_1, b)$$

The first conjunct eventually bottoms out in the predication $to'(e, e_1, y_1)$, among others. The second conjunct, the coercion relation, is established using $similar'$ (e, b, y_2). Finally y_1 and y_2 are identified using the axiom

$$(\forall e, x, y)similar'(e, x, y) \supset (\exists e_1)to'(e_1, e, y)$$

relating *similar* to the preposition used to signal its second argument.

A greatly abbreviated proof graph for this interpretation is shown in Figure 16.5. I have ignored the determiner and used dots to avoid the details of composition within NPs.

In languages that have a freer word order than English has, many of the elements displaced from their unmarked position can be treated similarly.

5   Ataxis

Bolinger (1988) discusses a number of examples of what he calls "ataxis." In

> The plane crashed with no apparent survivors.

the adjective "apparent" does not really modify "survivors," say, in contrast to *real* survivors. Rather, it is the quantifier "no" that is apparent. The meaning is that the plane crashed with apparently no survivors. In

> He held some of the most powerful men in the world at his complete mercy.

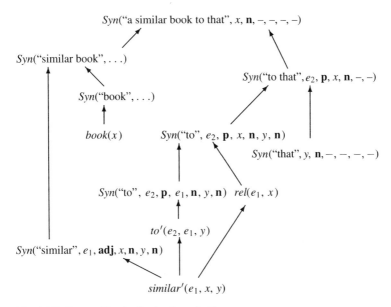

Fig. 16.5. Parse of "a similar book to that".

his mercy is not complete. Rather the holding at his mercy is complete. In

> We appreciate every automobile you ever purchased.

"every" quantifies purchases, not automobiles (and "appreciate" similarly takes purchases and not automobiles as its logical object). In the most likely reading of

> She lost her first tooth.

"first" really modifies the loss, not the tooth – she had her first loss of a tooth. Similarly, in

(5)   John smokes an occasional cigarette.

it is the smoking and not the cigarette that is occasional.

Bolinger defines ataxis as "the tendency for more routinized syntactic processes to invade the domain of less routinized ones." He talks about "migrant modifiers." In addition to the above examples, he gives a number of attested examples that sound less good but are nevertheless easily understandable.

Bolinger quotes Tommola (1978) as saying, "the listener . . . focuses his attention on the content words in the message, and interprets them in the light of normal experience, predicting and building up a representation of what the speaker intends to convey. This strategy makes it possible for him to predict the correct internal relationships between message units even independent of any syntactic structure."

He further quotes him, "Speech comprehension proceeds with fairly little direct reference to grammar as formulated by linguists."

In this paper, I take a less radical stance. Grammar is used where the meaning derived from it makes sense. However, there are other interpretive devices that can be applied when it fails to make sense. Metonymic coercion is one such device, and in an important class of applications of metonymic coercion, the coercion function is taken from the explicit content of the sentence itself, that is, from the logical form that is recognized by virtue of the "grammar as formulated by linguists." Bolinger's examples of ataxis yield to this approach.

Consider sentence (5). The adjective "occasional" requires an event for its argument, but its explicit argument is a cigarette, which is not an event. The reference to the cigarette must be coerced into a reference to an associated event. The main verb of the sentence provides that event – the smoking of the cigarette. It has the cigarette as one of its arguments, and consequently can function as the desired coercion relation.

Figure 16.6 gives a somewhat abbreviated proof graph of this interpretation. Where y is the cigarette, the nonmetonymic predication that syntax alone would give us, $occasional'(e_3, y)$, is coerced into $occasional'(e_3, e_1)$, and the coercion relation that effects this is $smoke'(e_1, j, y)$.

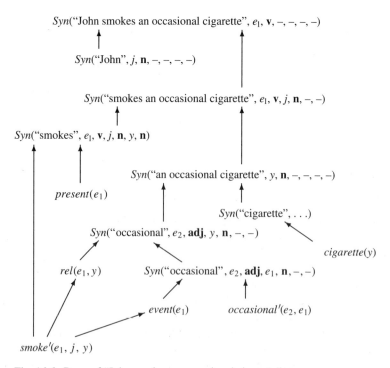

Fig. 16.6. Parse of "John smokes an occasional cigarette".

Of course, the most salient event associated with cigarettes is smoking them, regardless of the rest of the sentence, so in

> An occasional cigarette can't be harmful.

the coercion will again be to the smoking. However, this salient event is overridden in such sentences as

> John buys an occasional cigarette.
> John eats an occasional cigarette.

where the coerced events are the buying and the eating, respectively.

Bolinger's other examples yield to the same approach.

6   Container Nouns

In the sentence,

(6)   John drank a cup of coffee.

John did not drink the cup; he drank the coffee. Similarly, in the following sentences, the real participant in the action designated by the main verb is not the grammatical object (or the object of "with") but the object of the preposition "of".

> John ate a bag of potato chips.
> John bought a tank of gas.
> John visited a large number of friends last week.
> John shook hands with a group of men.

Without coercion, the relevant part of the logical form of sentence (6) would be

$$Past(e_1) \wedge drink'(e_1, j, x) \wedge cup(x) \wedge of(x, y) \wedge coffee(y)$$

That is, in the past there was a drinking event e_1 by John j of a cup x where there is an "of" relation (to be pragmatically strengthened to "contains") between x and a portion of substance y describable as coffee. The cup does not satisfy the selectional constraints on the logical object of "drink" that it must be a liquid. The "of" relation between x and y is used to coerce the logical object from x to y.

This interpretation is illustrated in Figure 16.7.

7   Distributive and Collective Readings

There are two entities associated with plural NPs – the set of entities referred to by the NP and the typical element of that set. In

> The men ran.

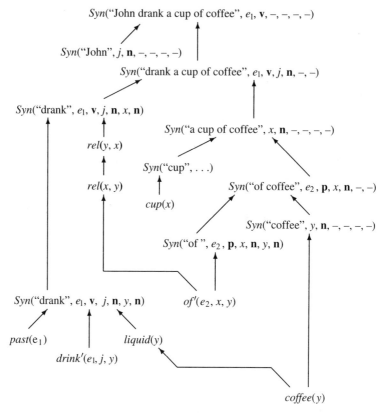

Fig. 16.7. Parse of "John drank a cup of coffee".

each individual man must run by himself, so the predicate *run* applies to the typical element. This is the distributive reading. In

The men gathered.
The men were numerous.

the predicates *gather* and *numerous* apply to the set of men. This is the collective reading of the NP. The sentence

The men lifted the piano.

is ambiguous between the two readings. They could each have lifted it individually, the distributive reading, in which case the logical subject of "lift" would be the typical element of the set, or they could have lifted it together, the collective reading, in which case it would be the set, or the aggregate.

Typical elements can be thought of as reified universally quantified variables. Their principal property is that they are typical elements of a set, represented as *typelt(x, s)*. The principal fact about typical elements is that their other properties are inherited by all the elements of the set. Functional dependencies among such elements are represented by independent predications discovered during interpretation. Difficulties involved in this approach are worked out in Hobbs (1983, 1995).

Compositional semantics in the approach taken here is strictly local, in the sense that composition rules acting at a level higher than an NP cannot reach inside the NP for information. The *Syn* predication associated with NPs only carries information about the entity referred to, and in the case of plural NPs, only about the typical element. The details of how the internal structure of NPs is analyzed will not be explicated here; it is in Hobbs (1998). Here we will only note that one of the properties made available by this analysis is the typical element property, $typelt(x, s)$. Thus, to simplify the example, we will assume that the lexical axiom for the word "men" is

$$man'(e, x) \land typelt(x, s) \supset Syn(\text{"men"}, x, \mathbf{n}, -, -, -, -)$$

That is, if e is the eventuality of x being the typical element of a set s of men, then x can be described by the word "men." We will also assume there is an axiom that says that if x is the typical element of s, then s is a set.

$$typelt(x, s) \supset set(s)$$

In cases where the collective reading is the correct one, there must be a coercion from the typical element to the set. This can be effected by using the typical element relation, $typelt(x, s)$, as the coercion relation. That is, distributive readings are taken as basic, and collective readings are taken as examples of metonymy.

Figure 16.8 illustrates the interpretation of "Men gathered." The predicate *gather* requires a set for its argument. The explicit subject x of the verb phrase "gathered" is the typical element of the set of men, rather than the set itself. Thus, there is a coercion, in which the predication $typelt'(x, s)$, relating x to s, is used as the instantiation of the coercion relation $rel(s, x)$.

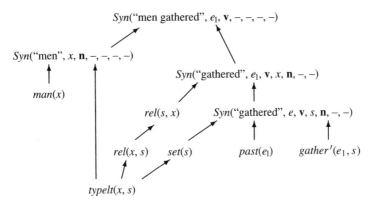

Fig. 16.8. Parse of "Men gathered".

The opposite approach could have been followed, taking the basic referent of the NP to be the set and coercing it into the typical element when the distributive reading is required. This approach is perhaps more intuitively appealing since a plural NP by itself seems to describe a set. However, in the majority of cases the distributive reading is the correct one, so the approach taken here minimizes appeals to metonymy.

8   Small Clauses in Disguise

The intended message of the sentence

(7)   This country needs literate citizens.

is not that this country is underpopulated, but that more of the population that it already has should be literate. Thus, the sentence really conveys the same message as the sentence

> This country needs its citizens to be literate.

The logical object of the *need* relation is not the set of citizens, but the eventuality of their being literate.

A teacher who says to a class whose enrollment is already determined,

> I want motivated students.

can only mean that he or she wants the students already in the class to be motivated.

Once again, this phenomenon can be viewed as an instance of metonymy where the coercion function is provided by the explicit content of the sentence itself. In particular, the word "literate" conveys a relation between the eventuality of being literate and its logical subject, the typical citizen. This relation becomes the coercion relation, coercing the logical object of "need" from the typical citizen to the literacy eventuality.

In the formal notation, the sentence initially conveys

$$need'(e_1, x, y) \land literate'(e_2, y) \land citizen(y) \land typelt(y, s)$$

The country x needs y where y is a typical citizen and is literate. After coercion, the interpretation is as follows:

$$need'(e_1, x, e_2) \land literate'(e_2, y) \land citizen(y) \land typelt(y, s)$$

Now it is the literacy of the citizens that is needed. The coercion relation between e_2 and y is provided by the predication

$$literate'(e_2, c_2)$$

This interpretation is illustrated in Figure 16.9.

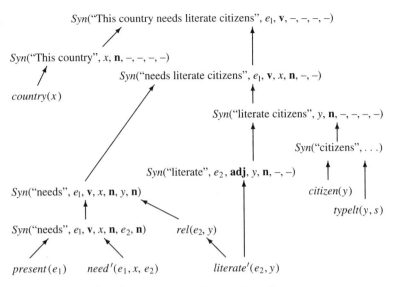

Fig. 16.9. Parse of "This country needs literate citizens".

9   Asserting Grammatically Subordinated Information

In uttering the sentence

(8)   An innocent man was hanged today.

it is quite likely that the speaker means to convey primarily not the fact of the hanging, which is probably mutually known, but rather the innocence of the victim. That is, the new information is not, as in the canonical case, the predication associated with the main verb, but a predication associated with a grammatically subordinated element, a prenominal adjective. That is the primary assertional claim of the sentence.

The logical form of the sentence, without coercion, will contain the predications

$$hang'(e_1, x, m) \wedge innocent'(e_2, m)$$

That is, e_1 is a hanging of the man m by someone x, and e_2 is m's innocence. The entire sentence would normally be described by the *Syn* predication

$$Syn(\text{"An} \quad \text{innocent} \quad \text{man} \quad \text{was} \quad \text{hanged}$$
$$\text{today"}, e_1, \mathbf{v}, -, -, -, -)$$

where the sentence is taken to be a description of the hanging event e_1.

In section 2, it was stated that in the IA framework, the job of an agent is to interpret the environment by proving abductively, or explaining, the observables in the environment, thereby establishing that the agent is in a coherent situation.

When the observable is an utterance by a speaker i to a hearer u of a string of words w, the most plausible explanation is that w is a grammatical, interpretable sentence (or an otherwise coherent text) describing an eventuality that the speaker wants the hearer to believe or to adopt some other cognitive stance toward. For the purposes of this chapter we will take the goal to be the hearer's belief. Thus, the linkage between syntax and compositional semantics, represented with *Syn* predications, and pragmatics, involving the predicates *goal* and *believe*, is effected by axioms of the following flavor:

$$Syn(w, e, \mathbf{v}, -, -, -, -) \land goal(i, e_0) \land believe'(e_0, u, e)$$
$$\supset utter(i, u, w)$$

That is, if w is a grammatical, interpretable sentence describing the eventuality e and a speaker i has the goal e_0 that a hearer u believe e to obtain, then (defeasibly) i will utter to u the string of words w. This axiom is used to explain the occurrence of the utterance.

In the case of sentence (8) the pragmatic part of the interpretation would seem to be

$$goal(i, e_0) \land believe'(e_0, u, e_1)$$

involving a belief in the hanging event, whereas what is wanted is

$$goal(i, e_0) \land believe'(e_0, u, e_2)$$

involving a belief in the innocence.

This again can be seen as an instance of metonymy where the explicit content of the sentence is used as the coercion relation. The desired top-level *Syn* predication is

$$Syn(\text{"An \quad innocent \quad man \quad was \quad hanged}$$
$$\text{today"}, e_2, \mathbf{v}, -, -, -, -)$$

indicating that the innocence is what the sentence asserts. The metonymy axiom (1) decomposes this into

$$Syn(\text{"An \quad innocent \quad man \quad was \quad hanged}$$
$$\text{today"}, e_1, \mathbf{v}, -, -, -, -) \land rel(e_2, e_1)$$

The first conjunct is proved as it is normally, yielding the parse tree and the logical form of the sentence. The transitivity of *rel* decomposes the second conjunct into

$$rel(e_2, m) \land rel(m, e_1)$$

The first conjunct is established using *innocent'*(e_2, m), and the second conjunct is established using *hang'*(e_1, x, m) and the symmetricity of *rel*.

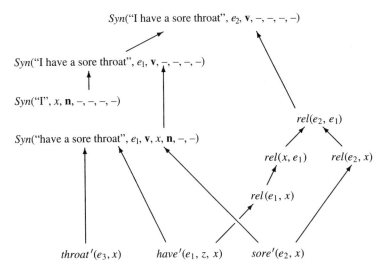

Fig. 16.10. Interpretation of "I have a sore throat".

In a sense, we have coerced the sentence "An innocent man was hanged today" into the sentence "The man who was hanged today was innocent."

Similarly, in

(9)   I have a sore throat.

it is not the possession of a throat that is being asserted, but the soreness of the throat the hearer already knows the speaker has. This can be viewed as an instance of metonymy as well. The explicit assertion of the sentence, the possession, is coerced into the soreness of what is possessed. The possession is related to the throat and the throat is related to the soreness, both by properties that are explicit in the logical form of the sentence and are thus emminently accessible.

This example requires that both possession and soreness be possible coercion relations, that is, instances of axiom schema (4):

$$have'(e_1, z, x) \supset rel(e_1, x)$$
$$sore'(e_2, x) \supset rel(e_2, x)$$

These coercion relations compose through the transitivity and symmetricity of *rel*.

Figure 16.10 shows an abbreviated version of the proof graph for the interpretation of example (9). The having e_1 is taken as the eventuality conveyed by the verb phrase, but that is coerced into the soreness e_2, using as a coercion relation a composite of the having and the soreness.

The sentence "I have a sore throat" is coerced into the sentence "My throat is sore."

These two examples used Metonymy Axiom (1). The eventuality is coerced, rather than one of its arguments.

I have not said what constraint forces this coercion, but it could be the constraint that what is said should be informative, an instance of the more general principle that one does not usually have the goal to achieve a state that already holds.

A similar story can be told about examples in which high stress changes what is asserted or alters our interpretation of predicate-argument structure. For example, in

> John introduced Bill to MARY.

the assertional claim of the sentence is "It was Mary that John introduced Bill to." In

> John didn't introduce Bill to MARY.
> John only introduced Bill to SUE.

the high stress forces a coercion of the arguments of *not* and *only* from the e such that $introduce'(e, j, b, m)$ to the e_0 such that $Mary'(e_0, m)$. It was not Mary that John introduced Bill to. It was only Sue that John introduced Bill to.

High stress indicates new information, and the new information in a sentence is generally what the speaker wants the hearer to believe. The coercion is one way to bring the intonation and the rest of the interpretation into correspondence with one another. Similarly, in example (8) the word "innocent" is likely to be given high stress.

In Hobbs (1995), it is shown how a similar move is a key part of an account of how the correct interpretation of monotone-decreasing quantifiers can be extracted from a flat logical form. Essentially, the sentence "Few men work" is reinterpreted as "The men who work are few."

10   Conclusion

Metonymy is a pervasive phenomenon, and metonymic interpretation is a powerful interpretive device. In generation, it can be used to achieve economy of expression wherever a sufficiently salient coercion relation will yield an unambiguous interpretation. Among the most salient relations are those provided by the explicit content of the text itself. Allowing these as possible coercions, we see how a combination of syntax, compositional semantics, and metonymic interpretation can explain a diverse set of supposedly syntactic phenomena.

The examples discussed in this chapter all lie on the boundaries between syntax, semantics, and pragmatics. That they all yield to the same solution illustrates the utility of a framework in which the three areas are modelled in a uniform fashion.

Acknowledgments

This research was funded by the National Science Foundation under Grant Number IRI-9304961 (Integrated Techniques for Generation and Interpretation) and Grant Number IRI-9619126 (Multimodal Access to Spatial Data).

References

Bolinger, D. 1988. Ataxis. In Rokko Linguistic Society (ed.), *Gendai no Gengo Kenkyu (Linguistics Today)*, Tokyo, Kinseido, pp. 1–17.

Hobbs, J.R. 1983. An Improper Treatment of Quantification in Ordinary English. *Proc. 21st Annual Meeting, Association for Computational Linguistics*, Cambridge, Massachusetts, pp. 57–63.

Hobbs, J.R. 1985. Ontological Promiscuity. *Proc. 23rd Annual Meeting of the Association for Computational Linguistics*, Chicago, Illinois, pp. 61–69.

Hobbs, J.R. 1995. Monotone Decreasing Quantifiers in a Scope-Free Logical Form. In K. van Deemter and S. Peters (eds.), *Semantic Ambiguity and Underspecification*, CSLI Lecture Notes No. 55, Stanford, California, pp. 55–76.

Hobbs, J.R. 1998. *The Syntax of English in an Abductive Framework*, manuscript.

Hobbs, J.R. Stickel, M., Appelt, D., and Martin, P. 1993. Interpretation as Abduction. *Artificial Intelligence* 63: 1–2, 69–142.

Nunberg, G. 1995. Transfers of Meaning. *Journal of Semantics* 12: 109–132.

Pollard, C., and Sag, I. A. 1994. *Head-Driven Phrase Structure Grammar*, University of Chicago Press and CSLI Publications.

Tommola, J. 1978. Expectancy and Speech Comprehension. In V. Kohonen and N.E. Enkvist (eds.), *Text Linguistics, Cognitive Learning and Language Teaching*, Suomen Sovelletun Kielitieteen Yhdistyksen (AFinLA) Julkaisuja, No. 22, Turku, Finland, 49–69.

17 Generative Lexicon Meets Corpus Data: The Case of Nonstandard Word Uses

ADAM KILGARRIFF

Abstract

There are various ways to evaluate the *Generative Lexicon* (GL). One is to see to what extent it accounts for what we find in text corpora. This has not previously been done, and this chapter presents a first foray. The experiment looks at the 'nonstandard' uses of words found in a sample of corpus data: "nonstandard" is defined as not matching a literal reading of any of the word's dictionary definitions. For each nonstandard instance we asked whether it could be analyzed using GL strategies. Most cases could not. The chapter discusses in detail a number of nonstandard uses and presents a model for their interpretation that draws on large quantities of knowledge about how the word has been used in the past. The knowledge is frequently indeterminate between "lexical" and "general," and is usually triggered by collocations rather than a single word in isolation.

1 Introduction

The GL claims to be a general theory of the lexicon. Pustejovsky identifies "the creative uses of words in novel contexts" (Pustejovsky, 1995, p. 1) as one of two central issues which GL addresses, where other formal theories have remained silent. He asserts as a principle that "a clear notion of semantic well-formedness will be necessary in order to characterise a theory of possible word meaning" (*ibid*, p. 6) and identifies a generative lexicon as a framework in which a core set of word senses is used to generate a larger set, according to a set of generative devices. Most work in the GL tradition has been concerned to identify and formally specify those devices.

This suggests a method for evaluating the theory against corpus data. If GL is a good general theory, then all meanings of all words as found in the corpus will be in principle analyzable according to the methods characteristic of GL. A GL analysis of a nonstandard meaning of a word takes the word's base meaning and applies one or more of the generative devices to give the nonstandard meaning. Given the youth of GL theory, one would not expect all varieties of the devices to be specified, so we would not expect every nonstandard word use to be analyzable according to one of the meaning-composing operations already discussed in the literature. Nonetheless, it is generally possible to say whether a nonstandard use

312

is related to a standard use in a way which would fall under some process of composition, if the catalog of processes were complete.

2 Polysemy (in the Lexicon) and Nonstandard Uses (in the Corpus)

The GL makes two sets of predictions, and in this section they are distinguished, the better to focus on the one that is the topic of this chapter.

Pustejovsky (1995) introduces the GL with reference to a set of sentence-pairs such as

> The glass **broke**.
> John **broke** the glass.

He then argues that earlier approaches to the lexicon had no option but to treat these two types of uses of "break" as distinct senses, not only for "break" but also for all the other ergative verbs, so missing a generalization and making the lexicon far bulkier than it need be. By contrast, in the GL, "break" is underspecified for transitivity, no duplication of senses is required, and the lexicon is more compact. This suggests a lexicon-based method for empirical evaluation of the GL: given the set of pairs of two senses of the same word in a pre-existing dictionary, how much of the time can the relation between the two be accounted for by the GL? This is a question of great interest for the GL, and has been investigated at some length in (Buitelaar, 1997; Butielaar, 1998).[1] If it is the predictions of the GL for polysemy that are to be scrutinized, then a lexicon or dictionary is the appropriate object to investigate.

The GL also makes predictions about how words may be used, which go beyond anything listed in existing lexicons. A "theory of possible word meaning" will account for novel uses of words. To investigate the coverage of the GL in relation to these, we need to look in a corpus.

3 What is Nonstandard Use?

To test whether GL accounts for novel word uses, we must first identify a set of them. This involves distinguishing standard and nonstandard uses of words.

"Standard" and "nonstandard" are loaded terms. A "standard" case tends to be the kind of case that a particular theory has a vested interest in. Textbook examples of sense extension or logical polysemy simply assert that one use of the word is "standard," another is "extended" or similar. For our task, such a relaxed strategy is not viable. Identifying "standard" or "central" or "core" or 'prototypical' uses of a word is an arduous and challenging intellectual task for anyone – linguist or lexicographer – whose job it is to do it in a principled and systematic way.

---

[1] See also the close study of sense pairs in (Kilgarriff, 1993).

The standard/nonstandard distinction must not be confused with productive uses of language. Consider the use of "see" to mean 'understand.' There is a substantial literature on the productive or semi-productive process underlying the meaning transfer (Lakoff and Johnson, 1980; Sweetser, 1990) yet there is nothing non-standard about the use of "see" in "I see what you mean." Conversely, 'productive' implies a rule, so to assume that all nonstandard uses were productive would be to prejudge the issue that the experiment sets out to test.

The current experiment calls for an operational definition of '(non)standard'. The only possibility the author is aware of is to use an existing dictionary. We then classify any corpus occurrence that fits a dictionary definition of the word as 'standard', and misfits are classified as 'nonstandard'.

This may seem unpalatable. Dictionaries are imperfect artifacts, produced for particular markets, under time constraints, by teams of people some of whom are more skilled than others. Any two dictionaries will differ in the meanings they say words have at innumerable points. All of this sets them at a great distance from the theoretical realm GL inhabits and makes them seem clumsy tools for evaluating the theory.

It also may be objected that a dictionary is too detailed, or too coarse-grained, for the current exercise. It may be objected that a dictionary is too detailed because it specifies, as separate senses, those productive uses that the GL would explain as the outcome of generative processes. But this objection misses the mark because, as discussed above, the experiment aims to look at nonstandard uses, not the polysemy question. The divide between the two issues will be redrawn by the selection of a dictionary but both questions remain, and the nonstandard uses, according to a particular dictionary, still remain a valid dataset regarding which we can ask, *are they accounted for by the GL?*

A dictionary may be too coarse-grained because it sweeps two uses into a single sense where it is the achievement of the GL to explain the difference between the two readings. Thus, "enjoy" can take a verb phrase ("enjoy doing something") or a noun phrase denoting an event ("enjoy the party") or a noun phrase denoting a physical object with an associated telic reading ("enjoy the paper"), and the GL analysis demonstrates how the third is implicit in the first, given the appropriate lexical entries and coercion mechanisms. However, dictionaries do not specify the three distinct readings as separate senses. In general, it may frequently be the case that the grain-size assumed in GL work is too fine to be spotted by strategies using dictionaries. A different methodology would be required to investigate how many phenomena there were in a corpus sample that **were** susceptible to GL analysis.

Many of the distinctions that the GL provides analyses for will fall through the net of the dictionaries' senses. However, that does not invalidate the ones that are caught by the net, as a suitable dataset for the experiment. Some alternations that have received GL analyses do also give rise to distinct senses in dictionaries. For example the 'container' and 'containee' readings of "cup" are each assigned their own sense in (LDOCE, 1995). Moreover, if the GL is a general theory of the lexicon, it should account for novelty whether or not the novelty was closely related to existing GL analyses.

Close reading of definitions from a published dictionary does not provide an ideal method for distinguishing standard from nonstandard uses of words. However, the method has no fundamental flaws, and there is no better method available.

4   Experimental Design

The design was as follows:

- take a sample of words
- take a set of corpus instances for each
- choose a dictionary
- sense-tag
- identify **mismatches** to dictionary senses
- determine whether they fit the GL model

The materials used for the experiment were available from another project. This was SENSEVAL (Kilgarriff and Palmer, forthcoming), an evaluation exercise for Word Sense Disambiguation programs, which needed a set of correctly disambiguated corpus instances to evaluate against. The HECTOR lexical database (Atkins, 1993) was used. It comprises a dictionary of several hundred words and a corpus in which all the occurrences of those words have been manually sense-tagged by professional lexicographers.

For Pilot SENSEVAL, the corpus instances were tagged twice more (again by professional lexicographers), and where the taggers disagreed the data was sent to an arbiter. The taggings thereby attained were 95% replicable (Kilgarriff, 1999; Kilgarriff and Plamer, forthcoming).[2]

4.1   Sample of Words

In most GL work, words to be studied have been hand-selected according to the interests and hypotheses of the researcher. For a study such as this (and indeed any study that explores the viability of the GL as a general theory of the lexicon) it is essential to approach sampling more systematically. A random sample of the words available in the HECTOR dictionary was used.[3] The words investigated were "modest," "disability," "steering," "seize," "sack" (noun), "sack" (verb), "onion," "rabbit," also "handbag" (taken from a different dataset).

---

[2] We are most grateful to Oxford University Press for permission to use the Hector database, and to the UK EPSRC for the grant that supported the manual re-tagging of the data.

[3] The approach to sampling of which this was a degenerate version is described in detail in (Kilgarriff, 1998a).

4.2   Sample of Corpus Instances

The HECTOR corpus is a 20-million word corpus comprising mainly journalism, books, and magazines. It was a pilot for the British National Corpus, and some of the data is shared with the BNC. Around two hundred corpus instances per word were randomly selected from all the HECTOR data available. The exact number of corpus lines per word varied according to the BNC frequency of the word, its level of polysemy, and the number of its corpus lines that turned out to be personal names, of the wrong word class, or otherwise anomalous. There were usually two sentences of context available, the sentence containing the word and the preceding one, but occasionally more and occasionally less, depending on the structures available in HECTOR.

4.3   Dictionary

The HECTOR dictionary was produced in tandem with the sense-tagging of the HECTOR corpus, so the HECTOR dictionary entries are probably more closely tied to the corpus evidence than any published dictionary. Only a sample of several hundred entries were prepared, and they were never polished and double-checked for publication. The entries include more examples than standard dictionaries, and provide more explicit information on lexico-grammatical patterning.

4.4   Sense-Tagging

The basic task was to assign each corpus instance for a word to one (or more) of the meanings in the HECTOR dictionary entry for that word. The task had been done once already prior to SENSEVAL and was done twice more for SENSEVAL. The options available to the taggers were:

- simple assignment of one sense
- more than one sense, e.g., "1" or "2"
- sense plus suffix: suffixes were:
    - P for proper-name use, e.g., "Peter Rabbit"
    - A or N for adjectival or nominal use of a sense that wasn't standardly adjectival/nominal
    - M for metaphorical or metonymic use
    - X for other exploitations of the sense
    - ? for awkward and unclear cases
- T, P, U for Typographical errors, Proper names (where the use is not also a regular use of the word – cf. the P suffix) or Unassignable

Some words were easy and quick, others hard and slow. The average time taken was one minute per citation.

4.5   *Identify Mismatches*

For this experiment, it was necessary to identify all those cases that were not covered by literal readings of dictionary entries. We took all those instances where there was anything less than complete agreement by all three taggers on a single, simple sense (e.g., without suffixes) and re-examined them. That is, all those cases where there was any disagreement, or where there were suffixes, or where there were disjunctive answers, were re-analysed. This cast the net wide, and in some cases over half the data was re-examined. Each of these cases was then classified as standard or non-standard by the author.

4.6   *GL?*

For the nonstandard cases, the author then also assessed whether a GL-style analysis might plausibly apply.

5   Examples

Different words behaved in different ways, and in this section we make some comments on each of the words in turn. A number of corpus citations are provided, as that serves to demonstrate the nature of the exercise and the sensitivities required for the analysis of nonstandard word use.

The numbers in brackets following each word give, first, the number of corpus instances that were re-examined specifically for this exercise, and second, the complete sample size for the word.

5.1   *modest (164/270)*

The HECTOR lexicographers had split the meaning of "modest" between nine senses, in contrast to 3 (CIDE, 1995), 4 (LDOCE, 1995), or 5 (COBUILD, 1995) in other dictionaries. There was a high degree of overlap, and the sense distinctions could not be drawn sharply. (This supports findings in other exercises that this is characteristic of adjectives: They can be assigned to a wide range of nouns, sometimes more literally, sometimes less so, but it is the meaning of the modified noun that determines the sense of the adjective. Where the nouns do not fall into neat categories, nor will the adjective senses.)

Faced with this indeterminacy, the taggers often gave disjunctive or different answers. However, in none of the 164 cases of nonagreement was it appropriate to classify the corpus instance as a nonstandard use of the word.

5.2   *disability (29/160)*

HECTOR distinguished two senses, one 'medical,' for physical or mental disabilities, the other for anything nonmedical. However, the nonmedical, residual sense was marked 'chiefly legal.' This seems a lexicographic error, as most of the non-medical instances in the corpus were not legal either: the lexicographer should identify the technical, legal sense as distinct, and provide a third, residual sense for instances such as:

> Satie may well have lacked accomplishment, but like all major artists he managed to turn his **disabilities** to account.

The cases re-examined were either of this type, or names such as "Disability Alliance," which were clearly both the medical sense, and (parts of) names.

5.3   *steering (16/177)*

There were two senses in HECTOR:

- the activity e.g., "his steering was careless" vs.
- the mechanism e.g., "they overhauled the steering"

These are metonymically related. Most of the sixteen re-examined corpus instances were simple cases of underspecification, e.g.,

> it has the Peugeot's steering feel

One more complex case was:

> After nearly fifty years [as a bus driver] Mr. Hannis stepped down from behind the steering wheel

This is of interest because it makes passing reference to the idiomatic reading of "behind the steering wheel" in which it means 'to be the driving force behind (an organization).' Had Mr. Hannis's occupation been not bus-driving but managerial, the instance would have been clearly idiomatic. As it is, the sentence carries traces of both the literal and idiomatic readings.

5.4   *seize (53/259)*

HECTOR gives 10 'senses' for "seize" (excluding phrasal verbs). On closer inspection, it would seem that these 'senses' are better interpreted as features, as they are not exclusive and frequently co-occur. The HECTOR labels for the first five senses are 'grab,' 'hostage,' 'confiscate,' 'possess/invade,' 'opportunity.' These are all aspects of the meaning of "seize," which might or might not be evident in a particular instance. Most of the re-examined cases were ones where more than one feature was salient, and the taggers had given two senses and/or given different ones. In

> [He] slipped out of the hands of the two [gangsters] who had seized him

both HOSTAGE and GRAB are salient. In

> Bruges Group Tory MPs claimed victory last night after seizing all the top places on the backbench European affairs committee

both OPPORTUNITY and POSSESS/INVADE are present. (OPPORTUNITY is implicitly present in a high proportion of instances: replacing "seize" by "seize the opportunity (to take)" would not, in most cases, change the meaning.)

Lexical semantics may seem a politically neutral territory but this is not always so. Consider

> ... examine charges that Israeli soldiers were intimidating local residents. Al-Haq, a human rights organisation on the West Bank, charged soldiers with non-registration of property seized, assault and tearing up identity cards.

If your sympathies are with the Israelis, this is CONFISC. If they are with the Palestinians, it is POSSESS/INVADE.

Research of this kind cannot readily be done by anyone who is not a native speaker, and it is also as well if the researcher is from the same culture as the intended readership. Consider

> Tolley drove uppishly at a half-volley and was caught at short mid-wicket; Lord, cutting without due care, was seized at gully off Tim Wren

Enquiries of people who are not British[4] are met with blank stares. The context is of course cricket, and what happened was that the ball was caught. (The object of "seize" is "Lord", who hit the ball that was caught. The relation between the ball and Lord is metonymic. The cricket use of "catch X" where X is a player is a distinct sense in LDOCE3 and CIDE, the complication here being that the verb is not "catch" but "seize".)

5.5   sack/v (5/178)

Four of the five re-examined cases were errors. The fifth,

> And Labour MP, Mr Bruce George, has called for the firm to be **sacked** from duty at Prince Andrew's £5 million home at Sunningwell Park near Windsor.

is nonstandard because the CEASE-EMPLOYING meaning of "sack" is specified in HECTOR as taking a person as its direct object. Here, the object is the company. This is an instance that the GL could in principle account for.

5.6   sack/n (7/82)

The instances re-examined were typing errors, two instances of "sack race,"[5] one instance with insufficient context to determine the sense, and one non-standard use

---

[4] Nor from the West Indies, the Indian subcontinent, Australia, New Zealand, or South Africa, one might suppose.

[5] A kind of race in which the contestants stand in a sack, which they hold around their waist, and hop; usually encountered at school sports days and village fêtes.

based on a metaphor:

> Santa Claus Ridley pulled another doubtful gift from his sack.

(Ridley is a British politician.)

5.7   *handbag (30/715)*

The "handbag" data has a different origin: the British National Corpus. It was analysed as part of a different study, reported in (Kilgarriff, 1998b) with goals similar to the current exercise. Thirty nonstandard instances were found, comprising metaphors, handbag-as-Thatcher's-symbol, handbags-as-weapons, the idiom "dance round your handbag," and exploitations of the idiom in the sublanguage of nightclubs, where "handbag" denotes a music genre. There was just one instance that potentially supported a GL analysis:

> She moved from handbags through gifts to the flower shop

("Handbags" denotes the handbag department of a department store.)

5.8   *onion (34/214)*

The lexical entry distinguishes PLANT onions from VEGETABLE onions, and ten of the re-examined cases bridged that distinction, e.g.:

> Plant the sets two inches apart in rows 10 inches apart to produce a good yield of medium-sized onions.

There was a simile and a metaphor, in which a speeding tennis ball is likened to an onion. Other anomalies included instances in which onion and derivatives were being used as medicine, as a decorative feature, and for dying. In each case, neither the PLANT nor the VEGETABLE sense was more applicable than the other.
In

> It's not all frogs legs and strings of onions in the South of France

we have a cliché of Frenchness rather than a vegetable, and in

> In Leicestershire, machine drivers have their own names for river plants, such as 'water onions' for the true bulrush

the occurrence belongs to a sublanguage and is signalled as such.
For purposes of counting numbers, just the tennis ball metaphor and the 'water onions' were counted as nonstandard, though clearly other decisions could have been made.

5.9   *rabbit (52/224)*

This was the most fecund of the words. First, the word enters into a large number of names, and these accounted for half the instances re-examined. There were:

- Rabbit (Winnie the Pooh's friend)
- Peter Rabbit
- Crusader Rabbit
- Brer Rabbit
- (Who framed) Roger Rabbit
- The White Rabbit
- Care For Your Rabbit (book title)
- Super Rabbit:

    > Now Oxfordshire grain growers are facing a new enemy, the Super Rabbit. Super Rabbit is different from anything ever seen before in the county because he seems pretty well indestructible.

- Sumo Rabbit and His Inescapable Trap of Doom (song title)

"Rabbit" also brought the issue of representations to the fore. HECTOR included a *toy* sense of rabbit, which might seem an innocent choice. However the data included

> Some people learn by watching videos of the great players, Borg, McEnroe, Navratilova, and Evert. I thought it would be fun to make Monica an animated film of a rabbit playing tennis set to music, and this was a success.

> It contains three drawings of Cecily Parsley, the rabbit innkeeper, a hand-painted Christmas card and two amateurish Lake District views.

> Playboy was described as a pleasure-primer, its symbol was a rabbit and its bait was the Playmate of the month, the girl who was unfolded in the center wearing a staple through her navel but not much else.

> Marie Holmes as the nervy Piglet, John Nolan as the garrulous Owl, and Judy Eden as the troublesome Rabbit all perform competently, and Anne Belton, as Kanga, fusses in matronly fashion over young Roo (Jonathan Eden) and the other animals.

To try to unpick just this last example: there was a toy rabbit, belonging to Christopher Robin, called Rabbit. Christopher Robin's father, A. A. Milne, wrote stories about Rabbit in which he imputed to it some TOY- and some ANIMAL-properties. The books of the stories were published and became popular and now have been turned into a play so a person (Judy Eden) now "pretends" to be this TOY-ANIMAL individual.

"Rabbit" also supports a number of conventionalized metaphors and collocations with both literal and metaphorical meanings: "frightened rabbits," "froze like rabbits," "running like rabbits," "rabbit holes, hutches" and "warrens" all occurred in the data. Only "rabbit warren" was explicitly mentioned in HECTOR.

There are several instances that allude to magicians pulling rabbits out of their hats:

> The violins waved and swayed like cornstalks in the wind. The drummer, white haired, might have been a conjuror drawing **rabbits** from his instrument's interior.

This is a distinct sense in the HECTOR entry, so the instances are allocated to it and correspondingly classified as standard.

6   Results

Of 2276 corpus instances examined, there were 390 where the lexicographers had not all agreed on the same unique tag in the first pass. Of these, on closer examination 41 instances were found to be nonstandard word uses. Thus just under 2% of the corpus instances were nonstandard.

Of these, just two, or 5%, were plausible candidates for GL treatment.

The quantitative results are presented in Table 17.1.

Table 17.1. *Experimental results, showing, for each word, the size of the dataset (Sample), the number of instances re-examined (Re-ex), the number of those which were classified as nonstandard uses (NS) and the number of those which were plausibly accounted for by GL analyses (GL)*

Word	Sample	Re-ex	NS	GL
modest	270	164	0	0
disability	160	29	0	0
steering	177	16	0	0
seize	259	53	0	0
sack/n	178	5	1	1
sack/v	82	7	1	0
onion	214	34	2	0
rabbit	224	52	7	0
handbag	712	30	30	1
TOTALS	2276	390	41	2

7   Discussion

The exercise puts the spotlight on the dictionary as much as on the words. Many readers will have granted the argument of section 3 that a published dictionary had to be used for this exercise, but may now feel this argument must have been flawed and that there must be a more tolerable strategy than working to the vagaries of one particular dictionary. The author can only agree that it would be nice if there were one.[6]

41 of the 2276 instances in the dataset were identified as nonstandard, and just two of these – the "handbag department" use of "handbags" and the use of verbal "sack" with a company rather than an individual as object – were identified as candidates for GL-style analysis. As is evident from the examples, another analyst would probably not have arrived at identical figures, but they would, in all likelihood, have pointed to the same conclusion: GL analyses will only ever account for a small proportion of nonstandard word uses.

The evidence points to the similarity between the lexicographer's task, when s/he classifies the word's meaning into distinct senses, and the analyst's when s/he classifies instances as standard or nonstandard. The lexicographer asks him/herself, "is this pattern of usage sufficiently distinct from other uses, and well-enough embedded in the common knowledge of speakers to count as a distinct sense?" The analyst asks him/herself, "is this instance sufficiently distinct from the listed senses to count as nonstandard?" Both face the same confounding factors: metaphors, at word-, phrase-, sentence- or even discourse-level; uses of words in names and in sublanguage expressions; underspecification and overlap between meanings; word combinations that mean roughly what one would expect if the meaning of the whole were simply the sum of the meanings of the parts, but which carry some additional connotation.

7.1   Lexicon or Pragmatics?

For many of the nonstandard instances, an appropriate model must contain both par-ticular knowledge about some nonstandard interpretation, and reasoning to make

---

[6] Some GL literature (e.g., (Copestake and Briscoe, 1996)) points to co-predication and related am-biguity tests as a way of identifying the distinct senses. The proposal is explored at some length in (Kilgarriff, 1998b). It suffers from numerous drawbacks. First, there is simply no inventory of senses available, which has been developed according to these criteria. Second, different speakers very often disagree on the acceptability of the test sentences. Thirdly, the relation between evidence from co-predication tests and the pretheoretical notion of a word sense is far from clear. (Cruse, 1986) argues that the tests are criterial for the notion of a distinct sense, but his methods are not based on corpus or lexicographic evidence or systematic sampling of the lexicon and bear no relation to lexicographic practice. (Geeraerts, 1993) presents a critique of the logic of the tests. Experiments to explore the relation between linguists' ambiguity tests and lexicographers' polysemy judgments are currently underway.

the nonstandard interpretation fit the current context. The "particular knowledge" can be lexical, nonlexical, or indeterminate. Consider

> Alpine France is dominated by new brutalist architecture: stacked rabbit hutches reaching into the sky . . .

In this case, the particular knowledge, shared by most native speakers, is that

- 'rabbit hutch' is a collocation
- rabbit hutches are small boxes
- to call a human residence a rabbit hutch is to imply that it is uncomfortably small

The first time one hears a building, office, flat, or room referred to as a rabbit hutch, some general-purpose interpretation process (which may well be conscious) is needed.[7] But thereafter, the BUILDING reading is familiar. Future encounters will make reference to earlier ones. This can be seen as the **general** knowledge that buildings and rooms, when small and cramped, are like rabbits' residences, or as the **lexical** knowledge that "hutch" or "rabbit hutch" can describe buildings and rooms, with a connotation of 'cramped.'

It is the compound "rabbit hutch" rather than "hutch" alone that triggers the nonstandard reading. Setting the figurative use aside, "rabbit hutch" is a regular, compositional compound and there is little reason for specifying it in a dictionary. Hutches are, typically, for housing rabbits so, here again, the knowledge about the likely co-occurrence of the words can be seen as general or lexical. (The intonation contour implies it is stored in the mental lexicon.)

That hutches are small boxes is also indeterminate between lexical and general knowledge. It can be seen as the definition of "hutch," hence lexical, or as based on familiarity with pet rabbit residences, hence general.

To bring all this knowledge to bear in the current context requires an act of visual imagination: to see an alpine resort as a stack of rabbit hutches.

A different sort of nonstandard use is:

> Santa Claus Ridley pulled another doubtful gift from his sack.

Here, the required knowledge is that Santa Claus has gifts in a sack that he gives out and this is a cause for rejoicing. There is less that is obviously lexical in this case, though gifts and sacks play a role in defining the social construct, 'Santa', and it is the co-occurrence of "Santa Claus," "gifts," and "sack" which triggers the figurative interpretation.

---

[7] As ever, there are further complexities. "Hutch" and "warren" are both rabbit-residence words that are also used pejoratively to imply that buildings, etc., are cramped. A speaker who is familiar with this use of "warren" but not of "hutch" may well, in their first encounter with this use of "hutch," interpret by analogy with "warren" rather than interpreting from scratch (whatever that may mean).

As with "rabbit hutch," the figure is not fresh. We have previously encountered ironic attributions of "Santa Claus" or "Father Christmas" to people who are giving things away. Interpretation is eased by this familiarity.

In the current context, Ridley is mapped to Santa Claus, and his sack to the package of policies or similar.

These examples have been used to illustrate three themes that apply to almost all the nonstandard uses encountered:

1. Nonstandard uses generally build on similar uses, as previously encountered
2. It is usually a familiar combination of words which triggers the nonstandard interpretation
3. The knowledge of the previously encountered uses of the words is very often indeterminate between 'lexical' and 'general.'

Any theory that relies on a distinction between general and lexical knowledge will founder.

7.2 Lexicon Size

The lexicon is rife with generalization. From generalizations about transitive verbs, to the generalization that "hutch" and "warren" are both rabbit residences, they permeate it, and the facts about a word that cannot usefully be viewed as an instance of a generalization are vastly outnumbered by those that can. GL aims to capture generalizations about words.

Given an appropriate inheritance framework, once a generalization has been captured, it need only be stated once, and inherited: It does not need to be stated at every word where it applies. So a strategy for capturing generalizations, coupled with inheritance, will tend to make the lexicon smaller: It will take less bytes to express the same set of facts. GL is associated with a compact lexicon, in this sense.

However, a compact, or smaller, lexicon should not be confused with a small lexicon. The examples above just begin to indicate how much knowledge of previously encountered language a speaker has at his or her disposal. Almost all the nonstandard instances in the dataset call on some knowledge that we may not think of as part of the meaning of the word and that the HECTOR lexicographer did not put in the HECTOR dictionary, yet that is directly linked to previous occasions on which we have heard the word used. The sample was around 200 citations each per word: had far more been data examined, far more items of knowledge would have been found to be required for the full interpretation of the speaker's meaning.[8] The sample took in just nine words. There are tens or even hundreds

---

[8] The issue of what should count as an interpretation, or, worse, a **full** interpretation leads into heady waters (see e.g., Eco, 1992). We hope that a pretheoretical intuition of what it is for a reader or hearer to grasp what the author or speaker meant will be adequate for current purposes.

of thousands of words in an adult vocabulary. The quantity of information is immense. A compact lexicon will be smaller than it would otherwise be – but still immense.

7.3   *Quotations*

Speakers recognize large numbers of poems, speeches, songs, jokes, and other quotations. Often, the knowledge required for interpreting a nonstandard instance relates to a quotation. One of the words studied in SENSEVAL was "bury." The "bury" data included three variants of Shakespeare's "I come to bury Caesar not to praise him," as in:

> [Steffi] Graf will not be there to praise the American but to bury her . . . [9]

We know and recognize vast numbers of quotations. (I suspect most of us could recognise, if not reproduce, snatches from most top ten pop songs from our teenage years.) Without them, many non-standard word uses are not fully interpretable. This may or may not be considered lexical knowledge. Much will, and much will not, be widely shared in a speaker community: The more narrowly the speaker community is defined, the more will be shared. Many dictionaries include quotations, both for their role in the word's history and for their potential to shed light on otherwise incomprehensible uses (CIDE, 1995).

An intriguing analogy is with the memory-based learning (MBL) approach to machine learning. In MBL, all instances are retained and a new instance is classified according to the familiar instances that it most resembles. The approach has recently been shown to be well-suited to a range of natural language leaning tasks (Daelemans, van der Bosch, and Zavrel, to appear). In MBL, where numbers of instances are similar, they will contribute to future classifications jointly, so do not appear to have roles as individual recollections in memory. Exceptional instances, by contrast, play an explicit role in classification when a new instance matches. Correspondingly, for standard word uses, we do not think in terms of individual remembered occurrences at all. For instances with a touch of idiosyncrasy, like Mr. Hannis's "fifty years [. . .] behind the steering wheel," or strings of onions as a cliché of Frenchness, we probably do not but might. And for "not to praise but to bury" cases we do.

A proposal in the literature which informs this discussion is (Hanks, 1994). Hanks talks about word meaning in terms of "norms and exploitations." A word has its normal uses, and much of the time speakers simply proceed according to the norms. The norm for the word is its semantic capital, or meaning potential. However, it is always open to language users to exploit the potential, carrying

---

[9] For further details on the "Caesar" cases, and a discussion of other related issues in the SENSEVAL data, see (Krishnamurthy and Nicholls, 1999, forthcoming).

just a strand across to some new setting. The evidence encountered in the current experiment would suggest an addendum to Hanks's account: It is very often the exploitations that have become familiar in a speech community that serve as launching points for further exploitations.

In the 1995 book, Pustejovsky reviews recent work by Nunberg, and Asher and Lascarides, and draws the moral that:

> polysemy is not a monolithic phenomenon. Rather, it is the result of both compositional operations in the semantics, such as coercion and co-composition, and of contextual effects, such as the structure of rhetorical relations in discourse and pragmatic constraints on co-reference. (p. 236)

Our evidence endorses this weaker view of the role of generative devices, and adds that a prominent role in the analysis should be taken by extensive knowledge of how words have deviated from their norms before.

8   Conclusion

We have described an experiment in which the merits of GL as a general theory of the lexicon, which accounts for nonstandard uses of words, were scrutinized. The experiment looked at the nonstandard uses of words found in a sample of corpus data, and asked whether they could be analyzed using GL strategies. The finding was that most of the time, they could not.

This by no means undermines GL analyzes for the kinds of cases discussed in the GL literature. Rather, it points to the heterogeneity of the lexicon and of the processes underlying interpretation: GL is a theory for some lexical phenomena, not all.

A model of the interpretation of nonstandard word uses was sketched in which speakers and hearers have access to large quantities of knowledge of how the word (and its near-synonyms) has been used in the past. The knowledge is frequently indeterminate between "lexical" and "general," and is usually triggered by collocations rather than a single word in isolation.

There are numerous disputes in linguistics that circle around the question of storage or computation: Is the structure recalled from memory, or computed afresh each time it is encountered.[10] The GL is a theory of the lexicon that gives the starring role to computation. The evidence from this experiment is that, while complex computations are undoubtedly required, so too is a very substantial repository of specific knowledge about each word, the kinds of settings it normally occurs in, and the various ways in which those norms have been exploited in the past.

---

[10] A preliminary version of this chapter was presented at a conference entitled *Storage and Computation in Linguistics*, (in Utrecht, the Netherlands, October 1998).

References

Atkins, S. 1993. Tools for Computer-aided Lexicography: the Hector Project. *Papers in Computational Lexicography: COMPLEX '93*, Budapest.

Buitelaar, P. 1997. A Lexicon for Underspecified Semantic Tagging. In M. Light (ed.), *Tagging Text with Lexical Semantics: Why, What and How?* Washington, April. SIGLEX (Lexicon Special Interest Group) of the ACL, pp. 25–33.

Buitelaar, P. 1998. CORELEX: *Systematic Polysemy and Underspecification*, Ph.D. Thesis, Brandeis University.

CIDE. 1995. *Cambridge International Dictionary of English*. Cambridge University Press, Cambridge.

COBUILD. 1995. *The Collins COBUILD English Language Dictionary, 2nd Edition*. Edited by John McH. Sinclair, *et al.*, London.

Copestake, A., and Briscoe, E.J. 1996. Semi-productive Polysemy and Sense Extension. In J. Pustejovsky and Br. Boguraev (eds.), *Lexical Semantics: The Problem of Polysemy*. Oxford University Press, Oxford, 15–68.

Cruse, D.A. 1986. *Lexical Semantics*. Cambridge University Press, Cambridge.

Daelemans, W., van der Bosch, A., and Zavrel, J. 1999. Forgetting Exceptions is Harmful in Language Learning. *Machine Learning, Special Issue on Natural Language Learning*, 34: 11–41.

Eco, U. 1992. *Interpretation and Overinterpretation*. Cambridge University Press, Cambridge.

Geeraerts, D. 1993. Vagueness's Puzzles, Polysemy's Vagueness. *Cognitive Linguistics* 4: 223–272.

Hanks, P. 1994. Linguistic Norms and Pragmatic Exploitations or, Why Lexicographers Need Prototype Theory, and Vice Versa. In F. Kiefer, G. Kiss, and J. Pajzs (eds.), *Papers in Computational Lexicography: COMPLEX '94*, Budapest, 89–113.

Kilgarriff, A. 1993. Dictionary Word Sense Distinctions: An Enquiry into Their Nature. *Computers and the Humanities* 26: 365–387.

Kilgarriff, A. 1998a. Gold Standard Datasets for Evaluating Word Sense Disambiguation Programs. *Computer Speech and Language*, forthcoming. Special Issue on Evaluation of Speech and Language Technology, ed. R. Gaizauskas.

Kilgarriff, A. 1998b. 'I don't believe in word senses.' *Computers and the Humanities* 31: 91–113.

Kilgarriff, A. 1999. 95% Replicability for Manual Word Sense Tagging. *Proc. EACL*, Bergen, 277–278.

Kilgarriff, A., and Palmer, M. 2000. Guest editors, Special Issue on SENSEVAL: Evaluating Word Sense Disambiguation Programs. *Computers and the Humanities 34*.

Krishnamurthy, R., and Nicholls, D. 2000. Peeling an Onion: The Lexicographers' Experience of Manual Sense-tagging. *Computers and the Humanities*. Special Issue on SENSEVAL, (eds.) Adam Kilgarriff and Martha Palmer 34: 85–97.

Lakoff, G., and Johnson, M. 1980. *Metaphors We Live By*. University of Chicago Press, Chicago.

LDOCE. 1995. *Longman Dictionary of Contemporary English, 3rd Edition*. Ed. Longman, Harlow.

Pustejovsky, J. 1995. *The Generative Lexicon*. MIT Press, Cambridge.

Sweetser, E. 1990. *From Etymology to Pragmatics: Metaphorical and Cultural Aspects of Semantic Structure*. Cambridge University Press, Cambridge.

PART IV

Building Resources

18   Introduction

FEDERICA BUSA AND PIERRETTE BOUILLON

The goal of this part of the volume is best explained by the recent interest in evaluating which lexical semantics resources are available for Natural Language Processing (NLP) and whether a methodology can be established for building large-scale semantic knowledge-bases.[1]

The papers address the topic of understanding and structuring word meaning from the particular perspective of building NLP systems. Here, the problem of how to represent word meaning has fairly strict requirements: It affects the choice of particular data structure as well as the specific architectural requirements for a computational lexicon.

All of the contributions in this section present practical questions and dilemmas that are not usually faced in theoretical research. The first issue is one of methodology: Can existing semantic resources (viz. ontologies) be reproduced by identifying a consistent set of criteria? This is an important question, because a positive answer would mean that we have achieved an understanding of how to model conceptual knowledge independently of domains and people's intuitions.

The second issue is whether existing lexical semantics frameworks provide the basis for developing a large-scale resource on systematic grounds. Although related to previous question this problem is also relevant to the notion of "scalability." In other words, if a particular framework makes certain claims about how meaning should be structured to account for a limited number of linguistic facts, is the suggested structuring sufficiently general to cover a large corpus? Furthermore, were that corpus to become even larger, would the lexicon scale up easily to cover the newer data? More or less explicit answers are found in the different contributions.

Finally, the papers that follow are also concerned with establishing the boundary between lexical knowledge and world knowledge. In particular, lexicon design requires criteria that allow for a systematic structuring of information in both domain specific and general lexicons. In absence of such criteria, the designer is left to his/her own intuitions.

---

[1] The reader who is most familiar with the field may have guessed the implicit reference to the European EAGLES effort in the domain of lexical semantics and most recently its American offspring. EAGLES stands for Expert Advisory Group on Language Engineering Standard. It is funded by the European Commission with the goal of establishing standards in different areas of NLP: morphosyntax, syntax, speech, lexical semantics, and evaluation.

Federica Busa, Nicoletta Calzolari, and Alessandro Lenci elaborate on such foundations in the context of building the SIMPLE architecture. Nilda Ruimy, Elisabetta Gola, and Monica Monachini discuss more specific issues tackled in developing the SIMPLE model. Finally, Piek Vossen presents an alternative architecture: the EuroWordNet project.

The three contributions in this section describe general purpose resources that can be used in a variety of NLP tasks. What remains an open-ended question is whether such general purpose lexicons and ontologies are actually useful and usable when they are constructed independently of specific NLP applications. This will remain a controversial and unanswered question to be verified once these knowledge resources will become available.

19 Generative Lexicon and the SIMPLE Model: Developing Semantic Resources for NLP

FEDERICA BUSA, NICOLETTA CALZOLARI,
AND ALESSANDRO LENCI

Abstract

In this paper, we present recent extensions of *Generative Lexicon theory* (Pustejovsky, 1995; Pustejovsky, 1998) in the context of the development of large-scale lexical resources for twelve different European languages: the SIMPLE model.

The development of lexical resources must be guided by an underlying framework for structuring word meaning and generating concepts, which satisfies both ontological considerations as well as the need to capture linguistic generalizations. The model presented here is a proposal toward this goal.

1 Introduction[1]

The development of formal frameworks for computational lexical semantics should respond to two needs: capturing the richness of language as revealed in both meaning variation and systematic polysemy, and providing a viable and testable model for building large-scale lexical resources for natural language processing.

In this paper, we address these topics from the dual perspective of theory and applications. The theoretical aspect motivates a generative framework for structuring and generating concepts. The practical aspect focuses on the implementation of the GL-based framework within the EU-sponsored SIMPLE project,[2] which involves the development of harmonized large-scale semantic lexicons (10,000 word senses) for twelve different languages.

Such a task has tackled questions that are at the core of lexical semantics research. The development of twelve harmonized lexicons requires mechanisms for guaranteeing uniformity and consistency of the representations. These mechanisms, in turn, guarantee that within the same language, consistent formal devices apply cross-domain and cross-categorially. Finally, the multilingual component translates into the problem of identifying linguistic independent elements of the semantic vocabulary for structuring word meaning. Without detailing the specific

---

[1] An earlier version of this paper Busa, Calzolari, Lenci, and Pustejovsky *Building a Semantic Lexicon: Structuring and Generating Concepts* was first presented at the IWCS-III in Tilburg in June 1999.

[2] SIMPLE stands for *Semantic Information for Multipurpose PLurilingual Lexica*, sponsored by DG-XIII of EU, within the LE – Language Engineering Programme, and coordinated by Antonio Zampolli.

aspects of the project, we will focus on the formal backbone that explicitly addresses these questions.

2   Semantic Classes and Lexical Semantic Description

Explicitly defined ontologies play a very important role in lexicon design: The meaning of an item is partly determined by the position in the ontology occupied by the concept or concepts it expresses; they allow the lexicon designer to have a clear and comprehensive view of the overall semantic relations between the lexical items in the knowledge base.

The general principles underlying the design of most current ontologies are based on two main assumptions. The first is that the ontology is taken to be a conceptualization of the world as we understand it; as a result elements of the ontology are identified in terms of language independent criteria. The second is that the links between nodes determining the major conceptual partitions often reduce to ISA relations only.

These design principles not only give rise to a number of problems, which are discussed in much recent work on ontologies (cf. Guarino, 1998), but, in addition, there are entities that cannot be included within flat taxonomic models, except with the use of fairly complicating (and ad hoc) multiple inheritance mechanisms (cf. Pustejovsky and Boguraev, 1993).

To illustrate the difficulty of structuring ontologies principally along the ISA relation, consider the nominals below, which cannot be classified according to standard type-subtype relations:

(1)   a. John hit the target on the wall. (*physical_object*)
      b. Fiat has not yet reached the $1 billion target for this year.
        (*abstract_scalar_quantity*)
      c. John's target is Mary's affection. (*abstract_mental*)

(2)   a. The main component of relativity theory states that . . . . . (*proposition*)
      b. Your car will not run without this component. (*physical_object*)
      c. Your formula is missing a key component, namely two atoms of hydrogen. (*natural_kind*)

(3)   a. Il collegamento fra Roma e Bologna è chiuso. (*road*)
        The link between Rome and Bologna is closed.
      b. Il collegamento fra le pagine web. (*virtual_object*)
        The link between web pages.
      c. Il collegamento fra Roma e New York. (*flight/route*)
        The link between Rome and New York

The examples in (1)–(3) show that the ISA relation of these nouns can only be determined in context. The behavior of nouns such as "target," "component," and "link" provides a clear indication that, in many cases, the semantic potential of a lexical item is not reducible to a single descriptive component of an entity it denotes, but carries additional information along multiple dimensions (see also Chomsky, 1995; Moravcsik, this volume). Without this starting assumption, not only are the number of senses encoded for the nouns in (1)–(3) proliferated in a potentially unbounded way,[3] but there is no deterministic criterion for specifying the supertype of these entities.

Verbs raise similar issues. The most common approach to verb meaning is to define a finite set of "semantic" classes, which should be indicative of properties of the members of that class. Classes are either identified with a verb's syntactic behavior (cf. Levin, 1993) or with a set of primitive predicates (Jackendoff, 1992; Dowty, 1979). The development of a large-scale resource, such as SIMPLE, requires a set of reliable criteria for explaining what it means for a given predicate to be a member of a certain semantic class. In general, current lexical semantics models define verb semantic classes along one single parameter; thus class membership remains in general an open and difficult problem. Although these approaches can inform a number of decisions, they do not to directly provide the guiding principles for designing an ontology. Consider the following examples:

(4)   a. The boat <u>sank</u> in the middle of the Atlantic. (*change of location, change of state, motion*)

       b. The roof <u>collapsed</u>. (*destruction, change of location, change of state*)

(5)   a. The television <u>broke</u>. (*change of state*)

       b. The glass <u>broke</u>. (*destruction, change of state*)

As shown in (4) and (5), the verbs can be understood from multiple perspectives, thus fall simultaneously into distinct classes.

One of the main problems that the SIMPLE-GL framework has tried to overcome is the fact that existing ontologies cannot be replicated. The reason being that no set of design principles are currently available in the field and, as a result, knowledge engineers mostly rely on their own intuitions about the domain they are modeling or about language.

In this chapter, we present an alternative proposal to the current methodology for building ontologies that, we argue, is essentially centered around the question of *What is X?* Our goal is to capture additional aspects of word meaning that are equally important in language and equally necessary in the development of a computational lexicon. We will instead ask: *What is the conceptual structure of X, given its behavior in language?* Our model of the lexicon and of its underlying ontology starts with the relatively simple premise: how language talks about the world.

---

[3] In WordNet 1.6, for instance, words such as "target" and "link" are hyponyms of "abstraction," "event," "physical object," "psychological feature," and others.

3   Toward a Formal Framework for Ontology Design

The SIMPLE-GL model represents an attempt to develop a *grammar* that guides the structuring of the conceptual entities in the ontology in a deterministic fashion. The basic vocabulary relies on qualia structure for structuring the semantic/conceptual types. The perspective adopted here for the study of concepts is that all words have internal structure and differ in terms of complexity, which affects the way they compose in a sentence.

Consider the nouns "stone" and "chair." Both denote a *physical_object* along one dimension of meaning. They differ along other aspects. The first is the artifactual nature of "chair," which lacks with "stone," as shown in (6) and (7) below:

(6)   a. La sedia è riuscita bene.
            The chair came out well.
        b. #Il sasso è riuscito bene.
            The stone came out well.

(7)   a. Gianni ha cominciato una nuova sedia.
            Gianni began a new chair.
        b. #Gianni ha cominciato un nuovo sasso.
            Gianni began a new stone.

Furthermore, the two nouns also differ along another dimension, namely that of functionality, which is available with "chair," but not with "stone":

(8)   a. a good chair
            (good to sit on)
        b. ? a good stone

The expression in (8) is meaningless without a very specific context. It is certainly possible to imagine that the expression is uttered in a circumstance where an individual has picked one particular stone to sit on. What this shows is that aspects of meaning are not necessarily fixed at all times, but they are flexible enough to allow for recategorization when an appropriate context is available.

As said above, verbs also differ along distinct parameters, which also reflect the underlying complexity of their structure. Consider, for instance, the predicates "float" and "sink," which differ according to the causal dimension: "float" uniquely denotes a particular state or process, "sink" also encodes a causal component, which can be explicitly referenced by means of the adjunct headed by the preposition "from":

(9)   a. The boat sank from the explosion
        b. #The boat floated from the explosion

Returning to the examples in (1)–(3), from our concern of explaining how the set of admissible categories in the lexicon are motivated on linguistic grounds, and what are the constraints on concept formation, it is necessary to identify the core element that is common to all occurrences of the nouns. This is achieved by observing that an entity is a "target" if that entity fulfills a certain function in a given context, irrespectively of whether it is "physical," "mental," or "abstract." Similarly, anything can be a *"collegamento"* (link) as long as it connects two entities in a certain way, the specific way, however, can only be determined by knowing what those entities are. Finally, the type of the individual that is characterized as a "component" can be inferred only by knowing what type of entity that individual is a component of.

These examples by no means represent exceptional behavior, but in fact are quite pervasive in language, and it is clear that unless we have a way of structuring word meaning along such multiple dimensions, our model would fail to provide an appropriate semantics for them. In the next section, we introduce the syntactic vocabulary that allows for such a structuring.

4   A Syntax for Word Meaning

The SIMPLE project has provided an important setting for testing the viability of existing models of the lexicon. In order to express the different dimensions of meaning outlined above, we have tested the usefulness of qualia structure, which is summarized below:

- FORMAL ROLE – provides the information that distinguishes an individual within a larger set. It expresses the ISA relation which applies to all categories of the language.
- CONSTITUTIVE ROLE – expresses a variety of relations concerning the internal constitution of an entity or event.
- TELIC ROLE – expresses the typical function of an entity, the purpose for carrying out an event, i.e., what the entity is for.
- AGENTIVE ROLE – expresses the origin of an entity, or the coming into being of a property or of an event.

Qualia structure is generally understood as a representational tool for expressing the componential aspect of word meaning (Pustejovsky, 1995; Calzolari, 1991). However, as a syntax for constructing word meaning, it also provides a very powerful tool for studying the recursive processes that give rise to the different degree of complexity of concepts. Informally, this is described below, where $\tau_1 \ldots \ldots \tau_n$ represent possible conceptual types with different structural complexity:

(10)   a. τ_1 [FORMAL]
         b. τ_2 [FORMAL CONSTITUTIVE]
         c. τ_3 [FORMAL CONSTITUTIVE AGENTIVE]
         d. τ_4 [TELIC]
         e. τ_5 [AGENTIVE]
         f. . . . .
         g. τ_n [FORMAL CONSTITUTIVE TELIC]

Each qualia role in $\tau_1 \ldots \tau_n$ is an "independent" element of the vocabulary for semantic description, which enters into the construction of a concept.

Lexical items with different degrees of complexity, as determined by their internal semantic constituency, i.e., qualia structure, are organized in the lexicon in terms of a tripartite structure distinguishing between *simple types*, *unified types*, and *complex types* at the top level, (cf. Pustejovsky, 1998, this volume). This is schematically shown below:

(11)

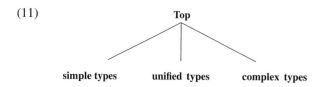

Intuitively, the type of a lexical item is *simple* if the item is uniquely defined in terms of a taxonomic relation to another entity in a hierarchy. Natural kind entities are such an example. Similarly, "information," "abstract," are also members of the set of *simple types* when they do not involve richer information concerning other aspects of meaning.

(12)

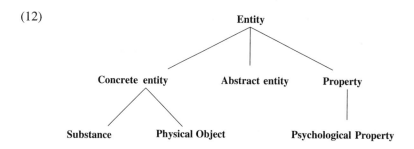

Unified types implement the principle of *orthogonal inheritance* (Pustejovsky and Boguraev, 1993), which allows a lexical item to fall into multiple classes along different dimensions of meaning. A *unified type* is created by recursively combining a simple or another unified type with additional elements from qualia structure. Artifacts, natural kinds with a specified instrumental property (e.g., "tool," "lever," "pet"), or complex events (e.g., "sink," "buy," "sell"), are an example. Finally, *complex types* model the properties of logically polysemous lexical items, which, however, we will not discuss in this paper.

While the four qualia roles provide the basic structuring of a semantic type, it is necessary to introduce distinctions to characterize precisely how each quale contributes to the overall typing of a concept. In order to capture a broad range of distinctions in the linguistic data, in the next section, we introduce the notion of *extended qualia structure*.

5   Extended Qualia Structure

When using a semantic vocabulary for structuring a large number of word meanings, it turns out that there are lexical items that share, on the surface, the same structural properties (e.g., they may involve a TELIC role), but they differ in their linguistic behavior.

The extended qualia structure addresses the concern of capturing more or less subtle linguistic differences while maintaining a systematic and consistent structuring of the lexical representations. This is achieved by specifying, for each qualia role, its *extended qualia set*, namely subtypes of that role that are consistent with its interpretation. For each element in the qualia set we also distinguish between *strong functional types* and *weak types*. The former are qualia roles that act like functions: given any type they create a new unified type. The latter simply add information to a type without changing its nature.

This difference can be viewed analogously to the notion of projecting categories in syntax. For instance, an adjectival phrase may attach to a noun phrase and build a restricted entity, which is again a noun phrase. Conversely, a noun phrase can combine with a verb phrase to produce an entity (i.e., a sentence), which is of a different type from those it is derived from.

The introduction of the extended qualia structure is motivated, minimally, by comparing the behavior of lexical items such as "honey," "petrol," or "car." As shown below, in (13), all nouns have the AGENTIVE role defined. However, in each case, the agentive expresses different modes of coming into being:

(13)   a.
$$\begin{bmatrix} \textbf{honey} \\ \text{type : } \textbf{simple} \\ \text{argstr : [arg1 : } \textbf{x:substance}] \\ \text{qualia : } \begin{bmatrix} \text{formal : } \textbf{substance(x)} \\ \text{agentive : } \textbf{produce(bee,x)} \end{bmatrix} \end{bmatrix}$$

       b.
$$\begin{bmatrix} \textbf{petrol} \\ \text{type : } \textbf{unified} \\ \text{argstr : [arg1 : } \textbf{x:substance}] \\ \text{qualia : } \begin{bmatrix} \text{formal : } \textbf{substance(x)} \\ \text{agentive : } \textbf{derived\_from(x,oil)} \end{bmatrix} \end{bmatrix}$$

       c.
$$\begin{bmatrix} \textbf{car} \\ \text{type : } \textbf{unified} \\ \text{argstr : [arg1 : } \textbf{x:phys\_object}] \\ \text{qualia : } \begin{bmatrix} \text{formal : } \textbf{vehicle(x)} \\ \text{agentive : } \textbf{make(individual,x)} \end{bmatrix} \end{bmatrix}$$

Note, however, that in coercion contexts, which represent a good way of testing the underlying event import of nouns, reference to the AGENTIVE role of the nominals highlights different constraints:

(14)   a. I finished the car
            (make the car)
       b. I finished the petrol
            (*make the petrol)
       c. #The bee finished the honey
            (*produce the honey)[4]

In Pustejovsky (1995), it is shown that with coercing predicates such as "finish," the AGENTIVE or TELIC role of the noun in object position determines the interpretation of the reconstructed event, unless, of course, the context provides a more "salient" event. In (14a), "car" readily makes available the creation aspect specified in the AGENTIVE role. Thus, we would expect all nominals with an AGENTIVE role defined to behave in the same way. This is not the case, however, with "petrol" and "honey," which do not allow a reading where the reconstructed event corresponds to that in the AGENTIVE role.

The same holds for the TELIC role. Consider the difference between "fish" and "swimmer." For "fish," the information concerning its typical activity, namely "swim," can be optionally encoded. For "swimmer," the TELIC role instead obligatorily expresses the characterizing activity of the individual (cf. Busa, 1996; for agentive nouns). This different properties of "fish" and "swimmer" are also reflected in the number of readings available with certain adjective-noun combinations:

(15)   a. an old swimmer
            1. a person who is old and who swims
            2. a person who has been swimming for a long time.
       b. an old fish
            1. a fish which is old
            2. #a fish which has been swimming for a long time.

Note that the availability of two interpretations in (15a) is not determined by the fact that "swimmer" is a morphologically derived noun. The degree of polysemy of an adjective-noun combination depends on the underlying complexity of the head noun. Thus, "old mill," for instance, can either be interpreted as a mill that is old (i.e., built a long time ago), or one that used to function in the past (cf. Bouillon, 1997; Bouillon and Busa, forthcoming).

---

[4] Type coercion may be sensitive to different types of agentive or telic qualia.

The AGENTIVE role of nominals such as "honey" or the TELIC role of "fish" are weak qualia, whereas those of "car," "petrol," and "swimmer" are strong qualia. Weak and strong qualia determine whether or not orthogonal components of meaning give rise to *simple* or *unified* types. For each role in the qualia set of one of the four top qualia, this property is explicitly marked by means of the subscripts S and W, as shown in the FORMAL type hierarchy below:

(16)

The hierarchy for FORMAL is actually quite simple and it only distinguishes between the standard ISA relation (i.e., a weak quale), and the result, (i.e., a strong quale), marking the resulting state for complex event structures denoting transitions.

The qualia set for the CONSTITUTIVE role involves a number of subtypes, which express different constitutive relations that contribute to the semantic description of various concepts (see also Climent, this volume):

(17)

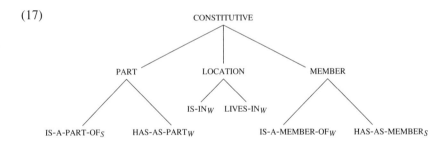

The strong CONSTITUTIVE types are involved in the construction of unified types such as "group," "organ," "headquarters," "component," "ingredient." We return to specific examples in the next section.

The TELIC involves a set of subtypes that distinguish lexical items according to a number of parameters. The first is discussed in Pustejovsky (1995) and concerns the distinction between DIRECT and INDIRECT TELIC. This expresses whether the entity that is defined is the object of the activity specified in the TELIC (e.g., "beer," is the object of the telic drinking), or whether the entity corresponds to the "subject." In this latter case, we distinguish whether the entity is an instrument (e.g., "knife" relative to "cut"), an agentive noun (e.g., "violinist" relative to "play the violin"), or whether the event is the typical activity of the entity (e.g., "fly" for certain kinds of birds). Finally, the PURPOSE TELIC is the one associated with verbs, expressing the goal of the agent for performing a given action:

(18)

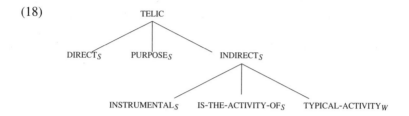

Finally, the AGENTIVE qualia set distinguishes between persistent and temporary properties of the event encoded therein. This is treated as an aspectual-like distinction, which is motivated by the fact that with certain nominals, the agentive role (i.e., AGENTIVE_PROG) encodes an event that has a progressive-like reading (with "pedestrian" or "participant," and also "grocery" and "laundry," for instance). AGENTIVE_PERF, instead, introduces a perfect-like interpretation of the event by expressing that all other properties of the lexical item are dependent on the prior occurrence of that event. In turn, AGENTIVE_PERF is distinguished for natural kinds, artifactual entities, and for causation involved in complex event structures.

(19)

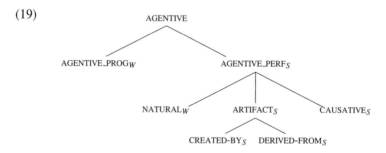

With these elements in place, in the next section we turn to the basic mechanisms for building concepts, and then present how the difficult cases discussed in section 2 can be handled in this model.

6   Building Concepts

The process of concept construction is recursive. The basic elements are provided by the set of *simple types*, which are further distinguished into *base category types*, the primary entities in the ontology (substances, objects, events, abstract entities, and their simple subtypes) and *functional types*, the extended qualia structure.

The set of functional types provide the organizing principles for lexical structuring: They combine with base category types to produce either *simple types* or *unified types*, according to whether the functional type is weak (f_w), or strong (f_s). The basic rules of composition for type construction are stated as follows, where 's' stands for a simple type, 'u' for a unified type:

(20)   a. for $a \in$ s and $b \in f_w$, the composition $g_1(a,b) \in$ s
       b. for $a \in$ s and $b \in f_s$, the composition $g_2(a,b) \in$ u
       c. for $a \in$ u and $b \in f_s$, the composition $g_3(a,b) \in$ u
       d. for $a \in$ u and $b \in$ u, the composition $g_4(a,b) \in$ u

It is clear that the above rules still require a set of constraints that determine whether there is an ordering to the composition, when two functional types can contribute to the creation of the same type and when this is not possible. All these questions are part of our ongoing research, and we have no definite answer at this stage. The fragment in (21) illustrates the process of type construction:

(21)

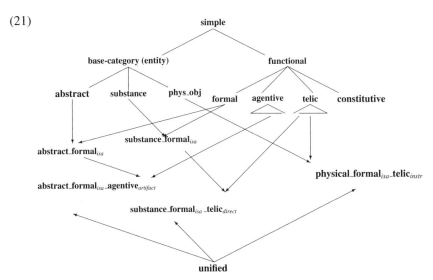

A unified type such as **abstract_formal**$_{isa}$**-agentive**$_{artifact}$ provides the basic type of entities such as "idea," provided that the event encoded in the qualia AGENTIVE$_{artifact}$ is specialized to be "mental process." If this type is further unified with specific types of TELIC, then other unified types such as "theory," "communication," or "plan" can be generated. Similarly, the type **physical_formal**$_{isa}$**-telic**$_{instr}$ would correspond to some natural kind that performs a particular function (e.g., "fire wood"). In turn, this could be specialized by unification with one of the subtypes of AGENTIVE, and so on.

For simplicity of exposition, in the tree above we have ignored the CONSTI-TUTIVE role, but the generation proceeds along similar lines. In fact, nominals such as "group" or "component," are top unified types, whose FORMAL role is underspecified, as shown below:

(22) a.
$$
\begin{bmatrix}
\textbf{group} \\
\text{type : } \textbf{unified: entity\_constitutive}_{member} \\
\text{argstr : } \begin{bmatrix} \text{arg1 : } \textbf{x:collective\_entity} \\ \text{arg2 : } \textbf{y:entity} \end{bmatrix} \\
\text{qualia : } \begin{bmatrix} \text{formal : } \textbf{isa(x,entity)} \\ \text{constitutive : } \textbf{has-as-member(x,y)} \end{bmatrix}
\end{bmatrix}
$$

b.
$$
\begin{bmatrix}
\textbf{component} \\
\text{type : } \textbf{unified: top\_constitutive}_{part} \\
\text{argstr : } \begin{bmatrix} \text{arg1 : } \textbf{x:top} \\ \text{arg2 : } \textbf{y:top} \end{bmatrix} \\
\text{qualia : } \begin{bmatrix} \text{formal : } \textbf{isa(x,entity)} \\ \text{constitutive : } \textbf{is-a-part-of(x,y)} \end{bmatrix}
\end{bmatrix}
$$

The representation in (22a) may be used to generate increasingly more specific concepts such as "flock," "herd," and so forth, by restricting the type of ARG2 to the appropriate entity.

Consider now the nominals "target" or even "product," which represent a problem for flat taxonomic ontologies. These nouns involve an underspecified FORMAL, linking to the top node **entity** of the *base category type* hierarchy, but are fully specified along other dimensions: TELIC for "target," and AGENTIVE for "product":

(23) a.
$$
\begin{bmatrix}
\textbf{target} \\
\text{type : } \textbf{unified:entity\_telic}_{direct} \\
\text{argstr : } \begin{bmatrix} \text{arg1 : } \textbf{x:top} \end{bmatrix} \\
\text{evenstr : } \begin{bmatrix} \text{e1 : } \textbf{e}_1\textbf{:event} \end{bmatrix} \\
\text{qualia : } \begin{bmatrix} \text{formal : } \textbf{isa(x,entity)} \\ \text{telic : } \textbf{aim(e}_1\textbf{,person,x)} \end{bmatrix}
\end{bmatrix}
$$

b.
$$
\begin{bmatrix}
\textbf{product} \\
\text{type : } \textbf{unified:entity\_agentive}_{artifact} \\
\text{argstr : } \begin{bmatrix} \text{arg1 : } \textbf{x:top} \\ \text{d-arg2 : } \textbf{y:top} \end{bmatrix} \\
\text{evenstr : } \begin{bmatrix} \text{e1 : } \textbf{e}_1\textbf{:event} \end{bmatrix} \\
\text{qualia : } \begin{bmatrix} \text{formal : } \textbf{isa(x,entity)} \\ \text{agentive : } \textbf{created-by(e}_1\textbf{,x,y)} \end{bmatrix}
\end{bmatrix}
$$

The solution just outlined explains straightforwardly why these unified nouns with an underspecified FORMAL receive so many interpretations in different contexts, and prove that an enumerative approach is not justified in light of the linguistic data. We now turn to verbs.

7   Verb Semantics

The model described in the previous section also provides the foundation for constructing the semantics for verbs. Again, the process involves our basic vocabulary of types. In this case, the set of *base category types* correspond to the ontology of events, and the *functional types* are the qualia roles for events.[5]

Events are structures that are constructed from a core predicate, a list of participants, and a set of logical operations over predicates (e.g., negation, temporal relations). The top base categories are primitive states and primitive processes. Stative predicates include locative predicates (i.e., "be-in," "be-at," etc.), possessive predicate (i.e., "have"), existence predicates (i.e., "be" and "exist"). Base processes involve predicates such as "move," "act," "experience," "feel," "say," etc. Functional types unify with base types to produce more complex event structures (i.e., unified types).

Consider the hierarchy below which presents a fragment of the general type-lattice for events:

(24)

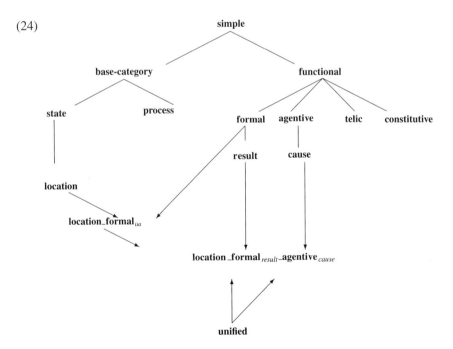

---

[5] For reasons of space, in this chapter, we have not said anything about the CONSTITUTIVE types for events. This does not change the nature of the discussion below.

The combinatorial possibilities deriving from our concept calculus give rise to a number of possibilities. Consider the relation between predicates such as "stay," "arrive," and "send," whose representation is given in (25)–(27):[6]

$$(25) \quad \begin{bmatrix} \textbf{stay} \\[4pt] \text{type} : \textbf{simple:location\_formal}_{isa} \\[6pt] \text{argstr} : \begin{bmatrix} \text{arg1} : \textbf{x:living\_entity} \\ \text{arg2} : \textbf{y:location} \end{bmatrix} \\[12pt] \text{evenstr} : [\text{e1} : \textbf{e}_1\textbf{:state}] \\[6pt] \text{qualia} : [\text{formal} : \textbf{at}(\textbf{e}_1,\textbf{x},\textbf{y})] \end{bmatrix}$$

$$(26) \quad \begin{bmatrix} \textbf{arrive} \\[4pt] \text{type} : \textbf{unified:location\_formal}_{result}\textbf{-agentive} \\[6pt] \text{argstr} : \begin{bmatrix} \text{arg1} : \textbf{x:entity} \\ \text{arg2} : \textbf{y:location} \end{bmatrix} \\[12pt] \text{evenstr} : \begin{bmatrix} \text{e1} : \textbf{e}_1\textbf{:state} \\ \text{e2} : \textbf{e}_2\textbf{:process} \\ \text{rest} : \textbf{e}_1 \textbf{ precedes e}_2 \end{bmatrix} \\[18pt] \text{qualia} : \begin{bmatrix} \text{formal} : \textbf{at}(\textbf{e}_1,\textbf{x},\textbf{y}) \\ \text{agentive} : \textbf{move}(\textbf{e}_2,\textbf{x}) \end{bmatrix} \end{bmatrix}$$

$$(27) \quad \begin{bmatrix} \textbf{send} \\[4pt] \text{type} : \textbf{unified:location\_formal}_{result}\textbf{-agentive}_{cause}\textbf{-telic}_{purp} \\[6pt] \text{argstr} : \begin{bmatrix} \text{arg1} : \textbf{x:living\_entity} \\ \text{arg2} : \textbf{y:entity} \\ \text{agr3} : \textbf{z:entity} \end{bmatrix} \\[18pt] \text{evenstr} : \begin{bmatrix} \text{e1} : \textbf{e}_1\textbf{:state} \\ \text{e2} : \textbf{e}_2\textbf{:process} \\ \text{rest} : \textbf{e}_1 \textbf{ precedes e}_2 \end{bmatrix} \\[18pt] \text{qualia} : \begin{bmatrix} \text{formal} : \neg\,\textbf{at}(\textbf{e}_1,\textbf{x},\textbf{y}) \\ \text{telic} : \textbf{at}(\textbf{e}_1,\textbf{z},\textbf{y}) \\ \text{agentive} : \textbf{act}(\textbf{e}_2,\textbf{x},\textbf{y}) \end{bmatrix} \end{bmatrix}$$

---

[6] For simplicity of exposition, we have ignored issues concerning the arity of predicates, the types of the arguments, and their relational constraints.

The examples above clarify how orthogonal aspects of meaning are built around a core locative predicate.

The model outlined above does not require assigning a priory semantic labels, but rather building a type (or a semantic class) that is attuned with the semantic contribution and the compositional behavior of a lexical item.

8   Building Lexical Semantics Resources

The relevance of this line of research for building resources is that types provide the formal specifications guiding subsequent encoding (see Ruimy, Gola and Monachini, this volume).

For purposes of bridging the ontology with the practical task of encoding the lexicon, we have created a "library" of templates that provide the constraints and conditions for a lexical item belonging to that type. In particular, in SIMPLE, each type, is associated with a template, which is isomorphic with the conceptual complexity of its type.

Templates are a practical tool with a central role in the lexicon-building phase. They provide the well-formedness conditions for a lexical item (i.e., *semantic unit*) to be of a given type; they are the general backbone to guarantee the highest level of consistency both within a single lexicon and among lexicons belonging to different languages. SIMPLE can thus be viewed as a "template-based framework" for lexicon development.

To illustrate how templates are used, consider again the lexical items "chair" and "target." To encode the actual entries, the lexicographers would choose the templates `physical_artifact_tool` and `telic`, respectively:

Examples:	all artifact tools, "chair," "lamp," etc.
Comments:	This field contains comments and linguistic tests
Semantic Unit:	<chair>
Template_Type:	physical_artifact_tool
Template_Sypertype:	
Unification_Path:	[physical_object | telic | agentive]
Domain:	General
Definition:	Dictionary definition
Selectional_Restr:	none
Formal:	isa(<chair>, <physical_object>)
Agentive:	created–by(<chair>, <make>)
Constitutive:	nil
Telic:	used–for(<chair>, <sit>)
Complexity:	unified

Examples:	all entities such as "link," "goal," etc.
Comments:	This field contains comments and linguistic tests.

Semantic Unit:	<target>
Template_Type:	telic
Template_Supertype:	
Unification_Path:	[top | telic]
Domain:	General
Definition:	Dictionary definition
Selectional_Restr:	none
Formal:	isa(<target>, <entity>)
Agentive:	nil
Constitutive:	nil
Telic:	telic(<target>, <achieve>)
Complexity:	unified

Note that in the above templates qualia-based information is represented as relations between words in the language. This is an implementation-dependent reason, which we will not discuss here.

The templates for verbs are quite similar, with the exception that they also contain information about the number of arguments, their selectional restrictions, and the event sort of a given semantic unit.

9   Conclusion

In this paper, we have presented a model for generating concepts out of a set of ontological categories that are grounded in linguistic behavior. We have shown that the model has a high degree of generality in that it provides the same mechanisms for generating concepts independently of their grammatical category. For reasons of space, we have not discussed adjectives, although they can be treated in the same way. In addition, the model allows for a fairly broad and clear coverage of the different types of concepts in the language, an aspect that is often lacking in existing lexicons, where the focus is on the representation of the clear, well-known cases, while the semantics of abstract entities is neglected.

To the standard approach of defining semantic classes along one dimension, we have opposed a framework whose development has been crucially concerned with capturing the multiplicity of meaning. We have argued that unidimensional models provide uninformative descriptions for underspecified lexical items and multiply senses without capturing underlying generalizations. Alternatively, assuming that lexical items differ according to which dimension of meaning may carry all the semantic load, the GL-SIMPLE model has clarified the nature of the underspecification of certain items. This takes into account the fact that lexical items may be highly underspecified along one dimension while providing a rich semantic contribution along other dimensions.

References

Bouillon, P., and Busa F. forthcoming. Where's the Polysemy? A Study of Adjective-noun Constructions. *Proc. Second Workshop on Lexical Semantics Systems*, Pisa, Italy, 6–7 April 1998.

Bouillon, P. 1997. *Polymorphie et Sémantique Lexicale: le cas des adjectifs*, Presse du Septentrion: Lille.

Busa, F. 1996. *Compositionality and the Semantics of Nominals*, Ph.D. Dissertation, Brandeis University.

Calzolari, N. 1991. Acquiring and Representing Semantic Information in a Lexical Knowledge Base. In J. Pustejovsky (ed.), *Proc. Workshop on Lexical Semantics and Knowledge Representation*, Berkeley, CA.

Chomsky, N. 1995. Language and Nature. *Mind* 104:000.

Dowty, D.R. 1979. *Word Meaning and Montague Grammar*. Kluver Academic Publishers, Dordrecht.

Guarino, N. 1998. Some Ontological Principles for Designing Upper Level Lexical Resources. *Proc. First International Conference on Language Resources and Evaluation*, Granada, Spain, 28–30 May 1998.

Jackendoff, R. 1992. *Semantic Structures*. MIT Press, Cambridge.

Levin, B. (1993). *English Verb Classes and Alternations*. University of Chicago Press, Chicago.

Pustejovsky, J. 1995. *The Generative Lexicon*. MIT Press, Cambridge, MA.

Pustejovsky, J. 1998. Specification of a Top Concept Lattice, Manuscript, Brandeis University.

Pustejovsky, J., and Boguraev, B. 1993. Lexical Knowledge Representation and Natural Language Processing. In F. Pereira and B. Grosz (eds.), *Natural Language Processing*. MIT Press, Cambridge, MA.

20 Lexicography Informs Lexical Semantics: The SIMPLE Experience

NILDA RUIMY, ELISABETTA GOLA,
AND MONICA MONACHINI

Abstract

Lexicography is often considered orthogonal to theoretical linguistics. In this paper, we show that this is a highly misguided view. As in other sciences, a careful and large-scale empirical investigation is a necessary step for testing, improving, and expanding a theoretical framework. We present results from the development of the Italian semantic lexicon in the framework of the SIMPLE project, which implements major aspects of Generative Lexicon theory. This paper focuses on the semantic properties of abstract nouns as they are conceptually more difficult to describe. For this reason, they are a good testbed for any semantic theory. The methodology – which has been developed to satisfy the requirements of building large lexicons – is more than a simple interface or a lexicographer auxiliary tool. Rather, it reveals how a real implementation greatly contributes to the underlying theory.

1   Introduction

"Unlike the mental grammar, the mental dictionary has had no cachet. It seems like nothing more than a humdrum list of words, each transcribed into the head by dull-witted rote memorization. In the preface to his Dictionary, Samuel Johnson wrote: "It is the fate of those who dwell at the lower employments of life, to be rather driven by the fear of evil, than attracted by the prospect of good; to be exposed to censure, without hope of praise; to be disgraced by miscarriage, or punished for neglect, where success would have been without applause, and diligence without reward. Among these unhappy mortals is the writer of dictionaries." Johnson's own dictionary defines lexicographer as "a harmless drudge, that busies himself in tracing the original, and detailing the signification of words. [...] we will see that the stereotype is unfair. The world of words is just as wondrous as the word of syntax, or even more so" (Pinker, 1995, 126–127).

Although Pinker is referring to morphological lexicons, his quotation applies also to semantic lexicons. Lexicography is often considered as a trivial routine activity, not really relevant from a theoretical point of view. In this paper, we argue that this is a highly misguided view. We draw our evidence from the practical experience gained in the framework of the SIMPLE project: building a noun ontology and encoding 7,000 Italian noun senses from a lexical semantics point of view.

350

2   The SIMPLE Project

The SIMPLE project (*Semantic Information for Multifunctional Plurilingual Lexica*) aims at building multilingual, multipurpose and harmonized computational semantic lexicons linked to the morphological and syntactic ones which were elaborated for twelve European languages during the PAROLE project. The goal of SIMPLE is to encode the semantics of nouns, verbs, and adjectives in view of Language Engineering applications. The 10,000 word meanings to be described consist of a lexical core common to all languages (i.e., the EUROWORDNET[1] 'base concepts,' see Vossen, this volume), the additional most relevant senses of the corresponding lexical units, and the most frequent words encoded in the PAROLE lexicons. The general approach adopted in SIMPLE follows the *Generative Lexicon* (henceforth, GL) (Pustejovsky, 1995; Busa et al., this volume), which constitutes the theoretical framework and the model underlying the set of top types that represent the core SIMPLE Ontology.[2]

3   Qualia Structure and the Dictionary

Pustejovsky defines the semantics of a lexical item as a structure involving different components (1995, p. 61).[3] One of these is *Qualia structure*, which is a rich and structured representation of the relational force of a lexical item (Pustejovsky, 1991; 1995; Moravcsik, 1975). What is peculiar about GL is that Qualia permits "a much richer description of meaning than either a simple decompositional view or a purely relational approach to word meaning would allow" (Pustejovsky, 1995, p. 76). That is, it expresses different/orthogonal aspects of word meaning instead of a one-dimensional inheritance (even multiple), which can only capture standard hyponymy/hyperonymy relations. For a detailed account of the GL theory, the reader should refer to the literature on this topic and, in this volume, to Pustejovsky; Bouillon and Busa; Busa et al. and Vossen.

The adequacy of qualia relations[4] for capturing key aspects of word meaning becomes apparent when consulting dictionary definitions. The elements of meaning easily map on the dimension(s) expressed via qualia roles. Furthermore, these

---

[1] See Vossen, this volume.

[2] See SIMPLE Specification Group, 1998.

[3] More formally there are four levels of representations: the argument structure, the specification of the event type, the *Qualia structure*, and an embedded transformation determining what information is inheritable from the global lexical structure. For deeper information, see (Pustejovsky, 1995, pp. 61–67).

[4] To remind very briefly the different aspects of a word's meaning are specified by each of the four qualia roles:
FORMAL: provides information for distinguishing an entity within a larger set;
CONSTITUTIVE: provides information about the internal constitution of an entity;
AGENTIVE: informs about the origin of an entity;
TELIC: expresses the function or purpose of an entity.

Table 20.1.

SemU	Dictionary definition
Materiale	Tutto cio'che serve per creare o costruire qualche cosa (TELIC: used for)
Material	*Everything which is used for creating or building something*
Manufatto	Oggetto fatto a mano o con attrezzi manuali (AGENTIVE: created by)
Artifact	*Object which has been made by hand or with manual tools*
Tuorlo	Parte centrale (CONSTITUTIVE: part of) dell'uovo
Yolk	*Central part of the egg*
Botte	Recipiente di legno (CONSTITUTIVE: made of) fatto di doghe arcuate tenute unite da cerchi di ferro (AGENTIVE: created by) che serve per la conservazione e il trasporto di liquidi, specialmente vino (TELIC: used for)
Barrel	*wooden container made of curved staves held together by metal strips used for keeping and transporting liquids, especially wine*
Organo	Ogni parte (CONSTITUTIVE: part of) del corpo animale o vegetale avente una particolare funzione (TELIC: used for)
Organ	*Each part of a (human/animal) body or plant having a particular function*
Banconota	Biglietto di banca emesso dalla banca centrale (AGENTIVE: created by) a cui lo Stato attribuisce valore di moneta legale (TELIC: used for)
Bill	*Bill issued by the Central Bank which is assigned the value of legal currency by the governement*

relations become particularly crucial for those sense definitions which have an underspecified genus term (see Table 20.1 below, especially the first definition).

Not all dimensions of meaning are always explicitly expressed in the definition of a lexical item. Some of them are inherited by virtue of its membership to a semantic type, as shown in Table 20.2 below.

Although qualia relations easily emerge from dictionary definitions, the formal expression of a specific value for a quale is sometimes quite problematic. Observe the definition of *"carta"* (paper): 'Materiale ottenuto dalla lavorazione di fibre di cellulosa, che si presenta in forma di fogli sottili e pieghevoli, adatti a vari usi' (lit. Material obtained from cellulose fibers which is usually constituted by subtle and folding sheets, which can be used for different purposes; Longman Dictionary def.: Material made in the form of sheets from very thin threads of wood or cloth, used for writing or printing on, covering parcels or walls, etc.).

The last part of the definition clearly conveys a TELIC information. It is indeniable that paper has some kind of use and this makes this information linguistically relevant. However, the TELIC information is totally underspecified as for a possible value. As a matter of fact, the appropriate TELIC relation could point to a number of words, such as: *"scrivere"* (to write), *"disegnare"* (to draw), *"stampare"* (to print), *"incartare"* (to wrap up in paper), etc., given the large and heterogeneous range of uses that paper may have. Hence, no unique semantic type can be found that could express a generalization over the different functions of *"carta."*

Table 20.2.

SemU	Dictionary definition	Inherited quale
Cazzuola	Attrezzo del muratore (AGENTIVE: used by)	Cazzuola
	di forma triangolare, per distendere la calcina (TELIC: used for)	↑
Trowel	*Mason tool triangle shaped, used for*	Instrument
	spreading cement	AGENTIVE: created by
Pane	Alimento costituito da un impasto di acqua e farina	Pane
	(CONSTITUTIVE: made of)	↑
	per lo piu' condito con sale lievitato e cotto al forno	Food
	(AGENTIVE: created by) in forme diverse	TELIC: used for
Bread	*Nutriment made of a mixture of water and flour*	
	generally seasoned with salt leavened and baked	
	in different shapes	
Sedia	Mobile su cui ci si siede (TELIC: used for)	Sedia:
	costituito da un piano orizzontale che poggia su quattro	↑
	gambe e da una spalliera (CONSTITUTIVE: made of)	Furniture
Chair	*Piece of furniture to sit on with an horizontal plane resting*	AGENTIVE: created by
	four legs with a support for the back	

On the other hand, defining at the lexical level the most prototypical usage of "*carta*" would certainly be restrictive, with the consequence that relevant information would be lost. Furthermore, it is worth noting that the different possible uses of paper that an individual assigns to it depends on the world knowledge of that individual. This variability gives rise to different encoding options:

(i) leaving the second member of the relation totally underspecified (both as to lexical realization and type assignment):

used_for (<carta_1>, <Word>: [SEMANTIC TYPE]);

(ii) instantiating the role as many times as necessary in order to cover all possible functions of the meaning being described:

used_for (<carta_1>, <scrivere>: [SYMBOLIC_CREATION])
used_for (<carta_1>, <disegnare>: [SYMBOLIC_CREATION])
used_for (<carta_1>, <stampare>: [SYMBOLIC_CREATION])
used_for (<carta_1>, <incartare>: [CAUSE_CHANGE_OF_STATE])
. . .

Moving from the theoretical model to the practical task of describing a selected set of entries has required a nonnegligible effort to establish a general methodology and fine-grained criteria guiding the actual encoding process.

Given the need to develop the twelve uniform lexicons, SIMPLE crucially relies on the notion of a structured set of templates, which are the result of combining the top-down approach for building the ontology with the bottom-up process of providing consistent semantic descriptions for related word senses, as they appear in dictionary definitions and corpora. From the theoretical point of view, the uniformity is guaranteed by the types and from the lexicographic standpoint by the *templates*. We turn to templates in the next section.

4   The Notion of Template and Their Relationship with Semantic Types and Qualia Roles

A template is a frame providing a structured cluster of semantic information for a word sense: It represents a guide for the encoding process. Templates constrain a semantic type to the core information for that type. Thus, from a theoretical point of view, a template also represents a generalization over various related semantic types (see Busa, Calzolari, and Lenci, this volume).

For example, the semantic types 4-WHEEL VEHICLES and 2-WHEEL VEHICLES encode respectively "car" and "bike." However, they are subsumed in a unique template VEHICLE because the core information of vehicles remains essentially the same: cars and bikes are both artifacts, they have same function of transportation and hence share the same place in the ontology. The "number of wheels" is a constitutive property rather linked to world knowledge. Such a characteristic may however be relevant in some contexts and may trigger a type shifting if the lexicographer chooses to mark it as a relevant feature.

To avoid the proliferation of types, templates are conceived so that the lexicographer can remain at a very general level, encoding "car" and "bike" in a very similar way. This would not be the case if the lexicographer's work was based on an hypothetical ontology distinguishing "fast vehicles" (skate, bike, skateboard, surf) from "motor vehicles" (car, truck, train, airplane).

To represent the properties of the underlying semantic types, templates are modeled by means of *qualia structure*, which has been extended in order to adapt it to the specific needs of the SIMPLE project.[5] First, given the necessity to meet specific technical requirements, qualia roles have been implemented as relations between semantic units (henceforth, Usems[6]) and sometimes as valued features, as shown in 2:

(1)   *has_as_part* (Usem1,Usem2),
         e.g.: (*armadio*, cupboard)
         has_as_part (<armadio>, <anta>: [Part])

---

[5] See Simple Specifications.

[6] Following the terminology of the GENELEX Model, word senses are encoded as *Semantic Units* or *Usems*. Each Usem is assigned a semantic type plus other sorts of information, which are intended to identify a word sense, and to distinguish it from the other senses of the same lexical item. Usems are language specific. Usems that identify the same sense in different languages will be assigned the same semantic type. For instance, the Usems for <dog> (Eng.), <hund> (Ger.) and <cane> (It.) will all receive the semantic type [ANIMAL] . The information which forms the content of the Usems in SIMPLE is therefore intended to provide the basis for future multilingual links between the different lexicons. Cf. SIMPLE Guidelines, p. 11.

(2)   *sex* = male, female,
        e.g.: (*leonessa*, lioness)
        sex = female

Moreover, in the process of developing the core set of templates for a large amount of lexical items, *Qualia structure* has been made simultaneously richer and stricter. It is richer, in that each qualia role has subtypes, that is, the set of possible values for each quale is enlarged (*Extended Qualia structure*). It is stricter, in that this extended set of values allows to express finer-grained distinctions for describing adequately the relationships holding between so many senses.

During the encoding process, the lexicographer is not allowed to change the template type, which contains the core mandatory information but only to add information in order to obtain a more complete and detailed description. In this sense, templates are a very severe guide: The theoretical background assumes for example that the opposition natural kind/artifactual object (AGENTIVE role), and the function of entities (TELIC role) is relevant and type defining, while other pieces of information are not. Nevertheless, some of this information can be used to distinguish subtypes.

In addition, for each of its actual use in a type definition, the relevance of a relation is marked with a different weight. The weight may indicate that the relation is 'type defining,' namely encoding an essential aspect of a word's meaning, for example, for "*musicista*" (musician) the TELIC relation IS_THE_ABILITY_OF (cf., Busa, 1996, Saint Dizier, this volume). Alternatively, a relation may convey optional or world knowledge information, e.g., for "*sedia*" (chair), the constitutive relation MADE_OF.

(3)
$$\begin{bmatrix} \text{<MUSICISTA>} \\ \text{WEIGHT} = \textbf{TYPE-DEFINING} \\ \text{TARGET} = \textbf{<SUONARE>} \\ \text{SEMR} = \textbf{is\_the\_ability\_of} \end{bmatrix}$$

(4)
$$\begin{bmatrix} \text{<SEDIA>} \\ \text{WEIGHT} = \textbf{OPTIONAL} \\ \text{TARGET} = \textbf{<LEGNO>} \\ \text{SEMR} = \textbf{made\_of} \end{bmatrix}$$

Consider furthermore, the template for VEHICLE, which contains an obligatory agentive information usually stating that vehicles are created by humans. However, "*cavallo da tiro*" (draft horse) is not an artifact, although it is a means of transportation. So, a change in this obligatory information may cause a type-shifting of the VEHICLE template. The complete expression "*cavallo da tiro*" may be construed either from the point of view of its function, i.e., as belonging to a new different subtype of VEHICLE or to a unified type involving the composition of types [ANIMAL and TELIC].

Table 20.3.

	Concrete	Human	Abstract
CONSTITUTIVE	How something is made of (the meronimic relations)	The membership relations	Connotation, domains
AGENTIVE	Natural kind vs. Artifact	Kind of Agents	Social and conventional source
TELIC	Function and use of objects	Social role of people	Frequently underspecified function

It is thus clear that building the Templates has involved addressing fundamental theoretical questions, which have contributed to fixing the interpretation of the qualia roles for different entities in the ontology, as shown in Table 20.3 below.

The table above illustrates that the same quale shifts its interpretation according to the domain of a given type (e.g., human, concrete, abstract). For reason of space, in the rest of this chapter we focus on the structuring of the types and the construction of the templates for abstract nouns, which still represent a serious difficulty.

5   The Representation of Nonconcrete Nouns

Qualia structure aims at providing a "uniform semantic representation" (Pustejovsky, 1995, p. 76), which should be able, in principle, to represent the meaning of all semantic classes of lexical items. However, qualia roles seem to be mostly defined for the semantic classes belonging to concrete nouns[7] and events.[8] The first difficulty concerning "abstract entities" is to define what an abstract noun. It is not our purpose to provide a theory of the subject. Rather, we will present the practical problems that we faced and the solutions we adopted.

In developing templates for nonconcrete nouns, we looked at nominals of different sorts, i.e., nouns which refer to:

(i) nonperceivable entities
   e.g., *"comunismo"* (communism), *"disciplina"* (discipline), *"libertà"* (freedom), *"anno"* (year);

(ii) mental objects, which are controversial as to their "physical/abstract" nature
   e.g., *"idea"* (idea), *"teoria"* (theory), *"pensiero"* (thought), *"immaginazione"* (imagination);

(iii) more complex concepts not clearly identifiable as abstract or concrete since they seem abstract although they usually apply to concrete entities

---

[7] A relevant part of Pustejovsky's examples is based on concrete nouns such as: "book," "knife," "dictionary," "novel," "newspaper," "car," "meal," "beer," etc.

[8] Events are strongly related to verbs and they will not be discussed here.

Table 20.4.

SemU	Dictionary definition
Pensiero	Qualsiasi rappresentazione mentale, prodotto dell'attivita' del pensiero o dell'immaginazione (AGENTIVE: result of)
Thought	*Any mental representation produced by thinking or imagining*
Pediatria	branca (*Constitutive*: part of) della medicina che studia (TELIC: purpose) le malattie del bambino (CONSTITUTIVE: concerns)
Pediatrics	*Branch of medecine that studies children's diseases*

    e.g., *"bellezza"* (beauty), *"forza"* (strenght), *"forma"* (shape), *"colore"* (color);

(iv) entities which present both a concrete and an abstract aspect
    e.g., *"linguaggio"* (language), *"segno"* (sign), *"numero"* (number), *"metro"* (meter);

(v) formal conventions rendered concrete by means of semiotic objects
    e.g., *"legge"* (law), *"azione"* (action), *"accordo"* (agreement): These are borderline items that have a twofold nature, abstract, and concrete.

In these semantic classes, deeper nodes (i.e., subtypes) have been identified trying to cluster word meanings as homogeneously as possible and following both our linguistic intuitions and dictionary definitions to create template types. Here again, as for concrete entities, TELIC, AGENTIVE, and CONSTITUTIVE dimensions appear in dictionary definitions. Nevertheless, qualia roles seem to be less adequate for capturing meaning dimensions of abstract nouns than they are for concrete nouns, because of the very nature of the former (see Table 20.4).

As observed for concrete nouns, a dimension may not be explicitly expressed in a sense definition, but rather inherited by virtue of its membership to a semantic type (see Table 20.5).

As shown in points (i) to (v) above, the class of abstract (or better, non-concrete) nouns is not homogeneous. The first step to organize it was to determine the structure of the ontology. Three main top classes were identified: **Abstract_entities**, **Representations**, and **Properties**.

Table 20.5.

SemU	Dictionary definition	Inherited Quale
Comunicato	Notizia d'interesse generale divulgata da un mezzo di informazione (AGENTIVE: result of)	Comunicato ↑
Message	*News on general topic broadcasted by an information media*	Information TELIC: indirect telic

6   The Templates for Abstract Entities

The type **abstract_entity** subsumes only nonperceivable entities, i.e., movements of thoughts, values and moral standards, fields of activity and domains, the legal sense of institutions, cognitive processes, time periods, and also the tricky class of formal conventions (see above). The resulting hierarchy is illustrated below:

1. **Abstract_entity**
    [1.1.] Domain
    [1.2.] Time
    [1.3.] Moral_standards
    [1.4.] Cognitive_Fact [ABSTRACT_ENTITY | RESULT AGENTIVE]
    [1.5.] Movement_of_thought [ABSTRACT_ENTITY | AGENTIVE]
    [1.6.] Institution [ABSTRACT_ENTITY | AGENTIVE | TELIC]
    [1.7.] Convention [ABSTRACT_ENTITY | RESULT AGENTIVE]

Templates were built for each of the semantic types above, in a way that reflects their different complexity. Types DOMAIN [*"agricoltura"* (agriculture), *"fisica"* (physics), *"medicina"* (medecine)], TIME [*"primavera"* (spring), *"domenica"* (Sunday), *"Rinascimento"* (Renaissance)], and MORAL_STANDARD [*"libertà"* (freedom), *"diritto'* (right), *"carità"* (charity)] are simple types. They only provide the information that their members are a particular type of abstract entities.

By contrast, the template type for INSTITUTION (*"società"* (company), *"scuola"* (school), *"banca"* (bank)) expresses that the members of this type are some kind of abstract entities that exist by virtue of the fact that they were created for a certain purpose. COGNITIVE_FACTS [*"teoria"* (theory), *"conoscenza"* (knowledge), *"idea"* (idea)] and CONVENTIONS are characterized by an AGENTIVE relation indicating a resultative aspect of their meaning. A general AGENTIVE relation has been assigned also to MOVEMENT_OF_THOUGHT [*"comunismo"* (communism), *"Romanticismo"* (Romanticism)] because they are social artifact.

6.1   The Templates for Properties

The class of **Properties**, which includes mostly deadjectival nominals, was not easy to structure. Structuring the hierarchy appears to be more of a conceptual operation rather than a linguistic one. In fact, the subtypes of PROPERTY have been called PHYSICAL_PROPERTY, PHYSICAL_POWER, PSYCH_PROPERTY, because no lexicalization exists. For the same reason, it appears difficult to draw a linguistic taxonomy of properties and to assign a *isa* relation other than a flat one (i.e., "*isa* (<Usem>, <property>)" to most subtypes). On the other hand, for NLP systems requirements, a distinction between abstract and concrete properties was necessary. For these reasons, we considered "abstract properties" those that are psychological [*"intelligenza"* (intelligence), (*"pensiero"* (thinking), *"bravura"* (bravery)] and social [*"potere"* (power), *"autorità"* (authority), *"giustizia"* (justice)].

"Concrete properties" have been clustered under the PHYSICAL_PROPERTY node ["*colore*" (color), "*forma*" (shape), "*larghezza*" (width)] and its subtypes [PHYSI-CAL_POWER: "*gusto*" (smell), "*udito*" (hearing), "*forza*" (strength); COLOR: "*rosso*" (red), "*giallo*" (yellow); SHAPE: "*triangolo*" (triangle), "*quadrato*" (square), "*cerchio*" (circle)]. The resulting hierarchy is illustrated below.

1. **Property**
   [1.1.] Quality
   [1.2.] Physical_property
      [1.2.1.] Physical_power
      [1.2.2.] Color
      [1.2.3.] Shape
   [1.3.] Psych_property
   [1.4.] Social_property [PROPERTY | AGENTIVE]

6.2 The Templates for Representations

The class of **Representation** contains more complex concepts, which are unified types (see Pustejovsky, this volume). It includes lexical items referring to symbolic entities, which take their values from a kind of social convention (AGENTIVE dimension) and which have a specific communicative function (TELIC dimension). For example, "language" is a system that conveys information given an amount of shared knowledge. Similarly, numbers have a value because of their position in a symbolic and conventional system. The type REPRESENTATION accounts for the concrete and abstract aspects that can be viewed as two sides of the same coin in the semantics of these nominals. Languages, for example, have both a material side (sounds or written symbols) and a mental counterpart (usually concerning meanings). The subtypes of the top node Representation bear the same AGENTIVE and TELIC dimensions and are therefore mainly distinguished through CONSTITUTIVE features and relations.

1. **Representation [entity | agentive | telic]**
   [1.1.] Language
   [1.2.] Sign
   [1.3.] Information
   [1.4.] Number
   [1.5.] Unit_of_measurement

7 The Qualia Relations for Nonconcrete Nouns

Abstract nominals present a double face: On the one hand they are intrinsically complex, on the other hand the information about their semantics is rather poor. Thus, capturing and formalizing their meaning had been not always easy. That is why some of these relations are very general compared to those used for concrete

Table 20.6a.

Constitutive relations and features	Examples
concerns ($\underline{1}$, <Usem>)	(<tax_1>, <finances>)
has_as_member ($\underline{1}$, <Usem>)	(<socialism>, <socialist>: [Ideo])
has_as_part ($\underline{1}$, <Usem>)	(<science_1>, <method>)
is_a_part_of ($\underline{1}$, <Usem>)	(<pediatrics>, <medicine>: [Domain])
is_in ($\underline{1}$, <Usem>:[Building])	(<school_2>:[Institution], <school_1>: [Building])
measured_by ($\underline{1}$, <Usem>)	(<lenght_1>, <metre>: [Unit_of_measurement])
property_of ($\underline{1}$, <Adj_Usem>)	(<beauty_1>, <beautiful>)
quantifies ($\underline{1}$, <Usem>)	(<litre_1>, <capacity>)
related_to ($\underline{1}$, <Usem>)	<second>, <two>
successor_of ($\underline{1}$, <Usem>)	(<primavera_1>, <winter>: [Time])
connotation = pos, neg, underspec	*freedom*: connotation = positive
dimension = 1,2,3	*rectangle*: dimension = 2
iterative = yes, no, underspec	*season*: iterative = yes
scalar = yes, no	*red*: scalar = yes
punctual = yes, no, underspec	*moment*: punctual = yes

Table 20.6b.

Agentive relations and features	Examples
agentive ($\underline{1}$, <Usem>: [Human])	(<marxism>, <Marx>: [Human])
result_of ($\underline{1}$, <found>: [Creation])	(<school_2>: [Institution], <found>: [Creation])
result_of ($\underline{1}$, <convention>)	(<language_2>, <convention>: [Cooperative_activity])
result_of ($\underline{1}$, <Usem>: [Process])	(<tax_1>, <istituire>)
source ($\underline{1}$, <society>)	(<power_2>, <society>)

nominals, as shown in Tables 20.6a–c[9] that illustrate relations used for describing CONSTITUTIVE, AGENTIVE, and TELIC aspects of nonconcrete nouns, respectively.[10]

Although specifying the target Usem of the relations, even the *is-a* relation (the classical genus term in Computational Linguistics) is difficult for abstract nouns, qualia constitute, in this case again, a valuable guide in permitting to structure the information that can be grasped. Qualia dimensions provide a useful means also for representing very underspecified nonconcrete nouns, not easy to formalize from a semantic point of view. This is the case of lexical items such as "*scopo*" (aim), defined as 'ciò a cui si tende, che si desidera ottenere,'[11] or "*obiettivo*," which only

---

[9] In the following tables, for simplicity of exposition, we are using directly the English word instead of giving the translation from Italian ones.

[10] In Tables 20.6b and 20.6c some relations are repeated when they are restricted differently, because they carry different information.

[11] For example, "everything to which one tends to, what one desires to obtain."

Table 20.6c.

Telic relations and features	Examples
telic (1, <Usem>: [Activity])	(<school_2>: [Institution], <teaching_1>: [Purpose_Act])
indirect_telic (1, <measure>)	(<litre_1>, <measure>)
indirect_telic (1, <represent>)	(<symbol_2>, <represent>)
indirect_telic (1, <Usem>)	(<message_2>, <inform>: [Give_knowledge])
direct_telic (1, <Usem>)	(<book_1>, <read>: [Acquire_Knowledge])
used_by (1, <Usem>)	(<language_2>, <community>: [Human_group])
used_for (1, <Usem>)	(<number>, <count>)

conveys a bare TELIC dimension. The same holds for *"origine"* (origin), *"causa"* (cause), *"motivo"* (reason), etc., which lexically instantiate the AGENTIVE quale and *"parte"* (part), *"modo"* (way), *"maniera"* (manner), which are intrinsically CONSTITUTIVE. For the encoding of these Usems, definable only in terms of Qualia dimensions, three template types were created, namely TELIC, AGENTIVE, and CONSTITUTIVE.

8   Conclusion: the Contribution of Lexicographic Practice to Linguistic Theory

In this chapter, we have presented a wedding of theoretical linguistic and lexicographic practice focusing on the semantic properties of abstract nouns. Abstract nouns are conceptually more difficult to describe: They are neither perceivable, nor measurable, and are not as easily understood as objects and concrete events. We have pointed out that the lexicographer's subjectivity, which always plays a role during the lexicon building process, affects even more the resulting analysis of abstract nouns. Furthermore, as far as the formal vocabulary is concerned, the difficulty to describe abstract nouns by means of qualia roles seems to be related more to the intrinsic complexity of abstract entities and properties rather than to the inadequacy of the Qualia theory. Rather, qualia structure has been especially useful to get around the problem of assigning the genus term to some abstract entities. In other words, for those nouns for which a genus term can hardly be found (e.g., "scopo" (aim)), qualia roles provide directly the interpretation, which is transparent in the structuring of the semantics. Besides, we have seen how the elements of meaning easily map on the dimensions expressed via qualia roles, as far as concrete nouns are concerned. We have presented a set of templates that reflect the semantic structuring of a type. These templates are used by the lexicographer for determining membership of a semantic unit to a given type. At first sight, templates may simply look like a lexicographer auxiliary tool to speed up the coding task. On the contrary, templates are not only an interface but an implementation of the underlying theory. In fact, we have described a template development process that involves addressing and answering theoretical questions.

References

Busa, F. 1996. Compositionality and Semantics of Nominals, PhD thesis, Brandeis University.

Moravcsik, J.M. 1975. Aitia as Generative Factor in Aristotle's philosophy. *Dialogue* 14: 622–636.

Pinker, S. 1995. *The Language Instinct. How the Mind Creates Language*, HarperPerennial (a division of HarperCollins).

Pustejovsky, J. 1991. The Generative Lexicon. *Computational Linguistics* 17: 409–441.

Pustejovsky, J. 1995. *The Generative Lexicon*. MIT Press, Cambridge, MA.

SIMPLE Specification Group. 1998. *Simple Work Package 2, Linguistic Specifications*, Pisa.

21   Condensed Meaning In EuroWordNet

PIEK VOSSEN

Abstract

This chapter discusses condensed meaning in the EuroWordNet project. In this project, several wordnets for different languages are combined in a multilingual database. The matching of the meanings across the wordnets makes it necessary to account for polysemy in a generative way and to establish a notion of equivalence at a more global level. Finally, we will describe an attempt to set up a more fundamental ontology, which is linked to the meanings in the wordnets as derived complex types. The multilingual design of the EuroWordNet database makes it possible to specify how the lexicon of each language uniquely maps onto these condensed types.

1   Introduction

The aim of EuroWordNet[1] is to develop a multilingual database with wordnets in several European languages: English, Dutch, Italian, Spanish, French, German, Czech, and Estonian. Each language-specific wordnet is structured along the same lines as WordNet (Miller et al., 1990): Synonyms are grouped into synsets, which are related by means of basic semantic relations such as hyponymy (e.g., between "car" and "vehicle") or meronymy relations (e.g., between "car" and "wheel"). By means of these relations all words are interconnected, constituting a huge network or wordnet. Because the lexicalization of concepts is different across languages, each wordnet in the EuroWordNet database represents an autonomous and unique system of language-internal relations. This means that each wordnet represents the lexical semantic relations between the lexicalized words and expressions of the language only: No artificial classifications (such as External-Body-Part, InanimateObject) are introduced to impose some structuring of the hierarchy (Vossen, 1998; Vossen and Bloksma, 1998). In addition to the relations between the synsets, each language-synset is related to an Inter-Lingual-Index

---

[1] EuroWordNet is funded by the EC as projects LE2-4003 and LE4-8328. It is a joint enterprise of the University of Amsterdam (coordinator), the Fundacion Universidad Empresa (Madrid and Barcelona), Istituto di Linguistica Computazionale del CNR (Pisa), University of Sheffield, University of Tuebingen, University of Avignon, University of Tartu, University of Brno, Bertin (Paris), Memodata (Avignon), Xerox Research Center (Grenoble), and Lernout and Hauspie (Antwerp). Further information on the project can be found at: http://www.hum.uva.nl/~ewn.

(ILI), connecting all these wordnets. In the database, it is possible to go from synsets in one language to synsets in any other wordnet that are linked to the same ILI-records and to compare the lexical semantic structures. This is illustrated in Figure 21.1 for the language-specific synsets linked to the ILI-record "drive." The ILI is an unstructured fund of concepts, mainly based on the synsets taken from WordNet1.5 and adapted to provide a better matching across the wordnets. Each ILI-record consists of a synset, a gloss specifying the meaning, and a reference to its source. No relations are maintained between the ILI-records as such. The development of a complete language-neutral ontology is considered to be too complex and time-consuming given the limitations of the project. As an unstructured list there is no need to discuss changes or updates to the index from a many-to-many perspective, and it is easier to deal with complex mappings of meanings across wordnets. Furthermore, it will be possible to indirectly see a structuring of a set of ILI-records by viewing the language-internal relations of the language-specific concepts that are related to the set of ILI-records. It is thus possible to get any hierarchical structuring, according to any ontology or wordnet that is linked to the index (including WordNet1.5). In Peters et al. (1998); Vossen et al. (1997), further details are given how lexical semantic structures or configurations can be compared in the EuroWordNet database.

Some language-independent structuring of the ILI is still provided by two separate ontologies, which may be linked to ILI records (see Figure 21.1):

- the Top Concept ontology, which is a hierarchy of language-independent concepts, reflecting important semantic distinctions, (e.g., *Object* and *Substance*, *Dynamic* and *Static*);
- a hierarchy of domain labels, which are knowledge structures grouping meanings in terms of topics or scripts (e.g. *Traffic*, *Road-Traffic*, *Air-Traffic*, *Sports*, *Medical*).

Both the Top Concepts and the domain labels can be transferred via the equivalence relations of the ILI-records to the language-specific meanings, as illustrated in Figure 21.1. The Top Concepts *Dynamic* and *Location* are for example directly linked to the ILI-record "drive" and therefore indirectly also apply to all language-specific concepts related to this ILI-record. Via the language-internal relations the Top Concepts can be further inherited to all other related language-specific concepts. The main purpose of the ontologies is to provide a common framework for the most important concepts in all the wordnets.

The development of the individual wordnets takes place at different sites, using separate tools and databases. To achieve maximal compatibility of the independently created results, we have determined a set of common Base Concepts. These Base Concepts play a major role in the separate wordnets, which is measured in terms of the number of relations with other concepts and their position in the

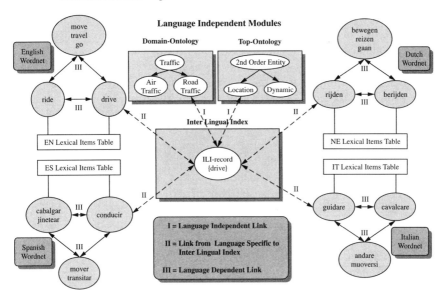

Fig. 21.1. The global architecture of the EuroWordNet database.

hierarchy.[2] Each site has made a selection in the local wordnets, and the translations of these selections into equivalent WordNet1.5 synsets have been merged to form a set of 1024 fundamental concepts (both nominal and verbal), which is shared by all sites. The further development of the wordnets takes place by encoding the language-internal relations for this set and extending it top-down to more specific meanings that depend on it. A special effort has been made to manually encode the relations for these concepts in a coherent and compatible way, so that the cores of the different wordnets are of sufficient quality. For that purpose, we have classified these Base Concepts in terms of the Top-Ontology mentioned above (Rodriguez et al., 1998).

The wordnets are (as much as possible) built from existing resources that still have a traditional structuring of senses against which the generative approach opposes (Pustejovsky, 1995). This means that different contextual interpretations are sometimes enumerated as distinct senses and in other cases collapsed or only partially represented. We see for example that WordNet1.5 only lists one meaning for "embassy" as the "building," whereas the Dutch wordnet gives separate meanings for the "building" and the "institute" for the equivalent "ambassade." In

---

[2] Base Concepts should not be confused with the Basic Level concepts defined by (Rosch, 1977). Base Concepts are typically more general and abstract, which is a natural consequence of the criteria for their selection. So whereas "table" may a Basic Level Concept we expect "furniture" to be a Base Concept.

the case of "school," both wordnets list both senses, but the Italian wordnet only represents the "institute." These inconsistencies make clear that the comparison of wordnets in the database will confront us with many situations in which meaning interpretations are distributed in different ways. To be able to make a decision over the compatibility of such mismatches, it is necessary to define a common policy for the treatment of sense-enumeration in the individual wordnets. This will be discussed in section 2 that deals with complex types in the individual word-nets. By specifying disjunctive and conjunctive combinations of interpretations or conceptualizations, it is possible to represent particular types of polysemy in a more condensed way. Nevertheless, other types of regular polysemy will still occur and in section 3 we will discuss how these can be grouped by introducing complex types in the Inter-Lingual-Index itself. Different partial reflections of in-terpretation across wordnets can then still be matched via more coarse meanings in the ILI that connect several of these interpret ations. Finally, the top-ontology concepts, mentioned above, can be combined to form complex combinations that can be applied to ILI-records, and thus indirectly provide a more systematic po-tential for interpretations for the synsets in the local wordnets linked to these ILI-records.

2   Complex Types in the Language-specific Wordnets

In WordNet1.5, multiple hyperonyms incidentally occur. The next example "spoon" has two hyperonyms "cutlery" and "container" that apply to the same synset:

> **spoon** – (a piece of cutlery with a shallow bowl-shaped container and a handle; used to stir or serve or take up food):
> -HAS_HYPERONYM: **cutlery** – (implements for cutting and eating food)
> -HAS_HYPERONYM: **container** – (something that holds things, especially for transport or storage)

In EuroWordNet we systematically use this option to encode combinations of meaning aspects in a single sense, resulting in complex types. Following (Vossen, 1995), three different complex types are distinguished, depending on the combi-natorial constraints of the hyperonyms:

- disjunctive hyperonyms
- conjunctive hyperonyms
- nonexclusive hyperonyms

Disjunctive hyperonyms are incompatible types that never apply simultaneously. We find many examples of these disjunctions among so-called *functionals*, which are nouns that refer to the participant in an event but do not restrict for the type of entity participating. The typical definition pattern for these nouns is a disjunction of genus words as shown in the following examples taken from the Longman

Dictionary of Contemporary English (Procter, 1978):

> **arrival** – a person or thing that arrives or has arrived
> **puzzler** – a person or thing that puzzles
> **threat** – a person, thing or idea regarded as a possible danger

The disjunction represents an open range of entity types that can play a certain role in the event. Alternatively, dictionaries may also enumerate different senses for the disjuncted types as is illustrated by the different senses of "threat" in WordNet1.5:

> **menace, threat1** – (something that is a source of danger)
> -HAS_HYPERONYM: **danger** – (a cause of pain or injury or loss; he feared the dangers of travelling by air;)[-HAS_HYPERONYM: causal agent, cause, causal agency] – (any entity that causes events to happen)
> **terror, scourge, threat4** – (a person who inspires fear or dread)
> -HAS_HYPERONYM: **person, individual, someone, mortal, human, soul** – (a human being)

Here we see that sense 1 of "threat" is linked to a nonrestrictive class "danger," which can be any "causal agent" (see also the head of the gloss: "something"), whereas sense 4 expresses the same concept restricted to "person." By distinguishing different synsets, it is suggested that these are also distinct concepts or senses, which is highly doubtful. As the more generic sense already suggests, anything can be a "threat," which means that we could need any number of synsets to express this range. Cases such as "threat" will in principle be encoded in EuroWordNet as a single sense using a so-called role-relation, possibly extended with a disjunctive range of hyperonyms:

> **threat**
> -ROLE_AGENT   threaten
> -HAS_HYPERONYM   person; *disjunctive*
> -HAS_HYPERONYM   thing; *disjunctive*
> -HAS_HYPERONYM   idea; *disjunctive*

The status of the multiple hyperonyms is indicated by the label *disjunctive* that can be added to a relation. Not all cases of disjunctive hyperonyms in definitions also represent an open range of types, as is shown in the following examples from LDOCE:

> **acquittal 2** – the act of declaring or condition of being found not guilty
> **adherence 2** – the act or condition of sticking to something firmly

In these examples, a fixed choice is given as the interpretation of the derived nominal between "act" and "condition." The combination of both is incompatible: the former denotes a dynamic event and the latter a static situation. Because we are not dealing with an open range of interpretations we have to assume that they represent different senses. Because the polysemy is regular it is still possible to generalize over this relation. This is however captured outside the language-specific wordnet, as will be explained in the following section.

Disjunctive ranges are not restricted to hyponymy relations only. In the following examples from WordNet1.5 we see that different senses of "door" are distinguished depending on the type of whole of which it is a part:

> **door 1** – (a swinging or sliding barrier that will close the entrance to a room or building; he knocked on the door; he slammed the door as he left)
> -HAS_HOLONYM: **doorway, door, entree, entry, portal, room access** – (the space in a wall through which you enter or leave a room or building; the space that a door can close; he stuck his head in the doorway)
> **doorway, door 2, entree, entry, portal, room access** – (the space in a wall through which you enter or leave a room or building; the space that a door can close; he stuck his head in the doorway)
> -HAS_HOLONYM: **wall** – (a partition with a height and length greater than its thickness; used to divide or enclose or support)
> **door 6** – (a swinging or sliding barrier that will close off access into a car; she forgot to lock the doors of her car)
> -HAS_HOLONYM: **car, auto, automobile, machine, motorcar** – (4-wheeled; usually propelled by an internal combustion engine; he needed a car to get to work)

The different holonyms of which "door" can be a PART are listed here as different synsets (sense 1 and 6 of "door"), suggesting that these reflect different concepts. Again, there could be any number of holonyms that have a "door" as a part. According to the principle that is applied here these would all result in different synsets for "door." In EuroWordNet, these meanings are combined in a single complex type listing the disjunctive holonyms in which it can be incorporated:

> **door**
> -HAS_HOLONYM   car; *disjunctive*
> -HAS_HOLONYM   airplane; *disjunctive*
> -HAS_HOLONYM   room; *disjunctive*
> -HAS_HOLONYM   building; *disjunctive*

Note that in the opposite situation conjunction of meronyms is the default:

> **car**
> -HAS_MERONYM   door; *conjunctive*[3]
> -HAS_MERONYM   wheel; *conjunctive*

---

[3] In general, absence of a label triggers the default interpretation in EuroWordNet. It is therefore not necessary to explicitly indicate *conjunction* of meronyms in the database as it is done in this example.

Conjunctive hyperonyms always apply simultaneously and thus can never be incompatible. Typical examples of conjunctive hyperonyms are found for specific lexicalizations of verbs in which multiple aspects are combined. In Dutch, we see for example that many verb compounds combine a resultative verb and a manner of motion and thus can be classified by both hyperonyms:

doodschoppen   to kick to death
-HAS_HYPERONYM   doden (to kill); *conjunctive*
-HAS_HYPERONYM   schoppen (to kick); *conjunctive*
opentrekken   to pull open
-HAS_HYPERONYM   openen (to open); *conjunctive*
-HAS_HYPERONYM   trekken (to pull); *conjunctive*

Here the conjunctive label indicates that both aspects are always implied in the meaning of the verb. In many other cases, the hyperonyms are nonexclusive: both aspects may apply simultaneously or one of both may apply:

knife
-HAS_HYPERONYM   weapon
-HAS_HYPERONYM   cutlery

Absence of the disjunctive/conjunctive label expresses optionality and compatibility of the perspectives.

Finally, disjunction and nonexclusiveness also apply in the reversed direction to the hyponyms of a class. As argued by both (Vossen and Bloksma, 1998) and (Guarino, 1998), there is an important difference between co-hyponyms that represent disjunct classes, such as "cat" and "dog" and hyponyms that can cross-classify with these disjunct types, such as "pet" and "draught animal." As a "dog" it is impossible to have "cat"-specific properties, but it is not unlikely that it has "pet" or "draught animal" properties. A similar observation can be made with respect to the substitution behavior of these co-hyponyms. We can refer to "dogs" with "pet" and "draugh animal" but certainly not with "cat." In this respect, the nondisjunct classes resemble the *functionals* discussed above, being orthogonal to the disjunct types. Because all relations in EuroWordNet are encoded separately in both ways, it is possible to use the same label *disjunctive* to differentiate the hyponyms if a class in the opposite direction (see below).

Nevertheless, there may be strong stereotypical preferences or restrictions to some types. The class of "pets" is in our culture typically associated with "cats" and "dogs" but not with "insects." On the one hand, we thus may want to express that the class of "pets" has "cats" and "dogs" as members but we do not want to classify "cat" and "dog" by all possible orthogonal classes that exist. There is a difference in status between the conventional classification of "dog" and "cat" as an "animal" and the classification as a "pet." The latter classification is more relevant to "pet" than for the members. To deal with this phenomenon, a separate label *reversed* is used to mark the implicational direction of a relation. The next examples then show the result when we combine the different kind of labeling and directions of relations that have been discussed:

- animate being
  - HAS_HYPONYM plant; *disjunctive*
  - HAS_HYPONYM person; *disjunctive*
  - HAS_HYPONYM animal; *disjunctive*
  - HAS_HYPONYM parent
  - HAS_HYPONYM winner
  - HAS_HYPONYM favorite
- animal
  - HAS_HYPONYM horse; *disjunctive*
  - HAS_HYPONYM cat; *disjunctive*
  - HAS_HYPONYM dog; *disjunctive*
  - HAS_HYPONYM pet
  - HAS_HYPONYM draught animal
- pet
  - HAS_HYPERONYM animal
  - HAS_HYPONYM cat
  - HAS_HYPONYM dog
- draught animal
  - HAS_HYPERONYM animal
  - HAS_HYPONYM horse
  - HAS_HYPONYM draught dog
- cat
  - HAS_HYPERONYM animal
  - HAS_HYPERONYM pet; *reversed*
- dog
  - HAS_HYPERONYM animal
  - HAS_HYPERONYM pet; *reversed*
  - HAS_HYPERONYM draught animal; *reversed*
- draught dog
  - HAS_HYPERONYM dog; *conjunctive*
  - HAS_HYPERONYM draught animal; *conjunctive*
- horse
  - HAS_HYPERONYM animal
  - HAS_HYPERONYM draught animal; *reversed*
  - HAS_HYPERONYM riding animal; *reversed*

Hyponyms that are not labeled as *disjunct* are thus orthogonal to the other co-hyponyms. Cross-classification is only excluded by explicit marking as *disjunct* classes. The label *reversed* here indicates that the conceptual implication is the other way around. A "horse" is a typical example of a "draught animal" but "draught animal" is not a typical class of "horse." In other words: the link from "draught animal" to "horse" is needed to define or explain the usage of the former and not the latter. Finally, we see that, in the case of "draught dog," the link to "draught animal" is indeed necessary to define it and consequently we have two hyperonyms that are *conjunctively* combined. This illustrates the difference in status of the multiple hyperonyms for "horse" and for "draught dog."

By means of disjunctive/conjunctive/reversed hyp(er)onyms it is thus possible to encode several generative aspects of meaning: open ranges of entities (disjunctive types) and different types of parallel classifications (multiple hyperonyms). In many other cases, the wordnets will however still contain polysemous entries, listing incompatible hyponymic relations. These will be discussed in the next section.

3   Complex Types in the Inter-Lingual-Index

We mentioned before that incompatible hyperonyms that do not represent an open range of entities are kept separate in the wordnets. Among these are many cases of regular polysemy that apply to larger groups of conceptual classes (e.g., the "building/institute" polysemy mentioned in the introduction). As suggested, inconsistent listing of the regular polysemy in the wordnets may result in a situation that the local synsets of, for example "university," cannot be matched across wordnets. Hamp and Feldweg (1997) describe how such polysemy can be accounted for in a specific wordnet for German. To limit this danger in EuroWordNet for all involved wordnets, we extend the ILI with globalized senses that represent sets of more specific but related senses of the same word. In Figure 21.2, we see that the original linking of Dutch, Italian, and Spanish equivalents for "university" have been extended with an EQ_METONYM relation to a new so-called *Composite* ILI-record "university," which contains a reference to two more specific meanings. Via the EQ_METONYM relations the synsets can be retrieved despite of the different ways in which they are linked to the more specific synsets. It is not necessary that the metonymy-relation also holds in the local language. In this example, only the Dutch wordnet has two senses that parallel the metonymy-relation in the ILI. The Italian and Spanish example only list one sense (which may be correct or an omission in their resources). In the case of Spanish there are multiple equivalences to both senses of "university," whereas the Italian synset is only linked to the "building" sense. The Spanish synset is in fact equivalent to the new Composite ILI-record.

As a side effect, the relation between the two Dutch senses is now expressed via the metonymy-equivalence relation to the more global Composite ILI-record. The Composite ILI-record may also create metonymic relations between different forms that represent the same semantic relation, such as *"universiteit"* (university institute) and *"universiteitsgebouw"* (university building) in Dutch. This shows that productive interpretations from a complex type such as "university" can have different realizations in languages. Whereas one language may express these interpretations with the same form (resulting in polysemy), another language may use different compounds or derivations.

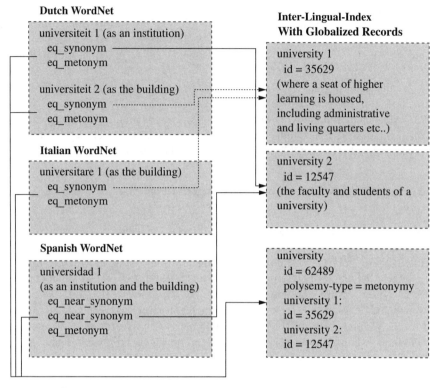

Fig. 21.2. Inter-Lingual-Index with a Composite ILI-record for "university".

Similar globalized records are added for *generalizations*. Generalizations apply to explicit enumeration of meaning specialization. For example, in the Dutch resource there is only one sense for *"schoonmaken"* (to clean) which simultaneously matches with at least four senses of "clean" in WordNet1.5:

- make clean by removing dirt, filth, or unwanted substances from
- remove unwanted substances from, such as feathers or pits, as of chickens or fruit
- remove in making clean; Clean the spots off the rug
- remove unwanted substances from - (as in chemistry)

The senses in WordNet1.5 do not seem to be incompatible but merely differentiate different contexts and objects that are involved (without being complete). The Dutch equivalent could be used in any of these situations as well. Such extreme proliferation of meaning occurs quite often in WordNet1.5. On the one hand, this is a good feature for an interlingua, because we can very precisely establish equivalence relations; on the other hand, it makes it more difficult to comprehensively establish equivalence between synsets across the wordnets. It is clear that arbitrary listings of such specializations may lead to similar situations as described above that synsets across wordnets are linked to different specializations and thus cannot be matched. By introducing a single generalized meaning for cases such as "clean" that groups these specializations, and by adding an EQ_GENERALIZATION relations from the relevant synsets in the wordnets to the generalization, we will achieve a better matching.

Finally, there is a specific globalization relation, EQ_DIATHESIS, to capture sense differentiation due to diathesis alternations (Levin, 1993), e.g.:

> **Italian: cambiare (to change)** 1 intransitive (to become different) 2 transitive (to make different)
>
> **Dutch: bewegen (to move)** 1 intransitive (to change place or position) 2 transitive (to cause to change place or position) 6 reflexive ((of people, animals) to change place or position)

Here we see that Italian *"cambiare"* 1 and 2 (change) exhibit a transitive/intransitive alternation that correlates with a difference in causation. Something similar holds for different senses of *"bewegen"* (move) in Dutch, which refer as intransitives verbs to a noncausative change-of-position and as transitives to the causation of such a change (this also holds for *"mover"* (move) in Spanish and *"muovere"* (move) in Italian). This phenomenon is very widespread in all the resources that are used, including WordNet1.5, which forms the basis for the ILI. By adding a single meaning that abstracts from causation (and thus from transitive or intransitive realization), it is possible to get a more systematic encoding on the one hand and provide a more stable matching across the wordnets as well.

The generation of these equivalence relations is to a large extent done automatically (see Buitelaar, 1998; Peters et al. 1998; Peters, Peters, and Vossen, 1998) After extending the ILI with more global concepts, the EQ_METONYM, EQ_GENERALIZATION or EQ_DIATHESIS will be automatically generated for all synsets that have at least one of the specific ILI-records in the globalized ILI-records as the target of an EQ_SYNONYM or EQ_NEAR_SYNONYM relation. There is no need for the local wordnet builders to consider each of these equivalence-extensions manually. Note that this procedure will also generate a relation when interpretations are represented by different word forms in languages, as has been suggested for Dutch compounds such as *"universiteitsgebouw"* (university building). This brings in a new perspective in the discussion. If realization of generative meanings is not limited to polysemy, it is less clear where one should stop. In theory, there could be a vague language that uses a few forms and extreme degree of polysemy, or a language that uses an extreme amount of forms, each with an unique interpretation. In the interlingua, we could build in any level of sense-grouping or globalization but it is not clear what is a natural or practical level per se. The granulation of the ILI is now determined by the English language (as represented by WordNet1.5), which has a tendency to use polysemy rather than derivation or compounding (as in, for example, more Germanic languages).

4   Complex Types of Top-Concepts

The above discussion showed that a well-designed interlingua or language-neutral ontology may have many benefits from which all the linked wordnets can profit. We also demonstrated that the separation of the interlingua from the language-specific realizations may help to clarify the way meaning is proliferated in the lexicalized vocabulary of languages. Still, the sense-groupings in the ILI mainly serve a practical purpose: to improve the matching of synsets across the word-nets. As we explained in the introduction, it is not feasible to develop a complete language-neutral ontology within the limits of this project, and without knowing in what respects languages differ. The ILI is therefore still nothing but an index for matching meanings, without much structure. This being said, we nevertheless have began to provide a more fundamental specification of the meanings in the form of a top-ontology of 63 semantic distinctions. This ontology has been applied to a set of 1024 so-called Base Concepts (BCs) that play a fundamental role in establishing the relations in the different wordnets (Rodriguez et al., 1998). These Base Concepts are represented as ILI-records and thus indirectly give access to the linked synsets in the local wordnets.

The first starting point for the top ontology is that the wordnets are linguis-tic ontologies, representing the lexicalization patterns of languages. We therefore used semantic distinctions which are common in linguistic paradigms: Aktionsart models (Dowty, 1979; Pustejovsky, 1991; Vendler, 1967; Verkuyl, 1972; Verkuyl, 1989); entity-orders (Lyons, 1977); Aristotle's Qualia-structure (Pustejovsky, 1995). The second starting point is that the ontology should reflect the diversity of the set of common BCs. In this sense, the classification of the common BCs in terms of the top-concepts should result in homogeneous Base Concept Clusters with an average size. Large clusters will be further subdivided and very small clusters will be generalized. Finally, we can mention as important characteristics:

- the Top Concepts are hierarchically ordered by means of a subsumption relation but there can only be one super-type linked to each Top Concept: multiple inheritance between top-concepts is not allowed.
- in addition to the subsumption relation, Top Concepts can have an opposition-relation to indicate that certain distinctions are disjoint, whereas others may overlap.
- there may be multiple relations from ILI-records to Top Concepts. This means that the BCs can be cross-classified in terms of multiple Top Con-cepts (as long as these are not disjoint): i.e., multiple inheritance from Top Concept to Base Concept is allowed.

It is important to realize that the Top Concepts (TCs) are more like semantic features than common conceptual classes. We typically find TCs for *Living* and for *Part* as meaning components or facets but we do not find a TC *Bodypart*, even though this may be more appealing to a nonexpert. BCs representing "body parts" are now cross-classified by the conjunction of *Living* and *Part*. The reason for this is that the diversity of the BCs would require many cross-classifying concepts where *Living* and *Part* are combined with many other TCs. Furthermore, it turned out that the BCs typically abstract from particular features but these abstractions do not show any redundancy (i.e., it is not the case that all things that are *Living* also always share other features). An explanation for the diversity of the BCs is the way in which they have been selected. To be useful as a classifier or category for many concepts (one of the major criteria for selection), a concept must capture a particular generalization but abstract from (many) other properties. Likewise, we find many classifying meanings that express only one or two TC-features but no others. In this respect, the BCs typically abstract one or two l evels from the cognitive Basic-Level as defined by (Rosch, 1977).

Following (Lyons, 1977) we distinguish at the first level 3 types of entities:

> **1stOrderEntity (always concrete nouns)**   Any concrete entity (publicly) perceivable by the senses and located at any point in time, in a three-dimensional space.

> **2ndOrderEntity (nouns, verbs, and adjectives)**   Any Static Situation (property, relation) or Dynamic Situation, which cannot be grasped, heard, seen, felt as an independent physical thing. They can be located in time and occur or take place rather than exist; e.g., continue, occur, apply

> **3rdOrderEntity (always abstract nouns)**   An unobservable proposition that exists independently of time and space. They can be true or false rather than real. They can be asserted or denied, remembered or forgotten (e.g., idea, thought, information, theory, plan).

Because the number of 3rdOrderEntities among the BCs was limited compared to the 1stOrder and 2ndOrder Entities, we have not further subdivided them. The 1stOrderEntities and 2ndOrderEntities are further subdivided according to the hierarchy given in Figure 21.3, where the superscripts indicate the number of assigned BCs. For a more complete description of the BCs and TCs see (Rodriguez et al., 1998). Here will only discuss the most important distinctions.

4.1   Classification of 1st-Order-Entities

The 1stOrderEntities are distinguished in terms of four main ways of conceptualizing or classifying a concrete entity:

> **Origin**   the way in which an entity has come about.
> **Form**   as an a-morf substance or as an object with a fixed shape, hence the subdivisions Substance and Object.
> **Composition**   as a group of self-contained wholes or as a part of such a whole, hence the subdivisions Part and Group.
> **Function**   the typical activity or action that is associated with an entity.

1st Order Entity^1
Origin^0
 Natural^{21}
  Living^{30}
   Plant^{18}
   Human^{106}
   Creature^2
   Anima^{123}
 Artifact^{144}
Form^0
 Substance^{32}
  Solid^{63}
  Liquid^{13}
  Gas^1
 Object1^{62}
Composition^0
 Part^{86}
 Group^{63}
Function^{55}
 Vehicle^8
 Representation^{12}
  Money Representation^{10}
  Language Representation^{34}
  Image Representation^9
 Software^4
 Place^{45}
 Occupation^{23}
 Instrument^{18}
 Garment^3
 Furniture^6
 Covering^8
 Container^{12}
 Comestible^{32}
 Building^{13}

2nd Order Entity^0
Situation Type^6
 Dynamic^{134}
  Bounded Event^{183}
  Unbounded Event^{48}
 Static^{28}
  Property^{61}
  Relation^{38}
Situation Component^0
 Cause^{67}
  Agentive^{170}
  Phenomenal^{17}
  Stimulating^{25}
 Communication^{50}
 Condition^{62}
 Existence^{27}
 Experience^{43}
 Location^{76}
 Manner^{21}
 Mental^{90}
 Modal^{10}
 Physical^{140}
 Possession^{23}
 Purpose^{137}
 Quantity^{39}
 Social^{100}
 Time^{24}
 Usage^8

3rd Order Entity^{33}:
theory;
idea;
structure;
evidence;
procedure;
doctrine;
policy;
data point;
content;
plan of action;
concept;
plan;
communication;
knowledge base;
cognitive content;
know-how;
category;
information;
abstract;
info;

Fig. 21.3. The EuroWordNet Top-Ontology.

These classes are comparable with Aristotle's Qualia roles as described in Pustejovsky's Generative lexicon, (the *Agentive role, Formal role, Constitutional role*, and *Telic Role*, respectively: Pustejovsky, 1995) but are also based on our empirical findings to classify the BCs. BCs can be classified in terms of any combination of these four roles.

The main classes are then further subdivided, where the subdivisions for *Form* and *Composition* are obvious given the above definition, except that *Substance* itself is further subdivided into *Solid, Liquid*, and *Gas*. In the case of *Function*, the subdivisions are based only on the frequency of BCs having such a function or role. In principle, the number of roles is infinite but the above roles appear to occur more frequently in the set of common Base Concepts. Finally, a more fine-grained subdivision has been made for *Origin*, first into *Natural* and *Artifact*. The category *Natural* covers both inanimate objects and substances, such as stones, sand, water, and all living things, among which animals, plants, and humans. The latter are stored at a deeper level below *Living*. The intermediate level *Living* is necessary to create a separate cluster for natural objects and substances, which consist of "living material" (e.g., "skin," "cell") but are not considered as "animate beings." Nonliving and natural objects and substances, such as natural products like "milk," "seeds," and "fruit," are classified directly below *Natural*. As suggested, each BC that is a 1stOrderEntity is classified in terms of these main classes. However, whereas the main classes are intended for cross-classifications, most of the subdivisions are disjoint classes: a concept cannot be an *Object* and a *Substance*, or both *Natural* and *Artifact*. This means that within a mainclass only one subdivision can be assigned. Consequently, each BC that is a 1stOrderEntity has at least one up to four classifications:

> **fruit**   Comestible (Function); Object (Form); Part (Composition); Plant (Natural, Origin)
>
> **skin**   Covering (Covering); Solid (Form); Part (Composition); Living (Natural, Origin)
>
> **cell**   Part (Composition); Living (Natural, Origin)
>
> **life 1**   Group (Composition); Living (Natural, Origin)
>
> **reproductive structure 1**   Living (Natural, Origin)

Finally, with respect to *Composition*, it needs to be said that only concepts that essentially depend on some other concept, are classified as either *Part* or *Group*. It is not the case that all persons will be classified as Parts because they may be part of group. *Group*, on the other hand, typically depends on the elements as part of its meaning. The default interpretations is therefore to be an independent *Whole*.

4.2   The Classification of 2ndOrderEntities

As explained above, 2ndOrderEntities can be referred to by nouns and verbs (and also adjectives or adverbs) denoting static or dynamic Situations, such as "birth," "live," "life," "love," "die," and "death." All 2ndOrderEntities are classified using two different classification schemes, which represent the first division below 2ndOrderEntity:

> **SituationType**   the event-structure in terms of which a situation can be characterized as a conceptual unit over time
>
> **SituationComponent**   the most salient semantic component(s) that characterize(s) a situation

SituationType reflects the way in which a situation can be quantified and distributed over time, and the dynamicity that is involved. It thus represents a basic classification in terms of the event-structure (in the formal tradition) and the predicate-inherent Aktionsart properties of nouns and verbs. The *Situation-Components* represent a conceptual classification, resulting in intuitively coherent clusters of word meanings. The *SituationComponents* reflect the most salient semantic components that apply to our selection of Base Concepts. Examples of *SituationComponents* are: *Location, Existence, Cause.*

Typically, *SituationType* represents disjoint features that cannot be combined, whereas it is possible to assign any range or combination of *SituationComponents* to a word meaning. Each 2ndOrder meaning can thus be classified in terms of an obligatory but unique *SituationType* and any number of *SituationComponents*. Following a traditional Aktionsart classification (Dowty, 1979; Vendler, 1967; Verkuyl, 1972; Verkuyl, 1989), *SituationType* is first subdivided into *Static* and *Dynamic*, depending on the dynamicity of the Situation:

Dynamic   Situations implying either a specific transition from one state to another (Bounded in time) or a continuous transition perceived as an ongoing temporally unbounded process (e.g., event, act, action, become, happen, take place, process, habit, change, activity. Opposed to *Static*.

Static   Situations (properties, relations, and states) in which there is no transition from one eventuality or situation to another: nondynamic (e.g., state, property, be). Opposed to *Dynamic*.

In general words, *Static Situations* do not involve any change, *Dynamic Situations* involve some specific change or a continuous changing. *Static Situations* are further subdivided into *Properties*, such as length, size, which apply to single concrete entities or abstract situations, and *Relations*, such as distance, space, which only exist relative to and in between several entities (of the same order):

Property   Static Situation, which applies to a single concrete entity or abstract Situation (e.g., color, speed, age, length, size, shape, weight).

Relation   Static Situation, which applies to a pair of concrete entities or abstract Situations, and which cannot exist by itself without either one of the involved entities (e.g., relation, kinship, distance, space).

Dynamic Situations are subdivided into events that express a specific transition and are bounded in time (*BoundedEvent*), and processes that are unbounded in time (*UnboundedEvent*) and do not imply a specific transition from one situation to another (although there can be many intermediate transitions):

BoundedEvent   Dynamic Situations in which a specific transition from one Situation to another is implied; Bounded in time and directed to a result (e.g., to do, to cause to change, to make, to create).

UnboundedEvent   Dynamic Situations occurring during a period of time and composed of a sequence of (micro-)changes of state, which are not perceived as relevant for characterizing the Situation as a whole (e.g., grow, change, move around, live, breath, activity, hobby, sport, education, work, performance, fight, love, caring, management).

The *SituationComponents* divide the Base Concepts into conceptually coherent clusters. The set of distinctions is therefore based on the diversity of the set of common Base Concepts that has been defined. As far as the set of Base Concepts is representative for the total wordnets, this set of *SituationComponents* is also representative for the whole. As said above, a verb or 2ndOrder noun may thus be composed of any combination of these components. However, it is obvious that some combinations make more sense than others. The more specific a word is, the more components it incorporates. Just as with the 1stOrderEntities, we therefore typically see that the more frequent classifying nouns and verbs only incorporate a few of these components. In the set of common Base-Concept, such classifying words are more frequent, and words with many *SituationComponents* are therefore rare. Below are some examples of typical combinations of *SituationComponents*:

- Experience + Stimulating + Dynamic + Condition (undifferentiated for Mental or Physical)
  Verbs: cause to feel unwell; cause pain
- Physical + Experience + SituationType (undifferentiated for Static/ Dynamic)
  Nouns: sense; sensation; perception;
  Verbs: look; feel; experience;
- Mental + (BoundedEvent) Dynamic + Agentive
  Verbs: identify; form an opinion of; form a resolution about; decide; choose; understand; call back; ascertain; bump into; affirm; admit defeat
  Nouns: choice, selection
- Mental + Dynamic + Agentive
  Verbs: interpret; differentiate; devise; determine; cerebrate; analyze; arrange
  Nouns: higher cognitive process; cerebration; categorization; basic cognitive process; argumentation; abstract thought
- Mental + Experience + SituationType (undifferentiated for Static/ Dynamic)
  Verbs: consider; desire; believe; experience
  Nouns: pleasance; motivation; humor; feeling; faith; emotion; disturbance; disposition; desire; attitude
- Relation + Physical + Location
  Verbs: go; be; stay in one place; adjoin
  Nouns: path;course; aim; blank space; degree; direction; spatial relation; elbow room; course; direction; distance; spacing; spatial property; space

The 1stOrder en 2ndOrder TCs can thus be combined in a partial lattice. Combinations of TCs have been applied to the BCs to get the most specific description that was still considered to be valid in the local wordnets. This resulted in 124 clusters for the 1stOrderEntities (491 BCs) and 314 clusters for the 2ndOrderEntities (500 BCs). The TC-combinations can be seen as complex types assigned to the ILI-records that represent the BCs. These types do not represent metonymic relations as discussed in the previous section but more direct presuppositions or entailments. They predict a range of interpretations corresponding to the combination of TCs. Possibly, more complex types can be derived for more specific concepts than the BCs but this has not been realized in EuroWordNet. In principle, the complex types should carry over to all the synsets in the local wordnets that have a (direct) equivalence relation with the BC. The implications can then be further distributed to all the hyponyms of the concepts in the local wordnets. As we have discussed, multiple hyperonyms can result in complex types as well, and thus also in further combinations of these basic implications in the local wordnet. Figure 21.4 illustrates this for "spoon" in WordNet1.5, which inherits via the multiple hyperonyms both the single feature *Function* from "container" and the feature-combination *Artifact* and *Object* from "artifact object." In this example there is some redundancy because of the diamond hyponymy-structure.

However, it is important to realize that the Top Ontology does not necessarily correspond with the language-internal hierarchies. Each language-internal structure has a different mapping with the top-ontology via the ILI-records to which they are linked as equivalents. For example, there are no words in Dutch that correspond with technical notions such as 1stOrderEntity, 2ndOrderEntity, 3rdOrderEntity,[4] but also not with more down-to-earth concepts such as the functional 1stOrder concept *Container*. These levels will thus not be present in the Dutch wordnet. From the Dutch hierarchy it will hence not be possible to simply extract all the "containers" because no Dutch word meaning is used to group or classify them. Nevertheless, the Dutch "containers" may still be found either via the equivalence relations with English "containers," which are stored below the sense of "container" or via the TopConcept clustering *Container* that is imposed on the Dutch hierarchy (or any other ontology that may be linked to the ILI). Figure 21.4 shows a fragment of the Dutch wordnet in which there is no equivalent for "container" nor for "artifact object" and "artifact."

The dotted line from the ILI-record "container" to *"lepel"* (spoon), indicates a so-called EQ_HAS_HYPERONYM relation to a more general ILI-record that can additionally classify the concept. This information can either be transferred from Word-Net1.5 or it can explicitly be encoded to represent the Base Concept "container" in Dutch in the form of all the important hyponyms. This demonstrates another possibility to combine top-ontology types in the local wordnet. If a language-specific concept is more complex, inclusive than any of the ILI-records, it is possible to link

---

[4] The opposite situation also occurs. Words such as *"iets"* (a thing, event or idea; anything) or *"zaak"* (thing or concept) are more abstract than the top-level concepts.

Top Ontology

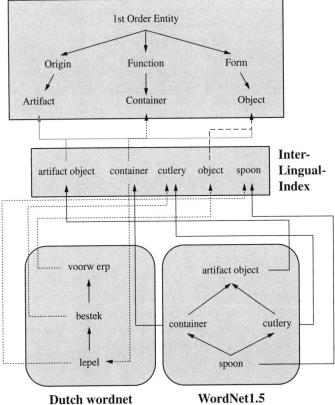

Fig. 21.4. Complex types in the Top Ontology and the local wordnets.

it to multiple ILI-records via the EQ_HAS_HYPERONYM relation. Any top-concept associated to these ILI-records will transfer to the language-specific meaning.

This discussion clearly shows that the realizations of interpretations, even from a generative point of view, is a matter of the language. Even though we demonstrated that is possible to set up a powerful and predictive system for deriving complex meanings, still, each language represents a unique lexical mapping to these meanings or aspects of these meanings.

5   Conclusion

It will be clear that both the individual wordnets and the multilingual database as a whole will profit from a generative approach, which reduces the (often inconsistent) enumeration of interpretations and improves the mapping across languages. For the separate wordnets, the possibility of disjunctive and conjunctive hyperonyms or hyponyms (and holonyms or meronyms) makes it possible to capture the different facets of meaning in a single sense or synset. For the multilingual database as a whole, the more coarse sense groups in the ILI will provide a smoother matching of meanings across the wordnets. We have seen that different lexicalizations of meaning aspects, either via polysemy, compounding or derivation, can thus still be interconnected. Finally, we described the EuroWordNet top-ontology, which represents a more fundamental language-independent structuring of the ILI in the form of complex types. Although this top-ontology has stronger predictive power, it is nevertheless limited to a smaller set of so-called Base Concepts, which play a major role in the individual wordnets. These implications can however still be carried over to the specific meanings in the local wordnets via the system of language-internal relations.

The current top-ontology is just a basic lattice of distinctions, in which the axioms and implications are not further formalized. The current ontology does not formally express how for example *Function* relates to *2ndOrderEntities* and we thus cannot differentiate Action-Result patterns of polysemy or derivation from Action-Agent patterns. The flexibility of the lattice was needed during the development phase and the formalization was not necessary for encoding the basic semantic relations in the wordnets. However, we would like to further extend this lattice with a formalization in the near future. This would more fundamentally explain how lexicalizations of meanings in the vocabularies of languages are related to more fundamental complex types, and consequently, give a better context to predict other extensions or derivations of meanings.

References

Buitelaar, P. 1998. *Corelex: Systematic Polysemy and Underspecification*, PhD, Brandeis University.

Dowty, D. R. 1979. *Word Meaning and Montague Grammar: The Semantics of Verbs and Times in Generative Semantics and in Montague's PTQ*, Reidel, Dordrecht.

Guarino, N. 1998. Some Ontological Principles for Designing Upper Level Lexical Resources. In A. Rubio, N. Gallardo, R. Catro, and A. Tejada (eds), *Proc. First International Conference on Language Resources and Evaluation*, Granada, pp. 527–534.

Hamp, B. and Feldweg, H. 1997. GermaNet: a Lexical-Semantic Net for German. In P. Vossen, N. Calzolari, G. Adriaens, A. Sanfilippo, and Y. Wilks (eds), *Proc. ACL/EACL-97 Workshop on Automatic Information Extraction and Building of Lexical Semantic Resources for NLP Applications*, Madrid, pp. 9–15.

Levin, B. 1993. *English Verb Classes and Alternations*. University of Chicago Press, Chicago.

Lyons, J. 1977. *Semantics*. Cambridge University Press, London.

Miller, G., Beckwith, R., Fellbaum, C., Gross, D., and Miller, K. 1990. *Five Papers on WordNet*. CSL Report 43, Cognitive Science Laboratory, Princeton University, Princeton.

Peters, W., Peters, I., and Vossen, P. 1998. The Reduction of Semantic Ambiguity in Linguistic Resources. In A. Rubio, N. Gallardo, R. Catro, and A. Tejada (eds), *Proc.*

First International Conference on Language Resources and Evaluation, Granada, pp. 409–416.

Peters, W., Vossen, P., Diez-Orzas, P., and Adriaens, G. (1998). Cross-linguistic Alignment of Wordnets with an Inter-Lingual-Index. In N. Ide, D. Greenstein, and P. Vossen (eds), *Special Issue on EuroWordNet. Computers and the Humanities* 32: 221–251.

Procter, P. (ed.) 1978. *Longman Dictionary of Contemporary English*. Longman, Harlow and London.

Pustejovsky, J. 1991. The Syntax of Event Structure. *Cognition* 41: 47–81.

Pustejovsky, J. 1995. *The Generative Lexicon*. MIT Press, Cambridge, MA.

Rodriguez, H., Climent, S., Vossen, P., Bloksma, L., Roventini, A., Bertagna, F., Alonge, A., and Peters, W. 1998. The Top-Down Strategy for Building EuroWordNet: Vocabulary Coverage, Base Concepts and Top Ontology. In N. Ide, D. Greenstein, P. Vossen (eds), *Special Issue on EuroWordNet. Computers and the Humanities* 32: 117–152.

Rosch, E. 1977. Human Categorisation. In N. Warren (eds), *Studies in Cross-Cultural Psychology* I. Academic Press, London, pp. 1–49.

Vendler, Z. 1967. *Linguistics and Philosophy*. Cornell University Press, Ithaca.

Verkuyl, H. 1972. *On the Compositional Nature of the Aspects*. Reidel, Dordrecht.

Verkuyl, H. 1989. Aspectual Classes and Aspectual Distinctions. *Linguistics and Philosophy* 12: 39–94.

Vossen, P. 1995. Grammatical and Conceptual Individuation in the Lexicon, PhD., *Studies in Language and Language Use* 15, Amsterdam, IFOTT, University of Amsterdam, Amsterdam.

Vossen, P. 1998. Introduction to EuroWordNet. In N. Ide, D. Greenstein, and P. Vossen (eds.), *Special Issue on EuroWordNet. Computers and the Humanities* 32: 73–89.

Vossen, P., Diez-Orzas, P., and Peters, W. 1997. The Multilingual Design of EuroWordNet. In P. Vossen, N. Calzolari, G. Adriaens, A. Sanfilippo, and Y. Wilks (eds), *Proc. ACL/EACL-97 Workshop Automatic Information Extraction and Building of Lexical Semantic Resources for NLP Applications*, Madrid, pp. 1–8.

Vossen, P., and Bloksma, L. 1998. Categories and Classifications in EuroWordNet. In A. Rubio, N. Gallardo, R. Catro, and A. Tejada (eds.), *Proc. First International Conference on Language Resources and Evaluation*, Granada, pp. 399–408.

Index